Praise for *American Eve*

"In *American Eve,* Paula Uruburu, making magnificent use of Nesbit's memoirs, letters, and photographs . . . places the notorious murder in a new context. . . . A master of detail . . . the effect is magical . . . *American Eve* is a real page-turner."
—*The New York Times*

"Uruburu has a fine sense of time and place, which comes through in her portrait of New York at the turn of the century."
—*The Washington Post*

"Uruburu's smart, historically savvy narrative is as riveting as the juiciest gossip fest, and the postcard photographs of the sixteen-year-old Evelyn, with her saucy-innocent eyes and rosebud lips, are . . . well, to die for."
—*O, the Oprah Magazine*

"[Told with] breathless, sensual panache . . . A tale oft-told, but never as diligently and lovingly researched as here, an operatic story—not of celebrity or the American Dream but of sex, class, and power."
—*Los Angeles Times*

"Uruburu . . . succeeds in humanizing her mordantly self-aware subject."
—*Vogue*

"*American Eve* uses the scandal to address our eternal fascination with rich and famous people behaving badly."
—*The Seattle Times*

"Riveting . . . the most sympathetic and comprehensive history of Nesbit to date."
—*Newsday*

"With the publication of *American Eve,* a first-rate work of narrative-driven historical research and biography, Nesbit's place in this pantheon of iconic women is assured—and undeniable. . . . Here, in Uruburu's capable hands, it rivets us."
—*The Buffalo News*

"*American Eve* colorfully re-creates the nasty underbelly of the Gilded Age—its religious cruelties, class oppression, and obsession with pubescent sexuality. Nesbit's tragedy underscores how dangerous desire can be."
—*New York Post*

continued . . .

"Uruburu draws some valid comparisons between then and now in this tell-all biography of one of the first in a long line of tarnished 'It' Girls."
—*Booklist*

"Richly detailed . . . readers will appreciate the parallels between Nesbit's 'It' Girl status and our own celebrity-obsessed culture."
—*Publishers Weekly*

"Uruburu sees the sensational, salacious career of Evelyn Nesbit as a cautionary tale about a preternaturally beautiful pubescent Red Ridinghood surrounded by hungry wolves in the dark woods of early-twentieth-century Manhattan."
—*Kirkus Reviews*

"Paula Uruburu serves up an intriguing and meticulously researched slice of American history. Evelyn Nesbit typified the glorious excesses of the Gilded Age, and this story has everything: sex, deception, drama, and a lurid love triangle, all culminating in the crime of the century."
—**Karen Abbott, author of** *Sin in the Second City: Madams, Ministers, Playboys, and the Battle for America's Soul*

"Of all the famous beauties of a hundred years ago, Evelyn Nesbit is the only one who would still turn heads today. Paula Uruburu's triumph is to fix this very modern-looking girl in her proper time and place, and also to describe the New York of the early 1900s so vividly that we feel we, too, could be strolling toward the Twenty-first Street apartment where the teen was seduced by Stanford White—or sitting in Madison Square Garden on the fatal evening that White was shot dead."
—**Mike Dash, author of** *Satan's Circus: Murder, Vice, Police Corruption, and New York's Trial of the Century*

"By centering her book on the ever-fascinating figure of Evelyn Nesbit—the stunningly beautiful chorine whose sexual charisma still burns through the Victorian photographs that adorn the book—Uruburu has produced not only a tour de force of historical crime writing and an illuminating social history but a rollicking piece of storytelling: a work that brings to life an entire glittering era while maintaining a breathless narrative pace."
—**Harold Schecter, author of** *The Devil's Gentleman: Privilege, Poison, and the Trial That Ushered in the Twentieth Century*

"In *American Eve* a beautiful young woman, a lecherous prince of New York, and an unstable husband show us how the national sport of media-fed scandal began. Before the story ends, one man is dead, another is locked away, and Paula Uruburu has given us a look at an age of excess that looks remarkably like our own. It is page-turning history at its best."

—Michael D'Antonio, author of *Hershey: Milton S. Hershey's Extraordinary Life of Wealth, Empire, and Utopian Dreams*

"Wonderfully absorbing . . . A lurid tabloid story of yore brought to fresh life and relevance with remarkable insight, verve, and wisdom. Old New York is laid bare in all its decadence and the cult of pubescent beauty traced to its source, all with worldliness, wit, humor, compassion, and suspense. The result is a real page-turner."

—Phillip Lopate, author of *Waterfront: A Walk Around Manhattan* and *Writing New York*

"Tragic now when a century ago it seemed merely scandalous, the story of Evelyn Nesbit is a gripping cautionary tale for those who believe Paris Hilton, Britney Spears, and Lindsay Lohan are the first of their kind. How is it that after a century of feminism, young, beautiful women still crash and burn for an eager public? Using newly available family sources, Paula Uruburu tells Evelyn Nesbit's story in all its darkness and terror."

—Honor Moore, author of *The Bishop's Daughter*

"Paula Uruburu has given life to the tragic American story of the poor, beautiful nymph whose fate is so often entangled with extreme wealth and the powerful man. Evelyn Nesbit is like a Dreiser heroine—Sister Carrie, Jennie Gerhardt—though hers is a true story, harrowing in this writer's hands."

—Martha McPhee, author of *L'America* and *Gorgeous Lies*

"In *American Eve*, a fascinating evocation of a woman and her times, Paula Uruburu does more than just tell the story of Evelyn Nesbit. Sex, money, scandal, celebrity, doom—the whole cocktail of America's obsessions is served up here in this intriguing, addictive book."

—Zachary Lazar, author of *Sway*

For Dorothy —

American Eve

Evelyn Nesbit, Stanford White,

the Birth of the "It" Girl, and

the Crime of the Century

Paula Uruburu

Wild roses are best — as are dish roses!

RIVERHEAD BOOKS

New York

Paula Uruburu 6/11

RIVERHEAD BOOKS
Published by the Penguin Group
Penguin Group (USA) Inc.
375 Hudson Street, New York, New York 10014, USA
Penguin Group (Canada), 90 Eglinton Avenue East, Suite 700, Toronto, Ontario M4P 2Y3, Canada
(a division of Pearson Penguin Canada Inc.)
Penguin Books Ltd., 80 Strand, London WC2R 0RL, England
Penguin Group Ireland, 25 St. Stephen's Green, Dublin 2, Ireland (a division of Penguin Books Ltd.)
Penguin Group (Australia), 250 Camberwell Road, Camberwell, Victoria 3124, Australia
(a division of Pearson Australia Group Pty. Ltd.)
Penguin Books India Pvt. Ltd., 11 Community Centre, Panchsheel Park, New Delhi—110 017, India
Penguin Group (NZ), 67 Apollo Drive, Rosedale, North Shore 0632, New Zealand
(a division of Pearson New Zealand Ltd.)
Penguin Books (South Africa) (Pty.) Ltd., 24 Sturdee Avenue, Rosebank, Johannesburg 2196,
South Africa

Penguin Books Ltd., Registered Offices: 80 Strand, London WC2R 0RL, England

The publisher does not have any control over and does not assume any responsibility for author or third-party websites or their content.

All photographs are from the author's collection except those on pages 16, 194, 264, 293, 364, 366, and 372, which are from the Nesbit/Thaw family archives.

Frontispiece art: American Eve, at sweet sixteen, posted for the Campbell Art Studio.

First Riverhead hardcover edition: May 2008
First Riverhead trade paperback edition: April 2009
Riverhead trade paperback ISBN: 978-1-59448-369-1

The Library of Congress has catalogued the Riverhead hardcover edition as follows:

Uruburu, Paula M.
    American Eve : Evelyn Nesbit, Stanford White, the birth of the "It" girl, and the crime of the century /
Paula Uruburu.
        p.   cm.
Includes bibliographical references.
ISBN 978-1-59448-993-8
1. Nesbit, Evelyn, 1884–1967.   2. Models (Persons)—United States—Biography.   3. Celebrities—
United States—Biography.   4. New York (N.Y.)—History—20th century.   I. Title.
HD8039.M772U59   2008   2008005818
974.7'1041092—dc22
[B]

PRINTED IN THE UNITED STATES OF AMERICA

10   9   8   7   6   5   4   3

Come slowly, Eden!
Lips unused to thee,
Bashful, sip thy jasmines,
As the fainting bee,

Reaching late his flower,
Round her chamber hums,
Counts his nectars—enters,
And is lost in balms!

—EMILY DICKINSON

for Brian

Campbell Art Studio postcard photo
of Evelyn, 1901, The Tiger Head.

CONTENTS

INTRODUCTION

The Garden of the New World   1

CHAPTER ONE

Siren Song   7

CHAPTER TWO

Beautiful City of Smoke   21

CHAPTER THREE

Poses   37

CHAPTER FOUR

The Little Sphinx in Manhattan   53

CHAPTER FIVE

Florodora   79

CHAPTER SIX

Benevolent Vampire 97

CHAPTER SEVEN

Through the Looking Glass 131

CHAPTER EIGHT

At the Feet of Diana 145

CHAPTER NINE

The Barrymore Curse 163

CHAPTER TEN

Enter Mad Harry 177

CHAPTER ELEVEN

The Worst Mistake of Her Life 205

CHAPTER TWELVE

The "Mistress of Millions" 249

CHAPTER THIRTEEN

Curtains: June 25, 1906 269

CHAPTER FOURTEEN

Aftershock   *289*

CHAPTER FIFTEEN

Dementia Americana   *303*

CHAPTER SIXTEEN

A Woman's Sacrifice   *317*

CHAPTER SEVENTEEN

America's Pet Murderer   *357*

EPILOGUE

The Fallen Idol   *367*

ACKNOWLEDGMENTS   *373*

NOTES   *375*

FURTHER READING   *387*

Diana atop the Madison Square Tower, circa 1900.

❧

The Garden of the New World

For we must consider that we shall be as a city upon a hill, the eyes of all people are upon us. *—John Winthrop, sermon, 1630*

God gave me my money. . . . God has marked the American people as His chosen nation to finally lead in the regeneration of the world. This is the divine mission of America and all it holds for all the profit, all the glory, all the happiness possible to man. *—John D. Rockefeller, 1900*

Rockefeller did the things that God would have done had He been rich. *—Anonymous*

Nature is very cruel . . . and if civilization has overlaid us with delicacies and refinements, nature works on just as though social laws had no existence. *—Evelyn Nesbit,* Prodigal Days

A little more than half a century before a winsome, waiflike, and wide-eyed Evelyn Nesbit, not yet sixteen, found her way to the island of Manhattan, Nathaniel Hawthorne had written a modest allegorical tale titled "Rappaccini's Daughter." It is the story of an intense but immature medical student who becomes obsessed with an exquisitely lovely and innocent young woman. The girl has never ventured beyond the walls of her outlaw scientist father's garden, a man-made paradise filled with marvelous-looking but unnatural species of fatally toxic plants and flowers. The illicit garden is the envy of a less than brilliant rival scientist, intent upon finding his way into the forbidden sanctuary and learning the secrets of his seemingly untouchable rival. Upon seeing the splendid flora and the rare beauty of the girl, the young man wonders, "Is this the Garden of the New World?" only to find out subsequently that the girl and everything in the garden are poisonous as a result of her father's unsanctioned experiments. When he realizes he has become contaminated with the poison through exposure to the beautiful girl, the young man viciously turns on her and blames her for his condition. The girl, betrayed and brokenhearted, decides to sacrifice her life for him by releasing the poisons in her system via a lethal antidote. She dies slowly and painfully at their feet as the medical student, her father, and her father's rival look on, respectively horrified, mystified, and triumphant.

The island of Manhattan at the turn of the last century was uncannily like Hawthorne's fictional New World Eden. It was a walled-in, manmade wonder, filled with dazzling but lethal temptations, bitter rivalries, and dangerous secrets. It was run by a handful of powerful men, a number of whom acted with impunity outside the boundaries of conventional practices in their ruthless pursuit of both profits and pleasure. In what would prove to be a decade of overindulgence that would nearly devour itself and sink with titanic hubris only a few years later, the chosen class of calculating Calvinists who sat at the top of the food chain ruled over their classless empires of excess, believing they were blessed with "divine right." Having reduced their methods of acquisition "to an exact science," they amassed astonishing tax-free fortunes, lived in magnificent mansions, rode in fabulous private Pullman cars on the railroads they built and monopolized, and sailed on luxurious yachts that were themselves "floating palaces." When asked about his yacht, the *Corsair,* J. P. Morgan replied famously, "If you have to ask how much it cost, you can't afford it." It was social Darwinism at its best—or worst.

By February 1900, New York's John D. Rockefeller, the president of Standard Oil, asserted, "The growth of a large business is merely survival of the fittest, a law of Nature, and of God." Then he crushed all his competitors into blackened viscous muck. Within a year, months before Christmas, Pittsburgh's Andrew Carnegie gave himself an early present. He sold his interest in Carnegie Steel to New York's J. P. Morgan for a whopping $480 million. So, while the average working stiff's salary was slightly less than five hundred dollars a year, as the story goes, Carnegie retired on an estimated pension of $44,000—a day.

Yet with the exception of a fistful of trust-busting politicians, certain resolute muckrakers, and the occasional enterprising anarchist, the huddled masses seemed unable to comprehend and unwilling to consider the colossal inequality between themselves and America's staggeringly wealthy untaxed multimillionaires, men like E. H. Harriman, Russell Sage (who, it was rumored, was so cheap he didn't wear underwear), and Henry Clay Frick, who proclaimed that "railroads are the Rembrandts of investment." (The latter two even managed to survive violent attacks by anarchy-minded assassins.) These fittest Philistines "bought paintings like other people bought penny postcards," and even if the Vanderbilts, Whitneys, Goulds, and their socially well-bred peers did not always know good art, they knew what they liked to buy. If they didn't, they called upon Stanford White to decide for them.

The self-ordained purveyor and pillager of high art for America's highest society (whose approach to art was usually either a "disheartening middle-brow indifference or a more positively demoralizing vanity"), Stanford White was the most conspicuous partner of the preeminent architectural firm of the day, McKim, Mead, and White. Like White himself, the firm grandly embraced both the public and the private. Their jewels included the Admiral Farragut Memorial; the Tiffany, Whitney, Pulitzer, and Vanderbilt mansions; St. Paul's Church; Judson Memorial Church; the New York Herald Building; the girded wrought-iron wonder of Pennsylvania Station; and the marvelous Washington Square Arch, now New York City's most elaborate tombstone (being located near what was a potter's field for the indigent and then a burial ground for yellow fever victims, totaling somewhere in the neighborhood of 20,000).

Über-society impresario, aesthetic prophet, protean clubman, and all-consuming libertine, White was the creator of Manhattan's own "Garden of the New World." Morgan and Carnegie were two of its major share-holders (along with White himself). A block-long business and enter-tainment complex located at the northeast corner of Madison Avenue and Twenty-sixth Street, the Garden was an oasis of splendor situated adjacent to the formerly unassuming Madison Square. (The present-day Madison Square Garden arena, still colloquially called "the Garden," is actually in its fourth incarnation, located between Thirty-first and Thirty-third streets and situated on top of the second Pennsylvania Station.)

Overlooking the Garden's splendid and innovative open-air rooftop theater was its gleaming tower, modeled after the Giralda in Seville, and the tallest point (at the time) in an increasingly priapic city over which the preternaturally and passionately inspired White held sway. Topped with a gilded bronze and scandalously nude Diana, Madison Square Garden was White's supreme architectural achievement, the envy of those who sought a coveted office or studio within its tiled and terra-cotta confines—and the site of its creator's not so original sins, which would eventually cause him to be cut down in the shadow of the goddess. And prove his mortality. And all because of another goddess, one that was flesh and blood.

But if Manhattan at the turn into the twentieth century was a city overwhelmed by its own prosperity in some quarters, it was overpopu-lated with the teeming poor in others, where the bodies were less effec-tively hidden than those under the Washington Square Arch. It was a metropolis of mind-boggling incongruities and inequities, symbolically reflected in the proximity of Wall Street to the Battery Park seawall, beyond which stood the Statue of Liberty, and only slightly closer to New Jersey, Ellis Island. It was a city where an Astor-owned block on the Lower East Side crammed five hundred immigrant families into grue-some rat-infested tenements, regular firetraps with a death rate rivaling Calcutta's.

In the same general vicinity stood the forbidding Tombs Prison, behind whose thick granite walls and iron bars one multimillionaire's banjo-eyed, baby-faced son, the infamous Harry K. Thaw, would find himself for the brutal murder of the creator whose corrupted Garden stood at the roaring heart of a projected sky-scraping city he would never see. During two sensational trials that stretched over two years, with the private no longer assiduously guarded from the public, the curious crowds of ten thousand or more who mobbed the street below Thaw's prison cell could afford to buy a souvenir penny postcard of the Tombs or the "Bridge of Sighs," which connected the prison to the courthouse on Centre Street. Most spectators, however, scrambled to procure one of the hundred or more postcards of the murderer's devastatingly lovely child bride and White's former teenage mistress, the twentieth century's American Eve and "the cause of it all."

Much farther uptown, surrounding newly minted mansions, many designed by Stanford White and inhabited by the likes of Mrs. William Backhouse Astor (described in the newspapers as being "borne down by a terrible weight of precious stones"), there were ornate gates and formidable wrought-iron fences designed to keep out the "democrats without diamonds." But the ordinary citizen in New York City (and those beyond its environs) was nonetheless hungry for a tantalizing glimpse into the rarefied world that existed just within those gates and behind those Garden walls. "Envious, suspicious, hopeful of sin," the people would get what they asked for "in spades and blazing scareheads" once the murder of the century ruptured the nation's tight-laced consciousness on a hot night in June 1906.

New York City at the turn of the twentieth century was certainly a New World paradise for some, a circumscribed fantastical Eden with its own strange walls and boundaries. Some were clearly visible; others were less obvious but no less impenetrable. Unless, of course, you were young. And beautiful.

Portrait of Evelyn at age sixteen (1901), by Rudolf Eickemeyer Jr.,
that appeared in Cosmopolitan magazine.

⤙✥⤚

CHAPTER ONE

Siren Song

She was a human camellia with something of the . . . dying beauty of the Narcissus in her delicately-featured face. —*Newspaper clipping, 1907*

She had the face of an angel and the heart of a snake.
—*Augustus Saint-Gaudens*

Plain girls are happiest. —*Evelyn Nesbit*

The tantalizing idea of a tabula rasa—a shiny, new, unsullied century—loomed large in the collective consciousness of the majority of Americans in the final hours of 1899. The populace was precariously balanced on the razor's edge between two antithetical worlds. One was a quickly receding past still deeply mired in the old-fashioned, the other a fast-approaching future riveted to the often hazardously new-fangled, where limbs were routinely mangled or ripped out of their sockets in the grinding cogs of unfamiliar machinery, all in the name of progress. Yet while men of gilt-edged sensibilities and iron (or steel) wills forged ahead on a variety of fronts, delighted with their swift evolution, others resolutely clung to the quaint hem of Victorian virtue, identifying themselves as the defenders of the sanctity of wife and home. So even though the Sears-Roebuck catalogue in 1900 featured thirty-seven pages of accessories for horse-drawn carriages and not a single one for automobiles, the old world was fast succumbing to the new. And nowhere more emphatically and ecstatically than in "the garden spot of a spotless new century," the city that had appeared to Whitman in an earlier manifestation as "unruly" and "self-sufficient," whose "turbulent musical chorus" produced a perpetually mesmerizing siren song—the island its original natives had called Mannahatta.

Having emerged, however, from a series of nerve-bending depressions in the 1890s, many Americans were still struggling to simply recover and sit upright as the old century crawled steadily toward oblivion. Even a heavy dose of money offered little immunity from the unsettling apocalyptic feelings that seem to grip entire populations in the terminal phases of a dying age. But America was still naive and nubile enough on December 31, 1899, to believe in the healthy tug of renewed possibilities—despite intermittent pangs of self-doubt and an unspoken fear that the Day of Reckoning might be at hand. And even though a few of the babbling lunatic fringe indeed shouted in the streets that "the end of the world was nigh," the *New York Times* evening edition proclaimed blithely that the nation stood poised upon the "threshold of 1900 . . . facing a still brighter dawn for human civilization." And the average citizen agreed.

The idea of a clean, fresh slate certainly seemed infectious. And nowhere was there such a splendidly contagious sense of unreality and invincibility as the glowing metropolitan island where almost no one and nothing was ever average. For the extraordinary occasion, the city's most superbly unruly son, Stanford White, turned Madison Square Park into an marvelous fairyland with more than 3,000 miniature orange-hued Chinese paper lanterns hung on every available post and branch. The anticipation of a new millennium was absolutely electric as the last minutes of the withering 1800s hung suspended in the frigid air, overripe and ready to drop.

And then midnight erupted. The Venetian plaster was barely dry in the uptown Fifth Avenue fiefdom where "the Four Hundred" popped Pommery Sec corks and toasted the new year from Mrs. Astor's exclusive ballroom on high. Meanwhile, in the lower reaches of Mott Street and below Canal Street, the less refined fired off revolvers into the blue-black sky, unconcerned in their soused serf revelry as to where the bullets might

land (two were killed and three wounded, according to the newspapers the next day). That night, in the choppy waters surrounding the
island, Standard Oil's omnipresent tugboats sounded their horns, while
the intermittent hooting blast of steam whistles from the ferries rippled
joyfully across both the Hudson and East rivers. Snow flurries had begun
to fall just before midnight, softening the effects of bone-chilling darkness. Illuminated in shimmering, spidery staccato bursts and explosive
flashes by a barrage of Chinatown fireworks set off exactly at midnight
near the Brooklyn Bridge, the wayward flakes flickered and pinwheeled
like multicolored confetti. It was as if God Himself had joined the
celebration.

The "loads of babies given up to the streets of the Bowery" who had
waited impatiently for the signal, blew excitedly into lead-painted tin
penny whistles. Gaggles of frowsy women clanged and banged on iron
skillets and pots with metal spoons from the stoops of swarming tenements. Thin-legged feral street Arabs blew across the mouths of empty
bottles of rotgut they found in the alleyways they slept in, imitating the
tugboat horns in the distance and becoming giddy and light-headed from
the alcoholic fumes.

The *New York World* announced the next morning that the 1800s were
gone forever, replaced by a "brisk, bright, fresh, altogether new 1900 . . .
good for a clean one hundred years. . . ." That same morning, from the
White House, the new century's first president, William McKinley, who
embodied the nation's self-satisfied and slightly overblown sense of inde-
structibility, issued his New Year's statement of good cheer, wished the
electorate well, then went back to bed, exhausted from hours of endless
handshaking at several balls the night before (a practice he had been
advised to curtail for reasons of personal security). That same night, in
Philadelphia, an exhausted and exceptionally striking young artists' model,
who the papers said had "taken the studios by stormy steamy surprise" a
year earlier, slept through the noisy celebrations around her in the streets
and saloons, unaware that she was destined to "rock civilization" with her
own siren song within a matter of years and sink an entire gilded class in
the whole bloody process.

Seemingly overnight, the inhabitants of the brash and volatile island of Manhattan had already set the mood for their new century and the rest of the country—one of unrepentant self-absorption—but, typically, with little self-reflection. Amid the mirth and merriment, in the established tradition of American mythmaking, Gothamites also believed themselves to be self-made and self-sustaining. As such, some of the citizens seemed to adopt instantaneously a carpe diem attitude, which provided a convenient solution to the dilemma of dwelling on past sins they would nonetheless be doomed to repeat. Others, soaked in the spirit of change, embraced the dawn with both arms and plotted their heady campaigns for advancement. For many, the stuffy waltzlike circularity of the past was already being displaced with rousing Sousa marches or the audacious open-ended ragtime riffs of the "newest American Negro music." But the "barbaric harmonies" and dangerously diverting offbeat rhythms of ragtime shocked the whitest-bred decent majority. Perhaps there were a discriminating few within the rollicking mob who heard the imminent rumblings of political, economic, and social revolution that New Year's Day. If so, only a handful cared to listen, surrounded as they were by Mannahatta's deceptively jubilant dissonance and "turbulent musical chorus." The rest of the population, it seemed, was easily distracted. And easily seduced.

It also seemed that no matter what the hoity-toity, the hardworking, or hoi polloi pouring through Ellis Island at a rate of half a million a year overlooked in the humming and drumming of their daily lives, as the century turned, a magical metamorphosis was occurring. And, as critic Leo Marx asserted, the machine had entered the garden.

The telephone, the phonograph, the electric light, the "flickering tintype"—all the wonders of American inventiveness—seemed to have materialized overnight, sprung full blown from the fertile minds of an indomitable generation of technological demigods. The first rapid-transit subway system was geared to open in New York City as iron-nerved Irish, Italian, and Chinese sandhogs blasted and burrowed their way under the heaving metropolis. And, while the roaring el train rained blinding ash and hot cinders onto the hats and heads of the pedestrians below, the first American auto show was held in New York City. As expensive battery-powered hansoms began to appear intermittently on the streets of Manhattan, most at first were simply oversized toys for the inherently curious or idle rich. Stanford White was one of the former. The peripatetic architect immediately took a shine to the "horse-less carriage" and took advantage of the mobility it afforded him in his Herculean attempts to redesign and lift a reinvented city on his shoulders for all to admire. New York society interloper Harry K. Thaw was one of the latter. He was the first automobile owner to make headlines by driving a car through the plate-glass window of a shop on Fifth Avenue, ostensibly after an argument with a salesclerk. Maybe Thaw wanted to prove to the city's architects that their buildings, unlike their social clubs, were not inpenetrable. Or, if he couldn't "break into" New York society, perhaps he would simply break as much of it as he could into pieces. If not, he would have to find another way to infiltrate the private Garden of the New World. Perhaps by wooing its very own Eve.

AMERICAN EVE

Evelyn Nesbit, image of an age, its sins, its soullessness . . .

Most don't know that her given name was apparently Florence Mary. She was not-so-plain Flo to her family and "Flossie the Fuss" to the chorus. She was "Kittens" to Stanford White, "Evie" to John Barrymore, and "Boofuls" to Harry Thaw. She was "Mrs. Thaw the younger" in London, "Le Bébé" in France, and "Mrs. Harry" when in Pittsburgh. Schoolgirl. Florodora girl. Gibson girl. "Angel-child." "Snake-charmer." Vixen. Victim. The ur-Lolita. The very first "It" girl before anyone know what "It" was. She could be what anyone wanted her to be. And inevitably was, even if it wasn't what she wanted. To anyone familiar with E. L. Doctorow's novel *Ragtime*, the name Evelyn Nesbit may evoke the mauve-tinted crucible of the sentimentally inclined and cynically named Gilded Age.

Postcard pose of sixteen-year-old Evelyn for Sarony, 1901.

To others it may signify passion and perversion, murder and scandal, "love, hate, villainy, perfidy, and outraged innocence." The extinction of an era. And a red velvet swing.

Herself a product of the Victorian past but with an approach to life that was unconsciously and uncannily modern, Evelyn Nesbit unwittingly embodied the country's paradoxes and ambiguities at its trembling turn into the twentieth century. At times she seemed the very picture of nineteenth-century sentimentality and girlish purity, yet her naturally bewitching Mona Lisa smile promised something dangerously new and enticing. A self-inventory of her visible assets tells the story: the curled pink ribbon of a mouth (painted red only for the stage) contrasted with "slightly olive-hued" skin; huge, dark, sultry eyes set in an angelic face, all framed by a "profusion of burnished copper curls." It was an image that spoke of both the vitality and freshness of an antediluvian world and the brave new world of the Century of Progress. As with Eve before the Fall, Evelyn's natural charms and air of innocence created an overwhelming and immediate impression of incorruptibility in certain poses. Yet the deceptive maturity of her heavy-lidded gaze and ever so slightly open-mouthed expression of apparent self-satisfaction in photo after photo suggested an Eve who had already tasted forbidden fruit.

In those first few years of what would prove to be a thrilling and ingenious decade of crusaders and con men, cakewalks and coon songs, contradictions and coincidences, class wars and conspicuous consumption, Evelyn Nesbit became its most precious commodity, even though, as the newspapers reported, she had come to New York with "nothing but her looks." But her face was her fortune (as her parasitic mother well knew), and Evelyn's mercurial rise to fame and equally precipitous plunge into notoriety only five years later reflected the era's accelerated, intoxicating, and uniquely schizophrenic mood.

All the feminine myth and mystique of the ancient world seemed to coalesce with contemporary American freshness in Evelyn and form a "beguiling new creature." She was Freud's "eternal question," embodying both "contemporary social types like 'the charmer' and 'The New

Woman,'" as well as more universal abstractions such as "virtue, progress, etc., raised to nearly mythological proportions." Like the nation itself, she was poised fearlessly on the brink of uncharted discoveries but apprehensive about abandoning the illusion of security or sentiments of the past.

To the reporters who followed her every move and unprecedented rise as a celebrity before there was any discernible evidence of a singular talent to justify such attention (we of course no longer harbor any delusions with regard to the modern cult of personality), she was a startling silky contradiction, "a vision who assailed one's senses like a perfume at once delicate and heavy, overpowering and yet faint." As the American Eve, her delectable budding underage appeal proved irresistible to the renegade creator who wanted to cultivate her as the rarest flower in his Garden of too-earthly delights. Yet no matter how different she may have looked from one image or photograph to the next, the public felt they knew her. Women wanted to be her; men wanted to own her. She became a maddening object of desire, and tragically, a victim of her own beguiling beauty during the "gaudy spree," which she would help bring to a stunningly shameful end.

At first the publicity that swirled and hummed around Evelyn would have you believe that hers was a fairy-tale existence. She was seen as a modern-day Cinderella who came from a city of literal burning ash and coal to become the "glittering girl model of Gotham." She then made the precarious but inevitable leap from studio to stage. From there it was but a cakewalk to a life of luxury as the "mistress of millions" once she became Mrs. Harry K. Thaw, of Pittsburgh. Or so the newspapers said. And all before she was twenty-one.

An unwitting sexual anarchist draped in a crimson silk kimono and laid out seductively on a pure white polar bear rug, she could incite the wrath of reformers and excite the imagination of the public merely by sleeping. Once the "Madison Square Tragedy" tore its way into the headlines, the "little butterfly" generated more newspaper sales and publicity than Hearst himself could ever have manufactured. Through two trials riddled with theatrical tribulation and shocking revelations, she was the "pale flower" whose petals took on a "bruised pallor," with sympathetic observers wishing she had "grown wholesomely in a wholesome garden." Others, like the sculptor Saint-Gaudens, were less charitable, commenting just before he died, in 1907, that "she had the face of an angel and the heart of a snake."

Throughout her humiliating and protracted ordeal on the witness stand, Evelyn's ubiquitous and mesmerizing image—and what it represented to a nation of novice interpreters—captivated even the most cynical New York journalists. Irvin S. Cobb, a well-known syndicated columnist and social critic, described her as "the most exquisitely lovely human being I ever looked at—[she had] the slim quick grace of a fawn, a head that sat on her flawless throat as a lily on its stem, eyes that were the color of blue-brown pansies and the size of half dollars; a mouth made of rumpled rose petals." Yet even as her startling testimony helped push an unsuspecting and unprepared America into the modern age, while canny entrepreneurs sold hastily manufactured little red velvet swings on the street outside the courthouse, as quickly as Evelyn's star rose, it fell victim to the very culture that created and consumed her.

But hers is also a more intimate story. Of family. Of class. Of sex. And of monsters in human form. Perhaps the latter is not so surprising, coming at the vestigial end of the Edwardian era's preoccupation with such double-natured real and fictional monsters as Dracula, Dr. Jekyll and Mr. Hyde, Jack the Ripper, and Dorian Gray, all of whom, wrapped in the guise of men, seduced, defiled, dissected, or devoured women.

It really begins with two dead fathers, one who left no money and one who left too much. Then there are two grotesquely misguided mothers, one driven by her fear of poverty, who lived off her child, then abandoned her; the other aided and abetted by obscene wealth who indulged one son beyond all reason.

Alternately naive and manipulative, Evelyn's mother, who in all of Evelyn's recollections and letters is referred to as Evelyn Florence or simply Mamma, was the vigilantly neglectful mother who oversaw her teenage daughter's careers as a model and an actress, but who turned a blind eye to her dangerous liaisons with much older married men, which Mrs. Nesbit either clumsily or cleverly procured and tacitly promoted.

Mrs. Mary Copley Thaw, on the other hand, was the pathologically
overindulgent nightmare matriarch spawned by the merchant aristocracy
who sought to gild (and regild as many times as needed) the family name
at any cost, even though her tarnished family tree rivaled Poe's House
of Usher. Mrs. Thaw's overweening social ambition seemed to know no
bounds, even as her public philanthropy atoned for privately funding a
multitude of her son's dirty little sins. Once Harry Thaw committed cold-
blooded murder in front of nine hundred witnesses, his mother announced

Evelyn's mother, Evelyn Florence Mackenzie Nesbit,
circa 1902.

to the world that she was "prepared to pay a million dollars to save her son from the electric chair." But the cost was much higher.

Then there are the two men, the one described more often than not as a genius, the other as "not quite an imbecile." But whereas Stanford White was old money, the son of a Shakespeare scholar, Harry Thaw, in spite of the fact that his family roots reached back to post-Revolutionary America, acted out as if "nouveau riche," the self-indulged son of a coke and railroad "ironmaster" whose business acumen and philanthropic impulses Harry did not seem to inherit. White was driven by his passion for beauty and widely acknowledged as the vibrant force behind New York's startling metamorphosis at the start of the twentieth century, transforming a dingy brownstone city into one of wedding-cake white and terra-cotta. Among White's feats were his personal decoration of the Metropolitan Opera House with 15,000 white roses and the ability to transform a portion of his Garden into Venice, complete with Grand Canal and gondolas. Thaw, on the other hand, was a "pygmy wastrel" who was routinely dismissed as a twitchy "good-for-nothing" and only driven to distraction. White was a true pagan, and in his relentless search for rare and beautiful objects, he roamed the globe and put the unobtainable within reach—for a price. Thaw was a pious debauchee who considered himself a modern knight errant, but who was closer to the Marquis de Sade. Yet both men were uncannily, incurably hedonistic, impulsive, controlling, and carnivorous. Stanford White's gargantuan appetite for beauty and incomparable artifacts took him to Tuscany and the Tenderloin, where ultimately his hush-hush "hive of moral lepers," two-faced Falstaffian duplicity, and private transgressions led to a spectacularly dramatic public murder. His sinister and decidedly darker doppelgänger, Harry Thaw, a fraudulent Savonarola and deluded savior, operated in weirdly similar ways—all the while believing he was acting as an agent of divine providence. And then there was Evelyn.

It was in early December 1900 that fifteen-year-old Florence Evelyn Nesbit arrived in New York City, where the only thing that distinguished her from thousands of other girls in similarly deprived and unguarded circumstances was an astonishing beauty that was "infinitely appealing." It would be described by columnist Dorothy Dix as "vague and intangible as that of the lily, or any other frail and delicate thing. It lay over her face like a gossamer veil." It was a veil that was as enticing for what was concealed as for what it revealed to the gaze of insatiably curious onlookers. Until the veil was lifted.

British postcard photograph
of sixteen-year-old Evelyn, 1901.

Five-year-old Evelyn with Pittsburgh playmate.

CHAPTER TWO

కుఖమ

Beautiful City of Smoke

Sentimentality is as much out of place in an autobiography as it would be in a time-table or phone book. —*Evelyn Nesbit*, My Story

In spite of marked improvements in diagnoses, triage, and treatment, due ironically to the unimaginable carnage of the War Between the States only twenty years earlier, medicine was far from being a sophisticated or reliable science, even as America advanced steadily upon the twentieth century. The average life expectancy was only forty-nine for men and fifty-one for women, and the infant mortality rate was distressingly high, as was the number of deaths of mothers and/or infants during childbirth. People of every age died with awful and chilling regularity from cholera, consumption, pneumonia, diphtheria, typhus, and smallpox, while infants and children died routinely from illnesses such as scarlet fever and whooping cough.

Yet as a light snowfall muted the slate grays and dingy browns of the landscape in and around Tarentum, the girl known as Florence Evelyn Nesbit was born on December 25. Fortunately, against significant odds, there were no complications for either mother or daughter. Those would come about sixteen years later.

The year was 1884. Or perhaps 1885, depending on whose version one takes into account. Over the years, Mrs. Nesbit lied about her daughter's age so many times to accommodate assorted and potentially sordid circumstances that her selective memory meant that eventually even her daughter couldn't be 100 percent certain of her own age. As Evelyn relates in several letters, an unfortunate fire consumed all records in her hometown. As a result, verifying her age in order to qualify for social security posed a problem in her later life, which her daughter-in-law remembered as well. When pressed by reporters during her daughter's rise to fame, however, Mamma Nesbit was nevertheless pretty certain that Florence Evelyn made her debut in an even-numbered year.

The place we know for sure was Tarentum, located twenty-four miles up the Allegheny River from the steel-driven city of Pittsburgh, which at the time had the dubious distinction of being named the "dirtiest city in America." Those unfortunate enough to have to scrape out a living in the deep choking cramp of the steel mills and coal mines were also forced to inhabit ramshackle row houses that weren't much better than the dark holes they toiled in for pennies a day. They were, however, only a cobblestone's throw (if one had a good arm) from the sprawling suburban estates and magnificently manicured lawns of several of Pittsburgh's brand-spanking-new Millionaires' Rows, whose imposing mansions and mock-English gardens sat podgy and stodgy and secure behind colonnades of trees, enormous boxwood hedges, and decorative gilded gates. Their impressive occupants were looked upon as emblems of progress, with eighty-room summer "cottages" in Newport and seats on the New York Stock Exchange. They viewed their world through steel-colored glasses and saw Pittsburgh as "the beautiful city of smoke," while those who actually made progress possible by sweating out a precarious living six days a week, ten hours a day, considered it hell on earth. But, by comparison, on the farthest edges of the panting smoky city, in communities such as Natoria and Tarentum, in Evelyn's memory the sunny, rustic world of Victorian America lingered like a ripe Anjou pear in Indian summer.

According to Nesbit family legend, little Florence was such an exceedingly pretty infant that she attracted visitors from the neighboring counties for months after she was born. Two years and two months later, the Nesbits' second child, Howard, was born, physically more frail and congenitally less feisty than his sister, but with the same large soulful eyes and silken brunet hair. As they grew, Howard and the petite Florence were often mistaken for twins. Their heavy-lidded, unwavering gaze gave brother and sister a "constant expression of knowing and amused detachment" often startling to casual observers in children so young. Because of her special Christmas birthday, Florence Evelyn believed that she was destined always to "get twice as many presents as anybody else."

Her father, Winfield Scott Nesbit, was a man of great heart and small aspirations. Known as Win or Winnie to his family and friends, he was by all accounts a good-looking, soft-spoken, unimposing man named in honor of a fierce and flinty general (whose career stretched from the War of 1812 until the start of the Civil War, when he served briefly as the Union general-in-chief). He was also described as that rarest of animals, an unambitious lawyer, and therefore one to whom money, its acquisition, and its management were not a priority. Her mother, whose maiden name was Mackenzie, was considered a handsome woman with some talent for sewing; not surprisingly, she had been brought up to wish for

Photo postcard of Evelyn's house in Tarentum, Pennsylvania, circa 1907.

nothing more than to stitch herself securely into the cherished quilt of Victorian domesticity. She was blithely unaware of how the world worked beyond the limited sphere of wife and mother and therefore knew nothing about her husband's lack of business acumen, wrongheaded investments, or slipshod business practices. What she did know was that her homemade outfits were routinely praised by friends and neighbors who saw them on mother and daughter. Comfortably cosseted by womanly conventionality, the sometimes skittish Mrs. Nesbit nonetheless seemed perfectly content to be the wife of the amiable Win and go along with his plans for his children's future. Florence Evelyn, unlike the majority of girls in the country, who barely finished grammar school, would go to Vassar College and travel, while Howard would follow in his father's footsteps and become a lawyer.

For her first ten years (depending on which account one follows), Florence Evelyn's childhood was ordinary, no different from that of most girls living in seemingly bucolic towns across America at the time. But if, as certain "big city" social critics and hopeful prophets claimed, a sea change in social mores and sensibilities was seeping through the widening cracks of not-so-ironclad Victorianism, the greater part of hardworking, God-fearing Christians throughout America were still living in communities like Tarentum with populations of fewer than 2,500 people.

Like other young girls "from the provinces," Florence Evelyn went to picnics and spelling bees and attended Sunday school, where she sang in the choir. She fantasized about running off with the traveling circus in the summer, went ice-skating and sledding in the winter, and attended her first Pirates baseball game with her father when she was five. Part princess, part prizefighter, depending on her mood, Florence Evelyn lived for her father's praise, and he in turn doted on her. Of course as the head of the house and sole wage earner, Win was the central figure in the family and the dominant force in Florence Evelyn's life.

Unusually progressive about the intellectual capabilities of "the weaker sex," Winfield encouraged his daughter's early interest in reading by building a small library at home of her favorite books. The majority were the typical childhood fairy tales and fantasies, such as *Snow White* and *Sleeping Beauty*, with wonderfully vivid illustrations, charming princes, and happily-ever-afters. But Florence Evelyn read anything her father brought home for her, including the *Arabian Nights*, Arthurian legends, Greek myths, and popular dime novels, even though the latter were considered "books for boys." With pithy titles such as *Ragged Dick, Slow and Sure, Do and Dare,* and *Mark, the Match Boy,* the rags-to-riches stories the little girl read were full of high sentiment and often ludicrous plots that extolled the virtues identified as "pluck and luck." Their foremost literary proponent was Horatio Alger Jr., who sold more than 200 million copies of his prescriptive fantasies to post–Civil War American dreamers who wanted a blueprint for success. Of course, none of his faithful reading public knew that before he came to New York City, Alger had been run out of Cape Cod, Massachusetts, accused of "the abominable and revolting crime of gross familiarity with boys."

A vivacious and free-spirited child, Florence Evelyn bounced headfirst into all activities, particularly those she thought would please her father— singing, dancing, drawing, reciting from her books, playing the piano. She began music and dance lessons with her father's encouragement and practiced in earnest to learn "The Amorous Goldfish" and "Chin, Chin Chinaman" to please him. She knew in her heart that she was her father's favorite, although Win made a point of always praising both children for their efforts. Her mother, on the other hand, visibly favored Howard, whose sometimes distracted disposition and nervous temperament mirrored her own and threatened to make him into a mamma's boy. The children often accompanied their mother on visits to various relatives' farms in the outlying areas of Donnellsville and Allegheny, where young Florence Evelyn's inherent self-assurance made an immediate and lasting impression on those around her. One cousin remembers a comment her own mother made: she "despaired of Florence ever learning how to milk a cow," not because it was hard work, but because "the cow took up too much of her space."

When Florence Evelyn was around eleven (see note, page 378), a change in her father's job meant the family would have to relocate to

Pittsburgh. The Nesbits moved into a modest two-story saltbox house unexceptionally similar to the one they had left, and life continued to be pleasantly predictable. The children were enrolled in the grandly named Shakespeare Elementary School, and every day Win went to his offices on Diamond Street in the family's rockaway carriage, bought "on time" from Sears, Roebuck. But in less than a year, what had seemed like an eighteenth-century sentimental novel turned Dickensian.

At the age of forty, Winfield Scott Nesbit died without warning, of either a brain hemorrhage or virulent spinal meningitis. Since autopsies were not routinely performed, the local doctors were unable to determine the exact cause of death. But the consequences were no less inexorable and devastating for his stunned family. Encumbrances on the modest property left by Win Nesbit cut off virtually every source of income, leaving his inconsolable wife and children broken and broke.

The days immediately following Win's funeral, paid for largely by a contribution from his side of the family, were heartbreaking. Having seen their father active and happy in the previous weeks and months, at first both children refused to accept the news. Eleven-year-old Florence Evelyn demanded to see him. She threw herself at the locked bedroom door behind which Win Nesbit lay in stale grim silence on top of the bedcovers until his removal for burial. Mrs. Nesbit had thought it best that he be remembered alive, so there would be no final viewing for the grief-stricken children. Instead, their last image of him entailed handfuls of dirt thrown onto a pine box as it was lowered by ropes into the frost-covered ground while neighbors and family friends intoned the clichés of despair and solace. "Here today and gone tomorrow." "It was God's will." "He's in a better place." To the children, it was as if their father were nowhere—he had simply vanished overnight into the cold gray cosmos. It was almost unbearable.

As Evelyn recounts in her memoirs, within a month, the sheriff came and hammered a notice of foreclosure and eviction on the mourning Nesbits' door. An auction had to be held to sell off the family carriage (at a reduced rate, since there were still payments outstanding) and the entire contents of the house, from couch to clothespins. When the dreaded day came, Florence Evelyn, her mother, and Howard stood on the sidewalk for several hours without making a sound and watched like somnambulists while passersby eyed them curiously. Virtually all of their possessions were sold and carted away, including all the books in the library that her father had picked out for her and into which Florence Evelyn had carefully written her name after weeks and months of diligent practice to perfect her penmanship.

The three moved in with relatives temporarily, then the children were shuttled back and forth between various family members, sometimes together, sometimes separately. Meanwhile, a distraught Mrs. Nesbit tried to find work in the city's dress shops. Struggling to sort out her husband's desperately muddled finances, but with no idea how to proceed in the outside world and no comprehension of the vagaries or consequences of bad business investments, in spite of constant scrimping and deprivation, Mrs. Nesbit soon found herself and her children in the hopeless grip of mounting debt (which made the sale of the house to satisfy some of the debt problematic and contentious). Eventually, they moved into a poorly ventilated room in a boardinghouse, which smelled of mothballs, sauerkraut, and lye. Mr. Charles Holman, a friend of the family, eventually came to their rescue and paid the back rent they soon owed on that first of several cheerless boardinghouse rooms they would occupy.

According to Evelyn in 1934, "Gone [was] the sense of security [my father] had radiated." He had been "my sun and moon and I had been his little shooting star." With their world suddenly pitched into a darkness like the deepest hole made in the earth by Carnegie Steel, gone virtually overnight were even the smallest pleasures the Nesbits once enjoyed. Evelyn later wrote that at such a young age, she did not fully appreciate the hardships her mother now faced with her tidy, egglike world rudely cracked open and no one to help pick up the pieces. Nor could Florence Evelyn have predicted how her father's untimely death would deal the first of a series of blows to a mortally wounded childhood—just as no one could have foreseen how Winfield Nesbit's death would have ill-fated and calamitous consequences that would reach well beyond his modest grave in Allegheny County.

As the weeks wore on, the normally chatty Florence Evelyn drifted into melancholy silence, having decided to keep the only thing she owned, her thoughts, locked away from prying, ineffectual adults. And although she did not speak the words out loud (in childish fear of casting a spell that might come true), there were moments of absolute panic when she feared her mother also would simply vanish. Or die, perhaps by her own hand. Florence Evelyn worried anxiously for weeks, her head filled with improbable dime-novel scenarios that now seemed all too possible.

As for her mother, the adult Evelyn recalled, "Her grief was terrible. . . . In our strange new home she often gave way to uncontrollable weeping." On a miserably regular basis their mother would cry out with steadily increasing melodramatic self-pity, "What is to become of us?" apparently not realizing or seeming overly concerned about the effect this wrenching display might have on her desolate children. She would grab wildly at the borrowed sheets and lay prostrate on the single bed they all shared while the children looked on in mute horror, holding hands in a musty corner of their badly lit room.

Florence Evelyn felt utterly powerless and gradually resentful, and her fear of abandonment and poverty only grew with each new episode. Her mother would wring her hands and emit long, wounded sobs, which drove the children out into the hallway or onto the front steps of the boardinghouse to escape the pitiful sounds, their hands over their ears. Eventually, brother and sister developed the practice of sleeping with a pillow over their heads to try to block out their mother's miserable night-time lamentations, a habit that would persist into adulthood for both of them.

Having left his affairs in a state of utter disarray, Win Nesbit, the unambitious lawyer, had injudiciously thrown his family into the hands of lawyers and the courts. Mrs. Nesbit found herself attempting on a weekly basis to sort out the dismal condition of her husband's rapidly disintegrating estate. As young as she was, Florence Evelyn could see the toll it was taking on her mother's looks and demeanor. The girl grew to fear the idea of going to court, almost to the point of a phobia. She also observed that her mother's reaction after only a few months was to shun all those she had known under better circumstances. The once happy mamma the children had known no longer existed, having been replaced by a strange, fretful, morose creature.

Florence Evelyn watched in amazement as her mother, only in her early thirties, suddenly willed herself, without warning or explanation, into an unconvincing pose of suffering silence. Here today. Gone tomorrow. Refusing to see even her closest friends, either out of shame or pride (another thing she couldn't afford), Mrs. Nesbit tried deliberately (if only intermittently and unsuccessfully) to obliterate her past and, it seemed to her bewildered children, her husband's memory. One day she no longer spoke his name either fondly or through acid tears. Even his picture was put away in a box on a closet shelf. Florence Evelyn and Howard could only surmise that their mother expected them to follow her example. Out of sight, out of mind.

This innate ability of her mother's to abruptly shut down (if only for brief periods), turn off her emotions, and get on with life in spite of catastrophe was a model of behavior Florence Evelyn observed with guarded curiosity, then hastily adopted. To cope with their sudden father-less, homeless, and penniless condition, sister and brother also developed an emotional resilience often mistaken by strangers as sullenness or gla-cial indifference. Shutting down or detaching themselves emotionally from a painful situation became a routine survival tactic; they learned to stifle or crush their own raw feelings so as not to upset their mother and thus avoid another harrowing scene. By her behavior, Mrs. Nesbit also progressively alienated any friends who offered assistance. Nor would she relent to seek help from either her own or Winfield's family, unless, as she said, there was absolutely no other alternative—which was almost always the case. But Mrs. Nesbit's abrupt lapses from leaden silence into abys-mal crying jags only hardened Florence Evelyn's resolve not to become a weak and pitiful hysteric, even though they alarmed the girl with their ferocity and physically sickened Howard.

Eventually, with no money whatsoever, the Nesbits moved in with Evelyn's maternal grandmother. However, this arrangement didn't last very long, and as she described it, "My earliest recollections of Pittsburgh are almost as painful as my later recollections." The penny-pinching family of three then moved to Cedar Avenue in Allegheny. More often than not, they had only one meal a day, and it was meager. Depending on one's point of view, Mrs. Nesbit either heroically, stupidly, or pathologically persisted in thinking she could somehow provide for herself and her children, despite all evidence to the contrary. She again borrowed some money from friends rather than family, and rented a house not far away in Shadyside on Fifth and South Highland Avenue with the intention of taking in boarders, figuring she could put her homespun skills to some practical use. It was a venture that would prove remarkably unsuccessful. And portentous.

FIRST EXPOSURE

According to Evelyn, it was a scorcher of a Sunday in August 1897, which for most people in Pittsburgh at that time meant sweating out the Sabbath heat from the front porch of their hard-won homes with either store-bought or improvised fans and lemonade. A barely perceptible, metallic-colored cloud of mill residue dissipated in the hot sun over the railroad tracks near Florence Evelyn's so-called home, which felt as impermanent to her as it did to the boarders.

Since it was Sunday, she was bored "almost to tears," with no friends and nothing to do. Howard was nowhere to be found, having taken to wandering off alone in search of nothing in particular. As she sat on the top step of the boardinghouse stoop, envying the neighbors who had lemonade and store-bought fans, Florence Evelyn noticed a man strolling down Cedar Avenue with a camera in his hand. Always one to take the initiative, the girl called out to the man, a local photographer. He stopped and turned around to see who was asking in such a small, eager voice to have her picture taken.

What he saw was twelve-and-a-half-year-old Florence Evelyn, whom he later said looked to him about eight or nine, running down the walk from the steps of the depressingly respectable boardinghouse. Everything about her seemed delightfully small except her thick hair and large piercing eyes. As he later recalled, she was "extremely pretty," almost unnervingly so, with a "childish abundance of curls" held barely in check by a blue ribbon. Like all Florence Evelyn's clothes, the dainty blue ankle-length dress with a matching waistband that she wore was one of her mother's designs. The man, who had the professional's eye for detail, remembered her worsted black stockings and thin-soled shoes resembling ballet slippers.

He watched as she eyed the camera in his hands and smiled in a way that seemed alternately flirtatious and shy. She asked him again if he would take her picture, and put one hand behind her skirts in a demure pose. He complied, struck by the openness and enthusiasm of the girl, and promised to send a copy of the picture to the boardinghouse. For some reason, although he noted the address, he had neglected to ask her name. Nonetheless, the man was so affected by the charming girl that he had the photo printed in a local Pittsburgh paper. He framed the original photograph and kept it on a shelf in his studio, little realizing that he was the first in a long line of professional photographers who saw something unique in this uncommon and willing little natural model.

But no matter how much they scrimped, the family seemed always on the verge of utter insolvency. In a telling indication of things to come, her mother, out of willful ignorance, wanton desperation, or monstrous calculation, exploited the pathetic state of affairs by sending her appealing prepubescent daughter to collect the weekly rents from the boarders, figuring that Florence Evelyn's looks would soften those who might not otherwise pay their rents on time. Needless to say, the overwhelming majority of boarders were middle-aged men; many were drummers (salesmen) or some equally transient type, while a number of them had no identifiable profession or particular social graces. Much later in life, Evelyn related to her daughter-in-law that even at such a young age, she sensed it was inappropriate for a child to knock on strange men's doors to ask for rent money: "Mamma was always worried about the rent," Evelyn recalled in 1915, but it was "too hard a thing" for her to actually ask for it every week, "and it never went smoothly." Although Florence Evelyn obeyed her mamma, the leering faces and sometimes glassy-eyed stares of the boarders, who smelled of whiskey or worse, made the twelve-year-old extremely uncomfortable. So did the comments a few felt compelled to mutter under their breath while squeezing their grimy two dollars' weekly rent into her small, soft hands.

But even Florence Evelyn's nascent charms could not keep the boardinghouse running at a profit, and little more than a month or so after the incident with the photographer, she and her mother had to relocate to a smaller boardinghouse solely as tenants. Out of necessity, Howard was conveniently sent once more to stay with an aunt outside Pittsburgh. One can only speculate on the jumble of feelings churning within Mrs. Nesbit, whose fears and ineffectuality forced her to hide from her relatives and to place Howard, so she said, out of harm's way (out of sight, out of mind) while she and her alternately hardheaded and dreamy daughter lived in the claustrophobic quarters of a room that Evelyn recalled in a letter "even mice rejected." One also wonders what nine-year-old Howard, who was far more sensitive and overtly needy than his sister, must have felt, living most of the time as if he were already an orphan. And an only child.

A deepening, double-edged fear of rejection and abandonment was imprinted indelibly on Florence Evelyn's young psyche, exacerbated by the constant upheaval and shuffling from one tedious boardinghouse to the next. Deprived of any sustained contact with other children (except her brother and occasionally her "country cousins"), friendships for the restless, lonely girl with anyone her own age were fleeting at best or for the most part nonexistent. Her growing inclination to quickly please or appease others and a sometimes desperate impulse to "smooth things over" (while keeping her true feelings to herself), together with her mother's ill-advised efforts to take advantage of her looks, made for a dangerous mix. Florence Evelyn's efforts to satisfy her mother were rarely rewarded with the kind of praise her father had lavished on her. Yet the girl's youthful naiveté and ambition gave her a sense of self-assurance and determination that were sorely lacking in her mother. The almost-teen wanted badly to be part of "the smart set" and believed that somehow her wishes would come true (in spite of her grandmother's saying that "if wishes were horses, beggars would ride").

In those rare moments when she didn't have to listen to her mother's harangues about where their next meal would come from, Florence Evelyn began to formulate a particularly whimsical but surprisingly durable fantasy life; she retreated into a snug and resilient soap bubble, whose transparent membrane allowed a view of the outside world, but at the same time refused to allow anyone or anything to burst it. The more her mother dragged her into the harsh light of stinging reality (eerily silent one moment, then wailing about the poorhouse and unmarked graves in some potter's field the next), the more Florence Evelyn retreated into her bubble. Her coping mechanism was to assume a dark-browed Irish silence as she honed her inherent knack for inhabiting two worlds simultaneously. Alternating between an almost too mature and matter-of-fact acceptance of a day's discouraging or disastrous events and the ability to escape at night into an admittedly adolescent but far more satisfying romantic fantasy world, a young Florence Evelyn would come to realize that even though dreaming was free, it could carry a great price.

Of course, Mrs. Nesbit's dilemma was certainly real and dire. Being a widow with two children approaching adolescence, no visible means of support, no social or public programs to offer assistance, a depressed and unstable economy, and no training of any kind that might be considered a profession, she didn't know where to turn. Nearly choking on the crumbs of her undigested pride, Mrs. Nesbit dropped her stoic pose one day and decided to ask for charity—from strangers—specifically, from Mrs. Mary Copely Thaw.

Mrs. Thaw was the granite-willed widow of one of Pittsburgh's wealthiest men and a prominent figure in her own not-so-small right. Mordantly overstuffed with good Christian works and self-righteousness, Mrs. Thaw modeled herself on England's Queen Victoria, whom she resembled (except that Mrs. Thaw was significantly taller). To that end, she wore only widow's weeds in public, as if in mourning for her life. Or the sins of others.

As Evelyn describes it, the Nesbits were living only a few long blocks from the hulking shadow of the Thaw family mansion. Named Lyndhurst, it was a menacing, medieval-styled structure newly built on Beechwood Boulevard, disguised as time-honored by a thin, spotty raw beard of freshly grown ivy. Mrs. Thaw, a devout Presbyterian, spent most of her time and a small part of her dead husband's immense fortune doing minor philanthropic work. She was known locally to give token amounts of money to needy families, which had prompted Mrs. Nesbit's dismal decision.

But, much to Mrs. Nesbit's shock and chagrin, when she steeled her nerve and rang the bell of the intimidating Lyndhurst to ask for a handout, she was rudely turned away by a gray-gloved servant, without ceremony or explanation. The humiliated woman practically tripped down the steps of Lyndhurst and returned to the boardinghouse. She did not tell her children about the incident, but as time passed, Mrs. Winfield Nesbit would never forget or forgive her mortifying affront on the doorstep of the high-and-mighty icy Thaws.

Florence Evelyn was aware that she had always sought her father's guidance, opinion, and approval much more than her mother's, whose energies had been directed toward the excruciatingly shy Howard. But the girl also recognized in an unconscious way that the cruel upheaval caused by her father's sudden exit tied her more closely to her mother, partly out of necessity, partly out of separation anxiety, and of course, one supposes, out of love. Most of the time, the girl felt sorry for her mother, and regretted when her own natural stubbornness caused her easily dismayed mamma additional stress.

But Florence Evelyn was fast approaching a new stage in her young and vulnerable life. She noticed how people, men and women alike, invariably responded to her with smiles and kind words (unlike her mother). A finely dressed woman stopped her on the street one day and exclaimed, "What a lovely child! Those eyes will break many a heart someday!" It soon began to filter through to the girl, however opaquely, that in the reduced family unit comprised of her mother, herself, and Howard, the magnetic center had slowly but surely shifted to her.

In January 1898, according to Evelyn, after the family had lived nearly

two years under the threat of absolute destitution, an acquaintance suggested to Mrs. Nesbit that she might find work in Philadelphia as a
seamstress. Weighing her options, Mrs. Nesbit saw that indeed there
were none. After yet another sniffling good-bye, this time at the noisy
Pittsburgh train station, "where dust could fill your mouth if you kept it
open too long," Florence Evelyn and Howard were sent back "to the
country" to live with an aunt. But with the deplorable economic climate
(the miserable lingering effects of the depression caused by the Panic of
1893), even those relatives were hard-pressed to make ends meet. So
within weeks after their arrival, brother and sister were summarily shipped
by their aunt to a family in Allegheny with whom their mother had been
friendly several years earlier. Almost imperceptibly, however, as the weeks
slogged by, the sea change in sensibilities that seemed so sluggish to the
advance guard began to surge, even in landlocked Pennsylvania.

Photo of Evelyn that inspired L. M. Montgomery's character
Anne of Green Gables, circa 1901.

CHAPTER THREE

Poses

Have you ever noticed the thought in the eyes of a pictured girl? . . . Ever seen a . . . model whose eyes were not vacant? The artist's model is either an auto-hypnotist or a mental gymnast. I think I was the latter.

—*Evelyn Nesbit*, My Story

Several weeks had wasted away since Florence Evelyn and Howard arrived on the doorstep of their distant relatives, veritable strangers who were as kind as could be under their own pinched circumstances. But self-preservation and the taint of resentful stinginess began to pervade the otherwise clean country air as four more weeks passed, with no word from Mamma Nesbit or money for the upkeep of her children. As their portions got smaller and the chores more demanding, the refugee Nesbit children, who had been taken out of school, began to wonder if they'd ever see their mother again, each fearing the worst but with unblinking childish optimism still capable of hope.

Then one day the jubilant word came—their mother had finally secured a job for herself in the City of Brotherly Love. Although she was a salesclerk and not a dress designer or even a seamstress, Mrs. Nesbit had managed to join the hustling bustled and burgeoning shirt-waisted new female workforce of America at Wanamaker's department store. Wanamaker's was Philadelphia's premier castle of commerce and the first store in America to install an elevator, far safer than the treacherous skirt-grabbing "escagators" whose interlocking slatted teeth threatened every day to pull women shoppers into the bowels of the basement.

Having saved enough money after a month of cutting yards of ging-ham, chintz, and velvet from huge bolts of fabric behind the sewing counter, Mrs. Nesbit sent for her exiled children. After perfunctory good-byes to their ersatz guardians at the station gate, Florence Evelyn and Howard were put on a train in Pittsburgh, with the conductor given instructions to "put them off in Philadelphia." Along with their measly belongings, Florence Evelyn had insisted on taking the "family" cat. When her thirteenth birthday/Christmas passed without any notice or presents, the girl pretended the cat had been a gift (when in fact it was a stray she and Howard found in an alleyway behind the neighborhood butcher shop). Every conductor who discovered the drowsy red tabby, wrapped contentedly in a flimsy tattered shawl on the girl's lap, wanted to throw it off the train. But each in turn took pity on the astonishingly pretty little waif and thin-boned, sad-eyed boy and let the cat be. There were no other children traveling alone.

Upon their arrival, Evelyn and Howard were introduced by their mother, who had taken the day off from work, to their new lodgings. The children narrowed their eyes and took in the sparse furnishings and tight quarters in the usual back room (always cheaper than a front room) on the second floor of yet another run-of-the-mill boardinghouse. They shrugged their shoulders in what had become for them an automatic ges-ture of blank acceptance. And then, within a few scant weeks of barely getting by on her moderate salary, serving the wives of middle managers and the maids of the well-to-do (and just after enrolling the children in the neighborhood public school), Mamma Nesbit announced that she had found positions for both of the children at Wanamaker's. This meant their schooling would be interrupted, indefinitely, as it had more than half a dozen times already.

At first Florence Evelyn was overjoyed at the prospect of being con-sidered adult enough to have a job. But not long afterward she felt a pang of sadness mixed with guilt that she would not be able (or so it seemed) to fulfill her father's dream that she go to Vassar. Nor did it seem likely that Howard would ever become a lawyer, especially if he couldn't get out of the fifth grade. Howard characteristically said little about his new job as a stock boy and seemed quietly resigned to not attending yet another nameless, unfriendly brick-faced school.

As her mother ripped down the hems of her homemade dresses to make her appear older (since only girls under sixteen wore knee-length skirts), a wistful Florence Evelyn also felt the increasingly familiar twinge of bitterness at having been moved around so much that she was never able to form any real friendships with anyone her age. Her apprehension at having been taken out of school again (perhaps permanently) grew as the weeks went by, so she tried whenever possible to read. Luckily, it didn't cost anything, since she could borrow books from the public library, and the few books that were occasionally left behind by boarders in the common sitting room she squirreled away and kept as her own.

Six days a week for twelve hours a day, Florence Evelyn, dressed in a dowdy starched uniform apron and newly hemmed ankle-length skirts, was a "floater," a sometime floor girl, sometime stock girl, sometime counter girl whose job it was to make sure all departments maintained a full supply of goods. Although her small hands and slight build, exaggerated by the oversize uniform apron, indicated to some apprehensive customers a girl of perhaps no more than eleven, Evelyn's mother assured the management that her daughter was sixteen. But even with their combined earnings from Wanamaker's, things were still bad enough that frequently the three Nesbits had only one meal a day, of little more than a cup of coffee and shredded wheat or mustard sandwiches (scraping to the bottom of a jar that Howard had pilfered from the grocery section of the store, with his mother's tacit approval). This diet did little to stabilize Howard's shaky constitution, and even though the severely strapped family hadn't been together in Philadelphia for long, Howard had to be sent away again, this time to the farm of another aunt near Tarentum "for his delicate health."

"My mother wept bitterly over this necessary parting," Evelyn recalled, even though Mamma Nesbit had also permitted him to work twelve hours a day at the store, six days a week.

Discovered

Living on Arch Street in Philadelphia, however, marked the beginning of Florence Evelyn's "independent career" (or so she imagined). And even as the weary century seemed on certain protracted days to be dragging its stiffening limbs toward its final months, a confident Florence Evelyn began to believe that at least her tiny part of the fickle universe had irreversibly shifted its orbit once more for the better. The woman who ran the boardinghouse on Arch Street was married to a newspaperman, who counted among his friends a reporter named Charlie Somerville. The young newspaperman took note of the remarkably "pretty child" during a visit. But it was while meandering aimlessly down a neighboring street one frigid Sunday, a week before her fourteenth birthday, that Florence Evelyn saw the face of destiny reflected in a store window—her own. It seemed inevitable. She was discovered.

As she peered into a specialty dry-goods window, admiring the variety of "outta sight" fabrics inside and picturing the birthday dress her mother could make from any one of them (had they been able to afford it), Florence Evelyn noticed in the reflection of the window an elderly woman staring intently at her from behind. Struck by the girl's unblemished porcelain skin set against dark tresses hidden partly under her coat, the woman approached the eye-catching girl, who turned to face her observer. In her longish cloth coat, with its twice-rolled sleeves and tatty muffler, decorated with cat hairs and wrapped carelessly around her neck and shoulders, Florence Evelyn seemed neither child nor adult but rather some strange combination of the two. She appeared like a china doll dressed in hobo hand-me-downs or one of those "darling diminutive performers from Barnum's museum" the woman had seen once in a daguerreotype. The girl's expression was also disconcerting; it seemed simultaneously immature and knowing, although what appeared at first to be rouge on her cheeks was simply the effect of the frigid wind, which whipped down the nearly deserted street.

"Would you like to pose for a portrait?" the woman asked.

An amused and noncommittal Florence Evelyn shrugged. Like most adolescent girls, she alternated between smug vanity and desperate insecurity about her appearance, particularly given the patchy, well-worn state of her clothing, usually made from mismatched pieces or remnants her mother took home from work. Today she thought this woman's offer was some kind of joke. The lady introduced herself as Mrs. Darach, a local portrait painter and miniaturist. A skeptical Florence Evelyn replied that she would raise the subject with her mother. The woman invited the girl to come to her studio on Chestnut Street later that day with her mother. On the way home, the usual formless fantasies of fame and fortune began to take on a more distinct shape in the girl's thoughts, fusing all the "formulaic fictions" she had already read that allowed young girls of that period to "create possibilities for their future."

In 1934, Evelyn would recall that up to that point, her mother had still not found a position anywhere to suit her self-proclaimed artistic talents, "that she kept failing all the time." She would testify during the first trial that her mother had tried very hard at first to secure a position as a dress designer, then as a seamstress. But the market demanded someone with a proven commercial record, someone who had been to Paris, someone with at least a little practical business experience "who had at her fingertips the latest mode," none of which Mrs. Nesbit had. So Florence Evelyn told her mother about the encounter.

After only brief hesitation (once it was established to Mrs. Nesbit's satisfaction that the person who requested the sitting was a woman), she agreed to the visit. That afternoon, Florence Evelyn began her career as an artist's model, sitting for five hours and earning a dollar for her efforts.

"I was as proud as though I myself combined all the genius of Michelangelo and Rosa Bonheur," she wrote. The pair stared in amazement at the crumpled bill, which her mother then stuffed reverently in a small cracked pitcher on their dresser. Perhaps it also began to dawn on Mrs. Nesbit that her daughter's potential as a breadwinner might put an end to their days of eating shredded wheat.

Another woman whom the new model and her mother befriended in

Philadelphia was the sister of a well-known and respected artist, John Storm. Florence Evelyn, already a "looker" and a "peach" (words she had heard from several boarders) needed neither the latest fashions nor make-up to enhance her natural gifts. After hearing of the girl's first sitting, at his sister's suggestion, Storm asked Mrs. Nesbit for permission to paint her daughter's portrait. Starting the very next week, and every Sunday after that, Florence Evelyn went to the elderly Storm's house and posed for him.

On Saturdays, when she wasn't working at the department store, and nearly every Sunday, she would sit for several hours in a studio, her head cocked to one side while the light was good, pretending to savor the fragrance of a fake flower or peering longingly out a window facing a brick wall across the alleyway. Sometimes as she sat having her thick hair braided then unbraided for the fifth time by her mother (to enhance the waves), Florence Evelyn looked up at the skylight, through which the sounds of the street filtered, along with the late-afternoon sunlight. Spending all her days either in the hectic store or in a musty, somber studio, if she wished that she could be outside, meeting people her own age and being carefree, she kept it to herself.

On most days, Mamma Nesbit seemed to have lost any hesitancy about the suitability of her daughter's posing for artists, be they men or women. The way Evelyn rationalized it in later years, "when I saw that I could earn more money posing as an artist's model than I could at Wanamaker's, I gave my mother no peace until she permitted me to pose for a livelihood." She adds, tellingly, "her objections crumbled under the force of necessity." To her delight, Florence Evelyn was eventually able to shed her ill-fitting apron for good—and for the more enticing attire (or lack thereof) of the professional studio model. Once posing demanded all of her time, the fourteen-year-old Florence Evelyn was ecstatic to be able to trade two jobs for one, thinking that now she might at least earn some freedom along with her wages.

It was through Storm that the eager little model was soon introduced to an emergent artists' colony, comprised solely of women, who shared a busy studio in the city not far from the Pennsylvania Academy of Fine

Arts, where all had been students. The group of three included Violet Oakley, a painter and stained-glass artist who had studied under Louis Comfort Tiffany, and two aspiring and talented painter-illustrators, Jessie Willcox Smith and Elizabeth Shippen Green, each of whom was on the cusp of her own fame and independent career.

Oakley was instantly struck by an ethereal quality in the young girl's looks and demeanor. The latter two, who specialized in depicting children, saw in Florence Evelyn's smooth adolescent features, which still retained some of the roundness of childhood in spite of her poor diet, the perfect model for idealized children's heads. With an important commission for some stained-glass windows to be installed in a nearby church, Oakley engaged Florence Evelyn's services as a model immediately after meeting with her. In the girl's graceful, undeveloped figure, boyish in its thin, lean lines, she saw the perfect embodiment of a kind of ambivalent, classically androgynous spirituality wrestling with the sensuality of her face. Inspired by the girl's subtle Raphael-like beauty, Oakley used her almost exclusively as a model for her angels. Barefoot, draped in floor-length diaphanous white robes, with her waist-length profusion of dark hair uncoiled down the small of her back or pinned up in a loose chignon, Florence Evelyn was immortalized in a number of stained-glass images. As she recalled years later, "I believe I posed for a heavenly host of angels; there are a number of churches in Pennsylvania and New York whose windows have my face and figure etched into them."

But even as she remained fitfully unsure about the propriety of modeling in general, Mamma Nesbit said that she took comfort in the fact that most of the artists who regularly engaged her daughter's services were female, while the men were well beyond middle age and therefore "safe." Florence Evelyn soon began to model full-body for Willcox Smith and Shippen Green, and was given the chance to indulge her childish fantasies by dressing up in all kinds of fetching outfits and whimsical costumes, many of the type associated with her favorite fables and fairy tales. Invariably, as she posed in these costumes, the girl began to envision herself as the characters she knew so well. Although it often reminded her of the precious books she had lost, she was doubly thrilled by the prospect of playing dress-up and getting paid for it. According to the adult Evelyn, during this period (roughly between 1899 and 1900) she "lived again in a world of fancy, far from economic worries."

Moreover, as much as she adored the flowing angelic gowns and the Bo Peep flounces of lace and lavender, Florence Evelyn became increasingly enamored of the idea that these people who painted or sketched or sculpted or etched her believed she was pretty enough to be a professional model. Eventually, as word spread of the remarkably malleable studio girl from Pittsburgh, who, with a subtle glance or change in the sweep of her hair, could play a milkmaid or nymph, a goddess or a Gypsy, other artists joined the charmed circle.

By the time Florence Evelyn turned fifteen, after a year of modeling and earning a steady income, she was ecstatic over her blossoming career. But her mother, who was only thirty-four, was intensely miserable. As Evelyn recalled, "[Mamma] could never get used to the rush and tumult of the department store, the hard-bargaining women customers." As she fretted during certain dim hours of the evening that she wished Florence could go back to school and finish her education, Mamma Nesbit's chronic complaint was, "Oh, if I could only put to practical use my knack for designing!"

And yet, in spite of her protestations, once Mrs. Nesbit found they could live on her daughter's earnings alone, she quit her job at Wanamaker's, ostensibly to "oversee" Florence Evelyn's new career. As the spirited model was handed from studio to studio in the rush of her daily work, she soon met other artists, male artists, who were no longer "all mummified plums" but who engaged her services with no real fuss or feathers from her mother. Luckily for the little poser, they were all serious artists and not "the depraved dabblers" condemned by various moral watchdogs of the period. Two of the more prominent artists who hired the girl were George Gibbs and Mills Thompson, both of whom illustrated stories, magazine covers, and books like the ones Florence Evelyn's father had brought home for her back in Tarentum and Pittsburgh. Although her mother raised no more objections in public, Mrs. Nesbit griped privately and annoyingly in their room at night about the possible impropriety of it all ("too much like Lady Macbeth," an adult Evelyn conjectured). Mamma Nesbit's frequent complaint seemed to be, "An artists' model! It sounds Bohemian. I don't like it."

Nonetheless, as she had in response to her father's death and her family's abrupt plunge into poverty, Florence Evelyn alternated between an unspoken resignation to the reality of her present circumstances and habitual episodic flights into dreamland, particularly during those long hours of immobility staring at nothing or the back of a canvas.

Having to fight the natural adolescent inclination to fidget, to move her head "exactly in the direction the artist did not want her to look," gradually, she said, she learned the value of patience as she sat absolutely motionless. But being unable to move or speak turned out to be exasperating most of the time for the normally animated teenager. She remembers the mental tricks she was compelled to perform to combat the teeth-grinding monotony of sittings. These sessions, she said, sometimes led her down "fantastic avenues . . . and secured angles of vision which perhaps I should not ordinarily have secured." It also fostered in her a sense of independence, and a belief in opportunities she didn't think possible for a girl until then. As a result, going against the grain of cultural conventions and expectations of the day, young Florence Evelyn decided that while "a girl's dreams are never practical," she had "yet to meet the freakish being who looks forward to a life of mending and minding." It was a revelation. From that moment on, as far as she was concerned, "[a] healthy girl does most of her dreaming by night, and if I did any dreaming at all in the daytime, it was not of the career that lay ahead of me [as a housewife and mother]."

So, in place of real friendships and her father's love, Florence Evelyn began to substitute the admiration of others as a way to avoid thinking too much about her losses, her long hours of posing, her mother's own assumed pose of being concerned about convention versus commerce, and the unreasonable inequity of it all for her and Howard.

To everyone who saw her, the girl had a remarkably distinctive look that set her far apart from any other models and so-called beauties of the day. There was something magnetic and haunting about her large, smoky eyes and almost mournful half smile. It was an expression Evelyn adopted without effort—and without any prompting from the artists. Virtually all who came into contact with her or saw her image tried to articulate what that expression meant, but were left unsatisfied. It is perhaps the greatest irony that in describing in her memoirs what she was thinking or feeling during long hours of posing, Evelyn recalled that initially she was thinking about the most mundane things one could imagine. Or absolutely nothing.

Significantly, however, at an age when any adolescent's personality is merely percolating, when an unchecked ego can boil over (even if watched), the girl from Tarentum was being told by everyone around her that she was the loveliest thing they had ever seen. And she had to believe it, because respected artists were willing to pay for the privilege of using her as their model. She was already possessed of a healthy self-absorption (and with few possessions of any other kind), so it did not require much for fifteen-year-old Florence Evelyn to be taken by the attention. And since most girls that age do not need encouragement to become preoccupied with their looks, Florence Evelyn's new career only exacerbated her propensity for mirror gazing. The flattery and unqualified approval of professional artists caused her to study her reflection when she was alone, sometimes for hours. Her mother began expressing some distress over her daughter's growing vanity, but there seemed little she could (or would) do to control or even curtail it, since their livelihood depended completely on those looks.

It wasn't long, however, before the hardworking little model discovered to her dismay that the reality of tedious hours holding a pose in airless, cluttered studios that reeked of oils, turpentine, pipe smoke, stale coffee grounds, and moldy cheese in mousetraps was less appealing than she had initially thought. As she described it, her enthusiasm for being painted "died with an aching neck" and an empty stomach when certain artists refused to break for lunch. And she still missed going to school. Even though she fought it, the melancholy girl could not throw off the prickly veil of loneliness that dropped on her with uncomfortable regularity in the twilight hours. She found little solace in the infrequent visits of her increasingly withdrawn brother, who was still staying primarily with relatives, supposedly because of his delicate health. One could speculate that even though Howard was her favorite, Mamma Nesbit also found it more economical to have her son stay with family (to whom she sent no money), and that Howard's mental health was more likely at risk than his physical well-being.

The romantic notion that artists live on a higher plane than mere mortals was also soon dissolved for the much-in-demand studio girl. As the weeks and months went by, she learned that they were as concerned with money and the grasping mundane arena of materialism as was her mother. And as much as she enjoyed conversation with those painters and sculptors who, to her surprise, talked to her while working, Florence Evelyn wanted to find someone to talk to who wasn't "a dreary adult, always blah, blahing about making ends meet."

Whenever she could, she read on her own. Growing into an omnivorous if perhaps too indiscriminate a reader, particularly of novels, she made a concerted effort to master the classics she had taken out of the library when she could and would hold them reverently in her hands, at times even pressing the books to her chest as she slept. At the time, she had in her possession a copy of Zola's *Nana*, left in a closet at the boardinghouse "by an innocuous-looking old woman." She had heard something about scandalous French novels, and this particular one was "somewhat beyond" her comprehension. Nevertheless, she understood well enough that she could never get into college without first attending high school, and so late one afternoon, while posing, Florence Evelyn revived the idea of someday going to Vassar. She believed that if she worked hard enough, she would be able to save funds sufficient to fulfill what had been her father's dream for her. Ultimately, she would come to the conclusion that reading secured for her "a sense of proportion, the one sense that spells salvation to a girl upon whom is lavished the subtle [and not-so-subtle] flattery" of premature attention.

With a child's heart bound by adult responsibilities, as more time passed, the child-woman found herself in the unenviable and paradoxical position of literally inhabiting both worlds simultaneously. She was acutely aware that the money she earned was the sole support of her family—her mother constantly reminded her of the fact in case she had any ideas about quitting when she complained, however infrequently, that she was bored or tired. The image of her hysterical mother came back to Florence Evelyn again and again while she sat for hours on end, and during the night, her own inexpressible fear of sudden poverty often came more sharply into focus. Doing what she would throughout her life, however, Florence Evelyn decided to ignore adversity or try if possible to alter whatever bitter reality confronted her. Or shape it into something positive, chipping away wherever possible.

As an increasing number of eager painters and illustrators dropped by the studios where "the little Miss Nesbit" worked steadily in the "skylight world" week after week, several commented on the girl's potential as a professional photographer's model. The possibility for such a change appealed to the teenager immediately, since she believed that one had to hold a pose only for several minutes for a photograph (she was wrong). And, her mother offered, she could sit for any number of photographers in the same time that she now sat for one artist (she was not wrong).

Not long after the suggestion was made, Ryland Phillips, a Philadelphia photographer who had heard from John Storm about the fetching fifteen-year-old, arranged for her to sit for some photographic studies. Or rather stand. Throughout the session, Phillips had Florence Evelyn lean casually against a wall, clad in a floor-length milky white satin gown, with her hair falling softly to one side. Unlike the painters, who preferred her without makeup, however, the photographer put some eye makeup and lipstick on Evelyn, subtle touches that nonetheless gave her a startlingly more mature appearance. Phillips was extraordinarily pleased by the pictures in which, he said, she resembled "a young Aphrodite." He managed to have them printed in an art magazine, where they attracted a good deal of attention; they were then reproduced in the Philadelphia newspapers (and once again a year or two later in *Broadway Magazine*).

By late fall, the Philadelphia newspapers had begun reporting on the "strange and fascinating creature" whose face "shows a remarkable maturity of repose, though [she is] no more than fourteen years old." Although the issue of her correct age was already becoming a topic for debate, as Florence Evelyn's popularity grew, so did the demand for the privilege of photographing the "rare young Pittsburgh beauty" or capturing her "dazzling allure on canvas." As one reporter saw it, she exuded an "enchanting combination of youthful innocence and colossal self-possession." When one of the local shopkeepers on Arch Street remarked casually to the girl that she was going to shake up the new century that was just around the corner, she almost believed it.

As New Year's Eve 1899 approached and the final weeks of the 1800s

One of the Phillips photographs of fifteen-year-old
Evelyn posing in Philadelphia, 1900.

were peeled away, Florence Evelyn hoped that the much-heralded Century
of Progress that was about to unwrap itself would live up to the hoopla
and near hysteria she heard on every side. While her mother mulled over
the idea of another change in the scenery behind her uniquely photoge-
nic daughter, Florence Evelyn fantasized about how she might figure in
whatever awesome changes lay ahead in the pink new tomorrow of 1900
and all tomorrows after that. But not even in her wildest dreams could
she have predicted that the public's burning desire for the perfect emblem
of their imagined perfect new age would be realized in a girl from
Tarentum. The setting, of course, was already obvious.

Advertising pose of sixteen-year-old Evelyn as the Sphinx.

CHAPTER FOUR

The Little Sphinx in Manhattan

By 1900, questions of identity had become a social obsession. . . . But there was something new: the favored type was one variation or other of the American female. —*Martha Banta,* Imagining American Women

Vulgar tradition dictated that portliness in mature men of the dignified leisure class indicated wealth and opulence. The opposite was true for women— dictated to by the useless and expensive canons of conspicuous waste . . . under the guidance of the canon of pecuniary decency, the men find the resulting artificiality and induced pathological features attractive, so for instance the constricted waist. —*Thorsten Veblen*

Mrs. Nesbit kept turning over in her head the suggestion that her coveted daughter might have a more profitable career as a photographer's model in New York City. After a few more turns, despite Florence Evelyn's regular income posing for a satisfied spectrum of Philadelphia painters, illustrators, and sculptors, in mid-June of 1900, Mrs. Nesbit packed up her few belongings in a ratty carpet bag and set off for New York, alone, with no plan of action whatsoever, leaving her children behind once again. What she did take with her were some letters of introduction to a few well-known metropolitan artists—but she told herself that she would use them only as a last resort. In the meantime, a confused and anxious Florence Evelyn, who, for the first time since her father's death, had felt a pleasing sensation of security, was pulled off her pedestal and shunted back to Pittsburgh to stay with family friends, while Howard was once more planted on a family farm out in Allegheny from which he had already been uprooted twice before.

As the weeks stretched into months with no money and only a few perfunctory postcards from her mamma, a discouraged Florence Evelyn was alternately bewildered and annoyed. She wondered why she couldn't have kept working while her mother was away, especially since her mamma took all the modeling money she had earned in the last year and a half to allegedly stir this latest pot of gilt veneer. She wondered where and how her mother was looking for a position. She wondered why the New York artists weren't clamoring for her services, not knowing that for reasons only she knew, her mamma had felt it necessary to withhold the letters of introduction.

Instead, whether out of fear or sheer ineptitude, Mrs. Nesbit had once again borrowed money from the "good penny," their ubiquitous family friend Charles Holman, who was making a name for himself back in Pittsburgh, where he had positioned himself to become secretary to the Stock Exchange. At the time, Holman's continued charity to the little Nesbit family and persistent refusal to let her mother "isolate herself in widowhood" seemed an admirable thing to young Florence Evelyn, who never wondered how it was that her mother managed to communicate with Mr. Holman but not with her or Howard as she supposedly scoured Manhattan for work, month after month.

During one of her last sessions posing, the fetching model had begun to calculate how many hours she needed to work in order to pay back all the people her mother had "unhappily imposed upon" in the last year alone. But it now appeared that the career that had begun so unexpectedly and fortuitously was on the verge of ending just as suddenly. It briefly crossed Florence Evelyn's mind that in a fit of reactionary perversity, her mother had sabotaged her fledgling career out of jealousy, cutting off her nose to spite her daughter's prettier face. But at fifteen, all she could do was sit and wait and stare at the walls. And not get paid a penny for doing so.

As of late November, Mrs. Nesbit had not found a job, although it's anybody's guess where she looked, how strenuously, and what type of job she looked for in the five months since leaving Philadelphia. But the intensely vibrant, swirling city that offered such glorious opportunities to so many others seemed to wrap itself around Mrs. Nesbit like a winding sheet. Thrown eventually into a state of panic, then paralysis, by the sheer impossibility of it all, with the hatchet edge of winter approaching (if the *Farmer's Almanac* was accurate), after securing a second-floor, back-room apartment on Twenty-second Street, Mamma Nesbit finally sent for her refugee children. She supposed that if nothing else, they might all find positions at Macy's department store as they had at Wanamaker's.

With her sixteenth birthday only three and a half weeks away, an elated Florence Evelyn went alone back to the country on money borrowed from a family friend to reclaim Howard, while a third friend provided the money for the children's railroad tickets to New York (her mother apparently having spent all of Florence Evelyn's earnings during her five un-accountable months in Manhattan). The trip from Pennsylvania to Manhattan, however, was far less dismal than the one to Philadelphia a year earlier. Fully revived, Evelyn recalled in later years that on the way to New York she began to foment images of a "splendid future for her and her brother." Her mother was, noticeably, excluded from that particular vision.

As predicted, winter in December 1900 descended like a sledge-hammer. Reunited with her underdressed and overwhelmed children, according to the adult Evelyn, her mother continued to try to look for work as a designer or seamstress. Part of Florence Evelyn still believed (or hoped) naively that in New York City her mother would become a well-known designer, and that their combined efforts would finally pull the family for-ever beyond the relentless, grappling hands of unfeeling bank presidents, callous courts, and mustard sandwiches. But Mrs. Nesbit's nebulous efforts proved futile. Everywhere she went, the same questions were asked.

"Have you been to Paris lately?" Or, "Have you had experience with similar firms?"

She had even less success than she did in Philadelphia and Pittsburgh, since the impediments that had blocked her way in the other cities were magnified a thousandfold in New York. On the contrary, however, Manhattan offered exceptional head-turning possibilities for an aspiring young model of equally exceptional head-turning looks.

Even though the three Nesbits shivered in a poorly heated room for several days, Mrs. Nesbit maintained her profoundly puzzling and inexplicable inertia regarding the letters of introduction. When it seemed she was on the verge of capitulating, she confessed to Florence Evelyn that she was simply unsure how to proceed. Moreover, she said she was worried about the propriety of her daughter becoming a New York model. Staring at her mother's vexed expression and empty purse hanging limply on the closet door behind her, the girl asked why it was all right to pose in Pittsburgh and Philadelphia but not New York. Her mother had no answer. A day later, when the all-too-familiar press of insistent hunger squeezed them (each had only a cup of cheap java and a biscuit the entire day), Mrs. Nesbit surrendered.

She took the Ryland Phillips photos and a letter of introduction to James Carroll Beckwith, a well-known and respected New York painter. After seeing the photographs, Beckwith said he wanted to see immediately if this "perfectly formed nymph" really existed in the flesh. The very next day, the diminutive poser and her mother came to Beckwith's studio on Fifty-seventh Street and Sixth Avenue. The gray-haired artist was instantly struck by what one reporter would describe as "the soul of beauty trapped behind big melancholy eyes." Beckwith was particularly affected by her haunting pubescent loveliness and the uncommon mixture of innocence and ennui in her expression that others had already noted.

The artist took Mrs. Nesbit aside, spoke to her about the business side of posing, and said that indeed he would be very happy to use her uncommonly lovely daughter as his model. He gave his credentials, in a show of politeness, since it was obvious Mrs. Nesbit had never heard of him and knew nothing of his work or the New York art scene. Florence Evelyn listened intently from the sidelines. When Beckwith mentioned that he taught life classes at the Art Students League, the girl involuntarily gasped and waited nervously for her mother's reaction.

She had heard about the school while listening to conversations in the Philadelphia studios, and, true to form, when her mother understood that life classes meant "posing in the nude," she "went to pieces." Beckwith assured a frantic Mrs. Nesbit that he had no intention of allowing her little girl to pose like that, whereupon, in an uncharacteristic show of proactive involvement, Mamma Nesbit said she would see for herself, since she would be at all the sittings. Within a month, however, she seemed to have forgotten her pledge.

MODELING AND MIGNON

After only ten days in New York, Florence Evelyn was already scheduled to pose twice a week for Beckwith, whose staunchest patron was John Jacob Astor. The elderly painter expressed his concerns for her welfare and took a grandfatherly view of the sweetly inexperienced adolescent with her equally unsophisticated mother, particularly given all the dark and dodgy corners in a city where people whispered nervously about white slavery and the less morally scrupulous routinely sought to procure images popularly known as "mignon." These were photo postcards of barefoot, fresh-faced young women or girls in Gypsy-style or rural costumes. Only a few degrees of attitude and clothing removed from the more salacious French postcards depicting fully nude *"jeunes filles"* smuggled in from the Continent and circulated throughout the city's thriving pornographic underground, mignon photos were in some ways more disturbing and subversive, disguising pedophilia as sentiment and pandering to the closeted connoisseur of "young filets."

When Florence Evelyn told Beckwith one afternoon soon after she had begun posing for him that she planned to seek out additional modeling work on her own (since her mother seemed incapable of finding work but moaned incessantly about their not having enough money), the artist raised his hands in dismay.

"You are not the sort of girl," he cautioned, wagging his finger, "that should go knocking at studio doors."

He offered to give her some new letters of introduction to respectable artists in New York, men whom he described as "eminently safe." As he went to a dilapidated desk to search for pencil and paper, the girl's thoughts reached back to the Pittsburgh boardinghouse and the unsavory prospect of asking for the rent from boarders at her mother's urging. Thanks to Beckwith's intervention, however, the teen soon found herself posing for a number of legitimate artists, including Frederick S. Church, Herbert Morgan, and Carl Blenner, without having to knock on any strange men's doors.

At first her workload was fairly light, and the poses Florence Evelyn was asked to hold were not particularly difficult. With her "liquid brown eyes," "rosy Cupid's bow mouth," "softly rounded translucent shoulders," "wildly abundant tresses," and "the most perfectly modeled foot since Venus," Evelyn's Pre-Raphaelite looks were indeed an artist's dream in the flesh. As she eased back into life in the studios, within a scant few months, the "girl from the provinces" began to attract enough attention to become a particular favorite of the New York artists (just as she had in Philadelphia). She was soon in demand by a significant number of painters, sculptors, and illustrators.

One day a reporter came down to the boardinghouse to interview Miss Florence Evelyn, notable as the first of what would soon become a regular routine in her life. Her mother showed him the Philadelphia photographs, one of which was promptly printed in one of the New York evening papers. When the *Sunday American* published two big pages of photographs, the short fuse of modern celebrity was ignited. Even so, at such a young age and with so little knowledge of how the world worked, the adult Evelyn would come to believe after some reflection, "I do not know that to be brought into the public eye so young is the happiest of experiences." Nor was it something her mother was equipped to deal with, any more than she had been regarding her husband's hopeless finances.

Being interviewed by a bona-fide New York reporter was "a novel experience that first time," the adult Evelyn wrote in 1934, and slightly less satisfying each time after that, especially when she realized that her mother concealed from her how much money they had and how much she was paid for such frequent "exposure." As for Mamma Nesbit, she gradually adapted to her role as "manager" of her daughter's career, despite a complete and consistent lack of business sense and only intermittent concerns about the possible impropriety of life "in the studios" for a girl barely sixteen years old.

According to Evelyn thirty years later, when she began her career in New York City, "in the main they wanted me for my head. I never posed for the figure in the sense that I posed in the nude." As her mother would tell reporters, "I never allowed Evelyn to pose in the altogether as did Trilby"—although there is suggestive evidence to suggest otherwise. Evelyn herself describes a painting of her, done by Frederick Church in July 1900, that was hung in the Lotos Club in New York: "[I was] an Undine with water lilies in [my] hair, running down my bare limbs, [with] two striped tigers at [my] flanks." Another painting, done by Carroll Beckwith in 1901, shows a decidedly demure but partially nude young woman, her hair piled loosely on her head, in an open kimono with one breast exposed; the young subject stares almost straight ahead. It is titled *Miss N.*

While the tactic of putting a barely clad young female model in a diaphanous classical costume, surrounding her with cherubs in some spurious mythical setting, or laying her out in an "Oriental posture," helped both avant-garde and academic artists circumvent middle-class prudery (and sometimes avert censure), to those not interested in serious or high art, a studio model's real or thinly veiled nudity and seductive poses were either good for cheap titillation or an abomination. Such was the case with the obvious suggestiveness of many of young Florence Evelyn's poses, intensified by the low-cut, flimsy, or minimalist but strategically placed drapery she wore where less was significantly and scandalously more.

In a number of pictures, Florence Evelyn gives the appearance of one "just budding into girlhood," and at times a distinctly peaches-and-cream American girlhood. Another of Beckwith's paintings, depicting a demure and comely Evelyn in a long-sleeved, high-necked black and red velvet dress is simply titled *Girlhood.* However, despite her Irish-Scottish-English ancestry, her natural coloring—brunette hair, heavy-lidded dark eyes, alabaster skin, and full-lipped pouty mouth—struck all who saw her as strangely foreign and decidedly Oriental, a loaded word that conjured up "naughty visions" for Americans at the time. As a result, she was frequently asked to model in the garb of "an Eastern girl in Turkish costume, all vivid coloring, with ropes and bangles of jade" about her exposed neck and bare arms.

The striking exoticism in her images inspired men and women alike to make comparisons with legendary beauties of the ancient past. She was Venus, Nefertiti, and Cleopatra all rolled into one sultry and precociously erotic package that belied her years. She was, according to various reporters, Psyche, the Sybil, or "a Siren out of Homer." Struggling to find the words to describe the hypnotic effect she had on those who saw her newest pictures in his case, one photographer hit upon it exactly—her look was "innocence and experience combined." She exuded the egglike virginal fragility of Shakespeare's Ophelia one moment and the brazen sensuality of wicked Salome the next. It was mere speculation on the part of observers which pose might be closer to the truth.

To most who saw her pictures and photographs, Florence Evelyn appeared at times oddly detached, her expression tantalizingly inscrutable, enough to cause more than one reporter to refer to her as "the Little Sphinx." Her calm, unflinching gaze was, to the more reactionary, "a bold and impudent coquettish stare" that affected observers in the same way it had unnerved those who saw her when she was a young child. For most, trying to read something into the little Sphinx's eyes was a perplexing enterprise. It was like looking at a mirage—something of the depths might appear visible but was indistinct and tantalizingly beyond reach, perhaps even illusory. The serenely enigmatic expression on her face intrigued observers, most of whom assumed it was a look she was trained to give. In reality, it was as natural to her as breathing.

As a result, in keeping with the upbeat tempo of the times, like Cinderella stepping from the pages of her storybook, the little girl from the outskirts of the sooty city rose seemingly overnight from deprivation and obscurity to become what one reporter called the "glittering girl model of Gotham." Very quickly after that first interview, a steady stream of newsmen came around the boardinghouse, anxious to have a photograph of "Miss Florence Nesbit," the girl destined to "flash into public view as a famous beauty." This was also the beginning of some confusion on the part of reporters and the public. Since she was Florence Evelyn and her mother was Evelyn Florence, a number of times the names were confused, with captions that read Miss Evelyn Florence or Miss Florence Nesbit. *Broadway Magazine* published a two-page spread with the Phillips photographs, but with two different names, as if Evelyn were her own twin.

There was also continued confusion and speculation about how old she was, since her mother invariably increased Evelyn's age by two or three years to skirt the thorny issue of child-labor laws. But as Florence Evelyn's popularity rose, the prickly question of her age piqued the curiosity of more than one secret admirer—and sent a red flag up for the vigilance societies, particularly the one run by a bulldozing man who had been a Civil War general and who saw Manhattan as little more than "Gotham and Gomorrah."

COMSTOCKERY

Sex. The stark impropriety of living, breathing models stripped of their previously mandated flesh-colored body stockings. The dubious avant-garde practices of the Art Students League. In fact, the entire question of what defines art as opposed to pornography (particularly if children were involved) was but one battle being waged in the explosive culture wars of the newest century, where, according to Evelyn years later, girls like herself were "sacrificed by straight-laced morality on the altar of mid-Victorian prudery." It was a decade where the fanatically puritanical still covered piano legs so as not to expose "too much limb," while at the same time newly coined euphemisms for a woman's private parts proliferated, including such colorful phrases as daisy den, ivory gate, Cupid's crown, and Bluebeard's closet. Like the ancient serpent, the Ouroboros, with its tail in its mouth, the age-old bugaboo of sex wound itself up-, mid-, and downtown in self-propelled vicious circles—and inevitably coiled around Florence Evelyn.

When it came to sex, the "Naughty Oughts" were of course, for many, a dim and confusing time. Boys were dressed as girls when very young, and girls played boys onstage. One of the most popular productions of the day was J. M. Barrie's *Peter Pan*, the story of the boy who never wanted to grow up and become a man—and wouldn't when played by actress Maude Adams. The whole subject of birth control was taboo in a society where "prophylactic" meant a popular brand of toothpaste. Information, medical or otherwise, regarding sexual activity was virtually nonexistent for women (it would take another ten years for Margaret Sanger to begin her campaign to educate the public about such things, and she would face not only withering criticism but the constant threat of imprisonment). Men, meanwhile, did have contraceptives available to them in the form of sheepskin condoms, but only if they were urbane enough to be "in the know" and willing to procure them "under the counter." Otherwise, they relied on the ancient methods of withdrawal, dumb luck, abstinence, and perhaps prayer to prevent unwanted pregnancies.

There were skirmishes unfolding on a wide variety of sexually charged fronts even as Tom (and Dick and Harry) foolery of every illegal and immoral kind appeared ready to burst through the seamy cracks that were exposing themselves in various parts of the city. But those who were routinely engaged in nocturnal missions of dissolution found themselves

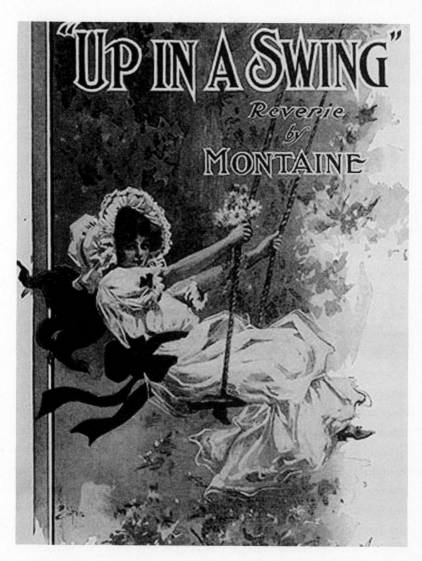

Typical image of innocent girlhood on sheet music, circa 1900.

locked in almost weekly moral combat with the one-man army named Anthony Comstock.

Defender of the innocents and crusader for purity, Comstock saw on the "alien island" of Manhattan a swarming battlefront, and the great campaign before him consisted of holding the line between what he believed was morally uplifting versus the eyebrow-raising immorality of nearly everything else, including the breezes blowing around the Flatiron building that lifted women's skirts. Decades earlier, Comstock made a name for himself as the sponsor of what are still known today as "the Comstock laws"—anti-obscenity legislation that makes it a crime to send any materials with sexual content through the mail (particularly those offering information on birth control).

Comstock made pronouncements almost daily, condemning the New Woman (one was arrested for smoking a cigarette on Fifth Avenue), the naturalistic novels of Stephen Crane and Theodore Dreiser, the Five Points area, beer halls, ragtime music, Sandow the strongman, amusement park rides, "saucy" sheet music, lotteries, dime novels, cigarette cards, Tin Pan Alley, bicycles, and even the aristocratic sport of tennis (an "ungraceful, unwomanly and unrefined game that offended all canons of womanly dignity and delicacy"). The only actual physical entertainment for women that was exempt from Comstock's reproach was swinging (in the literal sense, that is). He considered riding on a swing an innocent and innocuous form of exercise for young ladies, bound as they were to a male-dominated ideal of naive and girlish femininity that strove to keep them perpetually infantile.

Comstock attacked with equal force and watchfulness everything he believed offered fleshly or sinful distractions. A number of years earlier (when Teddy Roosevelt was still police commissioner), the sober-minded Comstock had tried to get the police to enforce the Sunday blue laws and close the saloons. But his success was limited and ultimately short-lived. His well-publicized campaign against all that he considered indecent came to be known as "Comstockery," so named by the curmudgeonly Irish dramatist George Bernard Shaw, whose frank and thought-provoking naturalistic plays such as *Mrs. Warren's Profession* and *Major Barbara* were specific targets of Comstock's conscience-hammering censorship. *Mrs. Warren's Profession* was closed after only one performance in New York, and several other plays suffered similar fates.

Comstock, who believed his work had been commissioned by God, saw himself as the supreme guardian of virtue fighting certain "jackals of the law." His lofty goal was to be accomplished through the assiduous enforcement of anti-obscenity laws. What's more, he was an officially sanctioned crusader, since he was designated a special agent for the Post Office. Within two years in his position, Comstock had "weighed in" with his opinions on pornography and initiated his own "bonfire of the vanities" by seizing more than 100,000 pounds of objectionable books and close to 200,000 drawings and photos. Yet while anything remotely associated with sex was anathema as far as the upstanding Society for the Suppression of Vice and its commander were concerned, those seeking lower and even horizontal pleasures could easily find them in the Tenderloin and Bowery, where an estimated 25,000 painted women who were "neither Parisian nor theatrical" walked the streets.

The rest of the female population of course navigated their way through the sometimes treacherous labyrinth of "social necessity," only to become part of the "sexual-marital bind." For some more enlightened social critics, these angels in the household differed perhaps only slightly from their unfortunate sisters, the city's "fallen women," since they too sold themselves and their modesty—only for a higher price. Described by author and journalist Charlotte Perkins Gilman, the sinister and deceptively oppressive social patterns that threatened to strangle any woman attempting to see through or escape them meant that "the same world exists for women as for men, the same human energies and human desires . . . [but] all that she may wish to do must come through a single channel and a single choice. Wealth, power, social distinction . . . not only these but home and happiness, reputation, ease and pleasure . . . all must come to her through a small gold ring."

"THE STATUE THAT OFFENDED NEW YORK"

But it was a large gold woman who was at the pivoting center of one of the most heated sexual debates of the day in New York. Comstock's most visible yet elusive enemies were "the infidels" Stanford White and his comrade in arms, sculptor Augustus Saint-Gaudens, who seemed intent

Collier's *cover satirizing Comstock's attempts*
to purify the Garden Diana.

upon thwarting Comstock's prissy and bullying self-righteous attempts at censorship. Rumors of scantily clad underage showgirls bursting out of pies at men's clubs in the city had already sent Comstock into spasms of rage, and when he learned that the maestro of such depraved entertainment had set his sights on a much more public form of "entertainment," he was beside himself.

White's desire for an ornamental figure to adorn the top of his radiant Garden Tower resulted in Saint-Gaudens's offering him a fittingly resplendent eighteen-foot sculpture of Diana, the goddess of the hunt (and chastity, wink, wink), which he had displayed at the 1893 World's Exposition. Modeled on Saint-Gaudens's mistress and clad only in her own natural beauty, the first Diana was too heavy to stand safely on her revolving ball-bearing perch. So the sculptor produced a more petite thirteen-foot version. Once in place, the lighter Diana spun effortlessly on her revolving golden hemisphere above the city, blown by the slightest gust of wind. Some joked that it was White's most elaborate pedestal yet for a Saint-Gaudens sculpture. But Diana proved more of a lightning rod than the weather vane she was purported to be. Almost as soon as the charmingly naked statue was placed atop White's tower, the luminous figure, which blazed serenely in the noonday sun, scandalized onlookers and provoked a variety of comments from shocked observers who must have had excellent vision, given their relative distance from the shining goddess.

According to one of the policemen patrolling Madison Square Park at the time, "People as has kids says as how she is immoralizing."

Several newspapers reported that there had been a "marked change in the character of the frequenters of Madison Square. Formerly this beautiful little park was the gathering place of children . . . but more generally what children come here are rushed through at breakneck speed . . . in their place the Square is thronged with clubmen armed with field glasses . . . Delmonico elegants, Casino Johnnies, and every other variety of local dude."

After seeing for himself that this divine body, adorned only in a thin veneer of gilt, stood in glaring promiscuous relief "against the clear blue of the heavens," which "rendered every detail of the modeling startlingly plain to the view," Comstock seethed with rage and demanded that it be taken down.

In seeming acquiescence to the already frustrated Comstock, White directed Saint-Gaudens to construct a gilded pennantlike drapery for Diana to "cover her modesty" (another euphemism for female private parts). Much to Comstock's vexation and White and Saint-Gaudens's orchestrated delight, the insubstantial drapery came detached and blew away within weeks of having been put in place. After that, in sparkling defiance, White proceeded to make sure that the Garden Diana could be seen even at night. Under his direction, she was daringly and dramatically illuminated from below by mirrors that reflected a ring of powerful incandescent arc lamps at her feet.

Ultimately, Comstock's campaign against the statue that offended decent citizens as far away as Philadelphia, like his efforts to close the saloons, failed. Nonetheless, it fueled his wrath and helped publicize his cause, however much he was preaching the converted. But it would not take long for "Saint Anthony of Comstock" to gain an ally and disciple in his crusade against White and other less visible voluptuaries: a man with money to burn (literally, since he sometimes lit his imported cigars with hundred-dollar bills to shock and amuse onlookers). Equally zealous but content initially to remain anonymous, Comstock's patron saint and private financier was none other than Harry K. Thaw, of Pittsburgh.

Fancying himself Sir Harry Trueheart, Thaw, like Comstock, was a puritanical vigilante who envisioned himself doing God's work—except that when no one was looking, "Mad Harry" used the devil's playground as his own (and, far from demonstrating Spartan discipline, was more likely to come home under his shield than on it). But like Comstock and his Society members, Thaw wanted to wipe out the "nest of vipers" he believed was preying on young girls in the city—particularly those vultures who thought they were above the law (eight stories, to be exact) in the obscene tower at Madison Square, where the "red-headed devil" who toyed with the most tender affections had yet to be caught red-handed in his love nest (the term coined supposedly in connection with White and his tower trysts).

*A rare image of Evelyn smiling in a
postcard photograph, circa 1902.*

AMERICAN DREAM GIRL

However much the tightly wound, tumescent life of Manhattan Island (and the rest of the nation that stretched beyond the Brooklyn Bridge and Diana's muted gaze) was under bully testosterone-fueled control, it was the flesh-and-blood goddess of innocent sexuality, Miss Florence Evelyn, whose image began to dominate the imagination of the public as the embodiment of fresh-faced youth and the always enticing American Dream.

A "slight striking almost fragile waif with a marvelous halo of hair," she was the living tabula rasa—pure, uninitiated, and ingenuous—and poised on the exhilarating threshold of fame. In the new century of teeming masses and mass marketing, with a population obsessed with iconographic images that symbolized the "one" (Uncle Sam, the Yellow Kid, Lady Liberty, Columbia, etc.), the "little girl from the outskirts of sooty city" was already on her way to becoming the icon of her age. It would not be long before she would be etched into the collective consciousness of America as its supreme symbol of irresistible and undeniable (if at times fickle) possibility, Charles Dana Gibson's "Eternal Question."

In early 1901, Violet Oakley, the stained-glass artist and muralist whom Florence Evelyn had posed for in Philadelphia, was in New York, commissioned by the All Angels Church on the Upper West Side to do a series of celestial scenes. Not surprisingly, she engaged her favorite model, and word quickly spread to the most remote bohemian borders of the metropolitan art world of the unassuming and supple studio girl who could "embody the essence of the shepherdess, coquette, or naiad" (although the issue of her costuming—or lack thereof—would continue both to titillate and offend, much like the Garden's Diana). As more painters and illustrators began to press for Florence Evelyn's services as a model, she found her admiring employers now included the most talented and recognizable artists of their kind, including those masters of "high indigo and mauve fantasies," Harrison Fisher, Howard Chandler Christy, Henry Hutt, and Archie Gunn.

Benefiting from a serendipitous convergence of timing and technology, photographs as well as other renderings of Florence Evelyn's image (such as chromolithographs, hand-tinted bas-relief photos, real-photo postcards, celluloid reproductions, and tipped-in gravures) were easily duplicated and soon widely in demand. Certain newspapers such as the *Sunday World* and the *Sunday American* had also just started to publish fashion pages featuring "living models" rather than the previously drawn and sometimes ridiculously disproportionate female figures. The photographer most responsible for this new trend in what was the beginning of modern fashion photography was Joel Feder, who had a studio on West

Evelyn as Gibson's
"Eternal Question," 1903.

Twenty-third Street. Immediately upon meeting "the most beautiful specimen of the skylight world," who had been featured in another issue of *Broadway Magazine* in an article on "The New York Studios," Feder attempted to engage Evelyn exclusively, offering her five dollars for a morning sitting or an afternoon and twice that for a whole day's posing. This was more than she made in a week posing for the typical fine artist. But Florence Evelyn was not yet ready to give herself to just one man or his eager albeit flattering attention. Nor did her mother want to cut off any avenues of potential revenue by choosing just one, no matter how tempting.

Modeling in costumes as she had in Philadelphia and once again acting out the fantasies she had read as a child only a handful of years earlier, Florence Evelyn was at times in thrall to her own image. Overcome now and then with adolescent self-absorption, she enjoyed suddenly seeing her face everywhere. And yet, as in Philadelphia, however much the idea of being the most sought-after model in the studios appealed to her teenage vanity, the posing she continued to do for painters and sculptors was increasingly dull, tiring, unglamorous, and time consuming. Inevitably, she preferred spending her time in front of a camera. Being a photographer's model for either commercial purposes or higher art was easier. And, as her mother had hoped, the rewards were more immediate and relatively lucrative, reaching as much as eighteen dollars a week.

As a photographer's model, Florence Evelyn routinely found herself dressed in a variety of beautiful outfits, a number of which were as unquestionably revealing as those she wore for the fine artists. But her mother did not object, and the money her daughter brought in every week paid for everything they had. One has to wonder what career choices or money the much-in-demand "little Pittsburgh peach" could have made with a professional manager or agent, since, like a leaf in a storm drain, Florence Evelyn's meteoric modeling career floated on the swells and eddies of the generosity, honesty, or whims of those who sought to engage her services, many knowing full well that her mother knew nothing about "the business of business." The fact that Florence Evelyn was able to rise so quickly and make a steady salary was at least a small wonder, since the unparalleled publicity she generated was virtually unplanned, and uncontrolled; very little of her success was the result of her mother's efforts. As her daughter-in-law described the situation many years later, "a very young Evelyn put her faith in her mother, the adult, to manage things and make the right career choices, and I suppose even a broken clock is right twice a day."

By the end of that first year in New York, Florence Evelyn could be viewed in the galleries of the Metropolitan Museum and on "arcade postcards" dispensed from drugstore machines on street corners. With conspicuous consumption rampant, it is not surprising that advertisers quickly saw in her beguiling features the ideal model for the newest female facial products and fashions. If the all-consuming desire of manufacturers was to create and sell an American look, then with the aid of rapidly developing innovations in the machinery of the print media, the growing popularity of new publications aimed primarily at female consumers, the latest methods of marketing an expanding number of new products, and the use of newly invented forms of mass communication, they had found their American dream girl.

Florence Evelyn was dubbed the "modern Helen" by one columnist, and her evocative and soon familiar face launched any number of advertising campaigns as canny entrepreneurs began to capitalize on her uncanny ability to appeal to both sexes and appear chaste and alluring at the same time. It wasn't long after her first blush as a New York studio model that Florence Evelyn could be found as the cover girl (or inside) of the growing number of women's magazines, whose inception reflected the demands made by the flourishing market of eager female consumers who were unwittingly willing "slaves of fashion." *Vanity Fair, Harper's Bazaar, Munsey's,* the *Woman's Home Companion,* the *Ladies' Home Journal, Cosmopolitan, The Delineator,* and other women's magazines routinely used Florence Evelyn, who undoubtedly helped boost their circulation.

Restricted circulation of a wholly different kind for female consumers was, however, the uncomfortable result of particularly punishing and macabre trends in the fashions being sold to women in those same magazines. Women were exhorted to wear hair rats, dead stuffed birds, or huge ostrich plumes on equally huge, unwieldy picture hats, and a variety of natural or unnaturally dyed animal pelts with limp heads, abrasive paws, and glassy, lifeless eyes. There were tight leg-of-mutton sleeves and "ear-shearing celluloid collars," irritating puffs and bustles big enough to hide a loaf of bread, which prevented easy sitting since they pressed merci-lessly on the lower spine. There were rib-crushing metal corsets worn over four additional layers of underclothes to create an unnatural cinched waist; skull-piercing hatpins, unforgiving tight kid gloves, and crippling high-button shoes, which had to be two sizes too small to be chic. There were heavy "hair-shirt" bathing costumes, bathing caps, and itchy black worsted stockings for the seaside, and ground-sweeping skirts on land, which picked up all the dirt and debris from the streets; these heavy skirts, which usually froze in the winter when wet with snow or slush, required

Artist's rendering of Miss Nesbit, 1901.

women to always have at least one hand free to liberate themselves from the tenacious ice and rubbish trapped within their treacherous trailing folds.

In 1901, being in fashion inevitably meant being incapacitated and in pain from head to toe, the result of "induced pathological features" for all aspiring models of "pecuniary decency." All, that is, but the nation's newest model, who would help to change the feminine ideal. In spite of her steady employment, Florence Evelyn could not afford most of what she modeled, and unless it was necessary for a photo session, the petite sixteen-year-old had no need for the confinement of corsets, bras, or layers of underclothing; she was happily unrestrained by the contraptions of comeliness and "vulgar tradition," which she nonetheless helped sell to an eager female population.

The Sacred and the Profane

Within a short time, Florence Evelyn (or some part of her) was selling everything from subscriptions for the *Woman's Home Companion*, Fairy soap, ocelot furs, Lowney's chocolates, Sunbonnet Oleo, and sewing machines to Rubifoam dentifrice, an early form of powdered toothpaste, which she admitted in later years "tasted like gritty talcum." Nor did it take long for the girl who had begun her career assuming childish heavenly poses to find herself on beer trays, cigarette and tobacco cards, celluloid pin backs, cigar labels, advertising fans, wallpaper, pyrographic pillows, playing cards, and pocket mirrors with the unfortunate "good for ten cents in trade" often written around the circumference of the mirror encircling her photo. Given out mainly in hotels from New York to Wyoming, these were innocent enough advertising tokens, although many of the men who were the predominant patrons in the hotels kept them in secret places, hidden from wives and girlfriends.

As part of her newly minted celebrity, Florence Evelyn also became the first recognizable and bona-fide pinup girl. She was a calendar girl for such notable entities as Prudential Life Insurance, Swift's Premium, Pompeian face cream, *Youth's Companion,* and Coca-Cola, for which the images of her marketed for public consumption were of the maidenly variety.

Another natural place for her image was sheet music, which was itself a kind of mania at the turn of the century. But while imaginary Daisys and Rosies had their place at pianos in countless households, the very real Florence Evelyn had songs written especially for her by lovesick admirers who paid to have their pieces published. One was Vincent Spadeo, who wrote the cleverly named "Nesbit Waltz," whose sheet music had on its cover a photo of Evelyn identified as the "Kimono Girl." Another piece was written by a smitten physician from New Jersey and titled "Love's Pleading," also featuring a photograph of an angelic-looking Florence Evelyn and published in a Sunday supplement.

Looking back on the first months of her mercurial success at such an impressionable age, Evelyn recalls in her memoirs that her youthful dreams were still vague at that point, and nothing in particular grabbed her attention beyond the happy accidental career that landed her in the Garden of the New World. While she was not "insensible to the possibilities of a career on the stage," as she described it, her "enthusiasm was for the present." One thing she seemed sure of, however: given the limited sphere of influence and choices that she said bound women "like so many Chinese feet," she was determined she would never become a domestic drudge, a wifey, or a drone. As she describes it, by sixteen she "already look[ed] back upon the life domestic with the interests and curiosity which the mountaineer reserves for the plains he has quitted." She had seen what a dead end that proved to be for her mother and her wretchedly extinguished spirit. And so she began to nurture the notion that she should go on the stage.

As Florence Evelyn's father became a fond memory and a more remote presence in his daughter's mind, initially Mamma Nesbit seems to have attempted to make up for that void by becoming overwhelmingly, stiflingly present, relentlessly peddling and protecting her daughter (badly), sheltering her (badly) even as she exploited her youthful looks. But contrary to popular myth, Mrs. Nesbit was not the archetypal ambitiously shrewd and calculating stage mother, which meant that her daughter's accidental career seemed to move forward with its own careless and inadvertent momentum.

As the weeks passed, Florence Evelyn's theatrical urge buzzed in and out of her bonnet. By the fall of 1901, the model, her mother, and Howard were all living off her still small but respectable wages in a boardinghouse on West Thirty-sixth Street between Fifth and Sixth avenues. Although Florence Evelyn's earnings were more than what the three Nesbits combined had made at Wanamaker's, they were hardly enough to pull them all safely out of the shadow of sometimes mean and meager survival in the costly life of Manhattan. Nor were they likely to fund Evelyn's dreams of becoming one of the "smart set." Howard became an increasingly infrequent inhabitant and "lost soul," being sent away usually for at least two weeks out of any given month, since Mamma Nesbit fretted that the city might be an unhealthy place for such a sensitive boy.

And then the little Sphinx, her eyes trained in another direction, found a new audience, which, unbeknownst to her, included the Pharaoh of Fifth Avenue, whose realm had swelled from his estate, Box Hill, to Byzantine empires and back again to Broadway and the borders of the Bowery.

Evelyn in The Theatre *magazine, 1902.*

CHAPTER FIVE

Florodora

The only people who never talk about themselves are Japanese, bank robbers, and ambassadors. —*Evelyn Nesbit*, My Story

Tell me, pretty maiden, are there any more at home like you?
—*Song lyric from* Florodora, 1901

In a city alive with the constant clamor and din of distraction, Florence Evelyn found herself burdened with long hours of confined inactivity and nerve-racking silence, sometimes seven days a week. Her life had become a monotonous rusting chain of sittings and appointments, always lasting into the twilight hours—and almost always within arm's reach of her wearisome mamma, in tow like a barge incapable of pulling its own weight. So within only six months of her arrival in New York City, the unofficial queenlet of the studio and advertising hearts had already begun to seriously consider abdicating the stifling linseed-stained and flash-powdered skylight worlds she had reigned over, where the high point of her day was having a cup of oolong tea before posing again in absolute stillness for several hours. She also began to wonder if life in the alternately arid or oily airless studios might have a withering effect on her, and at the seasoned age of sixteen feared becoming merely a pressed flower, something formerly moist and thriving, crushed and forgotten between faded pages and kept on a shelf.

Invariably, the girl model also found herself thrust solely into the company of adults, mostly very grown-up men whose one desire, usually, was that she not speak or move. There were other times when, for a fleeting second or two, she felt that certain lingering looks on the faces of certain artists were not motivated "by a desire to simply achieve the right perspective." But as she reclined against a papier-mâché tree, her hand held out to a stuffed bird fastened to a simulated fountain with chicken wire, or fixed her engaging sphinxlike smile on a phantom object of affection, the more she was convinced that the stage offered greener façades.

Almost from the moment her enchanting face and supple figure appeared in the pages of Manhattan's magazines and newspapers, Florence Evelyn had begun to receive all manner of dazzling as well as less than shining offers of fame from theatrical "types" who had no knowledge at all of whether she possessed any talent. Most came in the mail; some came right to the front door of her boardinghouse. Theatrical producers, legitimate and spurious alike, showed up only days after some of her earliest modeling photos appeared in both the *Journal* and the *World*. The would-be managers laid at her dainty feet mock-up playbills and advertisements with her photos; they talked of commanding high salaries and assured her that she would be a star. One unwitting prognosticator said glibly that the little looker would be "the most talked-about girl in America."

But, whether it was her mother's tunnel-visioned skepticism about a notoriously fickle and, she suspected, low-paying profession or the near-sighted overconfidence of youth on Florence Evelyn's part, initially the teenager and her mother rejected outright anyone who offered her the chance to capitalize on her name through "freakish notoriety," not wanting to risk a week with no paycheck and a return to stale Weetabix.

Contrary to the popular notion that her mother pushed Evelyn from the womb onto the stage is the fact that Mamma Nesbit was more than reluctant to give in to Florence's growing desire to pitch posturing for "real acting." After all, she was making good money as a model—at times almost twenty dollars a week. "They" had developed a faithful clientele of metropolitan artists, illustrators, and advertisers in a relatively short time just as "they" had in Philadelphia, which guaranteed a steady income. As she fretted unceasingly over the family's financial state of affairs (with Howard at this point once again somewhere with somebody no doubt in need of something), Mamma Nesbit actively discouraged her daughter's theatrical ambitions. While neither she nor Florence Evelyn had any idea what a chorus girl's weekly salary was, even if her dreamy-eyed daughter didn't always take that into account, Mrs. Nesbit did her own accounting. There was, of course, the seedy reputation of the theater to consider (with its loose morals and tight costumes), but that aspect seemed of less consequence to Mrs. Nesbit than the monetary issue.

However, Florence Evelyn's disenchantment with the alternately mind-numbing and grueling life as studio, advertising, and photographer's model forced the issue to what would be the next obvious step. Having lived for half a year on the boisterous fringes of the Gay White Way, which shared its sketchy but enticing borders with a number of the studios where she worked, the impatient teen declared to her mother with appropriate histrionics, "I am going to be an actress!"

As young and inexperienced as she was, Florence Evelyn tried to reassure her mother that she could maintain a sensible perspective about her prospects of becoming an actress. She writes in 1934 that she was not stagestruck in the common sense, even though she did have the enthusiasm of every teenage girl whose "desire for the enlargement of life" sees no possible flaws in such an impetuous plan. As far as Florence Evelyn could see, being on the magical stage, where she could woo an audience full of living, responsive people, was a vast improvement over the decidedly mundane studios populated by dismally sedate artists, many of whom were on the far edge of "decrepitude." And, in addition to living in such close proximity to the theater district, having already had her picture featured in several theatrical magazines, the celebrated girl model was convinced that she could be "supremely indifferent" to the position she might occupy in the spotlight. As she described it years later, she only wanted to be "in it" and see what else the world had to offer her. And, unlike other girls, for whom the stage would be their first exposure to an admiring or appreciative audience, Florence Evelyn already knew the effect she exerted over people with a mere look or the upturn of her chin.

For several weeks, mother and daughter seesawed over the idea of her acting. As Evelyn describes it in one memoir, her mother never really stood a chance with her when she wanted something badly enough. After some inquiries, Mamma Nesbit discovered that her daughter could still pose by day and appear on the stage by night (just as she had worked all week at Wanamaker's and posed on weekends in Philadelphia). And so Mrs. Nesbit's attitude changed. Whether or not Florence Evelyn saw this too-familiar arrangement as an utterly unhappy alternative, she convinced herself that she could see her mother's point about the more practical side of having two careers—again: "the very material fact that . . . stage life would enable me to make a double income."

If this meant continuing in the alternately suffocating and chilly studios all day, depending on the season, it was the price she had to pay since, as her mother constantly reminded her, the "dollars counted horribly." In the end, the combination of Florence Evelyn's pie-in-the-sky persistence and her mother's unrelenting hand-wringing about money proved to be deciding factors. One can't help but sense an undercurrent of desperation in the adult Evelyn's recollections about this decision, which imply that she was more anxious to distance herself from the grim specter of poverty than she was eager to sustain two simultaneous careers again at such a relatively immature and vulnerable age.

"Fate," however, as she wrote, "was moving me inexorably in the direction I was to take."

But not everyone was pleased at this proposed shift in the focus of her still unformed professional life. Neither Frederick Church nor Carroll Beckwith approved, and when Evelyn told the much-admired Beckwith during a modeling session of her intentions to pursue a career on the stage, he exploded in anger, scolded her, threw down his brush, and paced up and down his studio.

"That is preposterous!" he said. "I don't approve. You are barely sixteen—still a child!"

But instead of showing appreciation for the painter's paternal concern, a petulant Evelyn balked at his characterization of her as a child and silently fumed throughout the session. She fared no better with the avuncular Church, whose more gentle insistence also focused on her inexperience and youthful vulnerability; at his urging she came close to abandoning her thoughts of the stage, because, as she remembers it, "he lent art a meaning that made deserting it seem like a sacrilege."

THE BABY FARM

Over the course of several months early in 1901, Florence Evelyn had received a number of letters from a Mr. Marks, a well-known and legitimate theatrical agent who promised in illegibly scribbled letters the req-

This is my pussy

Double-entendre postcard image of Evelyn
from her Florodora *days.*

uisite fame and fortune. With no knowledge of the business of Broadway and no ability to discern a genuine from an insincere offer, Mrs. Nesbit and her daughter initially paid little attention to these letters. However, when Marks wrote again in May, saying that he could arrange an introduction to John C. Fisher, the manager of the *Florodora* company, the curtain lifted.

Just as things Oriental had found their way into the popular culture and marketing of the day, so had the Philippines, newly accesible because of the Panama Canal. *Florodora,* a "spicy little musical dish," was the most popular show on Broadway. Playing nightly at the Moorish Casino Theatre, nicknamed the "temple of feminine pulchritude," *Florodora* was set in a mythical Philippine Island.

There is little doubt that in spite of Florence Evelyn's attempts to paint her mother's initial reaction as anxious and reluctant to have her go on the stage, it didn't take long for Mrs. Nesbit to rethink her position. To hear Evelyn tell it in 1934, "I overruled my mother's objections and went with her one day to Mr. Fisher's office."

The well-publicized fact that several former *Florodora* soubrettes had managed to snag millionaire husbands may have also factored in the final equation for Mamma Nesbit's about-face.

Manager Marks met them at the theater. His flamboyant dress—the requisite black derby, black-and-white-checked suit, and diamond-studded bully-boy red tie—struck Mrs. Nesbit as "vulgar." Sixteen-year-old Florence Evelyn, however, thought it was "spiffy."

When they entered the office, Marks immediately began to pitch his newest find. Fisher held up his hand and took his partner Riley aside. Fisher then approached Mrs. Nesbit and asked about her qualifications for the chorus, mistaking the girl's mother as the one who had come for the audition. Marks let out a laugh as Florence Evelyn jumped up from her seat and declared that she was the one who wanted the job. Fisher looked over the five-foot-nothing girl in her homemade skirts, with her hair tied behind her and no makeup.

"So, you want to be an actress?" he asked with mock solemnity.

He turned to her mother.

"Madame, I'm not running a baby farm!"

He went on, explaining that even if he were willing to snatch her from the cradle and allow this little miss to join the company, Comstock's Gerry Society (which focused specifically on child labor) would be at his door, flaming swords of decontamination drawn and warrants in hand before you could say Diamond Jim Brady. Comstock, with the aid of the district attorney's office, had of late been stepping up his efforts to crack down on underage children working adult jobs in "depraved environments." The theater of course was a particularly sensitive area with Comstock, who saw the entire theater district as an "open sore" spreading filth in the streets. To Comstock, its unsavory atmosphere lured unsuspecting young girls from their homes with promises of overnight success and untold wealth, only to infect them and to have them end up, as he was quoted in one newspaper, "bejeweled Bathshebas, besotted, bedeviled, broken-hearted or brothel-bound."

Although Fisher smiled condescendingly at her, a devastated Florence Evelyn broke into instantaneous and very real tears. She looked at her mother in desperation, but Mrs. Nesbit returned an equally distressed look.

"All right," said Fisher, unable to resist the girl before him, whose wholesome, unpainted face was so striking against her dark mass of hair. "There is a rehearsal going on upstairs." He offered to let her take a look at it, and in less than thirty minutes, the specter of the Gerry Society seemed to have vanished from the producer's mind, displaced no doubt by thoughts of what an impact this unusually beautiful girl would make in his company. He asked her if she knew how to dance.

"A little," she replied, suddenly shy and somewhat apprehensive, her dancing (as well as singing and piano) lessons having been abruptly ended back in Pittsburgh when her father died. A woman who played the piano was sent for. Florence Evelyn did an impromptu dance, and offered that she could carry a tune as well.

"The stage manager was keen on my coming into the theater," the

adult Evelyn recalls, but Fisher was less than enthusiastic and said he
would "let them know." It was not because he thought the girl lacked
enough talent to fill an anonymous spot in the chorus. If anything, he
speculated that she might be a "find." The real issue was her age. He took
Mrs. Nesbit aside and told her frankly that her daughter's only chance of
joining the company was to "be a little reticent" about her real age. If she
did this, he would be willing to give her a trial, even though her diminutive figure, thin, narrow shoulders, and perfectly smooth face indicated
someone only playing at adulthood—and not very convincingly. Mrs.
Nesbit offered no resistance. The very next morning, the first day of a
month of rehearsals began for the model turned chorus girl while her
mamma attempted to juggle her schedule of modeling appointments to
accommodate the rehearsals.

By the end of the month, the former stock girl was a *Florodora* chorus
girl. Because of her luxurious brunette hair and sultry eyes, she was cast
as an unnamed "charming Spanish maiden." Putting on costumes and
makeup, spending hours doing repetitious actions, being directed to look
a certain way or strike a certain pose was nothing new to her. She had
learned from the business end of the so-called glamour of the studios,
and now, somewhat to her disappointment, she would get the same view
of the stage.

When thinking back on this first phase in her theatrical life, Evelyn
recalls that her initial reaction to the general shabbiness and banality of
the reality of life in the theater did not dampen her enthusiasm completely. Her heart rose at the prospect of being onstage. And, as she
already had in other ways in her short life, she quickly dropped her illusions and accepted the machinery of the whole enterprise, the long hours
of hard work, and the frequent run-down state of the sets, where "a beautiful garden from the front of the house is drab, tattered and discolored
close up," and "lovely dresses as seen from the auditorium are too often
bedraggled and soiled upon close inspection." Even if the reality of the
theater was a "bare, cold barn of a floor, inexpressibly dull when seen in
the unromantic light of morning," and knowing that hers would be an
insignificant part, Florence Evelyn prepared herself with juvenile high

spirits. Anxious to perfect herself for her anonymous part, the girl considered the world she was about to enter as a "terra incognita" with the promise of novel and exciting rewards all its own.

While the other chorus girls went backstage after their number to the communal dressing room, Florence Evelyn would stand in the wings and watch the featured sextet "dancing gracefully . . . and wonder a little ruefully whether [she would] ever be tall enough or skillful enough to do the work they were doing. . . ." As she writes, "in my innocence I regarded them as the most wonderful part of the show, and, certainly the best paid." For the girl who, until recently, always seemed to just barely keep her family's head above the bog of insolvency (if one were to believe her mother), the evidence of the sextet's success was, for her, the beautiful clothes and jewels they wore offstage. While performing in their wedding-cake gowns, with seven layers of lace like strawberry icing, their long throats decorated with black velvet chokers and wearing long black gloves as they clutched pink parasols, the sextet seemed the height of smartness and elegance to the girl from Allegheny County. Their signature number, "Tell Me Pretty Maiden," was the highlight of the show each night and frequently the cause of a standing ovation by enthusiastic audience members—predominantly male—before the number was even completed.

Each night, as the dapper, clean-shaven, square-jawed Gibsonish men in their gray cutaway coats, black silk top hats, and pearl gray gloves got down on their knees to serenade the six buxom, statuesque *Florodora* beauties, the audience clapped with delight, waiting for the response to the question "Are there any more at home like you?" And every night a new cordon of stage-door Johnnies then went to wait outside to find out.

While appearing in the show, the youngest member of the company was billed as Florence Evelyn. Her constant primping and preening, however, caused her to be christened "Flossie the Fuss" by the cast and crew. After weeks of teasing, the fledgling chorine considered giving herself a *nom de théâtre* to go with her new career, one that she hoped would put an end to her unwelcome nickname. Two months and a day later,

"Flossie the Fuss" disappeared when Florence Evelyn insisted that her new name was Evelyn Nesbit. Another perhaps unintentional but no less compelling reason may have been to assert herself and coincidentally usurp her mother. If there was going to be an Evelyn Nesbit, she would be it. So she dropped Florence for good (although her mother and the family back in Pennsylvania continued to refer to her as Florence). Her mother said nothing.

In her memoirs, Evelyn tried to dispel the objections that "ever excite the moralist" when it comes to the stage's bad influence on the young and unsuspecting.

"I can speak only for myself when I say it did not corrupt me. If being brought into contact with people who are loose of speech or who have exaggerated views on the flexibility of morals is corruption, then the streets of New York, of Paris, of London, of any city, are unfit for a young girl."

To the adult Evelyn, if life in the theater entailed "a certain freedom of speech and a certain frankness in dealing with relationships which exist between people," it also offered the "protection which comes from the destruction of illusion." The way she remembered it years later, Evelyn saw that there was, contrary to popular belief, a keen appreciation of duty toward the inexperienced among the theatrical people with whom she was involved at this early point in her life. As she put it, "I can speak only for myself that such anxiety was displayed to hide the ugly truths from the novitiate." This was due in large part, of course, to the fear of the crusading Saint Anthony of Comstock, who had set his sights on the theater, with its exploitation of fresh-faced femmes and its "injurious effects on susceptible young things."

Since the well-publicized and gorgeous little Evelyn would be the obvious object of such scrutiny, the company made a particular effort to "treat her with kid gloves" and keep her in the dark about certain facts of life on and off the stage. Although the naturally curious Evelyn quizzed her fellow chorus girls and talked to a number of worldlier if not wiser cast and crew people around her about life in the big city, they now dubbed her "the Kid" and "not one of them attempted to lift the veil," which hid certain realities from her eyes. As she put it, invariably when she came within earshot of a particularly juicy conversation, the next and only thing she would hear was "Shhhhh! The kid."

Nonetheless, she did pick up a few opinions while appearing in her first show, not the least of which involved the typical chorus girl's impressively "frank egotism . . . a quality which is neither to be despised nor condemned." Evelyn wrote that the other girls in the chorus "had got the trick of thinking aloud, and found speech to be an excellent substitute for thought. I found it took years of study before I could disentangle the real intentions of a girl from her often vehemently expressed view. I have heard people—men especially—who have complained bitterly of the inconsistency and deceptive powers of girls engaged on the stage . . . her code, her method, is unchanged throughout all the centuries."

Right from the start, Evelyn enjoyed the cast-member camaraderie with those she considered her first real friends, and she claimed that initially, girls she barely knew were willing to do everything they could to help her adjust. Still frequently caught up in her own adolescent sense of self-consciousness when it came to expressing herself with words rather than clichéd expressions, Evelyn admired their ability to put into words what others would only think, especially when compared to her own self-censoring tendencies. How much she may have learned from their thinking out loud is unclear, even as she recognized that their substitution of speech for actual thought could lead to troubling inconsistencies.

She also came to observe human nature at its less than admirable, but saw the audience rather than the actors as posing a threat: "It is harder to please the low brow than the high brow. It is always the man who has just jumped on his wife who hisses at stage villainy the loudest."

In all her memoirs Evelyn refuted the "provincial accusation" that theatrical people are wholly artificial and insincere. "You must remember," she would write, "that the average girl who joins a chorus is one who has little or no opportunity for tasting the comforts of existence. Their early days have been spent very often amid the most straitened circumstances. . . . Girls who have not had the benefit of an education often disregard the fact that there is no discreditable aspect to poverty, and because people will look down upon them on account [of that poverty], they disguise their real selves." Half the artificiality of the theater, she would assert, is due to a "monstrous misconception as to what is essential in a woman."

Whether or not Evelyn was able to see things more clearly than the average aspiring actress, one wonders if subconsciously she knew that she also fit snugly into the typical pattern of most of the girls she met. Evelyn wrote, "It is her first object to secure a line of parentage. . . . The formula does not vary very considerably. A ruined or dead father—a life of noble self-sacrifice and eventually the theater. These are the stories which one hears on every hand from the girls of the chorus. . . . It is very pathetic. A little country mouse who finds herself amid her smartly clad sisters undergoes an ordeal beside which a mere appearance before the foot-lights is as nothing . . . whatever ambition there is concentrated upon a desire to shine before her newly found friends."

As for the men she observed, the mature Evelyn wrote, "I know of no more interesting subject to the average man than himself. . . . All men lie when speaking of themselves, and however good or pious they may be, they exaggerate their own qualities." What the typical chorus girl came to understand about her role, both in the literal and figural sense, was that "she sings, she dances and she dresses with this central thought in mind: I must arouse the interest of men." Evelyn saw this pattern was not much different for the general population of women. Like the chorus girl, "women in other walks of life do exactly the same thing. . . . They are obeying the same instinct that animates the chorus girl." It's just that "their invitation may be more subtle and intimate." The chorus girl's opportunity comes after the show, but too often the encounter is disap-pointing. "I am always sorry for the girl and have very little patience with the disillusioned man, who has to begin all over again reconstructing his ideal as he goes on to discover what was the charm which attracted him to this or that particular member of the chorus."

About her own feelings at this point in time, like most teenagers, Evelyn said she had only a "vague and nebulous" idea as to which direc-tion her ambitions should run.

"In those days I lived very much in the present," she wrote.

Apart from the fascination of actual performing, the hurry and excitement of preparations, the exhilaration of the music, the plaudits of the audience, and the rush of changes made at breathless speed all combined to stimulate her as yet untarnished and freewheeling outlook on life. Of course, she acknowledged, after the shows there were numerous parties "given by boys to girls": "We always went in bunches to these parties. One girl would invite the other, and we would go off to a cafe for supper, and afterwards to some apartment where we could dance. . . . I would emphasize the perfect innocence of these frolics. . . . There was nothing in them but harmless amusement."

Rector's was the particular favorite of the theatrical crowd as well as the so-called new cast of characters dubbed "the midnight supper society." Nicknamed the "cathedral of froth," Rector's stood on Broadway between Forty-third and Forty-fourth, and it was the place where "one could go to forget and two could go and be forgotten." It had a number of eye-catching features, not the least of which was a huge electrified griffin (the mythological beast with the head and wings of an eagle and the body of a lion) affixed over the doorway of its Greco-Roman façade. Beneath the talons of the griffin whirled New York's first revolving door. The sparkling "glass squirrel wheel," as it was called, was a clever attention-grabber for curious passersby and a risqué skirt grabber for unsuspecting female patrons who often found themselves "with their skirts flared up in folds nearly past their knees." The regulars, however, knew how to whirl through the wheel with "nary a ruffled feather."

According to Evelyn, her mother took a dim and conservative view of her partying. Confronting her mother in the wee hours of the morning, Evelyn confessed that it gave her the sense of being "the product of a novel and decadent generation." She also came to see in her later years what she couldn't as a teenager, having been let loose, so to speak, in Manhattan while her mother, apparently, sat home waiting: that their temperaments were remarkably and irreconcilably different, and that she shared something of her father's trusting eagerness to try new things, while her brother, Howard, shared her mother's cautiousness. She remembered vividly the apprehension she felt at coming home late, awaiting her mother's inevitable and reproachful "Oh, Evelyn!" (Mamma Nesbit used her daughter's *nom de théâtre* only when she wanted to indicate disapproval.)

But if all the teenager cared about was having fun, followed by falling into bed out of sheer exhaustion, oblivious to her mother's criticism of her imagined outrageous conduct, then Mamma Nesbit's chief concern was that Evelyn not ruin a good thing by losing any precious beauty sleep. Apparently, the possibility of Evelyn's moral ruination wasn't enough of a concern for her mother to put an end to posing, performing, and partying for her underage daughter.

Still very young and immature in spite of her innate intelligence and her role as the family's breadwinner, Evelyn, unlike most of her chorus girl friends, enjoyed what she describes as her "childish interests," which a number of potential suitors around her recognized. Some fled in a panic, while others found flirting with dynamite all the more enticing. Amused by her delight at mechanical toys, a fact that should have underscored for them her minor status, to hear Evelyn tell it, many were then "careful to speak so innocuously in front of me as to be downright banal."

Although alcohol was readily available to the chorus girls, underage or not, it was used more as a prop than anything else. Some of the girls drank, Evelyn recalled, because they thought it was the thing to do: "A cocktail was less a pleasure than part of the ritual of good fun; champagne was something rather amusing," and she doubted whether any of the girls really liked it, but "since nobody took very much, little harm was done." With her mother's voice always in the back of her mind, fearful that drinking might indeed spoil her looks, Evelyn learned how to nurse a glass of sparkling wine for an entire night, limiting herself to "a little liquor and lots of soda water." She was also painfully aware that she needed to be fresh enough in the morning for her modeling work.

With a typical teenage tendency to view life in this period as some kind of haphazardly structured musical comedy, Evelyn saw herself as a character in "theatre-land," an indiscriminate but intriguing place where one had to "learn the ropes or hang trying." It differed only slightly from her previous incarnation as a fourteen-year-old model in the uncharted territory of the "artistic set," where ordinary girls were "inspired to vacuity by the monotony of sittings." As Evelyn asserted a mere year and a half after her first career had begun, she felt she had "worked things out" for herself, managing to balance two careers to her mother's none, and walking the fine line between childhood and adulthood, reason and foolishness, in loco parentis.

The earliest slapdash days and hectic nights of Evelyn's new life in theater-land passed quickly but happily enough, yet making friends, only to have them vanish overnight to another cast in another show in another city, intensified Evelyn's chronic if subconscious fear of the impermanence of life. It was the one aspect of the profession that she disliked, the constant entrances and exits, and it was only in the small, quiet moments few and far between that her thoughts drifted back to her father. Given her mother's resolute refusal to voice her own sense of loss and festering resentment at having been thrust into poverty by her husband's miscalculations, it is not surprising that eventually Evelyn relegated him to "a hidden place" where he became for her "a fond memory," "like the pleasant ghosts of people who came and went" in her life.

When pressed to think about her childhood in later life, Evelyn said that the happy times seemed few and far between; they existed for her as if in a dream and only now and then could she "by some trick of memory ... recall the men and women who contributed to that careless period" of her life:

"Happy times," she wrote in 1915, "are hard to remember ... a happy childhood may be expressed in the character of [those] who [have] been fortunate enough to experience it."

Nonetheless, with the unadulterated vitality of youth, Evelyn continued to pose by day and perform onstage seven nights a week, rushing to modeling appointments, then performances, then parties around town in the midst of a silly, hilarious blur of other chorus girls. She would always come home, but at one or two o'clock in the morning, "suddenly full of healthy sleepiness," her mother's grousing barely registered as Evelyn burrowed in between their very own sheets to recuperate. One had to wonder if there would ever be anyone who could keep pace with the impressionable little Sphinx "with the heart-stopping scarlet stare," someone who could hold her interests long enough to make an impression on her.

STANFORD WHITE
McKIM, MEAD & WHITE

Notable New Yorker photograph of
Stanford White, circa 1900.

CHAPTER SIX

Benevolent Vampire

He was a generously big man—and infinitely mean; he was kind and tender—and preyed upon the defenseless. . . . A crude expression offended him; yet in some things he was shameless. —*Evelyn Nesbit*, Prodigal Days

Stanford White was a member of a small clique of men who had vicious tendencies . . . performed frequently without remorse, with the sense that he and his friends were immune to the laws of the land.
—*Evelyn Nesbit*, My Story

September 1901 was nearly a week old, and although Evelyn was only a "utility girl" in her third giddy month in the New York City production of *Florodora*, her nightly presence onstage in the "temple of feminine pulchritude" made her a not-so-obscure object of desire for some prominent and powerfully connected devotees. One was the well-known director of "the Garden" at Madison Square, who had seen the show forty times since it had opened. And there was the usual coterie of bankers, businessmen, and robber barons. More than slightly farther uptown, however, at the Pan-American Exposition in Buffalo on that same Saturday, a different kind of drama was about to unfold, one that threatened to shatter the cavalier confidence of a barely broken-in century. And in an unlikely setting named the Temple of Music.

President William McKinley stood at the head of a long queue of men in straw boaters and women with colorful parasols. The line snaked its way around the Greco-Roman-style building where many had waited patiently in a late-summer sun for hours to shake the president's hand. Although a number had struck up pleasant conversations amongst themselves, one young man, whose hand appeared to be bandaged, waited his turn in colorless, edgy silence. When he reached the president, before anyone knew what was happening, he raised the hand waist-high, covered not by a bandage but a handkerchief. Two shots rang out, fired into the president at point-blank range. The noise reverberated with callous force through the great hall. A stunned Secret Service man stood by, stupidly immobile, "while a Negro man who had stood on line behind the assassin wrestled him to the floor before he could fire a third time."

A wounded but conscious McKinley was rushed to the nearest hospital. One of the bullets had miraculously deflected off a brass button on his vest. But the other had torn its way into the fleshy part of his considerably fleshy stomach. As the news spread, a stunned nation held its breath. It was the opinion of the attending physicians that although the bullet was not fatal, speed in tending to the bleeding wound was still a priority. The only doctor available to operate was a gynecologist, and neither he nor his assistants bothered to put on caps or gauze masks as they hastily probed the deep hole for the offending bullet. They closed up McKinley with a cauterized sewing needle from Woolworth's.

At the same time, the young man who had shot the president was already in custody. He was Leon Czolgosz, born and raised in Michigan (in spite of, as one paper put it, "his ugly-sounding foreign name"). He told authorities that he had purchased the gun, a .32-caliber nickel-plated revolver, for three dollars and ten cents (plus seventeen cents' postage) through the Sears, Roebuck catalogue. A self-proclaimed anarchist, Czolgosz had targeted McKinley, not because of any specific political beliefs the president espoused, but rather as a symbol, "an empty figurehead." Several hours later, as the would-be revolutionary sat in a cell, the doctor and his assistants wiped the clotted blood from their hands and closed up the president without finding the second bullet. Nonetheless, they declared the operation a success. The nation exhaled.

The following day's reports indicated that the president seemed to be improving. Then, just as suddenly as the attack had come, McKinley began to fail. Eight days later, Czolgosz graduated from anarchist to assassin as the president "expired," the victim not of a fatal gunshot but of a botched operation—he died of gangrene.

Justice was extremely swift but not exactly painless for Czolgosz, who was sentenced within a matter of weeks to the electric chair. New technology being what it was, the deadly-looking apparatus did not quite work as promised. After several sweat-stained attempts by the nervous executioners, who increased the voltage with each try, as the room filled with the young man's cries and the choking odor of burning hair, the assassin was finally and satisfactorily electrocuted (duly reported in gruesome detail in the newspapers). On the day that McKinley died (September 14), Theodore Roosevelt, who had been sworn into office immediately, promised to get the nation back on track. And, as one paper optimistically announced a week later, just like that, "Night turned into Day."

And it was only one week later, during a matinee of *Florodora*, that the wheels of Florence Evelyn's fate switched tracks once again, engineered by an unwitting, pleasantly plumped chorus girl by the name of Nell King. The thirty-something Nell, who had recently replaced Florence Clemmons as one of the featured sextet, was the bosomy mother of fellow chorus girl Edna Goodrich. Although Nell posed as her daughter's sister when the stage-door Johnnies came sniffing around (hoping to hook herself a "bigshot rich fish"), their little secret was well-known to the whole company. This particular day, Nell was on a mission.

Stanford White, who had been very open-handed of late to both her and her daughter, asked Nell to arrange for Edna to "bring the little Spanish maiden" to a luncheon he was planning. As Nell was well aware, with a man of such tremendous sway in the dominion of theater-land, the question wasn't if but when the task would be done. And since, as noted by one critic, "ornament was his passion" (at least one of them), White needed the darkly lovely little maiden to brighten his inventory of rare finds. In his expert estimation, the architect calculated that she would outshine all others.

Nell wiggled and flounced her way through small cliques of actors, stagehands, and various crew members in the cavernous backstage of the Casino Theater, looking for the Kid, who was fretting nervously in the wings. Evelyn wanted desperately to make a good impression on every audience at every show and prove herself to the company. Always anxious before a performance, she went through a little ritual, repeating a childhood nursery rhyme, which she chanted to herself "to chase away the butterflies." Nell spied Evelyn half in shadow as she played absent-mindedly with the vibrant multicolored scarves wrapped around her small-waisted peasant skirt. As Evelyn silently mouthed her incantation, Nell interrupted the ceremony by putting her hand on the girl's exposed shoulder.

"Do you think you can get your mother's permission to go to a lunch party with Edna and some of her 'society friends'?" she whispered.

Evelyn looked up at her, distracted, waiting for her cue. Nell repeated the question and Evelyn answered that she wasn't sure. She told Nell that her mother had been hovering more carefully as of late, still apprehensive about the "bad air" of the stage and nervous about crossing paths with Mr. Comstock and his prowling vice patrol, whose exploits were recounted almost daily in the papers. Like all respectable once and future middle-class women of the times, Mrs. Nesbit did not want to be accused of raising her daughter improperly. She surmised, if only dimly, that there was a darker side to life behind the footlights that might reflect poorly on her if she were suddenly thrust in the spotlight, and had to confess she had lied about her daughter's age—repeatedly.

Yet while she continued to accompany Evelyn to some of her modeling engagements during the day, Mamma Nesbit was not a presence at the theater where Evelyn performed eight times a week, including matinees. Her only attempt at guidance was the inane advice that Evelyn should avoid much contact with show people. Mrs. Nesbit, who was not about to try her own idle hands at gainful employment again, did not consider the absurdity of her words or the foolishness her actions. With her daughter bringing home her combined salaries, Mamma Nesbit reckoned it was worth the sacrifice.

That evening after dinner, Evelyn's instincts proved accurate. As she stood by the only window in their one-room apartment, she broached the subject: "Mamma, can I go to a society luncheon party with Edna Goodrich?"

Mrs. Nesbit considered the question. "I want to know more about these society people," she said. This of course was as ludicrous as her admonition about avoiding show people, given the fact that Mrs. Nesbit knew next to nothing about the New York social scene (but had given permission for Evelyn to perform nightly in front of hundreds of men, the vast majority of whom had little or no connections to any kind of society). Nonetheless, perhaps suspicious that any so-called society connections Edna might have would be of the dubious supper-society variety (which included everyone from jockeys and gamblers to Buffalo Bill Cody to "regular Broadway sharpies" such as Diamond Jim Brady, the "overdressed belch"), Mrs. Nesbit refused to give her consent.

Nor did she want to jeopardize the mounting interest of a Mr. James Garland, a millionaire banker, who had taken a fancy to her little girl after seeing her in *Florodora* every night for two weeks running from a coveted front-row seat. Several weeks earlier Garland had asked one of the librettists to introduce him to the little Spanish maiden, then "abruptly but with marked courtesy" asked if he might call on her mother. Evelyn gave some sort of evasive reply and promptly ran out the door, not giving it another thought. But a few days later, returning from a matinee, she found Garland sitting in the common front room of their boardinghouse talking to her mother.

As far as Mrs. Nesbit was concerned, Garland provided more than enough society for both of them on his Sunday yachting trips up the Hudson, for which they had a standing invitation. She was apparently less concerned (if at all) about the fact that the dour banking baron was a married man more than four times Evelyn's age, old enough to be her grandfather.

The disappointed Spanish maiden went back to Nell King the next day.

"Mamma says she doesn't think it's such a good idea."

Wanting badly to please White, and fearing that Edna might tumble from her present position of favor, Nell was unwilling to take no for an answer. For several days, she pestered Evelyn, who simply repeated her mother's reply. But White had specifically requested that Edna bring the dark-haired, diminutive chorine to his luncheon, and he was a man used to having his orders followed—as one would a blueprint. Nell decided to alter her line of attack. She arrived the next day at the boardinghouse in the West Thirties between Fifth and Sixth avenues in White's electric car, which visibly impressed Evelyn's mother.

"I assure you that everything is on the level," Nell said to Mrs. Nesbit. "The party is with some of the nicest people in New York society." She provided a laundry list of people's names, none of whom would actually be at the party (and some of whom were dead). With such smiling reassurance from another mother, coupled with the fact that it was not a dinner party, Mrs. Nesbit agreed to let Evelyn go. Nell heaved a busty sigh of relief as she got back into the car and adjusted her bosom. She knew the Pharaoh of Fifth Avenue would be pleased.

The day of the much-anticipated luncheon, an exhilarated Evelyn was in danger of wearing a hole in the already threadbare carpet, pivoting from mirror to bed to window to mirror. Mamma Nesbit pleaded with Florence to stand still as she dressed her in a simple homemade white outfit with black piping, pleated skirt, and a large white sailor's collar. Made from any available materials, including the occasional curtain or bedspread, the dresses Mrs. Nesbit made for Evelyn (to save money on buying new clothes) were the only remnants of her self-professed talent with needle and thread.

This particular dress was markedly different from those Evelyn wore back in Philadelphia when her mother had intentionally lengthened all the hems of her dresses and stretched her age to secure her the job at Wanamaker's. On this occasion, her mother made the skirt so that it would fall just at the knee, signifying a deliberate albeit useless gesture to turn the clock back on Evelyn's already amputated childhood. Indeed, without any stage makeup, her long hair tied in back with a large black taffeta ribbon, Evelyn looked less like a chorus girl and more like a girl in grammar school. Almost immediately upon her entrance into the theater world, Evelyn's age sparked rumors and speculation both back-stage and in the yellow press. Certain green-eyed actresses insisted that they knew for a fact that she was at least twenty, while others suggested that her slyly ambitious mother covered up the fact that Evelyn was in fact not even fifteen in order to get her on the stage and satisfy the Gerry Society. The fact that her mother began to shave a few years off her own calendar only obscured the truth further.

As for the "Goodrich sisters" (who also lied about their ages), neither realized the implications at the time of White's insistence that Edna bring Evelyn to lunch. Confident that White's habitually roving eye was still fixed on her shapely, more mature nineteen-year-old daughter, Nell was either too empty-headed or too full of herself to think that the sophisticated clubman could find the wraithlike, undeveloped child more attractive than ample Edna. She was woefully wrong.

Edna Goodrich arrived at the Nesbits' boardinghouse in a hansom cab, attired in a floor-length lavender dress that White had commented on approvingly several weeks earlier. Her brown hair was swept up in a fashionable pompadour and held in place with an artificial orchid and a multitude of hairpins. Before Edna could get out, Evelyn ran from the building and down the steps. She nearly vaulted into the cab.

"Where are we going?" she asked Edna, who acted more than a little patronizing as they pulled away from the curb.

"You'll see," she said with a slight smile as she adjusted the decorative lavender buttons on her bodice. She gave Evelyn the once over.

"Sweet costume," she added.

After having been cooped up in a monotonous succession of identical boardinghouse rooms, claustrophobic stockrooms, cluttered yet hollow studios, and bare-boned rehearsal halls for what seemed an eternity, the teenager, eager for friendship and expanded horizons, was in a state of euphoria. As she later put it, at that point in her life and on that particular day, "I loved everybody and everything. I thought the stage a lovely, enchanted place . . . since I had no experience to tell me differently."

To Evelyn's immense disappointment, however, the cab did not stop at the Waldorf or any of the posh hotels she thought a likely destination and ached to see. Instead, it came to a halt at a nondescript, almost shabby building on West Twenty-fourth Street off Broadway fronted by a toy shop owned by FAO Schwarz. The girls stepped from the cab, and Edna paid the driver with money White had given her, then dismissed him with a wave of her kid-gloved hand. As the pretty pair started to walk toward the doorway, Evelyn was momentarily distracted by some brightly painted mechanical toys in the window, especially a tin monkey dressed in a jaunty red fez and plaid vest who climbed a wire tree up to a bunch of tin bananas. Edna smiled again at Evelyn's immaturity, and pulled her by her collar inside the darkened hallway.

Then, as if by magic, the worn, narrow door in front of them opened automatically. To Evelyn, "it was all delightfully mysterious," appearing to her like something out of one of the dime novels she had read back in Tarentum. The girls made their way up the stairs, at the head of which another door opened in the same marvelous way. Intrigued, though beginning to have some qualms as to what lay beyond the murkiness of the second stairway, Evelyn stopped halfway up and asked, "Where on earth are we going?" Suddenly, a disembodied voice boomed out of the shadows.

"Nowhere on earth, dearie."

Evelyn shrank back, then hesitated, as a reassuring Edna nudged her with her elbow.

"It's all right, believe me," she whispered.

The two were ushered into a room that Evelyn described in 1934: "The sudden plunge from that dingy street entrance into this room was breathtaking. The predominating color was a wonderful red . . . heavy red velvet curtains shut out all daylight. There was plenty of illumination— yet I could find no lights anywhere. . . . Fine paintings hung on the walls. . . . The furniture was Italian antique, beautifully carved. There was a table set for four."

The great White stood to one side like an urban potentate, surveying his handiwork and amused by the reactions of the "little dolly" to his startling and innovative lighting effects. White's dramatically designed but camouflaged up lights revealed certain expensive objets d'art placed around the room with random artfulness. The indirect lighting threw a suffused rosy glow over the entire setting—the luxurious arabesque folds of floor-to-ceiling burgundy moiré drapes, overstuffed divans upholstered in crushed crimson velvet, and Oriental silk cushions and pillows the color of claret and cinnamon thrown promiscuously around the room. Evelyn attempted to appear as nonchalant as her companion, but to little avail. She saw in an instant that this setting easily transcended the feeble-minded glamour attempted by the theater. The place struck her as some-thing out of *The Arabian Nights*. She gazed at the scene again, half expecting the carpets to rise and fly around the room. She was less impressed, however, with her host.

Evelyn recalled that at first, White's above-average size "was appall-ing," and that "he seemed terribly old." In fact, being nearly three times her age, at forty-six, White appeared ruggedly but terminally advanced in years to the silky-skinned teenager. Since the table was set for four, Evelyn hoped that the fourth guest might prove a more appealing "date." Then, as if from nowhere, an even older man plodded into the room. He intro-duced himself as one Reginald Ronalds, whom Evelyn described as "dis-appointingly old," "not at all . . . a Don Juan." Semi-formal introductions of a sort were made, and as the four sat down to lunch, Evelyn was far more interested in the meal and the ambience than the man who had her brought to what was one of several of his hideaways.

"It was less of a pleasant social function than a very serious business [for me]," she confessed.

Having been on such frequent and intimate terms with the throb of hunger, Evelyn viewed the lunch that White had sent in from Delmonico's as a miraculous feast. As a child back in the farm country of Allegheny County, she had loved food of all kinds (a trait that continued through-out her life), and the architect commented approvingly on her "honest appetite" as she filled her plate with large pieces of lobster Newburg (Delmonico's invention), blackberry preserves, deviled eggs sprinkled with paprika, sweetbreads, hot rolls, and cool oysters on ice. It was like

Thanksgiving and Christmas rolled into one. Edna watched with disdain as she pushed some jellied cucumber around her plate with a cocktail fork.

It only became clear to Evelyn years later (as described in unpublished letters as well as her memoirs) that White's fascination with her, which became increasingly obvious as the afternoon progressed, was due to the fact that she was simply and intriguingly different from the norm—even to a man addicted to the extraordinary and capable of routinely performing remarkable feats, such as converting the Waldorf into the court at Versailles. But the tide had already turned as far as White and his self-selected cabal of connoisseurs, aesthetes, and fellow artists were concerned. For them, the sand had all but run out for the hourglass figure. The days of Anna Held and Lillian Russell were numbered. As for the generally restrained female population, trussed up in torture devices, corseted within inches of asphyxiation, they sorely needed a new model. And, as White recognized, Evelyn was the newest. It was something neither Edna nor her mother had counted on when they agreed to facilitate the tête-à-tête that afternoon.

As Evelyn would write: "Edna Goodrich was a big girl, plump and voluptuous—a type very popular in the Gay Nineties and the early part of the [twentieth] century. I was smaller, slenderer; a type artists and, as I learned later, older, more experienced men admired. I had discovered in the studios that artists cared little for the big-breasted, heavy-hipped, corseted figure, preferring to paint the freer, more sinuous, uncorseted one with natural, unspoiled lines."

Throughout the afternoon, most of the fun was had at Evelyn's expense. White teased her for her short, childish white frock and loosely bound long hair. At lunch she had her first real glass of expensive champagne. "I was permitted one glass, no more," she wrote. White had been adamant on that issue. Nonetheless, she loved the "irresponsible happiness of that party," and was pleasantly surprised by her host's apparently inexhaustible capacity for playfulness. Ronalds left during the cherry pie à la mode (another invention of Delmonico's), having some business to attend to down on Wall Street. White then asked the two girls if they would like to see some other rooms upstairs. They nodded enthusiastically and ascended two more flights of another darkened stairway, which led to a room at the top floor of the building.

Unlike the bold and subtler variations on shades of red below, the predominating color of this room was a deep forest green. Yet as Evelyn peered into the room, also illuminated by concealed lighting, amid the haze of green, two startling red objects suddenly materialized once her eyes adjusted to the light. One was a cardinal's hat, hung from the ceiling as an irreverent lampshade. The other was a "gorgeous swing with red velvet ropes around which trailed green smilax, set high in the ceiling at one end of the studio." As Evelyn approached the swing, White suggested teasingly to Edna, "Let's give this kiddie a ride."

Without hesitation, Evelyn jumped onto the swing. White grabbed the velvet ropes and Evelyn's small hands simultaneously as he pulled her backward, then thrust her forward with a vigorous push. A second and third push sent her soaring into the air in the direction of a large, multicolored paper Japanese parasol suspended by an undetectable string White had put into Edna's hand. He instructed Edna to pull at the string that moved the parasol up or down, and he encouraged Evelyn to kick at it. The closer she got, the happier he seemed. He clapped and shivered with delight each time Evelyn's dainty foot pierced the gaily decorated paper. As the colorful parasol twirled like a kaleidoscope before her eyes, again and again a giggling Evelyn broke the thin membrane of the paper until another had to be put in its place. White always made sure he had a replacement on hand.

The heady combination of a glass of good champagne, sumptuous food, and the lush surroundings of his fantastic enchanted forest, combined with White's visible admiration for her charms, proved intoxicating to Evelyn beyond anything she had ever imagined possible. That afternoon she and the architect laughed until their sides ached, and his reactions to her childish responses seemed gleefully real and equally juvenile. Except for the alcohol, even Saint Anthony of Comstock might have found little to complain about. Evelyn did not, on that first visit, see a different room, one that would play a crucial role in setting the stage for future tragedy.

As captivated as White was with his new playmate, at about four o'clock, he looked at his watch, stating that he had some business to attend to. He took Edna aside for a moment, who then sidled up to Evelyn. She told Evelyn that White wanted her to visit his dentist, and that she would take her. It was explained to Evelyn in the cab that White wanted her to fix a front tooth that spoiled her otherwise faultless beauty. Although it was barely noticeable in photographs, the tooth was slightly discolored (having been chipped during an ice-skating mishap as a child). Although both girls went to the dentist, only Edna saw the dentist dur-

Posing for Metropolitan Magazine, *1902.*

ing the visit, while Evelyn sat in the polished oak-paneled waiting room, which smelled faintly of sweet gas and burnt rubber.

Evelyn noticed that Edna seemed petulant during the ride home and increasingly bad-humored. She related her experiences of the day to her mother, who seemed puzzled about a number of things, not the least of which was why a society man would have such a gorgeous establishment in the heart of the business district. Evelyn, of course, didn't realize that Edna had picked up clear signals that White had found "a new bon-bon." The tip-off was the desire to fix her teeth. It wasn't long before Edna and her mother stopped speaking to Evelyn altogether. Nor did Evelyn have an answer for her mother about the reason for the wondrous apartment and unlikely location.

"Unsophisticated enough not to be able to find answers to our questions," Evelyn later wrote, "Mamma and I dismissed our lack of understanding, attributing it to our small-town ways."

Several days after, White sent a letter to Evelyn's mother, asking "in his illegible scrawl" for her to call at 160 Fifth Avenue. The chronically insecure Mrs. Nesbit appeared flustered, not knowing whether this was a home or a place of business. She asked her daughter whether it would be proper to call at either. Evelyn simply shrugged her shoulders and offered once again that White was a well-known society man. Several days later, in spite of vague misgivings about impropriety, Evelyn's mother met with White at the address he gave, which he had assured her in a phone call was his office.

The interview went "smashingly." Late in the afternoon Mrs. Nesbit came back, talking nonstop about Mr. White's kindness and concern for "his little Spanish maiden." She related how White had seen her from afar in the show "a number of times," and that after seeing her up close, he expressed the desire to have his dentist tend to Evelyn's tooth. Her mother saw this as a particularly generous if curious gesture, but White assured her that he had done the same for all the girls in *Florodora*.

"It was rather a fad of White's, this teeth-seeing," Evelyn recalled. Not sensing any great urgency, however, neither Evelyn nor her mother followed up on White's unconventional if gracious offer.

Several days later, White invited Evelyn to a second luncheon. This time the request came through Elsie Ferguson, a fleshy, blond chorus girl appearing in *The Strollers*, a musical comedy playing at the Knickerbocker Theatre, next door to the Casino. Much to Evelyn's delight, where Mr. White was concerned, her mother no longer had any objections to her attending any parties. That afternoon, Elsie Ferguson's "date" for lunch was a man named Thomas B. Clarke, who dealt in priceless Chinese porcelains and antiques. When he arrived, looking as he did with a shock of white hair and slightly bent like the silver-headed cane he carried, Clarke appeared to Evelyn an antique: "[He] looked to me as old as Methuselah." (Evelyn heard some years later that Ferguson eventually married Clarke's son.)

The four sampled fresh pastries from a Mulberry Street bakery, and after the roast partridge and quail, White produced a two-pound box of Lowney's chocolates, which he placed gingerly on Evelyn's small lap. He winked at her, acknowledging that she had been one of their models. Her host's effortless charisma proceeded to win Evelyn over. She started to see him in a new light and soon considered both his personality and barrel-chested appearance to her liking, including his bristling walrus-like brush of a mustache and "hair that stood up like velvet pile." Friends and acquaintances all agreed that he was a vigorously charming and arresting figure, routinely described in the papers as "masterful," "intense," and "burly yet boyish."

Evelyn also enjoyed his candid manner and ready laugh: "He was a compendium of information on all subjects, likely and unlikely. He was an authority and teacher. . . . [He] suggested his own genius by his appreciation of genius both contemporary and past." He was, she writes, one of those men "gifted by Nature beyond the average," and her growing impression of him, which her mother had felt immediately, was that "he was very kind, and that he was safe. True, he wasn't the 'romantic' type, but he was handsome in a way that appealed, a charming, cultured gentleman whose magnetism undid all my first impressions of him. He emerged as a splendid man, thoughtful, sweet, and kind; a brilliant conversationalist and an altogether interesting companion."

Numerous other men, most of them frequent patrons of *Florodora*, had already tried unsuccessfully to attract Evelyn's attention. Some anonymously sent uninspired bouquets or paltry boxes of candy; others, like a Mr. Munroe, sent weekly mash notes, all of which she ignored. As several weeks went by, it was clear who dominated Evelyn's thoughts. She spoke incessantly with her mother of White and his engrossing lifestyle. She repeated like a mantra the list of guests and the variety of food he had at his splendid parties, which she now attended frequently and where, among others, she met everyone from Annie Oakley to Caruso.

It pleased Evelyn that when it came to Mr. White, her mother's conversation was equally filled with superlatives. The only one, it seemed, who wasn't a fan of Stanford White was Mr. James Garland.

Although Mrs. Nesbit, not wanting to close any gates of gilded opportunity, had continued to allow Garland to provide Sunday entertainment on his "floating palace" for her daughter and her, her preference for White, whose generosity seemed limitless, was clear. And, just as Mamma Nesbit began to ponder what to do about the other married millionaire in Evelyn's life, Garland himself brought up the subject. After Evelyn casually mentioned having attended a Stanford White soirée, Garland's face clouded over.

"If you continue to associate with Mr. White, we must end our relationship," he said, as if scolding her.

An astonished Evelyn, who never considered that the elderly Garland had more than a sociable interest in her (and who she figured at the time was interested in a romantic relationship with her mother), listened as he continued, "I have most serious intentions regarding you. Right now I am divorcing my wife . . . but if you insist on going with a man like White, I cannot see you again."

Evelyn was flabbergasted, and gave a little nervous laugh, hoping that her mother would know what to say. Her mother said nothing.

"Why?" a puzzled Evelyn finally asked.

"Because," said Garland with disdain, "he is a voluptuary." Evelyn didn't know what the word meant, but she did know that White's personality and gay parties were infinitely more appealing than anything Garland had to offer, yacht or no yacht. Moreover, if there had been some under-standing, unspoken or otherwise, between Garland and her mother regard-ing Evelyn's future, the little Spanish maiden had never been let in on the negotiations. Impressionable but precocious, if she gave any thought to the subject of marriage at all, Evelyn invariably considered it a dead end and a trap. She had exhibited no desire to trade the stage for a cage, gilded or otherwise, and when considering Garland specifically, as she put it, "I would as soon have married Santa Claus."

So, with her mother's unspoken approval, Evelyn left the rueful James Garland high and dry. He told Evelyn when they reached the dock to let him know if and when she ended her association with White. (The fact that Evelyn would be named in Garland's divorce suit provided great fodder for the prosecution during the murder trial.)

It is not surprising that a freshly captivated Evelyn saw in White, however unconsciously, a man like her father, who was attentive, irre-sponsibly fun-loving, and "extremely clever." As Evelyn put it, "Let me say here that cleverness in a man or woman has always been the supreme attraction." And just as White had an impressive arsenal of wit at his disposal, his special influence in the Broadway district was additionally attractive to the aspiring actress. Here was someone who could help the stage career he vigorously encouraged, which Garland had obliquely dis-paraged. And, to put the vanilla ice cream on the cherry pie, Mr. White, who had a wife and family with whom he seemed decidedly contented, was "safe." But if White was out of the ordinary, so too was the little girl from the suburbs of Pittsburgh who was not the type to take pleasure in the mere commonplace or the placid when offered the incomparable.

On their next luncheon date, Evelyn and White repeated the first afternoon's harmless uplifting entertainment with a session on the red velvet swing. As Evelyn rode the swing, a disaffected Elsie Ferguson, who had again accompanied her, stood by, wanting to preserve a more genteel image. Like Edna Goodrich, Elsie was unaware that White pre-ferred Evelyn's unsophisticated vitality. Then, while getting ready to push her again, White commented on the fact that Evelyn had not gotten her teeth fixed. She had no sufficient answer for him, saying simply that Edna had not moved to help her when they were at the dentist's office, nor did Evelyn or her mother consider it a priority.

White, however, decided to take the issue up directly with her mother again. He assured Mrs. Nesbit that as an artist, his interest in her daughter's appearance was "a purely aesthetic urge," and won her over to the idea more easily than her daughter, who had the same aversion regarding a trip to the dentist that most people have (particularly in those days of primitive foot-powered low-speed drills and sickly-sweet laughing gas administered via an ill-fitting, smothering rubberized mask). Mrs. Nesbit found herself "overwhelmingly grateful" for White's attention to her daughter, since they were too poor to afford the impossible luxury of such a visit. In less than a fortnight, Evelyn had her teeth worked on. She was now perfect.

THE BIG BAD WOLF

As Evelyn would gradually learn, White's modus operandi was always the same when it came to meeting his next conquest. He would invariably have a current favorite, an old friend, or his secretary, twenty-six-year-old Charles Hartnett, set up a rendezvous with a potential lust interest in one of his "snuggeries," usually at his studio apartment on Twenty-fourth Street or in the Tower studio at Madison Square Garden. Some of his accomplices were girls who had gotten too old—having passed eighteen; these were "innocent agents" who simply did his bidding, not realizing that they were helping usher the way for their own replacement. Others who worked on White's behalf "may have been of a less innocent character," Evelyn later surmised. Needless to say, White was anxious to keep his various "friends" "separate and distinct," absurdly so it seemed to a naive Evelyn at first. Once, when he invited her to a luncheon at his Twenty-fourth Street studio, where a second girl would be waiting, White cautioned Evelyn in the cab not to let the girl know about his acquaintance with Edna Goodrich. Evelyn giggled and enjoyed the fact that she was chosen to be the keeper of his "silly secrets." To

Evelyn, her mother, and the wider audience, the little chorus girl was his unofficial ward and he her sainted patron.

As Evelyn would describe on the witness stand, "men like White, the baser White with which the world is better acquainted, reduce their methods to an exact science." The formula never varied. With an appearance and manner that easily deceived them, Stanford White found easy pickings in young "peaches" and "tomatoes" eager to appear on the stage. He insinuated himself into their usually deprived lives, and engaged their mothers (those who had them) as willing or clueless conspirators. Setting himself up as benefactor and friend, White would eventually arrange a meeting out of the public eye. Even if by nature he was a kind man, the

Sixteen-year-old Evelyn wearing Stanny's
gift of a Red Riding Hood cloak.

fatherly attitude White showed toward those he had "marked down" was, as Evelyn came to see, calculated. A later editorial from the *Atlanta News* that labeled him as monstrous libertine also described how this "brilliant architect . . . was relentless and irresistible in his organized and well-prepared search for the honor and virtue of the young uncorrupted girls of the great metropolis in which he lived."

With Evelyn, White took the "shortest cut to [her] affections," both of which were intimately tied to her abbreviated childhood. In addition to her unmistakable love of sweets and food in general, it had become a well-known joke among the theater crowd that "the Kid" loved automata, the mechanical toys she lingered over in the shop window below White's apartment. So White furnished his life-sized dolly with a new toy each time she visited. She had her pick of anything she fancied in the FAO Schwarz window, an inoffensive and ironic front for White's hideaway. Nor did her mother consider these relatively expensive gifts of toys as anything but paternal kindness.

During the first impulsive month when he was actively pursuing Evelyn, White revealed himself to her as a man of tremendous powers and capabilities, one of which, unbeknownst to her, was the ability to juggle the affections of numerous girls simultaneously. But as far as Evelyn was concerned, he was a unique man, "large and generous in his dealings with his fellows; brilliant as an artist and scholar; kindly to a degree in his relations to those who needed his kindness." And in a culture where the norm regarding meals and food in general (even in 1901) was to "buy it, boil it, bolt it and beat it," White was a connoisseur and gourmand of the "Continental model," a man who took the act of eating as seriously as he did his art. With variety of taste and sensuous presentation as his foundation, White strove to make meals an aesthetic experience; whether it was teal and mallard or veal medallions and rack of lamb, his table was invariably a source of unending pleasure and an epicurean delight. It was a rule that applied to virtually everything in his life, especially his craving for mignon of a very particular type.

One day when she told White about the artists she had already posed for, he replied that they were all "old stuffs" and that he would introduce her to some real artists, including the foremost illustrator of the day, Charles Dana Gibson. As she would later write in regard to first seeing Stanford White, "he himself looked like an old stuff; at that point in one's life, anyone over twenty-five seemed ancient." For their next few meetings it was always the same. White never approached Evelyn directly himself; instead, he had her brought to him by other showgirl acquaintances. These clandestine meetings were well orchestrated, carefully planned down to the last detail, as one might expect from an architect whose own appetite for both fine and unrefined gratification and pursuit of perfection would ultimately be his downfall.

Her benefactor, as her mother now preferred to call White, began to send flowers regularly, while nearly every other day the aged Mr. Clarke, who was also apparently fascinated by Evelyn and moved by her constrained circumstances, sent huge baskets of fruit to her boardinghouse address. As she remembers it, she and her mother were appropriately grateful for this show of "polite attention." Going beyond what most would consider polite attention, however, White's next impressive act was to move daughter and mother (and Howard when he was well enough to be "in town") into the Wellington Hotel, where their accommodations included a drawing room, alcove, and private bath.

The apartment at the Wellington, decorated by the great man personally, was a shrine to sensuality. The color scheme was an enchanting snow white and rose red, a deliberate choice by White to appeal to his little maiden's love of fairy tales. Her bedroom had white satin walls, red velvet carpets, a huge white bearskin on the floor, ivory white furniture, and a bed draped in ivory satin, covered with rare imported Irish lace. The canopy of the bed was also draped in white satin, "ending in a huge crown from which protruded five thick white ostrich plumes." In imitation of the red velvet swing room in White's own apartment on Twenty-fourth Street, the small living room was done in forest green, decorated with swan planters, concealed lights, and a beautiful ebony piano. White also generously engaged a German piano teacher so that Evelyn could revive her piano lessons, for which she rewarded him by studying Beethoven, "especially to please him."

One day soon after the move, a package arrived for White's "protégée" containing a sage green hat, a soft green feathered boa, and a gorgeous English-tailored cloak of "an intriguing shade of American beauty red with long flowing lines and a boyish satin collar." With it came instructions that Evelyn was to wear the cape to a party that Friday night. Rather than become alarmed or suspicious that perhaps White had more than a philanthropic or avuncular interest in Evelyn, Mrs. Nesbit made her daughter a new dress especially for the occasion, and in record time.

The night of the party, she sent it on to the theater. After the performance, Evelyn was told by a stagehand that a carriage was waiting for her on the side of Twenty-ninth Street. As she approached, Evelyn saw that several carriages were waiting there (she wasn't the only chorus girl being wooed by the captains of industry and Champagne Charlies of Manhattan). Before she could inquire which one was hers, out from the dimness of the greengrocer's doorway across from where the line of carriages waited stepped White. He got into the carriage with Evelyn.

"Where are we going?" she asked.

White smiled puckishly.

"To my Garden," he said with a wink as the cab headed in the direction of Madison Square.

Evelyn, who was still wound up from the performance and the gifts White had sent earlier in the day, bubbled with anticipation and could not keep still in her seat. She had heard about the splendid parties White threw in his private apartment high above the city, but this was her first invitation. So many things were running through her head that she didn't think about why there was always a need for such furtive arrangements. When she finally asked him a week or so later, White said that he had a morbid fear of publicity and was by nature a very private man in spite of his public persona.

When they arrived at Madison Square Garden, White hurried his petite charge into the elevator, which lifted them with well-oiled, whirring efficiency to his personal aerie at the top. White had designed the eighty-foot tower so that the rooms, one above the other, were built around the elevator shaft with each taking the shape of a horseshoe. Since all the other rooms were offices (except for Peter Cooper Hewitt's studio), the building was empty at night.

Once the elevator opened to reveal the Garden's Tower room, Evelyn clapped her hands and stared at its wondrous Edenic design. There were dazzling azure-and-emerald-green Tiffany sconces around the room decorated with luminous red-eyed dragonflies that seemed to hover magically in the air. A huge gilt mirror ran around the full length of the room on the back wall, and reflected in the mirror was an equally long and luxurious tufted velvet couch the deepest shade of moss. An ebony grand piano filled one corner of the room; spread casually across it was a soft-green-and-lavender paisley shawl with deep-purple fringe. Poised on top of the piano was an exquisite bronze by the famed sculptor Frederick William MacMonnies titled *Bacchante*. A tempting row of hot hors d'oeuvres, Italian pastries, cheeses, and a platter bursting with fruit dipped in dark chocolate were displayed on a round rosewood table. Several huge bouquets of exotic flowers sat on side tables, their fragrance mixing with the scents of the food in an exceptionally heady blend. Perhaps the most striking floral feature was a spectacular arrangement of bird of paradise plants, which White had brought up from the wilds of exotic Florida. Their waxy green leaves formed fan-shaped crowns bursting with brilliant orange and purplish blue petals. Evelyn was spellbound.

Apparently, both Evelyn and Stanny, as she now chose to refer to her benefactor, shared a terrible sweet tooth. She picked up a sugarplum from the platter on the festive table and rolled it around in her mouth, savoring the pleasing texture. Stanny smacked his lips in playful mimicry, placed a chocolate-covered cherry between his lips, and smiled at her as he held out his hand. Evaluating Evelyn in her new dress and red cape, White, who bore more than a passing resemblance to the mustachioed new president, exclaimed, "Bully!" He spun her around in front of him and said appraisingly, "You look just like Little Red Riding Hood! We must have your picture taken in that cape." Excitedly he ran both hands through his distinctive brush of auburn hair. He then said that he would arrange for Evelyn to pose in the cloak for one of his photographer friends.

Aside from his urge to have their teeth fixed, White had developed the habit of having his favorite actresses photographed by well-known photographers, then pasting certain of the photos into private scrapbooks. One such "camera artist" was Rudolf Eickemeyer Jr., a portraitist and New York Camera Club member, who cofounded the Campbell Art Company. Another was Gertrude Käsebier, who counted among her subjects Mark Twain and Booker T. Washington. A third was Otto Sarony, well known for his theatrical subjects. Evelyn smiled and pulled on a stray ringlet that brushed her cheek.

"Mr. Breese?" asked Evelyn, having heard the name mentioned as one of White's photographer acquaintances through the backstage grapevine.

"No, no," said White, arching his eyebrows and drumming his fingers on the table, "not Mr. Breese."

White was all too aware that his friend, James Breese, founder of the Carbon Studio, was, like himself, quite the "rounder." It was well known that Breese specialized in society women (perhaps in more ways than one), and therefore White most definitely would not trust Breese with his newest and most extraordinary find.

"Someone else," White assured her, "who has won prizes for his studies." Eventually, Evelyn would pose for all of White's photographer friends. All but Breese.

He told his Little Red Riding Hood that he would arrange the whole thing one day soon, if her mother agreed. Evelyn acknowledged that almost anything he did seemed to agree with her mother, though she was sure the first question her mother would ask was how much she was to be paid by this photographer. While the issue of money was like a knotted apron string snagged somewhere in the back of Evelyn's mind (and inextricably bound to the image of her mother sobbing uncontrollably on some dilapidated bed), it was always in the forefront of Mrs. Nesbit's. Nor did her mother ever let Evelyn forget how easy it would be for them to slip back into the abyss of poverty. So, just as she had when she collected rents at twelve and began her first two jobs at fourteen, sixteen-year-old Evelyn found herself inescapably caught once more between two worlds—that of her childish fantasies (complete with wardrobe) and the very adult and not so innocent world of real-life wolves.

Evelyn stole a moment to look intently at White, taking him in against the brilliantly decorated background of a room filled to capacity with gorgeous objects. While becoming aware of her patron's capability for overindulgence, Evelyn was increasingly affected by Stanny's flattering and seemingly genuine concern over her welfare. She seemed to take special pleasure in the fact that unlike many of the anonymous stagestruck Johnnies who wrote her silly love notes and made impossibly exaggerated promises, Stanny didn't treat her with any great ceremony. He was, instead, courteous and considerate, always able to make her feel she was special. He kept to his word when he promised something and seemed to take a sincere interest in her life and fledgling career, "exercising an almost fatherly supervision" over everything she did. He was "particularly solicitous" as to what she drank, "mildly reproving, gently bantering, a man who kept one smiling" as he got her to do as she was told. As she described it, "He had a trick of suggesting disparagement without expressing it" (even though he was the one responsible for introducing her to expensive champagne in the first place).

That night, after finishing a glass of particularly pricey Moët & Chandon White had poured for her while she scooped out the contents of a cream puff with her pinky, leaving only the flaky shell on her plate, Evelyn was surprised by his response when she pushed her glass forward for a second drink.

"One is quite enough for a little girl," Stanny said, "and I want you to be a nice little girl."

"What do you think is a nice little girl?" she asked coyly, pushing her glass forward again. But White seemed quite serious. He took hold of her small hand and told her that nice girls didn't drink to excess or stay up late, that they went home to their mothers at an early hour. Of course, all things are relative, considering that when he told her this the time was close to one o'clock in the morning.

Suddenly, he decided to take her home, which Evelyn felt was a particularly dull way to end an otherwise spiffy evening. But as she sat next to an uncharacteristically quiet Stanny in the hansom cab, Evelyn mused about her ascending good fortune, her growing fondness for the influential and animated White, and the constant delights he placed before her. He drummed loudly on the apartment door in order to wake up Mrs. Nesbit to show her that he had delivered her daughter safe and sound. Apparently, Mrs. Nesbit was not losing sleep over her daughter's whereabouts now that she had turned over a portion of her parental responsibilities to Mr. White. It began to appear to Evelyn, however unconsciously, that indeed Stanny was more concerned for her welfare than her own mother.

Even if he could stay for only a few minutes, every morning Stanny came to the hotel with books for Evelyn to read, suggestions for her "cultivation" in art, music, and literature. He fed her ambitions for self-improvement, and her responsiveness was a refreshing change from the usual Broadway concubine, whose range of thought seemed limited to the world that existed between Madison Square and Twenty-third Street. He introduced her to Dickens, Shelley, Keats, Milton, and Tennyson. She told him that she was especially keen to read Shakespeare, so as the favored son of a Shakespeare scholar, Stanny started her on the sonnets, promising that he would soon unlock for her an astounding and magical world of words, "produced," he said reverently, "by the greatest writer who ever lived." He said this "almost breathlessly," she remembered, and it even seemed "there were tears forming in his deeply expressive eyes" when he spoke of it.

According to Evelyn, White and her mother also soon became "fast friends." He visited with Mrs. Nesbit on a number of occasions, always with flowers in hand and always courteous in his manner. Evelyn's mother was quite taken by his apparent anxiety over her daughter's well-being, and she began to impose on the architect's goodwill to include the sensitive thirteen-year-old Howard in his plans as well. When White generously offered to finance Howard's schooling, Mrs. Nesbit was ecstatic. Within a matter of days, a stunned and grateful Howard (who was once again staying with family members on a farm in Allegheny County) was sent to Chester Academy in another part of Pennsylvania, more than likely the only student with an expensive Persian rug in his room, courtesy of the family's benefactor. Mrs. Nesbit quickly came to profess this magnificent man as "eminently solid," one who seemed "heaven-sent" to the Nesbit family.

The family's as well as Evelyn's individual relationship with White grew more intense as his *Florodora* girlie became the most significant if inexperienced player in his elaborate production, the script of which had been written long before she came on the scene. She was not the first girl to ride on the red velvet swing. Nor did she have any say in how the relationship was to proceed or be conducted. But what did it matter to her, anyway? She was being treated like a sultana, and Stanny was her wizard-godfather, giving her books and candy and marvelous gifts, promoting her career, helping her family, and doing it all while whistling snatches of Beethoven and remaking Manhattan to his liking. And since her own mother never questioned the much older, very married man's involvement in her life, which might also seem innocuous to a casual observer, why should she?

But those few who knew White and his "peculiarities" more intimately waited with bated breath and feigned indifference for the other costly shoe to drop. They surmised that this was not going to be another Ruth St. Denis experience. St. Denis was a young dancer whose relationship with White several years earlier had never progressed beyond the platonic. It was clear that Evelyn was destined for something more.

Assuming at the time that James Garland had spoken against White out of jealousy, Evelyn never questioned—until it was too late—why although "Stanford White was a notorious man in New York, and . . . there was hardly a man about town who did not know him and of him, there were none who warned me" (besides Garland, of course). She would come to learn that Stanford White was a member of a small clique of men who had vicious tendencies. She wrote, "[I use] the word 'vicious' because it perfectly describes White's untamed, ruthless, and wicked actions, performed frequently without remorse, with the sense that he and his friends were immune to the laws of the land." And White clearly must have felt exempt from fear of discovery and immune to the possibility of retribution for his schemes of seduction, should they ever be exposed. If he had, as Harry Thaw later claimed, "ravished three hundred and sixty-eight girls," White seemed unconcerned about a number of things, including the possibility that his wife might discover his "dalliance" with underage girls in love nests set up from Gramercy Park to Westchester (if she didn't already know).

It wasn't long after Evelyn's first night in the Tower that White kept his word and brought her to the studio of Gertrude Käsebier. White had introduced a number of sitters to the talented Käsebier, many of them wealthy socialites whose homes he had designed and/or decorated. With a "sugar-daddyish mix of altruism and self-gratification that seems to have marked his relationships with these young women," White would make gifts to the showgirls of "a generous number of publicity prints." And of course, he would order some "for his own delectation." It was rumored that he had voluminous albums of the reigning beauties of the day, including a "big book of 500 photographs" filled only with images of the tantalizingly pubescent Evelyn.

On the day that White brought Evelyn to her, Käsebier studied the petite girl's delicate features from across the room. She drew White aside and subtly chastised him "for taking so young a 'protégée.' But the charitable White explained that he had "bought" Evelyn to rescue her from neglect and exploitation by her widowed mother, who had hired her out as an artists' model at an early age and was now "selling her to the highest bidder." He told the photographer that he had been educating the child, teaching her how to be beautiful, how to dress, and so on. Käsebier, struck by the remarkable mixture of ennui and expectation in the girl's face, considered that Evelyn didn't need to be taught how to be beautiful, but rather how to preserve her innocence. Still, Käsebier had cultivated a pleasant and at times almost playful relationship with the architect, who sat for her himself. So, at the architect's behest, she photographed the striking young showgirl. The resulting *Portrait (Miss N.)* became part of Käsebier's exhibit at 291, the influential fine-art gallery on Fifth Avenue and home to the Photo-Secessionists movement.

As Käsebier's biographer perceptively points out in her analysis of the iconic photograph, it is in fact innately sexier and more subversive than the ones Rudolf Eickemeyer Jr. would take of Evelyn on the bearskin rug that became infamous as evidence at the murder trials. Among the thousands of drawings and photographs of Evelyn, "none more fully suggests her ripe, youthful beauty as Käsebier's *Miss N*. Käsebier presents her as a coquette, recalling those in Alphonse Mucha's posters and other popular turn-of-the-century pictures. . . . In *Miss N.* she seems unnervingly close to the viewer, an effect that Käsebier achieved by cropping the top of her head and by photographing her slightly from above. Her upturned head seems about to offer a kiss while her right hand proffers a small Quimper pitcher. Yet her torso recedes, so that this temptress seems both to move forward and resist. Although her Empire-style gown suggests the past . . . the direct gaze shows Evelyn Nesbit is no coy eighteenth-century maiden."

Clearly, regardless of her own misgivings about her young subject's vulnerability, in *Portrait (Miss N.)*, Käsebier herself intuitively capitalized on the quality that was the essence of Evelyn's appeal: a nascent sexuality inextricably tied to an image of classical and seemingly unspoiled purity. But in spite of the whiteness of the gown that exposes equally white, narrow adolescent shoulders and yet primly covers her small breasts, there can be no mistaking the message conveyed by the angle and placement of the heart-shaped, fragile-looking white pitcher that Evelyn holds suggestively near her lap. There is nothing else in the picture to distract one from the sultry gaze of the subject, save perhaps the dark curves of the sofa behind Evelyn, which draw our eyes back to the dark curls of her hair and thus her face. And there is another contradictory message embedded in the photograph. While at the time young girls wore their hair down in long curls, it was the fashion for adult women to wear it piled on their head. In this photo, Evelyn's hair is done up like a woman's while two long curls hang down over her shoulder like a child's.

Within a mere few months after she made it to Broadway, Evelyn's star was indeed rising, if not on the stage, then behind the scenes. In early November 1901, Evelyn noticed that White had begun to take a greater interest in her mother's movements. As she described it, "He displayed a

Gertrude Käsebier's Mucha-inspired photograph Miss N., *1902.*

solicitude that took a significant shape." He knew the Nesbits had roots in Pittsburgh, and he knew that her mother often complained of being left alone during the long days and nights when Evelyn was modeling and performing. Mrs. Nesbit had, of course, abandoned any idea of acquiring work herself, now that White was always there to offer an additional twenty-five dollars a week to supplement Evelyn's small income.

The day finally came when White suggested to Mrs. Nesbit that she go back to Pittsburgh for a visit.

"It is never advisable to drop people out of your life," he told her solicitously. Mrs. Nesbit was at first reluctant to leave her adolescent daughter all alone in New York (even though she had left her in Pittsburgh and Philadelphia with virtual strangers). Evelyn had always been a free-spirited girl with a strong will, but that alone might be cause to worry. White smiled.

"I am here," he said. "She can hardly be alone when I am around to look after her."

For weeks during his visits, White took every opportunity to turn the topic of conversation to Pittsburgh. Not surprisingly, Evelyn's mother eventually agreed she would go, and leave Evelyn in Manhattan, while Howard would remain at the academy. With his customary generosity, White paid the entire fare and secured all the arrangements for Mrs. Nesbit. At his suggestion, before she left, Mrs. Nesbit insisted that Evelyn not go out with any person other than Mr. White while she was gone.

"Promise me you will see no one else while I'm gone," she said as she boarded the train, and "obey Mr. White." It was a promise Evelyn kept, only going to her scheduled modeling appointments by day and performances at night.

A few days after her mother left, Evelyn received a phone message from Stanny, asking her to come to a studio on Twenty-second Street. It was early in the morning, and by ten o'clock Evelyn was already on her way to the studio that belonged to Rudolf Eickemeyer Jr., the well-respected photographer Stanny had mentioned to Evelyn as having won a number of prestigious prizes for his work.

Evelyn in The Theatre *magazine, 1902.*

Beginning almost the minute she stepped through the door, Evelyn was coaxed into posing "for hours on end" by a doting Stanny. Presented with a dizzying variety of costumes, she was transformed into a rural, straw-hatted tomboy; a demure Quaker girl; a languid Turkish maiden. White orchestrated the event, confident that Eickemeyer's incredible eye for beauty and composition would enhance the naturally dramatic effects of Evelyn's beguiling looks and more studied theatrical poses aided by her costumes. As promised, Stanny posed her as Little Red Riding Hood, Pocahontas, and Little Bo Peep; he put a long blond wig on her so that Evelyn could imitate a Gainsborough girl. He personally put her hair up in a band of chrysanthemums, then arranged it so that it fell loosely about her soft shoulders. He draped furs around her and placed a strand of pearls in her hair. Like a magician, Stanny pulled costume after costume from a large trunk, which also provided an assortment of floral head-dresses and sheer-looking, flowing gowns. Several times when she went into the dressing room to change, White knocked on the door and asked if she needed any help. Each time she answered no.

Late in the afternoon, an inexhaustible White brought out "the most gorgeous of Japanese kimonos," which he had bought in Hong Kong especially for Evelyn (or so he told her) at a cost of several thousand dol-lars. When she put it on, the impression it made on White was obvious. He instructed her to sit on a huge, pristine polar bear pelt in a corner of the studio near some tapestries and the now-depleted large wooden trunk. Evelyn demonstrated her experience and natural versatility by assuming a number of poses in the kimono, her magnificent hair piled upon her head, with a few tawny wisps framing her delicate features. There was also a vivid contrast between her alabaster skin and the remark-able crimson-and-marigold shimmer of the kimono, further accentuated when set against the whiteness of the bearskin rug.

A childlike weariness fell upon Evelyn after changing costumes and posing nonstop for hours on end (with no meals to speak of). As her posture became more and more prone and her lashes flickered, Evelyn was like a languid candle, softening, then melting as she sank into uncon-sciousness. White himself fairly glowed with delight at the effect the impromptu scene produced. Having exclaimed finally that she could work no more, Evelyn, enveloped in her silk kimono, drifted asleep on the huge polar bear rug. In one of those rare serendipitous moments, Eickemeyer saw the opportunity for a unique and bewitching picture. He photographed the sleeping girl, and captured an impression that would, like the red velvet swing, become an indelible image connected to Evelyn as the "little butterfly."

The next day or so, when White stopped by his offices with Evelyn tagging by his side, he mentioned to his partner Charles McKim that "this little girl's mother has gone out of town and left her in my care."

"My God," was McKim's only comment.

The following day, White dropped his mask of paternal benevolence.

Infamous Eickemeyer photo of Evelyn as the "little butterfly," 1901.

Modeling pose, circa 1903.

CHAPTER SEVEN

Through the Looking Glass

Not even for the purpose of pleasing those who demand, according to the rules of melodrama, a more bitter and more prejudiced view, can I represent him other than he was. His failing we know—it was his one failing. —*Evelyn Nesbit, 1914*

If I write this . . . a little cold-bloodedly, I must do that or I should not write at all. I must tell all that is to be told, because around this night circled the tragedy which dragged me into the fierce light of publicity and of criticism. . . . It is more satisfactory for me to get outside myself and regard the big incident in my life from the outsider's point of view without fear, favor, or prejudice. —*Evelyn Nesbit, 1934*

A night (or two) after her marathon photo session, Evelyn received a note from Stanny inviting her to one of his by now familiar fêtes. During the murder trial, much would be made by the district attorney of Evelyn's inability to remember exact dates or days for the events that transpired after her mother's departure. As she would tell the court, aside from the fact that the events had happened five years earlier, until that unfortunate night, there was no reason for her to single out any particular day or evening as different from her regular routine. As she would testify, "No day or night from that period was particularly memorable in any significant way." For nearly three years she had posed countless times before, just as she had been a guest at numerous parties that White had thrown.

Around nine o'clock, Stanny's "little bon-bon" found herself in a cab sent for by him and directed to his apartment at Twenty-fourth Street. As she toyed with a pink silk bow on her sleeve, unconcerned about everything except what she would eat and who she might meet (since Caruso was in town), Evelyn wondered whom her mother might be socializing with back in Pittsburgh, and giggled, realizing that she was most likely already in bed.

Hungry and happy to be out and about, Evelyn whetted her appetite by thinking of the treats Stanny would probably have especially for her—chocolate-covered cherry cordials and bonbons (which he said were "almost as sweet" as Evelyn), imported four-berry preserves, sharp cheeses, pickled onions, the ubiquitous oysters, and lemon custard "for afters." She also looked forward to spending time in the sumptuous surroundings of the studio, with its hypnotic lights, thick Persian carpets, plush divans, and never-ending parade of diverting people who consistently expressed their own wonder at White's effortless brilliance in adding matchless and unbelievably rare objects to his collection with such frequency.

When asked to remember how she felt at the start of the evening (again more than five years later), Evelyn could only reply that she felt an overwhelming "sense of security and well-being," even though her mother was out of town and she was alone in New York, "since she was under the guardianship of Mr. White . . . with her mother's consent." As she would eventually realize, she was "utterly and entirely at his mercy." She described it in her memoir: "He dominated me by his kindness and by his authority. He abused the sacred trust which had been put into his hands. Nothing else matters."

Unlike her first entrance into the rooms at Twenty-fourth Street a little more than two months earlier, Evelyn entered without hesitation and with "something of a proprietary air," since she had come to regard "her benefactor" as "bound to [her] by some vague relationship." To her surprise and disappointment, however, even though the table was laid for a party, only White was there waiting. She looked around and asked where everybody was, thinking perhaps he had planned some sort of surprise. But a smiling Stanny was all apologies.

"Isn't it too bad," he said, holding out his hands to her, "that all the others invited have turned us down?"

A frowning Evelyn dropped into a large chenille chair, which was so big her feet didn't touch the carpet. She picked at the arm of the chair, as if annoyed. White noticed her immediate mood shift and asked her what she was bothered about. Evelyn replied that she was upset, thinking there would be no party now. She squinted her eyes petulantly and peered distractedly around the empty room.

"Nonsense," White answered, "we will have our own party." He pulled a chair next to his at the dining table, patted the seat, and said that they could have just as much fun without other guests—a tea party in the woods with only Alice and her Mad Hatter. And no tea. Evelyn flopped down, sitting with one leg beneath her in a way her mother would have frowned upon as being "unladylike," and characteristically shrugged her approval. She then began to fill her plate.

Throughout the meal the charismatic clubman did most of the talking, and since his brilliance always carried over into his conversations, she remembered, "I was not bored." He talked of meeting Thomas Edison recently and said that he would arrange for another party and invite him so that Evelyn could meet a real wizard. He produced a brightly painted cast-iron mechanical bank purchased especially for her in London and placed it in front of her on the table. It was William Tell and his son. White put a penny in the father's gun and told Evelyn to push a small lever. When she did, the penny shot into the apple on the son's head. Evelyn clapped with glee and asked him for some more pennies. She also asked for a glass of champagne, which he poured into a crystal flute. When she tried to sneak another a short time later, to her added delight, Stanny didn't seem to mind.

The jovial host then left Evelyn alone briefly. (This was not so strange to anyone who knew the architect, since he was always darting in and out of rooms, taking and making phone calls, wheeling and dealing his way across different time zones and continents at once.) She walked over to the piano and struck the first few notes of Beethoven's Fifth Symphony.

When he came back, she began to get ready to go home, grabbing the sleek red moleskin cape that White had given her.

"You're not going?" he said as he took the cape from her shoulders.

"Stay," he pleaded, "there's a lot in this house you have never seen and it will amuse you."

He gave her yet another flute of champagne and talked about artifacts he had bartered for or bought in order to furnish his and other homes of distinction. He described with glowing self-satisfaction particular items that he had purloined from China, Florence, Japan, and even more remote places around the globe.

"I have another room upstairs you have not seen," he said, piquing her natural curiosity. With that, he steered her up a tiny flight of stairs, which indeed she had never noticed before. Promising her "something special," White ushered her into a small back studio. Around the room were costly medieval tapestries, expensive paintings in equally expensive frames (most of which he had designed), as well as a smaller collection of antiques displayed prominently and lit dramatically from beneath. But most amazing of all to Evelyn was that

> the walls and ceiling [were] covered with mirrors, the floor with imitation glass. The mirrors . . . were so cleverly set together that they gave the appearance of being a solid sheet of mirror-covering. Here again, indirect lighting cast a soft glow over everything. At one side stood a large, moss-green velvet-covered couch, immense in so small a room. The multiple mirrors created an extraordinary effect; you saw yourself repeated in endless vistas.

It was a narcissist's dream. The novelty and unreality of the sight held Evelyn spellbound. She sat on the couch and had another glass of champagne, which Stanny offered. She was thrilled by the sight of her reflection at every turn and laughing because the bubbles tickled her nose—and because her benefactor seemed to have thrown caution to the wind with regard to the usual single glass of anything alcoholic. White looked at her expression and "smiled, as one who is pleased at a compliment." He reiterated the fact that he had ranged the world to furnish this sanctuary, as if trying to impress the little girl who had yet to graduate from the ninth grade.

Like a conjurer building to his best trick, White then pushed open some tapestry hangings in a doorway and revealed with a flourish a still smaller apartment off the so-called studio. It was "a little bedroom, all hung in chintz" and dyed the darkest purple of midnight. A small solitary table stood next to a four-poster canopied bed, which overwhelmed the ten-foot-square room. The curtains around the bed drew apart or together with the pull of a golden silken cord. The headboard, as well as the dome of the canopy and the wall next to the bed, were three solid beveled mirrors. Hidden all around the top of the bed were tiny electric bulbs, "and within easy reach a series of buttons regulating the lighting effects. By pushing the button an amber glow was cast about the inverted mirror overhead. Another push produced a rose coloring, and yet another a soft blue." She remembers that "with the room in darkness and only the bed lights working, the effect it produced was like the Fata Morgana. It also reminded her of "fairy-book descriptions of nymphs' palaces under the sea."

On the table was another bottle of champagne and a single glass. Evelyn laughed to herself. The only thing missing, she thought, was the white rabbit and a sign that read "drink me." Over the mantelpiece hung a provocative painting of a nude woman done by Robert Reid, a well-known muralist, and draperies the color of pinot noir hung from ceiling to floor in regal folds. Being less articulate than White perhaps would have liked, when he asked her what she thought, she simply commented how "pretty it all was" and then drifted back into the studio with the sensation she was floating. She played the piano for a little while, feeling slightly warm in the pit of her stomach, flushed in her cheeks, and somewhat "fraying around the edges."

Appealing to her love of "dressing up," White then produced from behind his back a "ravishing yellow satin Japanese kimono embroidered in festoons of deep purple wisteria." He drew her by the hand back into the bedroom, where a light-headed Evelyn stood again, as if mesmerized in front of the painting over the mantel. Her reverie was interrupted with the pop of the champagne cork, and she jumped at the noise. White laughed and took the only glass from the table, filled it, and offered it to her.

"Drink this," he said.

She did, and as she would testify during one trial, it seemed that "the wine tasted unusually bitter."

"I don't much care for this," she said, screwing up her face. White, however, encouraged her in a playful way to "drink it up" and warned her teasingly that such a sour face might stay that way permanently. So, minding what her mother had told her before she left about obeying Mr. White, Evelyn did. By the third or fourth sip, although it still tasted bad, she was reminded of something Stanny had told her numerous times about developing an educated palate.

Stanny began talking to his little bonbon "easily and naturally," commenting again on the room, and "there was nothing in his voice or in what he said that might suggest anything out of the ordinary."

Then, as she described it in 1914, Evelyn suddenly experienced "a curious sensation":

There began a buzzing and a drumming, a persistent thump—thump—thumping in my ears. I felt dizzy and sick, and the objects in the room became blurred and indistinct. The sound of his voice came to me [as if he were] speaking from a great distance—then all went black.

In 1934 she described the same moment this way:

And then, because of the unusual quantity of wine I had had, I lost all self-control. I grew dizzy; the room whirled around faster and faster. I "passed out." . . . Harry Thaw always maintained, afterwards, that the wine was drugged. I have never believed that to be so. I think it was simply a matter of too much champagne.

Whichever scenario was closer to the truth, the inexcusable result was the same. And whether or not the susceptible teenager was actually or wholly unconscious for some period of time—two hours? sixteen minutes?—all she knew was that when she opened her eyes in an approximation of some form of fuzzy awareness, she was lying on top of the silken sheets in the huge canopied bed next to Stanny, with midnight drawn tight around them. Stanny lay apprehensively beside her, taking in the contrast of her creamy skin against the violet folds of the sheets. She was clad only in "an abbreviated pink undergarment" that covered her small breasts, while White exposed "the naked body of his naked sins," only slightly receded in the "full flush of his extraordinary physical powers." She fixated blankly for a brief moment on the haphazard patterns of reddish hairs on his broad bare chest (and was not, at that point, aware of a thin reddish streak on her inner thigh).

In 1914, this is how she described the immediate scene that followed:

I could not realize what had happened. All that I knew was that something terrible had come to me and I screamed. With terror in his face, he tried to stop me. "For God's sakes don't!" he pleaded. It was horrible—horrible. I knew without understanding. What happened after I cannot tell.

In 1934, she added different details:

Catching a glimpse of my reflection in the mirror [above the bed], I think I let out one suppressed scream. I know I started to cry. I was utterly confused, still a bit dizzy, and terribly embarrassed and afraid.

Stanny hastily threw on a red satin robe, and gave Evelyn the purple-and-yellow kimono that had been tossed at the foot of the bed. She began to cry.

"Don't cry, Kittens," he said tenderly. "Please don't. It's all over. Now you belong to me."

He then sat up in the bed, took her upon his knee, petted her tousled hair, and kissed her on the neck and cheeks. He tried to soothe her and stop her sudden trembling. After dressing in embarrassed haste, as if she had forgotten how, Evelyn was driven home, where Stanny left her alone, in the earliest hours of the morning, sitting in a chair by the window. Unable to sleep, Evelyn was overwhelmed by a sense of immeasurable emptiness: "I felt nothing, neither repulsion nor hate. He was a strange being to me; an aspect of life [had been] revealed in a flash and chang[ed] all my perspectives."

As if still in a fog of intoxication, Evelyn rubbed her eyes and raked her mind, as if sifting through grains of sand, for even the smallest broken shells of information and misinformation she had come upon in French novels, the hootchy-kootchy doings she had heard joked about backstage, or the curious behaviors of tootsie-wootsies whispered about at parties. But none of it made any sense, and for a time she let her mind sink back into emptiness. Then her temples began to throb, and her "insides cramped in small waves of pain."

"This is what people made such a fuss about," she finally realized, arriving at the conclusion, "this, then, was what love meant."

Years later, confronting the criticism and skepticism of those who could not believe that she could have been a studio model and chorus girl and maintained her innocence much less her virginity until that night, even though she was sixteen, Evelyn countered: "I went . . . that night a child with no knowledge of the big and stunning facts of life. . . . If you say to me, 'How is it possible that you could live in such an atmosphere as you did, surrounded by significant evidence . . . that the world was less than the idyllic place you pretend, and still be innocent?'"

Her reply?

"There is an innocence which finds for evident evil an innocent explanation." Certainly her mother never told her anything about the "big and stunning facts" in a culture where the long shadow of Puritanism and "mid-Victorian prudery" kept girls in the dark about such things until marriage. Nor had Evelyn ever had so much to drink at one time, having previously heeded her mother's warning about spoiling her looks (and ruining their livelihood). Then there had been Stanny's own solicitous watchfulness, which years later she saw as having been motivated much more by his own self-interest: "He wanted control—of when I would have none."

She sat staring trancelike out the window in the yellow hours of the morning, her knees tucked under her chin, her arms wrapped around her legs, as alternating ribbons of blue-gray and orange rose together over the rooftops. Evelyn conducted for what seemed the hundredth time a mental inventory of White's character. Or the man she thought she knew as Stanny. Her reason and understanding teetered back and forth from moment to moment. Father. Lover. Protector. Seducer. All of White materialized before her like a roiling, boiling new planet suddenly careening through space on a straight path toward her. As she would later write, "He was a generously big man—and infinitely mean; he was kind and tender—and preyed upon the defenseless . . . a crude expression offended him; yet in some things he was shameless." She then hit upon the phrase that summed up for her in an instant the man who had stolen her trust and whose prodigious appetite seemed never quite satisfied: "He was a benevolent vampire."

It was in the same chair that Stanny found her when he called later in the morning, drumming on the door and then letting himself in when he got no response to his usual signal. He saw her illuminated by a shaft of sunlight, looking uncannily like the sadly beautiful, stony-eyed bust of Nefertiti in the Metropolitan Museum of Art, where not far away in the sculpture hall sat George Grey Barnard's marble statue *Innocence* (also known as *Maidenhood*), which Evelyn had posed for only a few months earlier.

Stanny immediately knelt before her and began pleading, half expecting the rage of virtue or shuddering tears of regret. He was therefore momentarily baffled by her stony silence. He kissed the hem of her baby-blue dressing gown in an extravagant show of remorse and shivered at its touch. Calling her his "Kittens," he then began to claim that he had not really done her "the greatest wrong of all." Evelyn seemed to look through him, motionless, the little Sphinx once again. Stanny proceeded to tell her in tones less frantic than urgent, but insistent, that everyone did what he and she had just done. In fact, he "ran on," telling her essentially that "everybody was bad . . . [and] evil was the basis of life."

He recklessly began to rattle off the names of people Evelyn knew, men and women, whom he painted in the same black hues as himself. No one was excluded—society people, stage people, "people of every rank and class of society, they were all steeped in evil." Seeing that his Kittens seemed unmoved by this argument, a persistent White altered his tactic slightly and tried to persuade her that at least he was no worse than these others; in fact, he was better, since he was willing to admit to his deeds. He began to illustrate his argument with countless stories, which Evelyn only half heard. He then shifted his focus again, stating with resumed strength his central thrust—that the worst sin of all was to be found out.

"That was unforgivable," he told her, and so she must "go along as if nothing happened" in order for people to still respect her.

Evelyn weighed his words against her understanding of what had happened in the last six hours and turned her head slightly as she slowly began to comprehend her newest position in the universe—and that immense part of it over which Stanny ruled.

"[It] was a terrible thing to talk. A girl must never talk; she must just keep things locked up in her bosom and confide in nobody," White continued, then added emphatically, "especially your mother, who would not see things clearly.

"To tell one's mother meant all the world knowing," he warned. White began to name names again, saying, "Look at Miss ———— and Miss ———— . . . If she hadn't told things about people she would be in a splendid position." He cautioned her repeatedly, ending this particular point with the ominous-sounding directive: "Don't talk, Evelyn."

The stunned girl continued to sit silent and oddly passive while White kept up his veritable barrage of words. What he didn't know was that the situation had already crystallized for the teenager. She was told not to tell. She had been told to obey him. And she had. The past two and a half years in the studios had been an extended series of daily sessions where she was told by the men in charge of her fate not to speak. Not to move. On the stage she was told how and where to move, when to speak, when not to speak, and how to hit one's mark. She knew as she stared out at the rooftops of the dreamlike city that White had made over in his own image that she was utterly powerless.

Still Stanny went on, "pleading, sometimes covertly menacing," and Evelyn listened, "dazed and bewildered as all the fair fabrics of [her] faith crumbled in the dust." If she was at all convinced as to the truth of what White was telling her, it wasn't so much that she knew he was right or that what he had done was acceptable. Rather, because of the huge discrepancy in their age, in class, in education, in wealth, in life experience, in sexual knowledge, in all the things that an adolescent girl can perhaps only dimly comprehend under the best of circumstances, she just didn't know any better. Nor did she have anyone to turn to.

Over the next few days, Evelyn contemplated what she had to substitute "for the place trust once inhabited." At first she felt absolutely nothing. Not repulsion. Not hate. Just a numbness. Stanny now seemed an alien being to her as an "aspect of life [was] revealed in a flash, changing all her perspectives." Years later, the adult Evelyn described needing a "new scaffolding, a shell from whence to work." At first she played the scene over and over in her head, but that proved too alarmingly hurtful. Then, as with all other unexpected turns in her short life, she decided she would just block out the pain. Just as she had the loss of her father. Just as she had the eviction from her home and the loss of all her childhood treasures. Just as she had all the unhappy or callous scenes that had punctuated her unpredictable and precarious existence up to that point. In its place she substituted "a dull sense of helplessness, accepting [White's] conception of life."

And love.

Falling back on both habit and well-honed psychic survival tactics, Evelyn dropped into wary, leaden silence. She would be especially sure not to enlighten her mother upon her return from Pittsburgh, unable to even imagine what her mamma's reaction might be. (And never admitting to herself that perhaps her mother had known better. And left anyway.)

What many people at the time of the trial claimed they could not understand (and something the district attorney would ask point-blank) was why she never expressed the obligatory deep-rooted horror of Stanny, the man who stole her innocence and violated her trust, either immediately after that fateful night or any time since.

Her answer was simple:

Neither then nor now can I conjure a pose as the conventional world demands. . . . Not even for the purpose of pleasing those who demand, according to the rules of melodrama, a more bitter and more prejudiced view, can I represent him other than he was. . . . I have no doubt in my mind that in many of the things he did he was actuated by the purest kindness. Such was the complexity of the man's character that he could at one and the same time be the disinterested patron and the scheming roué.

A monster in human form.

It was a momentarily frightening, then bitter revelation that broke upon her. She considered White's darkly elegant shape-shifting abilities that allowed him to seduce unsuspecting maidens with a minimum of blood-letting—although, unlike the typical vampire, Stanny surrounded himself with mirrors that helped dazzle his captives and reflected the glittering subterranean world he had created for his own amusement. In trying to describe her feelings about her "seduction" by the paternal White and her subsequent role as his teenage mistress, she wrote in 1915:

It may seem a shocking thing that I did not become melancholic or so depressed as to take no interest in life, but a healthy child . . . abhors bad memories and all the gloomy morbid machinery of introspection, and I found myself almost as I had been before that night, with interests as keen . . . though a change had come to me.

She continued, and not surprisingly, her train of thought ran to her father:

Doctors say that children who lose their limbs in accidents come to maturity with a sense of having been born as they are, without any recollection of previously having been better equipped for the battle of life. Young people who lose their parents . . . have the greatest difficulty in retaining a memory of those parents, however kindly and however apparently indispensable they may have been in their lifetime.

Having lost so much already, Evelyn knew that she had nothing else to lose. She then considered what she had to gain after having been robbed of the only currency of any value a girl had. So she accepted this new development in her relationship with Stanny and buried any halfhearted attempts at adolescent "gloomy" introspection or judgment. After twenty additional years of careful, calm reflection, viewing things through the lens of adulthood and subsequent experience, Evelyn concluded, "I would dare not say of him that he ruined my life. . . . He merely made a way for me, a painful way . . . which was inevitably mine." She also writes, "Stanford White was a great man. That is how I see him after all these years. That he did me wrong, that from certain moral standards he was perverse and decadent, does not blind my judgment."

So, instead of condemning him as a monster, Kittens took a deep breath and joined the routinely astounded and admiring coterie of friends and contemporaries who saw White as one of those men who "loom into life." After all, if tycoons and their socialite wives, great artists, musicians, writers, scientists, and inventors succumbed to his persuasive charms, who was she to resist? So the child-woman who "had nothing but her looks" gave herself over to this force of nature: "One remembers an earthquake without blaming or condemning the seismic forces which produced the phenomena. White was an earthquake which shattered to the foundations the fabric of innocence."

Accepting her fate, Evelyn did not rail at the natural or unnatural forces that brought her to Stanny. At sixteen, she decided it was "profitless to ask 'Why?'"

Seductive modeling pose, circa 1902–1903.

CHAPTER EIGHT

At the Feet of Diana

"Methinks," mused Petronius, "that one naked woman is more alluring than a thousand." —*Frederick L. Collins,* Glamorous Sinners

His art was loving; Eros set his sign. —*Ella Wheeler Wilcox*

According to legend, the only way a vampire can enter a potential victim's house is if it is invited across the threshold. Mrs. Nesbit, either foolishly or with contemptible consciousness, had done so with open arms. In trying to "keep the wolf from the door," she not only welcomed him in, but offered him exclusive rights to her daughter, then left. By the time the feckless Mrs. Nesbit returned from her ten-day Pittsburgh holiday, thanks to what she said was their benefactor's "wonderful thoughtfulness and generosity of spirit," it had become painfully clear to Evelyn that there was more than just a generation gap between herself and her mamma. An adult Evelyn came to believe that at sixteen, she was "probably the greatest enigma" the world offered her mother, and that she was "outside and beyond the range of her [mother's] understanding." At the time, Evelyn saw her mother as hopelessly old-fashioned, one of those people "who no longer desires to do the things which they criticize." Compared to Stanny's youthful exuberance, Evelyn's mother, who was in fact ten years younger than the architect, seemed to Evelyn "a relic of another age."

"I could not in my wildest moments," Evelyn said, "imagine her in her wildest moments greeting the dawn from the wrong end of the day." It appeared to her that her mother knew nothing about unconventional behavior except to condemn it, while Stanny reveled in it and damned the cost. Depending on one's perspective, White was "a connoisseur of beauty, of art, the epicure in all his fleshly wants" a "fashionable degenerate," or "an apostle of beauty in a nation that was maddeningly slow to embrace it." One thing Evelyn knew for sure—he was someone who could never let himself be limited by dreary, respectable "New Englandism" or, what she referred to in later years as "Pittsburgalism" ("a Pittsburgh provincialism that robbed your soul").

As promised, Evelyn obeyed her unorthodox father-lover and did not tell her old-fashioned mother what had happened as a result of her too-convenient absence. Instead, in spite of what Stanny had done and how he had done it, within a matter of days, Evelyn accepted her new role as his toy mistress and fell under the spell of her benevolent vampire—even though, true to form, he could only come out safely at night.

And because she was still only a girl, and he was a man from whom an entire city took its cues, the minor Evelyn also tumbled recklessly into major adolescent first love. Surrounded by luxury and sumptuousness whenever she was with Stanny, she easily and happily surrendered to it and to him. Nor was the forty-eight-year-old Stanny immune to the incomparable charms of his little Persephone, the newest diminutive queen of his dim and secret rites, caught in White's shadowy underworld, where "if a girl danced on the tables in the Tower room, she did not scratch the mahogany." For Evelyn was unlike any other girl he had ever encountered—she was the one about whom "penny-a-line newsmen waxed lyrical." She was "a soft petal torn from a rose," a "will-o'-the-wisp" with "languorous eyes" who "cast tender shadows wherever she walked." She was the "fluttering fair flower of American girlhood" who had, like Stephen Crane's Maggie, "blossomed in a mud puddle." And even if Stanny no longer needed to guess what mysteries hid themselves behind those "wells of paradise" and "coy half-smile," he nevertheless felt the familiar White heat of excitement at the possibility of further exploration.

As she describes her altered relationship with Stanny in the weeks and months following the night she came to call her "unvirgining" (in letters written late in life), Evelyn said in her memoir of 1934, "I couldn't help but marvel at this strange effect I had upon him. Whether at his office after hours or in the intimacy of his rooms, always when he first put his arms about me—or only touched me—he would start trembling."

During certain passionate and intense moments, she went on, "he would tell me I was a constant thrill," an irresistible angel dropped from heaven or a siren ascended from Neptune's realm.

"I was the type he adored and fell slave to." And much too unbelievably pretty to consider modesty a useful virtue.

And if Stanny found himself unusually and fatefully smitten, it was because this girl was a unique conquest, the holy chalice in a lifelong quest for pure animated organic perfection. According to even jaded reporters, upon first seeing Evelyn, "she bore no resemblance to any living woman ever seen." To Stanny, she was the ultimate combination of unfettered intellectual curiosity, singular precocious beauty, and an adorable lack of sophistication, all rolled into one willing and uninhibited child-woman, a real-life Miranda swept up in a tempest of his own devising. In addition, as a keen student of art history and profound lover of composition and color, Stanny, always the painter at heart, saw in Evelyn a Botticelli come to life. With her natural linear grace, smooth unspoiled lines, and unripe contours, she was a timeless masterpiece, her "humid parted lips when in repose" like those seen "in some of the old Italian Masters." And she was chiaroscuro incarnate, her unblemished skin "fairly glowing" in contrast to the dark spiced rum of her hair and eyes the color of oloroso sherry. As described by another reporter, she had "hair that in the shadows seemed violet-black but which in the sunlight took on a polished bronze hue." Infatuated with the mere idea of her and the pure sensuality of her appearance, there were times, Evelyn wrote, when Stanny wanted her so perfectly and utterly naked that she couldn't even wear hairpins in her hair. He would run his face with its bristling mustache or his "tender searching hands" through her long waves and toss aside any offending pin he might find. And just as with her "normal" studies, she seemed a rapt and eager student of the demimonde in

White's shadow world. In 1915 she would write, "In those days I lived very much in the present, and if conscience is an uneasy stirring as to one's future then I certainly had no conscience." Nor would she cry over spoiled milk if she could help it.

In letters she wrote, Evelyn recalls that when he was with her, either at the Garden after hours or in his studio apartment, he luxuriated in her sweet honeysuckle perfume and derived great pleasure from the idea that he was Pygmalion while she was his own charmed nymph—a modern Galatea undergoing a marvelous metamorphosis due to his skilled control and expert tutelage. In response, Evelyn acceded to Stanny's every whim and stimulus, and allowed herself to luxuriate in his generosity and powerful influence, aided by the balm of forgetfulness as to how he had used both to take advantage of her.

Over the course of several months, whenever they were together, Stanny invariably sought to combine her instruction with his delight; he wanted to open up the divine world of the arts and the wonders of aesthetic appreciation to this extraordinary ordinary girl who inspired a multitude of artists, but who routinely saw only the backs of canvases, while at the same time he wanted to worship at her irresistible "altar of bliss." Succumbing to the "subtle brew [of] kisses crushed to kisses" as the supreme "architect of desire," in the months following Evelyn's Dionysian initiation, Stanny behaved as if he had to possess her as completely as humanly possible. With her he could indulge himself in ways he could not with any of his other prized objects, since this one was not only gorgeous, but young and responsive and blissfully unguarded. Like the perfect champagne grape, he had picked her at the sweetest moment of her development, when she would be at her most deliciously erotic, susceptible to decadence, but without a sexual history and no equipment for passing sour judgments.

Often when the couple were alone at the Garden in the drowsy hours after midnight, the beaming creator and his petite American Eve would ride up in the elevator to its last stop and ascend to unrivaled heights by climbing the narrow spiral wrought-iron stairs through the cupola to the turreted top of his Tower. They would stand staring through the violet haze that defined the horizon; sometimes they just talked for hours as November's cool autumn breezes swirled around them through the fili- gree fretwork at the feet of the shimmering Diana, herself pivoting grace- fully and fearlessly in spite of being so fully exposed to all elements at such a dangerous and dizzying height.

Holding hands, Evelyn and Stanny would look out over the railing at his city; from their vantage point, the entire island appeared as a lush and simmering paradise, and they were the world's only two inhabitants. At times she would reach up as far as she could and touch the heel of Diana's foot, feeling a warm electric thrill run through her. As Evelyn gazed up at Diana with eyes "the color of blue champagne at midnight," White could see reflected in them the blinking starshine from above, mimicked in the tiny incandescent bulbs (which he turned on just for her) that looped the fringes of the empty rooftop theater far below them. Evelyn listened dreamily as Stanny told her of hallowed or mysterious places he had vis- ited and his extraordinary finds. He would then whisper to her that she was his most remarkable find, a tiny star dropped from the heavens, one he wished he could wear on his lapel.

To Stanny, she was his kiddie or sometimes his little sparrow (although her appetite was anything but birdlike). He would tease her, asking if she were "just a fairy out of wonderland," and then pinch her smooth white shoulders, feeling, he said, for her wings. She learned to respond to him in kind, which prompted White to remark to one of his friends that "Evelyn plays with me as a kitten." She could often see the effect she had on him; there were instances when he gasped in admiration at her exqui- site, unfolding, flowerlike loveliness, especially when a particular multi- hued light on his magical bed fell on her in a certain way, softening and enhancing the already exotic palette of her natural charms. Afterward, he would kiss her passionately and swear by the moon that he had never seen such perfection, reflected as it was from every conceivable angle by the surrounding mirrors. Had she read Shakespeare's play about star- crossed lovers before that time, she might have asked her considerably older Romeo to swear by the sun instead.

As her own intensifying affection for Stanny constantly renewed and reshaped itself, once the initial blush and shudder of sex was no longer a mystery, Evelyn began to flaunt her lithe and flexible figure, teasing him in ways he found irresistible. And, as she came to see it, they also transcended "mere sex." They were not just "Satyr Pursuing Nymph." As it would be described in one paper during the first trial, White was the "intellectual epicurean trying his master hand at a new medium," while another speculated that, "it must have pleased White's queer artistic whims to form her." Indeed, with her classic looks and natural gift for posing, refined in the skylight world during daylight hours, in the twilight time after business or the late evenings when White was free, Evelyn could become an enchanting *tableau vivant.* Stanny would put her in specific positions and arrange all the elements around her in a startling impersonation of the fabulous paintings he saw in the Louvre or sculpted figures he had imported from the porticos of Italy and Greece. The effect on him, she remembers, was palpable.

Because Evelyn was also just a "mere slip of a girl," yet athletic and graceful, Stanny could raise her with ease onto his broad shoulders or literally bounce her on his knees. There were times, after posing her as Olympia or Odalisque, complete with sequined and silken seraglio embellishments, when Stanny would lift the naked Evelyn onto his shoulder as she pretended to be the statue of Bacchante on his piano. He would place a wreath of fern leaves wound into a halo on each of their heads and ride her around the circumference of the Tower room, whirling past the realistic-looking orange trees scattered about with bulbs resembling actual oranges nestled in their branches (even though it was winter in New York). An ardent and equally naked Stanny would place one arm around the small of her back to steady her, while the giggling, limber Bacchante would hold a bottle of Pommery Sec by its neck in one hand, eating red grapes with her free hand and dropping them into the sparkling crystal flute that Stanny held up to her as they spun around the room. The two would ultimately collapse onto one of the plush sofas or oversized ottomans in childlike laughter, her luxurious hair falling out of its crown of leaves in a tangled cascade over his and her faces like sweet Spanish moss.

There were many occasions when Stanny would make her laugh so much "her ribs hurt." He joked about the attempts of lesser artists, who, in trying to re-create their own uninspired versions of beauty with other models, failed miserably. They might as well have been "bumpkins trying to put lipstick on a sow." At other times, in the intimacy of his rooms at Twenty-fourth Street, before having wild sex on one of the fashionable ferocious-looking tiger or lion skin rugs, Stanny would build a fire in the fireplace and throw something into it that sparked a temporary rainbow of shifting colors amid the rhythmically rising and falling flames. After his own flare of passion subsided, Stanny would put a now casually and shamelessly naked Evelyn on his red velvet swing, perhaps gloating about what a great private joke this was in light of Saint Anthony of Comstock's limited imagination and naive public approval of one of his favorite deviant pleasures.

Stanny would watch excitedly while Evelyn flew, as if weightless, in the direction of his unlimited supply of colorful parchment parasols, her bare feet arched and ready. The red-and-amber lick of the flames created a warming, hypnotic effect as they moved with her and cast arabesque patterns on the slender arc of her back and the smooth white crescents pressing on the red velvet seat. Again and again as he pushed Evelyn toward the glowing tin ceiling and spinning circles of paper, Stanny watched approvingly as her hair twisted behind her in lustrous brunette waves. Once she had broken the fragile bamboo ribs of the parasol and shredded its parchment into dangling ribbons, he gleefully threw it all on the fire and put another in its place, pulling the invisible string attached to the new parasol. And her heart.

A POORE ENCOUNTER

One afternoon Stanny arranged for Evelyn to have another sitting with photographer Rudolf Eickemeyer Jr. But this session was to be held at a house on East Nineteenth Street, which belonged to his friend, landscape artist Henry Poore. As was the case with nearly anything Stanny touched,

Poore's house bore the architect's unmistakable imprimatur of dramatic brilliance—it contained not only a floor-to-ceiling carved-stone fireplace that had been brought virtually stone by immense stone from an ancient castle in Normandy, but at the other end of the same room there was a remarkable life-size painting set in a recess in the wall instead of framed, normally hidden from view.

The trompe-l'oeil painting of a nude, fair-haired woman, standing on a Persian rug, was lovely in and of itself. But, as described by Evelyn in her 1934 memoirs, Stanny had a rug woven in the exact same color and pattern as the one the figure stood on in the painting. The actual rug began where the one in the painting left off and then folded over three short steps. The uncanny three-dimensional illusion it created "was startling," and according to Evelyn, "her skin seemed to glow like living flesh . . . she had evidently just returned from a ball, for a frilly costume lay where she had just stepped out of it . . . [and] in one hand she held a black mask." Only a small number of Poore's acquaintances were ever offered a privileged viewing of this painting in his private drawing room, hidden most of the time by a curtain drawn around the recess. Evelyn felt a little thrill at being one of those few.

On this particular day, Eickemeyer worked carefully to capture some new and enticing images for his professional portfolio (as well as for Stanny's personal album), which meant that in a number of the pictures she was dressed in exquisite kimonos and gowns, while in others she wore nothing but a smile. He labored for nearly an hour on one final plate, after which a kimono-clad Evelyn went downstairs to a lower bedroom to dress. Since it was December and nearly five, it was quite chilly and there was a small fire in the fireplace as well as the requisite fashionable black bearskin rug. It was too inviting for Evelyn to pass up, so she took off her kimono and sat, "quite alone and quite naked" before the fire, pensive and warm, just as if she were in one of Stanny's secret snuggeries.

"Suddenly," she recalls, "the door opened and a strange elderly man walked in. In my surprise I simply sat there open-mouthed, staring at him. He stood rooted to the spot in the doorway, staring back."

"I beg your pardon," the man finally said, gravely, and backed out, closing the door. Evelyn dressed quickly and within moments a frantic Stanny came running into the room. He asked if anyone had come in.

"Yes," stammered Evelyn, slightly bemused and slightly embarrassed. White ran out of the room, then back in again. She asked him who the man was and an uncharacteristically flummoxed White replied that it was his friend, Henry Poore.

"This is his house," Stanny said excitedly, "but I didn't want him to see you. What did you have on when he came in?"

"Nothing," she said.

THE WILD ROSE

After her engagement in *Florodora* ended, Evelyn next found herself in a part that again played up her sultry looks. Her role was "the Gypsy girl, Vashti," in the "gayety" being produced by George Lederer called *The Wild Rose,* which had come to Broadway after a run at the Garrick Theater in Philadelphia. Lederer stated to reporters in May 1902 that he was startled by the "Raphael-like vision of Miss Florence" when she walked into his office, accompanied by her mother, about six weeks earlier, looking for an "auxiliary place" in the chorus.

Lederer claimed that after interviewing the girl's mother, it was clear "she was as desirous of the girl's adoption of the stage as was the girl." One wonders about Lederer's (or the reporter's) ironic choice of the word "adoption." Clearly, more and more, Mrs. Nesbit seemed disinclined to assert motherly care or provide guidance for her daughter as long as Evelyn provided the weekly paycheck, supplemented every week by the liberal Stanny. Or perhaps, saying that the mother of the "eighteen year old aspiring actress approved" was Lederer's way of avoiding criticism and possibly jail by warding off the Gerry Society for hiring such a strikingly young-looking girl for his troupe (despite what her mother was willing to swear to regarding her daughter's age).

After first assuring himself that Evelyn could perform, by watching her rehearse, Lederer was then convinced that he had a "find." Both

Evelyn and her mother signed a "singular contract" supposedly giving Lederer exclusive control of the girl's services for a year.

It was soon rumored in the papers and gossip sheets (a rumor fed by Lederer himself) that he had named the production after his little Gypsy girl. It was also rumored that perhaps Stanford White had used his considerable influence to help his protégée move up from "utility girl" to featured player in this, only her second production. But according to the press at the time, the little model from Pittsburgh was perfectly capable

Evelyn as Vashti, the Gypsy girl, with
another chorus girl in The Wild Rose, *1902.*

of "paddling her own canoe" and "not only opening doors herself, but turning the heads of seasoned theatrical managers on her own." The extent of her acting talents, however, remained a question.

As it had with her modeling career, the publicity machine began working overtime once Evelyn began her run in *The Wild Rose*. A two-page article, which appeared in the centerfold of the *New York Herald* on May 4, 1902, told the story of the budding Broadway beauty and gave the details of her unique contract for *The Wild Rose* company. Its headline read, "Her Winsome Face to Be Seen Only from 8 to 11 p.m." This was accompanied by drawings and photos of "Miss Evelyn Florence in Various Poses."

Beginning first by examining the business end of show business, the article described how "rare loveliness in young womanhood is apparently a strikingly valuable asset in the inventories of theatrical managers whose productions depend for their success to a large extent on their possession of good-looking, shapely and graceful girls. . . . Only a few seasons ago only featured players were signed to exclusive contracts. Now a well-known purveyor of feminine loveliness has signed a new beauty whom he recently discovered to such a contract. This agreement has Manager George Lederer as party of the first part and Miss Evelyn Florence as its collateral subject."

This unique piece, a new type of public relations, and the so-called actual stipulations of Evelyn's contract would be quoted again when Evelyn made her first appearance in the July 1902 issue of *The Theatre* magazine. Unlike other chorus girls, who were destined to remain anonymous or relatively unknown (and certainly never would have their photos appear in such a prestigious and influential magazine, let alone occupy so much space), Evelyn was featured in two photos and would appear in another issue several months later (see page 127).

Articles began to appear with regularity, focused on Evelyn's budding Broadway career and filled with full-page photographs or drawings of the model-turned-actress Evelyn Florence (or Evelyn Nesbit or Evelyn Nesbitt). Each article sought a new angle for promoting this "fresh and fascinating theatrical find." One headline raised the question of whether

Prince Henry of Belgium would have married the young British society girl he did marry, a Miss Dolan, had he seen "this American Girl."

ONE-NIGHT STAND IN NEWPORT
(AUGUST 25, 1902)

As far as the press was concerned, a particularly newsworthy story involving Evelyn emerged when, in August 1902, it was announced that Mrs. Cornelius Vanderbilt, one of White's clients (and perhaps at his suggestion), had hired the entire company of *The Wild Rose* and its orchestra to perform at the fabulous "cottage" in Newport named Beaulieu, which White had designed for her. The papers reported that the "hundred or so citizens of lower Broadway were to entertain the 400" at Beaulieu and proclaimed cheerfully that, "Real Darkies Will Also Give a Genuine Cakewalk."

With the exception of two cast members and their well-known manager, the company from *The Wild Rose*, as well as "a troupe of nine Negroes engaged by the Lederer amusement company" were to set sail for Newport. Lederer did not accompany his players, feeling his presence was needed at the rehearsals of his new piece, *Sally in Our Alley*, at the Broadway Theatre, so his brother, James, went in his place.

The papers seemed as intrigued by this curious adventure as if it were an authentic savage safari, except clearly the view was that the unruly natives were the ones invading the little Rhode Island haven of civilization carved out of pink-and-white Italian marble. It was advertised that "Negroes will play in a pagoda erected in the theater for their accommodation and concealment, and "Williams and Walker will sing 'When Sousa Comes to Coon Town' and 'The Coon with the Panama'" (referring to the cigar). All of this, of course, was perfectly in keeping with the attitude of the age, in which tourists from Hoboken and the Bronx could see actual Zulu warriors "on display" at Coney Island in the same vicinity as the "Fairy Floss" concession stand, and an "honest-to-goodness Eskimo family" was camped on the boardwalk next to live babies in a new invention called an incubator.

It was also considered newsworthy that "Miss Mazie Follete and Evelyn Florence Nesbit who had expected under proper chaperonage to make the trip to Newport aboard the private yacht of a wealthy friend did not realize their expectations and took the plebeian route." "Miss Nesbit however was accompanied to the pier by a young man who if not the proprietor of a yacht certainly looked the part and dutifully toted the suitcase of the diminutive Evelyn." According to the story, although Evelyn was satisfied with her accommodations, Mazie Follete complained that she wanted a larger room with a bath, as her people suffer from a hereditary disease, a *"mal de mer."*

Stanny Claus

For Evelyn's seventeenth birthday, on the day before Christmas Eve 1901 (since, as she knew, her paramour would be spending the holidays with his family), a jolly Stanny turned his Garden Tower room into a wonderland, a veritable hothouse of flowers, even though it was December. There were American beauty roses, long-stemmed calla lilies, milky white gardenias, mauve and purple and green and yellow orchids, the largest number of hydrangeas she ever saw, and potted holly bushes placed around the room in splendid variations of color. To add to the effect, Stanny had sprinkled confectioner's sugar on all the blooms to simulate snow.

He sat Evelyn on one of the divans and told her to close her eyes. Then, for the little girl who had to pretend she had been given a stray cat as her only gift a few shabby Christmases ago, Stanny produced from behind his back an oversized red velvet stocking with "a lovely large pearl on a platinum chain . . . a set of white fox furs which were a novelty at the time . . . a ruby and diamond ring and two diamond solitaire rings." She jumped from the sofa and draped the furs around her shoulders, twirling and laughing, then kissing his hands and the tips of his fingers in appreciation. She teased him and called him "Stanny Claus" (a much better model than the stiffly tedious James Garland). Stanny told her she would have to be photographed with her furs and also laughed, perhaps imagining what kinds of artful arrangement he could achieve with such elegant props and his little Galatea.

True to his nature of never doing anything by half, as the weeks passed, Stanny continued to spend an immoderate amount of money he didn't really have on Kittens (and her mother and brother) in his acknowledged public role as patron and paternal protector. He had, for all intents and purposes, become Howard's father, a consequence of which was that

Postcard photograph of Evelyn wearing
Stanny's gift of white fox furs, 1902.

Stanny's secretary, who handled all of White's personal financial transactions, had also developed a relationship with young Howard that some suspected was of too intimate a nature, given the additional speculation that White's secretary was one of "Nature's bachelors."

In spite of his myriad professional obligations, Stanny made sure that Evelyn didn't suffer from lack of work in terms of theatrical auditions; she made brief appearances in such shows as *A Chinese Honeymoon* and *Under Two Flags,* even though the steady demand of modeling assignments for artists, illustrators, and photographers often pushed her fledgling acting career into the shadows, much to her dismay. On those glorious days when Evelyn was actually free from any kind of professional commitment, however, Stanny continued to take discernible pleasure in orchestrating her social calendar, filling her days with lighthearted distractions. There were steamboat excursions to Rye and Oakland beaches in Westchester across the Long Island Sound and picnics in Central Park, raucous outings to Coney Island to ride the Razzle Dazzle and only slightly more sedate evenings at the newly built and hypnotically incandescent Luna Park—all on Stanny's tab and always with a flock of other girls—but never, ever with Stanny.

Yet, while they were not exactly Svengali and Trilby, the master showman maintained a mesmerizing hold on his little dolly, even as Evelyn grew increasingly restless, weary of keeping secrets and being kept in the dark as one of them. She felt, every so often, a slow, dull, binding ache in her abdomen and attributed it to being trussed up in costume corsets, an occupational hazard, since she never wore one otherwise. But as the days continued to tip over nonchalantly into weeks, the wild rose began to wish intensely for some control over her own destiny. Or, at the very least, for selective amnesia.

White's impossibly hectic schedule made togetherness either physical or otherwise with Evelyn progressively more difficult, even after hours, when the protective cloak of darkness draped itself over Manhattan (the only time in any day Evelyn had come to believe was hers and Stanny's alone). Like a frantic vaudeville plate spinner always on the brink of losing control, White dashed back and forth between Broadway and his grand house, Box Hill, in St. James, Long Island, or between Fifth Avenue and somewhere on the Continent, tending to family obligations, overseeing a staggering multitude of projects (up to sixty at a time), cabling, cajoling, creating, and carousing—and secretly wavering on the brink of a personal financial crash.

But after months of clandestine coupling with the inexhaustible master designer, letting her heart fall into and then languish in his gifted but careless hands, Evelyn began to feel that she and Stanny had reached a kind of impasse. She knew he still cared for her, which she said later in life was not the same as love, "a slightly larger word than sex and therein lies the difference." And in spite of all the mooning popular songs about the subject, "Love with a capital L," Evelyn would come to believe, "could be a merciless word."

For her part, having misspent her "mossy rose" and squandered real affection on the ultimate fake fakir (whose feats of endurance continued to mystify and entertain his cult of co-conspirators), Evelyn was still an adorable fixture at the usual nocturnal Madison Square Garden revels. But if she began to feel that she had become just another lovely object to Stanny, desperately sought and despicably won, a prized possession increasingly neglected among an excess of superb acquisitions, she did not say so. Like a dark-haired diminutive Rapunzel trapped by fantastic circumstances in a magical Tower, she remained a kept girl, waiting for a princely rescue and the healing tears of happily ever after. In a weird way, all the elements of the Grimms' tale (which she had read back in Tarentum) were in place—the uncommon changeling child-woman, the hard bargaining, forbidden fruit, and feminine wiles. The only thing missing was the unseen watcher. Or so it seemed.

*Dashing Jack Barrymore in a postcard
photograph, circa 1902.*

～❦～

CHAPTER NINE

The Barrymore Curse

"Could You Be True to Eyes of Blue If You Looked into Eyes of Brown?"
—*Song title, 1901*

"If Money Talks It Ain't on Speaking Terms with Me" —*Song title, 1902*

As far as Evelyn could tell, she was Stanny's "one and only special dolly." But even as their furtive Dionysian relationship carried on with a kind of uncontrived momentum, White also continued to befriend and (in Evelyn's darkening eyes) be overly friendly with an unhealthy number of other young soubrettes. From Adora Andrews to Erminie Earle, Hilda Spong to Augusta True, Stanny's generosity ran the gamut from A to Z (and back again) as he paid for hospital or dental bills and sometimes rent and wrote affectionate notes and the like, which Evelyn didn't appreciate at all. Evelyn wrote Stanny her own love letters during a weeklong seaside holiday he had arranged for her in the sleepy south shore community of Freeport, Long Island. She wrote him every day from her hotel room and kept his responses in a silk-lined tufted pink jewelry box, already stuffed with expensive hatpins from Tiffany, a small hand-painted compact full of fashionable faux beauty marks, and theatrical baubles bought on lower Broadway.

But as time went on, Evelyn came to see that the majority of White's other girls fit a disturbingly familiar pattern. They were invariably underage, from poverty-stricken or disadvantaged families with dead or absent fathers; they were usually naive or emotionally needy, starved for attention, many feeling abandoned and sometimes desperately alone in the city. A handful might have been worldly beyond their years, or disillusioned with the romance of the theater, but whatever the scenario, Manhattan's "Lord of Misrule" did his best to keep them all sated and amused and spinning within arm's reach.

By January 1902, Evelyn was a month into bittersweet seventeen, a rebellious and reckless age when a child-woman who has convinced herself she must be in love can swing wildly between impulsive spite and the silly romantic sentimentalism encouraged by popular songs or by the continual and sometimes lavish attentions of an urbane lover who still shook with delight at her slightest touch. Although Evelyn never seemed to give much if any thought to the existence of Mrs. Stanford White, the "wifey" usually deposited safely somewhere out in Suffolk County, she racked her brain trying to find a way to bridle Stanny's interest in the countless Mazies and Daisies who populated the back row of each new show (whom she imagined were scheming to get a leg up, so to speak, on fame or fortune by taking advantage of Stanny's weakness for pretty young things).

She also knew what Stanny knew—that none of the rich old lobsters who came to see her perform who might offer her extravagant gifts and jewelry, even marriage, interested her in the least, since they "lacked the artist's immense and complex soul." So Stanny could act with impunity, secure in his knowledge that she had turned away probably half a dozen millionaires already and was compelled to share her "downy fan" with only him. It seemed as if she had taken to heart what he had said about the illicit nature of their affair and how "darker chocolate is much richer and sweeter than the milk variety."

One practice of Stanny's was particularly galling to Evelyn—his sending extravagant birthday bouquets to girls whose names he marked down in his little black book. Stanny's book was bursting at the seams (what with Ada, Anna, Bettina and Blanche, Bella, Della, Edna and Elsie; Dora, Flora, Gertie, and Goldie; Inez, Josie, Lottie, and Lydia; Mabel, Maggie, Maude, and Moiselle, Sadie, Susie, Violet, and Zanita), and one afternoon in a spasm of pique, Evelyn threw the infuriating thing into the wastebasket. An amused Stanny merely retrieved it, which drove her to distraction, but also to a plan of sorts, aimed at penetrating her lover's seemingly impervious heart.

Evelyn decided to fight fire with fire. Initially, she tried to stir up jealousy by accepting dinner dates with several eligible young bachelors, part of a clique at the Racquet Club. One was Bobby Collier, the son of the publishing magnate; another was James "Monty" Waterbury Jr., a well-known and handsome young polo star.

One night, in their sophomoric efforts to woo Evelyn, a number of these potential suitors played a game called "shadows." Making her stand on a chair behind a fairly translucent drape lit from behind, they fed her oysters over the top of the drape and then asked her to guess who had just given her the icy bluepoint splashed with a squeeze of lemon. When Stanny heard about this and other similar "dates," however, all he said was that she should be careful of "those boys." Clearly, as far as the renowned architect was concerned, none of them could hold a twelve-watt bulb to his far more inventive and mature parlor games or ultra-sophisticated lighting and visual effects. And then, one night, an inadvertent opportunity presented itself to Evelyn.

At one of Stanny's Tower affairs, as Evelyn sat at a small side table, nibbling on salty Russian caviar and savoring sweet African peaches in brandied melba sauce, perhaps rolling around in her mind Stanny's constant admonition that "a girl should never let herself get fat," Evelyn was approached by two men. The taller of the two was determined to obtain an introduction to the intriguing little ingenue and well-known model. As he extended his hand to her, Evelyn looked up to see John Barrymore, known as Jack at the time, sporting the whisper of a newly grown mustache, which he pinched several times out of nervousness.

The remarkably handsome twenty-one-year-old was the younger sibling of Ethel and Lionel Barrymore, both of whom were already well known as the newest generation of splendid talent produced by the combustible forces of the Drew and Barrymore acting families. Ethel was a favorite among Stanny's theatrical acquaintances and the reason why the

architect had befriended a disheveled and hungover Jack late one morning at the Knickerbocker Grille and added him to the privileged Tower
guest list.

Although he already showed ample evidence of the matinee-idol looks
he would become known for ("The Great Profile"), Jack had managed
thus far to escape the "family curse" of acting and, at least at this stage in
his life, did not consider habitual drinking to the point of stupefaction
another possible Barrymore curse. As described by one writer, "In the
considered opinion of his family and elders, the youth showed every
promise of being a bum." In fact, rather than follow in his family's prominent and perhaps intimidating footsteps, Jack had gone off in a slightly
different but nonetheless creative direction.

The gossip columns reported that the youngest Barrymore had
attended classes at the Art Students League, even though by his own
account he had only done so for a day "to get a good look at things." He
did show promise as a cartoonist and illustrator, although for some reason he lacked the ability to draw feet adequately, which might be a draw-
back for anyone but a Barrymore. One wonders if he had any legitimate
interest in developing his talents or whether he was just naturally attracted
to the colorful gypsy sensibilities of the art world, which shared its borders and a vagabond kinship with the theater-land he knew so well.
When the League's courses in life studies once again aroused the attentions of the omnipresent Comstock and his Society for the Suppression
of Vice, Jack was one of the first to defend the practice to his drinking
buddies at the Algonquin (if not in print, then at least in principle).

Life as a cartoonist seemed the perfect choice for Barrymore, who saw
and did everything in bold, broad, and often comic strokes. It suited his
overactive imagination and hyperactive temperament as he tossed around
in the territory of the fourth estate, where endless rumpled days trailed
off into long pickled nights in saloons and hotel bars with his newspaper
pals. A puny salary was offset by professional perks, not the least of which
were the thrill of deadlines and joining in the throbbing pulse of the
swelling city. And while it may not have generally been the case, there
was such a thing as a free lunch when Jack was around. He landed his

first job as a sketch artist at the *Morning Telegraph*. From there he progressed to Hearst's *Journal*, thanks to his sister Ethel's influence. And even though he was positively cocky, Jack wasn't proud and didn't mind relying on family or on the kindness of strangers and friends alike to pave and pay his way.

Jack had seen *The Wild Rose* more than a dozen times since it had opened in May at the Knickerbocker Theatre, even paying his own way at least half the time—and all because of the bewitching "brunette soubrette" who now sat within a dainty arm's reach. That night in the Tower room, as Jack looked into Evelyn's molten eyes, close up for the first time, his heart beat a two-step as it never had before. He was struck by not only her perfect girlish features but also a suggestive eagerness and perhaps a hint of recklessness in her eyes that matched his own. Here was a girl, he told himself, who wouldn't mind sawdust on her shoes. As for the impression he made on Evelyn, even though she had seen her share of dapper young men whom she could hold at bay for hours with her sphinx-like stare, the color rose perceptibly in her cheeks as he bent and kissed her hand. He was, she would recall in a letter, "positively Byronesque."

When White, who had been making the rounds of the room as host, stepped out for a moment to take a phone call, Jack seized the opportunity. He leaned in closely and whispered into Evelyn's ear, asking for her phone number. In pure Barrymore fashion, he wrote the number with a flourish on his frayed shirt cuff as she whispered it into his ear, leaving a deliciously indescribable floral scent on his collar. Whether or not he was aware that White had more than an avuncular or proprietary interest in Evelyn, within twenty-four hours of Stanny's departure for his annual two-week Canadian fishing trip, Jack took advantage of Alexander Bell's invention and the situation. The two made a date to meet for a post-show supper at Rector's. Whether she did it meaning to rouse Stanny from hopeless complacency or was simply swept off her feet by the charismatic cartoonist with the wicked smile, Evelyn quickly found herself irresistibly drawn to the rakish Jack, who had a distinct advantage over Stanny in that he could take her out in public. And in the daytime.

For the two weeks White was away, the heart-throbbing couple saw each other every day, while every night, Jack would meet his "Evie" at the stage door with a small corsage of violets that she said put to shame the vulgar bouquets of the typical stage-door Johnnies—and of the atypical Champagne Stanny. The mooning duo then invariably went off to supper and entertained each other "endlessly with jokes and stories" at Delmonico's or Sherry's. The backstage gossip soon spread that a certain ardent news-paper artist had been seen worshipping a familiar vision of feminine pul-chritude in the "cathedral of froth" and that the rapt duo sipped pink champagne from the same glass, champagne put on a prominent patron's tab. Another night at Rector's, Jack ordered a glass of milk, pulled two rose petals from his vest, and floated them on the surface. Then, much to the amusement of waiters and patrons within earshot, he professed pas-sionately, "Those are your lips."

Meanwhile, the very few who were privy to White's inner sanctum and thus suspected the real nature of his relationship with his "protégées," watched this public show of sugarcoated affection with some interest. Perhaps, a few thought, she would finally be the one—the sable-haired Pandora who could unleash the great architect's green-eyed monster. As rumors proliferated about the "love-struck youngsters," some of White's Broadway cronies mused about Barrymore robbing the roost while the cock was away.

Within days the whirlwind romance became public property. It was heralded in the *Herald,* which reported on Evie and Jack's "devoted cama-raderie." The *Herald* also noted that "in the afternoons they would drive or walk through the Park," and acted as if "they found each other conge-nial and all else dross." In *Town Topics,* it was reported that "the Bohemian Barrymore paid swift and tempestuous court to the Broadway Beauty." The *Morning Telegraph* said that "the wild Pittsburgh rose had moved her swain to dreadful poetic heights." Although it was hardly Shakespeare when it was printed, he described Evie as "a quivering pink poppy in a golden wind-swept space." This sent her over the moon with delight (even though she was kidded mercilessly backstage by the other girls: "Can I enter your golden windswept space?" they'd ask when entering the common dressing room). Since White had miraculously managed to live purely in the public eye as far as his intimate connection with his Kittens was concerned, the newspapers blithely reported that "Miss Nesbit . . . showed preference to none until Jack Barrymore. . . . Like two happy children, the after-theater Broadwayites began to see them with eyes for none other in the fashionable restaurants."

How they were able to eat in those fashionable restaurants is another matter. Even without his own money, the resourceful Jack continued to live off his family name and "off the cuff." It may have been something of a challenge at times, since, among many things, Stanny had cultivated in Evelyn a taste for quail, oysters Rockefeller, and Moët & Chandon. As for Evelyn's seemingly arbitrary attitude toward money, it can be explained as the result of having either too little or too much at her disposal at that point in her short life. Or as the result of being seventeen, by which time it seemed to her that life was either feast or famine, with no free lunch in between. Unless you were with Jack.

One of the people whom young Barrymore relied upon for financial buttressing was Frank Case, the Algonquin proprietor and a family friend. But Case became nervous over Jack's mounting tab, and it irked him to read about how the blissful duo were painting the town the same red that Jack's accounts were in. When Case raised the issue one night while Jack and Evie were dining on squab and pricey artichoke hearts, Barrymore revealed, perhaps for the first time with an audience, his hereditary gift. He jumped to his feet and threw his linen napkin on the floor, declaring with a flourish, "By God we'll go to a restaurant that doesn't insult its guests!"

With the embarrassed Evie at his side, the brash and shameless Barrymore packed his bags and left the hotel, neglecting of course to pay his substantial bill. The displaced couple drove around in a cab for hours in a futile search for a new hotel that Barrymore could call home. But the story was the same everywhere—no room at the inn. A political convention had taken every available room. Just after midnight, a somewhat deflated Byron with a drooping Evie still at his side came back to the Algonquin. He signed Case's name to a requisition in order to pay the dinner check and resumed his residence there. Evie went home in the same cab and paid the sizable fare with money from her allowance from Stanny.

Much to everyone's surprise—especially Evie's—Jack's "rushing" of his quivering pink poppy stretched from two weeks into two months. Stanny had returned from his fishing trip, and upon discovering the blissful pair's blossoming bond, he did what no one expected. He did nothing. He said nothing. At least, there were no indiscreet scenes of the sort some observers might have expected upon his return or even any private show of jealousy. It was clear that he had calmly abdicated his position as Evelyn's only paramour. If she had begun the romance in order to test the extent of Stanny's claim on her, the adolescent-fueled experiment seemed a tremendous bust.

Jack, however, unaware of the exact nature of Evelyn's relationship with her patron sinner, continued to make spontaneous and quixotic gestures, much to Evelyn's delight. Having never been courted in any remotely traditional sense nor allowed to initiate a personal relationship on her own "with someone her own age," Evelyn responded to Jack's romantic advances with enthusiastic and genuine affection. Of course, one may also wonder whether she took some additional rebellious pleasure in seeing someone she knew her fiscally minded, old-fashioned mother would not approve of—if the stories and rumors about the couple were ever to blow Mrs. Nesbit's way, since Evelyn hid her romance and Mamma Nesbit didn't read the gossip sheets.

In fact, it was only sometime near the end of the fifth week that the ineptly watchful Mrs. Nesbit finally got wind of Evelyn's budding love life with Barrymore and immediately demanded that it be terminated. She took hold of Evelyn one morning and asked if she "intended to marry that little pup." She didn't want White to think that his protégée was ungrateful and unworthy of his generosity and thus stop being generous. Nor was she about to let her obviously valuable daughter ruin her chances for fortune and lifelong security by marrying "a slick, penniless, hard-drinking ne'er do well who slept under the sun and lived beneath the moon." One millionaire, James Garland, had already sailed into the sunset. But even though her mother had issued the ultimatum that Evelyn stop seeing Jack at once, the teenager not only chafed at the edict, she did something she had never done before—at least not to such a degree and with such openness. She defied her mother.

"If Jack wants to see me, to marry me, even," she cried, "then I want to be with him!"

A stunned Mrs. Nesbit was thrown into a panic, yet she hesitated at first to tell White about the relationship, thinking ironically that their benefactor would be outraged by Evelyn's behavior and derail the gravy train.

Whether it was true or not, Stanny had come to view the romance as a frivolous and, as yet, platonic affair, having been told by a number of acquaintances "in the know" that it was a giddy juvenile crush that had not progressed beyond blissful hand-holding and bad poetry—Evelyn herself would write that throughout his life, Jack liked to tell everyone he met that "she was the only girl who ever said no to him." Perhaps by this time, Stanny was content to let the still precariously underage Kittens have her way. Or perhaps he was relieved to spend less time and energy worrying about ruinous exposure (which he had flirted with for so long, thinking back to the pie-girl incident), and more on serious private concerns, such as tremendous debts piling up and increasingly poor health. Perhaps he saw this as the perfect resolution to Evelyn's recent bouts of petulant possessiveness. Whatever the reason, Stanny stayed in the wings, content to watch the thing play itself out. Until Mamma Nesbit acted.

Finally deciding something had to be done and risking White's anger (so she thought) as well as the loss of her comfortable lifestyle, Mrs. Nesbit called upon Stanford White several times at his office. She asked for his assistance to break up the insolent couple, who she feared were going to elope. But White was reluctant to act in any way that might draw the wrong kind of attention to himself and arouse suspicions. Then, once again, Fortuna spun her wheel.

After a particularly happy-go-lucky night of eating "on the cheap"— cheese and breadsticks—at an Italian restaurant on lower Broadway and drinking "gallons of red wine," an intoxicated Evelyn, on the verge of passing out, was just conscious enough to realize she was too drunk to go home. Knowing her mother's opinion of Jack, and fearing Mrs. Nesbit's anger, the two went back to Jack's apartment at the Algonquin to sleep off the effects of the Mulberry Street wine. Filled with tipsy tenderness, Jack covered Evie with a cloak he told her his father, Maurice, had worn in a production of *The Count of Monte Cristo*. He promptly fell asleep on the floor next to Evie on a pile of secondhand books. If nothing else, it was a good story.

The following morning, at around eleven o'clock, Evelyn awoke with a start and a blinding headache and was now the one in a panic.

"Oh, my God!" she cried. "We're in for it now!"

Jack rubbed his eyes and went for a glass of water, his mouth like sandpaper and his head like "day-old turkey stuffing." Remarkably, until that evening, Evelyn had never stayed out all night (not even the night of her ruination). No matter what had gone on before, White had always managed to see that she returned home, even if it was four o'clock in the morning. The wave of nausea and pain in her stomach that rivaled the one in her head told her this all-night "frolic" could only have disastrous consequences.

Trembling and feeling queasy, Evelyn squeezed Jack's hand and held her knotted stomach all the way home in the cab ride. When they reached her apartment and gingerly opened the door, to their astonishment, a pale and tight-lipped Stanny stood alongside her irate mother, who was "shaking like an aspen." Mrs. Nesbit began to berate Evelyn, wringing her hands and shouting that she had ruined her reputation, that she had betrayed Mr. White, that she was lost, ungrateful, willful, and wicked. Evelyn burst into tears while Stanny stood to one side, puzzling over his next move. He decided to take Barrymore aside and ask him in a harshly paternal stage voice what his intentions were toward the girl. A gallant Jack replied without hesitation, "I want to marry Evie." White asked him the next obvious question.

"What will you live on?"

With his natural endearing theatrical flair and totally impractical inclinations, Jack replied, "We'll live on love."

It was a scene worthy of Chekhov. As a flushed and red-eyed Evelyn ran back across the room to Jack's side, on the verge of resuming her sobbing, Mrs. Nesbit broke out in crocodile tears. One can't help but think her crying was not caused by the thought of her daughter's moral ruination but by the idea that Evelyn had ruined any chances they might have had for continued soft and easy financial security. Stanny was sweating with apprehension, fearing that with all the bad feelings flying around the room, at any moment the curtain might finally be lifted on his own unconventional acts. If Kittens had wanted to expose his sins, this would have been as good (or bad) a moment as any. And, whether or not Jack meant what he said about marriage, he must have also suddenly wondered if Evie had heard and if he had been too hasty in his offer, given his free-spirited tendencies and severely reduced circumstances.

As the highly charged emotional scene unwound itself in the very apartment Stanny had decorated and maintained for Evelyn and her mother, Evelyn must have wondered what her next move should be. There is little doubt that she still had a strong emotional attachment to Stanny "in spite of that one thing" he had done and his subsequent behaviors. There is also the possibility that after spending the night on the floor of a sparsely furnished hotel room that Jack could not pay for, in the hungover, sobering light of day, Evie felt the familiar frightening specter of poverty rising in the back of her mind. Or, perhaps, she wanted to marry Jack but saw clearly that the combined force of her mother and Stanny, each of whom had controlled her life until this point, were not going to allow that to happen. She was, after all, still a minor.

Then, an unpleasant scene turned even uglier as Evelyn was whisked off to a doctor's office in the West Thirties to be examined at White's insistence. The next thing she knew, Evelyn found herself under lock and key in the office of Dr. Nathan Bowditch Potter, physician to the wealthy. A stern Potter questioned Evelyn for five or six hours as to the exact nature of her overnight tryst with Barrymore. Even though she was denied any food or drink until she talked, Evelyn remained stubbornly silent and refused to be examined. She folded her arms in defiance and chose instead to go hungry, flashing a scornful smile at one point, having gone without food many times before without any choice. And for a longer time.

It was clear that White's concern was whether or not Evelyn and Jack had been physically intimate. If this could somehow be determined, on the one hand, White might be off the hook should she turn out to be pregnant anytime in the near future—a disastrous possibility he had flirted with for nearly a year, relying presumably on whatever methods of prevention were then available. On the other hand, it might at least give him an excuse to remove her from the heady influence of the irresponsibly adoring Jack and thus get Mamma Nesbit off his back. Although the physician continued to grill Evelyn throughout the long day, she refused to say whether or not Barrymore had seduced her, and she was mystified by the peculiar treatment.

Late in the day, a weary Stanny entered the room and told the stubborn Evelyn, her arms still folded defiantly across her chest, the unbelievably shameless lie that she was "the only girl in the world who could point a finger at him." In spite of all the evidence to the contrary, even young habits die hard. Seventeen-year-old Evelyn, who wanted desperately to feel wanted and also be out of the room, accepted what Stanny told her and asked that he "square things with her mother." Then she asked for some roast beef.

The next morning, the star-crossed pair was summoned to White's Tower. As they stood before a now red-faced Stanny (Evelyn wondered whether it was bile or jealousy she saw reflected in his florid expression), the architect began to browbeat Barrymore in the same manner that the doctor had interrogated Evelyn. Knowing Jack's cavalier attitude, White expected to put a period to the whole episode. But, to his disbelief, Jack spun around on his worn heels to face Evelyn and asked, "Evie, will you marry me?" A startled Evelyn shot a glance at Stanny and stammered back, "I don't know." It was, of course, what she did know (which Jack didn't) that prevented her from giving any other answer.

White then took Evelyn aside and told her she should stay on the stage and become a great actress. Hadn't she just started rehearsing for a part in a new show, *Tommy Rot*, being produced by Mrs. Osborne's Playhouse? He added that he thought Barrymore was a little bit crazy, "that his father was in an insane asylum and that the whole family was a little bit queer," and that within a few days or perhaps years the younger Barrymore would be in an insane asylum, "lots of people thought so."

A day or so later, an incredulous Evelyn was informed by White that plans had been made for her to be sent by mid-October to an all-girl private school in Pompton Lakes, New Jersey. After the initial shock and a bolt of searing pain that shot through her abdomen, Evelyn described her feelings as "dismal" at the prospect of being "lifted out of the light and glitter of Broadway," only to be dumped into the quiet and peaceful dullness of what she perceived as "a convent school." But both White and Mrs. Nesbit insisted that she be penitent and obey, once again.

Whether or not White wanted to placate Mrs. Nesbit and avoid a scandal, or he truly wanted to end Evelyn's now doomed relationship with the good-for-nothing Jack, he acted as if he wanted her as far away from Barrymore as possible. Additionally, her banishment to the wilds of the Ramapos would provide Stanny much-needed relief from Evelyn's moodiness and the possibility of anyone finding out about his own libidinous indiscretions. Like Nell King and other mothers before her, Mrs. Nesbit no doubt wanted to stay in White's good graces and told Evelyn that she considered it only proper to do what Mr. White said.

The papers picked up the story almost immediately and reported that the "adored and adorable Miss Nesbit" would be leaving the stage "sometime in the coming months to pursue her studies and mind her mamma." Then fate played yet another nasty trick on Evie. As if the scenario weren't melodramatic enough, what with two men half in and half out of her life, neither of whom could give her wholly what she wanted or needed, a third emerged from out of the shadows. He had simmered there for nearly a year, plotting and pining, sending notes and keeping tabs, then materializing, like some haunted doppelgänger in a bad Gothic thriller, in the form of Harry K. Thaw. The unseen watcher.

A cracked Harry Thaw in the asylum, 1914.

࿔

CHAPTER TEN

Enter Mad Harry

The thousand injuries of Fortunato I had borne as best I could, but when he ventured upon insult, I vowed revenge.

—*Edgar Allan Poe, "The Cask of Amontillado"*

Home early [from Europe] and stopped in Newport. The first day I roamed among friends, tranquil, Mrs. Astor, Mrs. Mills, Mrs. Townsend Burden, the Nat Thayers, the Cornelius Vanderbilts (they out, they sent an invitation for a musical the day McKinley was shot; stopped it of course), and the Gerrys. Next day the Stuyvesant Fishes, the Belmonts and more, not so tranquil . . . Then home and then New York and first saw Evelyn.

—*Harry Thaw,* The Traitor

I t had been more than a month since *The Wild Rose* had ended and Evie's brief romance with Jack had been cut off at the root. Evelyn was also soon to be pulled from the production she had just started rehearsing for, *Tommy Rot,* in which she had another small role. Publicity photos taken of her by Otto Sarony were already in circulation by the producers, who had hoped to take advantage of Evelyn's exceptional and recognizable appeal, even though her part was still a minor one.

Once they confirmed for themselves the announcement of their inge- nue's impending departure, Mrs. Osborne and her partners were as unhappy as the crestfallen Evie—until they got something else they hadn't planned for—free publicity. As the word spread that the fledgling starlet was going to be "packed off to Pamlico"—the less formal name of

Mrs. deMille's school—the press had yet another provocative subject to explore regarding the "reigning model soubrette of Manhattan." The constantly shifting tide of chorines and minor cast members rarely merited so much as a mention in the papers, but Evelyn's impending transformation from showgirl to schoolgirl was news, even if her acting ability "had yet to generate any steam along the Hudson."

On certain days she tried to muster enthusiasm, reminding herself of the vision of Vassar in what seemed a lifetime ago. At other times she was visibly despondent and brooding, feeling rejected and betrayed by Stanny, incredulous that he had joined forces with her mamma in spite of the loyalty she had proven to him by not detonating any number of his explosive secrets. If she had hoped to get a different kind of rise out of Stanny by flaunting the dashing Jack under his nose, she had failed; and while the fallout of her all-night "frolic" was the kiss of death for her relationship with Barrymore, it also meant leaving behind both the studios and the Gay White Way, with its myriad distractions, not the least of which were her scads of male admirers.

While appearing in *Florodora* and *The Wild Rose,* Evelyn had grown accustomed to receiving "letters in shoals" from devotees young and old and mostly male. She had received more fan mail than anyone in the company of *The Wild Rose,* which did not endear her to either her fellow chorus girls or the so-called stars, a fact that would come back with a vengeance during the trials. The majority of the billets-doux and mash notes she received were signed. But others arrived daily at the theater by certain admirers who preferred to remain anonymous.

"Those are the married ones or the queer ones, you can bet," she was told by a stagehand.

For several days in a row, one anonymous would-be swain sent costly Japanese lotus flowers from the Waldorf to the theater where Evelyn was rehearsing until her "sentence to the nunnery" was to go into effect. When the unidentified admirer turned out to be a Wall Street magnate who eventually managed to meet with Evelyn (through a showgirl acquaintance) and offered her "diamonds and emeralds," Evelyn, who had learned not to inform her mother of such expensive attempts to win her affection, turned down his advances and his gifts without a second thought. The incredulous man, unwilling at first to take "no, thank you" for an answer, spent two weeks in a front-row seat, trying to comprehend how the lovely girl could be so unreceptive.

One series of anonymous letters that arrived daily for an entire week actually did make an impression upon Evelyn as having been evidently written by a "man of some refinement" who talked at length about books and animals, two of Evelyn's favorite subjects. In one early letter the unidentified admirer mentioned to Evelyn that he had seen her in *Florodora* (but on the advice of an acquaintance, did not elaborate on another little fact—that for an entire month he had watched her perform from the shaded security of a darkened theater box every night). This persistent correspondent began asking her out to lunch, which Evelyn politely declined each time, saying that she did not make it a practice of meeting with strange men. How strange she could not have imagined.

Soon after that, the mysterious would-be suitor sent another missive, and finally identified himself as Mr. Munroe. He praised Evelyn for being cautious with regard to meeting strangers and continued to write to her. Twice the letters contained a twenty-dollar bill. Each time Evelyn sent the money back, even though as her mother pointed out, it was offered "with all good charity and kindness." When he sent a dozen roses with a fifty-dollar bill wrapped around them, a miffed Evelyn ordered that the gift be sent back immediately, offended that Mr. Munroe seemed to have assumed that his previous bids for her attention simply had been too low. Unbeknownst to her, however, even though the flowers were sent back, her mother kept the fifty.

Although her curiosity was undeniably piqued by Mr. Munroe's doggedly sincere if slightly insulting campaign *de coeur*, and his language seemed to indicate that he was a man of some refinement, Evelyn continued alternately to pine for Stanny's undivided attention and to lament the loss of the devoted and demonstrative Jack, who decided that retreat was the better part of valor until he could find a solution to this extraordinary state of extracurricular affairs. Nonetheless, like a modern-day pubescent Penelope waiting for her distant and preoccupied Ulysses, Evelyn declined any and all would-be suitors, whether their invitations came through the mail or the men themselves confronted her at the stage door each night. Apparently it never occurred to her mother to question why.

As far as Evelyn could tell, like so many others who saw her on the stage, this Mr. Munroe was hopelessly smitten with her. She was blithely unaware that the gentleman author of the amusing letters had a much more sinister agenda, fed by irrational obsession, which was all part of his amateurish subterfuge. For Mr. Munroe was in actuality Harry K. Thaw—of Pittsburgh. Thaw was desperate to meet the alluring Evelyn and win her attention—and in doing so win her away from the clutches of her well-known benefactor, the man Thaw envied and despised. The rumor whispered among certain habitués of the theater district that Thaw secretly frequented was that in spite of his shining façade, White was a "wholesale ravisher of young girls," and Thaw suspected that "the poor little waif from Tarentum" might be in moral peril.

While it is not clear exactly when his loathing of the architect began, Thaw's moral outrage and desire to thwart White's presumed advances on unsuspecting young girls and "spoil his blasted eternal party" started at least a year or more before Evelyn even arrived in New York. There are several incidents that precipitated what began as essentially a one-sided feud, since White, until it was too late, never considered Thaw much of a threat to his lifestyle or his life.

Harry Thaw, in keeping with his mater's insistent desire for elevated social status, had naturally applied to a number of the elite men's clubs in New York City, and assumed he would be as welcome in Gotham as he had been in the various capitals of Europe. To his utter shock and outrage, the profligate Pittsburgher had been turned down by virtually every club or expelled almost immediately for "behavior unbecoming a gentleman." He had been turned down by the prestigious Metropolitan, the Century, the Knickerbocker, and the Players, and was expelled from the Union League Club, where in a well-publicized incident, "for a lark," Thaw had ridden a horse up the steps into the vestibule. Yet he continued to tell anyone who would listen that he had been blackballed from each of these establishments out of mere spite by certain of the more influential "old money" members. Exhibiting his tendency to become fixated on an object or person to the exclusion of all else, Harry came to blame one person for his public humiliation at being barred from the enviable New York social scene—the man who had been instrumental in designing and building most of the clubs—Stanford White. For his part, White didn't hide his dislike for the "Pennsylvania pug" when talking to acquaintances, and, as is the case, the talk got around. In his book *The Traitor,* Harry wrote his own account of his contact with White before Evelyn entered the scene.

The first time Thaw encountered White was when a mutual acquaintance, Craig Wadsworth, insisted after a bottle of champagne and some bluepoints at Rector's that they go to a party at White's Tower. Harry believed this to be his long-overdue entrée into the elusive social scene he craved. Not having been formally invited by the host, however, Harry chose to salute White from across the room when he arrived with Wadsworth, and then, according to him, "what happened was harsh." A Mrs. Fish, cousin to the Stuyvesant Fishes, had hooked up with Thaw and his companion, and soon after complained several times and very loudly that the food and the wine were "rotten." Another acquaintance of Harry's, George Keppel, who happened to have been at the party, suggested they leave, not because the food or wine was rotten but because of the scene the inebriated Mrs. Fish was making. They tried to slip away unnoticed but the stridently soused Mrs. Fish bullied her way into the elevator with them, and "the whole show was over" as she ranted on about White's awful food and even worse taste in decor. Although Harry offered no other comment after mentioning this incident, it is the link to a second one not long after, a social embarrassment that would make it into the New York gossip sheets.

Harry had arranged for a party with a number of shapely showgirls and as usual had spent a ridiculous amount of money for the cuisine, cocktails, and entertainment. But the day of the party, while sitting in Sherry's with one of his higher-society friends from Pittsburgh (who, unlike Harry's New York acquaintances, had no knowledge of Harry's lower-class interests), one of his "favorite girls," Frances Belmont (whose real name was Fannie Donnelly), stopped by his table to say hello. The socially hypersensitive Harry, who needed to maintain his status with the club boys back home, turned away from the embarrassed girl, fearful of acknowledging any acquaintance with what was too obviously a painted chippie of the theatrical sort. A fuming and mortified Frances decided to get even with the "hoity-toity" Thaw and retaliated by asking all of her friends to a party at White's Tower. The evening, in Thaw's mind, turned into a mammoth and very public disaster as the complete absence of "doe-eyed girlies"(reported in *Town Topics* a few days later) turned Harry's sexy soirée into a stag party. He angrily dismissed the "colored ragtime band" he had hired to perform, and his disappointed tuxedoed guests stood by as the shrimp *en coquille* and lobster salad spoiled. Staring at the uneaten teal on toast while the heavy cream dissolved into sweet puddles around the baked Alaska, a livid Harry blamed White for yet another public indignity.

After skulking in the shadows for the better part of a year, ultimately attending more than forty performances of *The Wild Rose* to outdo the number of times he heard White had seen *Florodora*, Harry Thaw finally decided to reveal himself to the girl he considered his "Angel-Child."

He arranged an afternoon meeting with her—except that he was going to meet her as Mr. Munroe. Employing the same tactics as his perceived adversary White (which others had tried as well), Thaw made a luncheon date with Evelyn through a showgirl acquaintance of his, Elba Kenny. Evelyn was mildly curious about meeting the mysterious Mr. Munroe, but knew from other girls that these kinds of things invariably went badly or didn't go at all. Figuring it might be a welcome distraction for her, with the unhappy reality of New Jersey hanging over her head, Evelyn agreed to the rendezvous. Elba asked her if she was excited, but Evelyn just shrugged; one lunch date was just as good or bad as the meal served, especially since she would soon be in Mrs. deMille's "nunnery" in the hinterlands of Pompton Lakes.

At three o'clock on the appointed day, the dainty Evelyn, followed by the rounder, taller Elba (whose bosom always announced her entrance first), spun effortlessly through the front entrance of Rector's. The Angel-Child was dressed in the latest fashion, thanks, of course, to Stanny. That afternoon she wore a clinging mocha confection with swirling silk skirts, a velvet bodice the color of creamery butter with velvet buttons, like chocolate pastilles, running almost a foot up each sleeve. On her head sat a dark brown opera hat with layers of netting that resembled Fairy Floss. It was smaller than the fashionably huge picture hats socialites usually reserved for strolling up and down Fifth Avenue, but on Evelyn, the less ostentatious effect was absolutely perfect. In spite of their difference in size and curvaceousness, next to Evelyn's spun-sugar sexuality, Elba was practically invisible.

After waiting patiently for twenty minutes or so, looking to gawking patrons like a tempting truffle in a Whitman "Fussy Assortment," a bored and annoyed Evelyn got up to leave. But anxious Elba held her there with the assurance that Mr. Munroe would appear momentarily. As if on cue, "Mr. Munroe" made his grandiose entrance. Then, right there during high tea, he fell to his knees and kissed the hem of Evelyn's dress as some of the bemused restaurant clientele and staff looked on. A startled Evelyn pulled back the folds of her skirts as if from a contagion, and the man stood, rising up to an unusual height of nearly six foot two. Impeccably dressed in an expensive Brooks Brothers suit, he stared intently down into Evelyn's enchanting face while ignoring Elba, bosoms and all.

"Do you know you are the prettiest girl in New York?" he blurted out.

A startled Evelyn said nothing, then characteristically shrugged and smiled politely.

Although Thaw invariably greeted people with a fatuous smile and an overeager handshake, accompanied by the phrase, "I am Harry K. Thaw—of Pittsburgh," he kept up his charade as Mr. Munroe. Initially, from a short distance, he had looked "sweet," but Evelyn's second impression of him upon closer inspection was an unpleasant one. Having been described in the Pittsburgh papers as looking like a "peeled turnip," Harry frequently had a "curious look in his eyes" and sometimes "a sinister brutality about the mouth," which Evelyn later said could just as easily curl up into an "idiotic grin." It reminded her of the well-known Steeplechase face, the grinning icon of Coney Island. One paper reported that Harry's rounded infantile countenance was dominated by "enlarged empty eyes" and a "somewhat pug nose," which was sometimes "improved with a trim mustache that barely reached his full thick lips."

Up close, his doughy baby face was particularly unsettling in contrast to his exceptional height. Of course, with the right lighting and sartorial embellishments, Harry could be considered handsome enough to charm most women, especially those who knew that he was heir-apparent to a $40 million coke and railroad fortune. But the Angel-Child was not most women.

Logo of George Tilyou's Coney Island
Steeplechase Park, circa 1900.

As Elba sat self-consciously sipping her Chinese tea, she listened to the one-sided conversation between a very earnest Mr. Munroe and a silent Evelyn. It was immediately clear to Evelyn that this was a man who "took his position in life very seriously and his world value too seriously" as he gesticulated with increasing energy and blinked his eyes for emphasis as he talked. In a flurry of words, one topic snowballed inoffensively into the next. But when Harry's ramble moved in an unflattering direction about one of Evelyn's chorus-girl friends (he called her fat and said that women should never let themselves gain too much flesh), Evelyn jumped to the girl's defense. He seemed taken aback by the assertiveness of her response, as if people had never challenged his views on anything before. They probably hadn't. Then, much to Evelyn's surprise, he suddenly introduced the subject of Stanford White.

Mr. Munroe's animated face turned solemn as he told Evelyn that she should keep away from White, "that he was very ugly, and not only that, he was married." Evelyn offered one of her inscrutable modeling looks and said she knew only good things about White. She shot a surreptitious glance at Elba, who simply stared into her teacup, as if trying to read the leaves. Thirty minutes had passed when Mr. Munroe rose up to his imposing full height and asked Evelyn where she was staying. Evelyn replied that she and her mother were happy in an apartment in the city but she declined to tell him where. She said she was not in the habit of giving strangers, even well-dressed ones, her address. But her answer was inconsequential. Mr. Harry "Munroe" Thaw already knew where she lived. He routinely employed a rather extensive and elaborate network of spies. He boasted to friends that his men "bested Pinkerton's" in ferreting out information, from Manhattan to Monaco. Indeed, he had learned about Evelyn's love of books and animals from "informants" who stretched back to his sacred smoky city.

For a brief moment, the flustered man seemed to be in suspended animation as he hovered over his diminutive dream girl, so deliciously and unbelievably close at last. He then bowed like the prep school boy he had been and said he had some pressing business matters to attend to. Evelyn countered by saying she had some urgent errands as well and pulled Elba to her feet. Harry listened intently to what he imagined to be the lisp of silk against skin as his Angel-Child and her girlfriend swept quickly through of the dining room and out the revolving glass door beneath the talons of the griffin. He automatically threw down a fifty-dollar bill and left.

For whatever reason, probably because his simpering expression and "goo-goo eyes" were so unsettling, Evelyn must have looked at his hands throughout the conversation because Harry's peculiar recollection over twenty years later was that "she liked my wrists and hands." Thinking back to that first encounter, Evelyn also recalled his hands, which like his face, were smooth as a baby's, indicating that "he had never labored at all in his thirty-two years." Had she known more about him, Evelyn would also have known that Harry never had the slightest interest in the family business. Any pressing matters he had were only in his head.

Upon immediate analysis of the encounter, Evelyn said she felt an overwhelming sense of relief when he left, and that at best this Mr. Munroe was just one of the throng of cordial-enough young men who admired her from beyond the footlights, which is where she wanted him to stay (young being relative, since he was almost twice her age, at thirty-two). She also figured that, as with many other potential Broadway swains, Mr. Munroe's curiosity had been satisfied, and that would be the end of things. She told a perplexed Elba that she had no desire to meet him again. Elba offered no response, nor did she disclose to Evelyn the true identity of her intensely infatuated admirer.

But Harry K. Thaw was used to getting his way, and he began to pursue Evelyn with what she initially saw as the same kind of flattering and harmless if overly zealous attention dozens of others had shown her. Eventually, they all admitted defeat. But not Mr. Munroe. As she put it, he "was persistent in pursuing me, everlastingly." Evelyn was, of course, unaware as to why he was so determined to win her or how he intended to, if need be, shatter the fragile bell jar of her existence. Nor did she know that the day after her first encounter with him, a fervent and undaunted Thaw had in fact gone to see her mother at their apartment at the Wellington to press his case for Evelyn's undivided attention. When Mrs. Nesbit opened the door, there stood Pittsburgh's infamous "squandering son of untold wealth," who in revealing his true identity to "the mamma" needn't have bothered to add "of Pittsburgh."

The shock of recognition nearly floored Mrs. Nesbit, who stood for a moment as if seeing a hallucination or some appalling apparition. Harry's outlandish escapades had been published from time to time in the hometown papers along with his photo, neither of which a prepubescent Evelyn had seen. But her mother had. Of course, Harry didn't know about the demeaning incident some years earlier at his own family's threshold, when their butler had dismissed "the mendicant mamma" with a wave of his gloved hand.

According to Harry, the brief meeting in the anteroom of the plush apartment did not go well.

"She was not enthusiastic," he wrote. "I knew why later. This mother should have known better."

Later that day, when Evelyn returned home from a modeling session, she mentioned to her mother the strange and uncomfortable lunch date she had endured the previous day. Predictably, Mrs. Nesbit neglected to mention her own disconcerting encounter with the same man, whose real identity she too withheld from Evelyn. She also failed to appreciate the irony of having turned a Thaw away from her door as he begged for her daughter's attention.

A week or so later, an unsuspecting Evelyn was invited to a pre-theater dinner by another actress friend. Among the dozen guests at the restaurant, coincidentally, was Mr. Munroe, whose seat was coincidentally right next to Evelyn's. She greeted this social ambush with her model's smile, which Mr. Munroe read as a coded sign of reciprocated affection. Throughout the sweetbread-and-mushroom patties, halibut, rice croquettes, currant jelly, almond cakes, and polite dinner conversation, not one of the eleven accomplices gave away Mr. Munroe's little secret. It wasn't until after the café noir and crème de menthe that, appropriately enough when entering the theater, the smiling man declared "with dramatic earnestness," his voice trembling with pride, "that he was not whomever Mr. Such and Such."

"I am not Mr. Munroe," he told Evelyn, with a sweep of his arm. "I am Harry Kendall Thaw, of Pittsburgh!"

As Evelyn later described it, "a disguised Napoleon revealing himself to a near-sighted veteran on Elba could not have made the revelation with greater aplomb." She continued: "It struck me as funny at the time . . . so characteristic was it that I do not think I ever knew him much better at any subsequent time than I did at that moment." According to her, the pie-eyed pursuer hung fire in the elegant lobby, waiting on twitchy tenterhooks for her reaction. Seventeen-year-old Evelyn gazed at him with some bewilderment, wondering from the tone of his voice what it was he expected her to do—"stagger back, turn pale?" She contented herself and Harry by exclaiming "Indeed!" There seemed little else to say.

"You've heard of me?" he replied, with a supercilious smirk. Evelyn said that when she was growing up as a girl in Pittsburgh, the name of Thaw carried with it the same weight that a name like Vanderbilt or Astor carried in Newport or New York. Anyone, she told him, who knew Pittsburgh knew of the Thaws. Harry went stiff with self-importance and grinned from ear to ear. And Evelyn flashed on the face of Steeplechase.

Speaking in his distinctive Gatling-gun manner, within the space of a few minutes, Thaw then disclosed to her the half-truths and irrational saga of his previous deceptions: why he had sent the flowers wrapped in bills, why he had felt it necessary to send letters under a nom de plume, and so on. He knew, he explained, that she was involved in a financially precarious career, which is why he sent money. He had meant no disrespect. Moreover, he said he knew what an impact his identity would have on her, because as Evelyn saw it through his eyes, "Harry Thaw, of Pittsburgh, was Somebody." And he had wanted to wait for the exact right moment to unveil himself to her, to throw off the mantle of ordinariness and thus make as big an impact on her as he could. He wanted, as he told her a week or so later, to "exceed theatricality."

Evelyn was simultaneously aggravated and amused, fascinated and annoyed by Harry's unbridled egotism. He also exuded a haughtiness that was irritating yet strangely compelling and symptomatic, she thought, of the obscenely nouveau riche. And, as she confessed years later, "even a pose, so long as it is consistently upheld, is impressive." That Harry seemed sincere about his patrimony she had no doubt. Little did she know, however, that there was another side of him, one which was beyond terrible. The newly polished and prosperous Thaws indeed had a family history, but Harry's own past was anything but brilliant. Known from New York to Monte Carlo for more than his money, Harry and his odd-ball, often juvenile, and sometimes hazardous antics, preferably played out among the less scrupulous denizens of the local theater districts (whose silence he routinely bought), were of singular interest to the saffron press. Worst of all, Evelyn had no idea of the depth of his veritable monomania regarding the great White.

Saint Vitus's Dance

At the time Evelyn began her acquaintance with "Mr. Munroe Somebody Thaw," she was apprised of the fact that he was heir to an estimated $40 million. But he was not the first adoring millionaire whose mono-poly money might be hers for the asking. Well aware of his eldest son's profligate propensities, the elder Thaw had stipulated in his will that the ne'er-do-well Harry receive a monthly allowance of only $2,500, a princely sum nonetheless in an age when a glass of Madeira and a steak dinner with all the trimmings at Delmonico's cost a dollar-fifty. But, when his father died, just after Harry's eighteenth birthday, the dot-ing Mother Thaw upped the ante to a staggering $80,000 a month (and maintained that for eighteen more shameful years, virtually all of which was also tax-free).

As early as 1894, Harry had made the local papers for chasing a driver down North Avenue in Cambridge with an unloaded shotgun, believing the man had cheated him out of ten cents' change. As the years pro-gressed, "Mad Harry" carried on with his juvenile behavior. But if Mother Thaw was ridiculously free with the family fortune when it came to

Harry, she kept a tight rein on bad press most of the time. So between Harry's own hush money and his mother's vigilant attempts at containment, Evelyn, like a lot of people, had been kept in the dark about Thaw's sinister side. When she met him, Harry told her about his last extended European holiday during which he had visited the Paris World's Fair, had gone ballooning, and had hired John Philip Sousa's band to entertain guests at a private party, where, according to Thaw, they "lifted the roof off." Someone quipped that Harry should be right at home in a balloon, since he was so "full of hot air." He had also gone mountain climbing in the Bavarian highlands and hobnobbed with royalty at the horse races in France. Evelyn was suitably impressed.

By 1898, without his hometown advantage, however, Harry had managed to bluster or bumble his way into the New York gossip columns— although not the club world he was determined to successfully infiltrate. It was reported that in spite of his above-average height, the younger Thaw had below-average intelligence and "appeared more like the perpetual undergraduate than the scion of a wealthy family." His inappropriate giggle when someone else's misfortunes struck him as funny was downright creepy, and even though he had been around the world several times (Rio, Barcelona, London, Paris, Rome, Vienna, Lucerne, Budapest, Constantinople, Cairo, Tangiers, Yalta), Harry only dabbled in adulthood; he wore his pseudo-worldliness like a mask at Carnival.

He believed the center of the world was wherever he was at the moment, and there was no one who could (or would) say differently. In a well-publicized incident in Paris three years earlier, Harry had thrown an extravagant dinner for himself and twenty-five of the most beautiful showgirls he could find. The price tag was estimated at $50,000. Among his guests was the well-known stage beauty Cléo de Mérode, a woman who had been courted by the king of Belgium. John Philip Sousa's band had provided the musical entertainment for that evening as well. The capper was that during dessert, each woman found a thousand dollars' worth of jewelry on her plate, surrounding the stem of her aperitif glass.

If Harry was notable for anything among his barroom acquaintances, it was a "touchy bluster that stemmed from frustrated snobbery." He was also easily bored. Of London he wrote, "The dances are tiresome. If Royalty comes, worse. You see rows and rows of girls, most tied to each chair." This, in fact, was a sight he was all too familiar with, though in a distinctly less staid way. He had done more than just dabble in bondage and flagellation in the bordellos from Pigalle to Budapest, and Harry's desire to handcuff or truss up women was but one variation on a sadistic theme that frequently ran through his one-note head.

No matter what the circumstances, Harry always walked quickly, with a long-legged, nervous gait, although to certain observers, "never seemed able to walk in a straight line." This inclination had been noted by an instructor at Wooster Prep School, which Harry attended at age sixteen. The teacher described his walk as an erratic kind of "zig-zag which seemed to involuntarily mimic his brain patterns." From there Harry went on to the University of Pittsburgh, where he barely tried his hand at law. After that, he enrolled in a special course at Harvard, where, by his own account, he "studied poker" and became a "cigarette fiend." During his brief tenure at Harvard, where he continued to be put off by the study of law, Harry's cigarette habit, combined with unspecified "immoral practices" and threats to fellow students and staff, got him hastily but quietly expelled.

Not only was he the product of a stern, distant father and a shamelessly suffocating mother, Harry Thaw, as it would subsequently be revealed at his murder trials, came from "tainted stock." Since infancy Harry was a problem child, his résumé studded with the bizarre. Given to long bouts of chronic insomnia, temper tantrums, and baby talk or wild incoherent babbling, all of which lasted well into his late adolescence, Harry duly impressed specialists, family physicians, nurses, and tutors with his tenacious and abnormal refusal to leave his infancy behind him. Among the list of childhood diseases (including whooping cough, scarlatina, strep throat, and mumps), perhaps Harry's most exotic illness was a bout of Saint Vitus's dance, although some later suspected it might have been a mild form of epilepsy. Saint Vitus's dance, a disorder associated with rheumatic fever, which Harry also had as a child, is characterized by jerky, uncontrollable twitching and movement of either the face or arms

and legs. In the Middle Ages it was considered a sign of demonic possession, and usually lasted about a month or two (unless the afflicted died
accidentally because of the fervor of an exorcist or cleric). In Harry's case,
no exorcist had ever been called, and so it seemed to linger for thirty-plus
years. But Harry Kendall Thaw knew the source of his torment—the
devil White.

When Harry was growing up, no one could discipline the truculent
troubled child. Only his exasperated father had tried, and only infrequently. Once the elder Thaw was dead and Harry was eighteen, there
was no one willing or able to strap him down. His siblings held him at
arm's length and mostly kept to themselves, watching with contrived
indifference as their mother fed Harry's insatiable narcissism. But because
he was a child of wealth and privilege, his bizarre actions were tolerated
as eccentric by his family and as spoiled by the staff, so that by the time
Harry reached his late teens, a repertoire of puerile behavioral aberrations
was firmly established as part of his inventory of adult quirks. He continued to speak baby talk (in his letters to Evelyn from prison, Harry wrote
to his "Boofuls," his "Tweetums," and to "Herself"). At other times, he
was given to "outbursts of uncurbed animal passion." He often amused
himself by throwing crockery or sharp, heavy objects at the heads of servants. He was reported to have pulled off the tablecloth and kicked his
pheasant and foie gras into the fireplace on several occasions when they
were not prepared as he had directed. Easily distracted, he could just as
easily become fixated on an idea to the exclusion of all else. It was also
reported that after a halfhearted suicide attempt while on a European
tour in his early youth, having attempted to cut his own throat, Harry
had been temporarily committed to a private sanatorium in England.
Yet all of this he managed to keep under wraps. Or rather, Mother
Thaw did.

Perhaps his mother's consistent myopia regarding Harry's aberrant
propensities was sheer denial, knowing that several members on her side
of the family had been institutionalized for insanity. Then again, perhaps
there was a more tragic and harrowing psychological explanation for Mrs.

Thaw's attitude toward her son. In a letter to a friend years later, Evelyn relates a horrendous event that she learned about soon after marrying Harry—a story that would give Freud nightmares. Apparently, Mother Thaw had given birth to a baby boy a year before Harry. But one night, while sleeping in the bed with his mother, the colicky newborn was accidentally smothered to death under one of Mary Copley Thaw's pendulous breasts. The child's name was obliterated from family records, and Harry was produced a year later.

For Harry, mother's milk and money were indistinguishable; Mary Copley Thaw paid for his best clothes and worst habits well into adulthood. And eventually, in spite of her best efforts, the entire world would see how far Mother Thaw would go to compensate for that horrible loss of her firstborn infant son, and try to deny the genetics of insanity when the family's numerous skeletons were dragged out of the closet and "put on exhibit in grinning succession in open court" after Harry's crime of passion.

Jekyll and Hyde

He was a zigzagging contradiction, part gentleman, part boor, part prude, part playboy (it is alleged that he was the person for whom the term as we know it was coined). He could be charming and tyrannical, sincere and pretentious, solicitous and sadistic. Unlike Evelyn, who possessed a marvelous "sensayuma" (her word, which appears in letters she wrote late in life), Harry took himself too seriously to detect even a whiff of humor in everyday things, except when it was inappropriate. Evelyn admits, however, that he did have "a kind, sweet, generous, and gentle side." As she stated years later for those who often wondered about her own sanity in marrying him, "I could not have loved a man who didn't have some of the finer qualities of humanity." It was this and only this "finer" part of Harry that he was careful to show to Evelyn during the early phase of their "friendship." Ironically, like the man on whom he was fixated, Harry

Thaw also led a double life, although his closet debauchery and depravity far outdid White's concealed life as a "notorious seeker of pleasure in strange ways."

Posing under another assumed name, Mr. Reid, Harry played at being a theatrical coach of some sort and scoured the Tenderloin district for gullible, unsuspecting prey. Once he had paid for a room as far as possible from any others in a less than respectable hotel, Harry would then pay an additional fee to various proprietresses for the privilege of having under-age, stagestruck girls come to his rooms for "tutoring." But the unortho-dox lessons Harry taught them were not what they expected. As Mr. Reid he would beat them with dog whips, handcuff them, tie them to chairs and headboards, put them in leg irons, scream in their faces and berate them, reportedly scalding at least one in a bathtub to punish her for her

Mary Copley Thaw and her son Harry, circa 1906–1907.

immoral disposition (thus earning him the nickname "Bathtub Harry"). Before his second trial, a woman named Susie Merrill, who ran a house "all of whose guests were of questionable morals," swore in an affidavit to these and other facts about Thaw's "queer" proclivities, which he had whetted in the most depraved corners of the Continent (in Paris, for example, he was considered "the most perversely profligate of all the American colony there").

Merrill described his modus operandi in her affidavit: "He advertised for girls from ages fifteen to seventeen. He had two whips, one like a riding crop, the other like a dog whip. On one occasion, I heard a young girl's screams. Then I saw her partly undressed, neck and limbs covered with welts. I found others writhing from punishment." Merrill estimated that Thaw had paid out about $40,000 over the course of two years to more than two hundred girls he had lured to her establishment. (Most of these facts would not come out until after the second trial, when, within weeks of offering to testify, Merrill died suddenly and mysteriously, unable to confirm her allegations under oath.)

After the evening of his unveiling, Harry would not leave Evelyn alone. He phoned her, pestered her with fervently written "mush" notes (his term), sent tokens of his esteem, did anything he could think of to earn her favor. At first all he managed to do was whip up the interest of the press, where it was reported that little Miss Nesbit "sent back two dozen pairs of the finest silk stockings and a Steinway piano delivered to her apartment, which already had one, thank you very much." According to one stage manager, "You have no idea how that child is annoyed by the attentions of men, especially of a man named Thaw."

Once she became fully cognizant of Thaw's determination to purloin her precious daughter, Mrs. Nesbit not only expressed her extreme distaste for him, she took every opportunity to try to curb any interaction between Evelyn and Harry. He was an all too gross and fleshy reminder of the part of her former life in Pittsburgh she wanted to stay buried. Nor did she want to anger White. It is also possible Stanny had gotten an ill wind of this new development and told Mrs. Nesbit that Evelyn should stay away from the devious and intractable Thaw. Why else would she have discouraged a multimillionaire's son (and an unmarried one at that) from pursuing Evelyn, not-so-past insults aside?

Nonetheless, going against her own instincts and half-cooked teenage lack of common sense, Evelyn ignored the warnings of her mother and Stanny. Not only did she stop discouraging Harry, she even grew to like him for what she characterized as his more "feminine" side. He was attentive to her needs alone, thoughtful, courteous, and sensitive. Coming immediately on the heels of the Barrymore breakup and the punishment that followed, her mother's and Stanny's disapproval were reason enough for Evelyn to permit her relationship with Harry to continue, even if motivated more by spite than sincere interest.

So, regardless of his more noticeable peculiarities, after almost four weeks, Evelyn formed "a genial friendship of sorts" with Harry Thaw. And at least at first, the "course of their friendship ran smoothly." She visited his rooms at the Knickerbocker Hotel one morning, where he showed her some old laces that she liked very much. He wrote in his memoir, "Had she told me, I should have given all to her." He wholeheartedly approved of her leaving the stage and returning to school, and told Evelyn very emphatically that the theater was no place for a nice little girl like her. Compared with Stanny's and her mother's, Evelyn felt that Harry's concern for her well-being was genuine. As far as she could see, he had nothing personal to gain in supporting the turnabout of her career path. As the time of departure for Mrs. deMille's school neared, Evelyn's love of learning, combined with Harry's unwavering and seemingly unselfish emotional encouragement, soon rekindled a spark she had thought permanently extinguished.

Privately, though, in spite of his vigorous endorsement of her leaving the stage, Harry couldn't help feeling frustrated by the fact that just when his lovely golden girl was within reach, she was to be snatched away and sent off to New Jersey. The school was one of any number that White could have chosen, but he apparently had some connection to it, either through Mrs. deMille and her theatrically inclined family, or as has been suggested, through the experience of sending other girls there and finding his secrets kept safe. He was also still providing for Howard's schooling, perhaps out of genuine affection for the boy or because of Mrs. Nesbit's not-so-subtle endless harping about her fatherless son.

Just before she left New York, Harry came to see Evelyn and, according to her, proposed marriage. She refused, politely, and told a dejected Harry that she liked him well enough, but that her life was too complicated at the moment. Of course, what she couldn't tell him was that she was not exactly the nice little girl he thought she was and she felt it hard to pretend otherwise. Nor could she tell him that the man he obviously despised was the one "who had spoiled her for anyone else." So she left in October, and in January 1903, a down-but-not-out Thaw went on an extended holiday to Monte Carlo and Cannes to relieve his frustrations, drink, and gamble excessively. And plan his next move.

Although Stanny had made "laborious arrangements" so that Evelyn's association with the theater should not be mentioned, it wasn't long after she arrived that the information leaked out. A number of pupils had heard of the new girl and others had seen her picture, so there was no denying the fact that she had been an artist's model and on the New York stage—a double threat. In addition, there was the intermittent and disruptive presence of reporters and photographers who sought to get an exclusive photo of Evelyn in her school uniform and on her way to classes.

While the parents of students from elite families were dismayed by the disruptive presence of a soubrette in the midst of their precious and impressionable daughters, it was a different story as far as their daughters were concerned. As Evelyn saw it: "I found myself among these girls as something of a heroine . . . a real live actress transplanted in their midst." Once the identity of Stanny's Kittens was out of the bag, the girls at the school quizzed Evelyn relentlessly about the New York stage and life in the studios, finding out that she was featured in some magazines they were not allowed to read or didn't even know existed. They all played at acting, putting on little skits and making homemade cosmetics with Evelyn's help. Having had to improvise due to lack of money in the not-so-distant past, Evelyn knew that "tooth-powder, laid on with a piece of cotton wadding, was an excellent substitute" for face powder.

"I shudder to think of the substitutes we employed for rouge and lip salve," she later wrote.

At first, a crushed Jack Barrymore, who had tried unsuccessfully to soak his sorrows in gin gimlets and boilermakers, made numerous attempts to contact Evelyn. He even went as far as Pompton Lakes, where he pinned poems and lovesick letters and drawings to the trees and bushes near the grass tennis court on the school grounds. But to no avail. That episode was over, and once again, force of habit and fear of poverty as well as the remnants of loyalty to Stanny and "their secret" forced Evelyn to take the path of least resistance and make the best of a disagreeable situation.

For several months at least, the little girl from Tarentum who had turned away millionaires and their floating palaces found herself once again on the lee side of normalcy. After classes each day, Evelyn participated in extracurricular activities that naturally involved some form of theatrics, however amateur. But there were other days when she felt strangely under the weather and had to take quinine water and cod liver oil to ease a persistent pain in her stomach. It was unlike anything she had ever felt, even after too much "disgustingly rich food" at one of the Garden's numerous feasts.

As with nearly every turning point in her life up until then, normalcy was relatively short-lived for Evelyn. For one thing, she was always just a postmark away from the intrepid Harry Thaw, who was determined to remain a presence in her consciousness, even as he sat in a casino on the Riviera. As he had from the start, Thaw kept up a steady correspondence with Evelyn, praising her innocence and determination to succeed in her studies and offering her his full emotional support. He also sent her gifts of food and clothing, inquired about her general welfare, and was still on his very best behavior. Then there was Stanny. In spite of his busy career, White paid a number of visits to the school to check on the progress of his "ward," and at other times, Evelyn went to see him in New York. According to one source, one day when White arrived at the school in a big touring car, he invited some of Evelyn's classmates for a ride. During the ride, his conversation was "of such a nature" that three of the girls insisted on being let out of the car and returned to the school on foot.

While it is not clear whether White knew of Thaw's attempts to foster a more significant relationship with Evelyn, when he did learn of Thaw's unshakable interest in his Kittens one day, Stanny told her again that she should stay away from him, just as he had warned her about the Racquet Club "boys." This, of course, was not unlike the warning Garland had given her about White, and White about Barrymore, and Thaw about White. And Evelyn had ignored them all.

Then, as bad luck would have it, two things happened to splinter yet again the insubstantial framework holding up Evelyn's trembling corner of the world. The parents of the girls whom Stanny offended during his joyride in the country caused an uproar. Each in turn demanded that Evelyn be taken out of the school. And while Mrs. deMille was trying to decide what to do, the decision was made for her—and Harry Thaw's window of opportunity to insinuate himself fully into his "Boofuls's" life was thrown wide open.

One day in late April 1903, just after classes finished, Evelyn felt a sudden searing pain in the area around her stomach, worse than any she had felt before. Within the hour it moved up her right side and seemed to burn for several more hours. Then she "turned absolutely green" and began to vomit from the pain. Mrs. Nesbit was contacted by the school nurse, who said she suspected appendicitis. Evelyn's frantic mother tried immediately to reach Stanford White, but he was out of town on business. She then turned to the next worst thing, the man she loathed, Harry Thaw, who had returned only recently from his European trip. Within the hour, Harry brought the second-best surgeon money could buy to the school (since his first choice, Dr. William Bull, was unavailable).

The doctor and two nurses arrived around six the next morning in an electric car Harry had hastily rented, and set up a makeshift operating room in the classroom where, appropriately, biology was taught (as well as geography). After a cursory examination, the doctor told a feverish and frightened Evelyn in rapid succession that her appendix was near bursting, that she could have died from peritonitis, and that she was to be anesthetized. The nurse also warned her that the aftereffects of the ether might cause her to vomit even more violently than she had for the last five hours or so. They left to wash up, and Harry entered the room.

Neither he nor Evelyn said a word—she was too feverish and nauseated to talk, and a gravely concerned Harry fell to his knees as he had the first day they met. He merely kissed her trembling hand. As a hazy Evelyn looked to her side, the last things she saw as she succumbed to the effects of the ether were a still-kneeling and distraught Harry, a chromolithograph of tropical plant species, and a map of the route for the Panama Canal. The operation was performed in haste, with the ether administered in large and unregulated doses from a big brown bottle on a soaked piece of cheesecloth.

During the operation, which took about an hour, Harry and Mrs. Nesbit discussed Evelyn's future in the gardens surrounding the school's main building, even though, as Evelyn felt at the time, "there seemed at that moment to be little future for me." When it was reported that the surgery had been a success, an elated Harry left, promising to come back as soon as possible. When Evelyn awoke from the effects of the operation and the ether a day later, there kneeling beside her was Stanford White.

Very soon after the surgery, everyone agreed that a severely weakened Evelyn should recuperate with a holiday. The doctor in particular warned her that she could not dance for at least a year if she wanted a full recovery, and she needed to be wary of infection. Harry sent his post-operative Angel-Child letters and lounging pajamas and candy and arranged for the manager of the Waldorf-Astoria to send her "no end of tenderloins." Thaw, who had been looking desperately for a means to worm his way more permanently into Evelyn's life, grabbed his chance. He suggested in a phone call to Mrs. Nesbit that an ocean voyage would help Evelyn recover quickly and that he could provide the means for such a trip. Mrs. Nesbit, who had always claimed to detest Thaw and had threatened to take a bullwhip to him, instead took advantage once again of an opportunity. She agreed to let Thaw make all the arrangements for the trip. What she did not count on but discovered too late was that Thaw planned to go as well, on a separate ship. His personal valet, William Bedford, a dapper Englishman who had been with the family for eighteen years, would accompany mother and daughter, and they would all meet in England.

Evelyn of course needed little persuasion. Stanny had held her spellbound for countless hours with stories of the great artists such as Tiepolo, Turner, and Raphael, "the magnificent architecture described by Vitruvius and Ruskin," and the marvelous scenery, often detailing his trips abroad and the "glorious feats of cultural exchange he performed—trading American oil and steel dollars for priceless artifacts and ancient treasures that would find a new home on Fifth Avenue or in Newport."

Harry, perhaps figuring his best chance was to "get to her" while in a weakened state, wrote Evelyn a day or so after her operation and asked once more if she would marry him. Even in the fog of recuperation she had the good sense to say no.

Did she do so because of lingering feelings for Stanny? Was she afraid of what Stanny's reaction might be to the news of Harry's sponsorship? Perhaps she was not completely convinced she liked Harry enough to marry him. Or, she liked him enough to tolerate his millions, but knowing how he apparently felt about purity and virginity, his favorite topics, decided she could not marry him. And of course, since Evelyn was well aware of Harry's "virgin complex," he might very well change his mind about her if he knew the lurid details of her relationship with White, which would have meant the end of her trip to Europe.

When Harry proposed for a third time to Evelyn, just before they were to leave, she again refused. In 1915 she wrote, "I realized that I could not marry any man unless he knew everything there was to know about me. This was a matter of common honesty."

Nor was she prepared to tell him the whole truth and nothing but. It is also possible that since Harry had been nothing but gentle, attentive, and generous to her up to that point, she didn't want to hurt his feelings—or incur his certain condemnation if he heard about her shockingly immoral behavior. He had already said how he disapproved of her being on the stage, that it was no place for a good little girl like her, and that he detested White. Of course, one of many absurdities is that, in addition to the occasional linking of the two in the papers (where White was always referred to as her avuncular benefactor), Thaw, through his veritable legion of informants and detectives, knew perfectly well (if not in any detail) that Evelyn might have had more than a social relationship with White. It was the reason he sought her out and marked her for his own. And while he didn't know the specifics, he certainly suspected the worst. Apparently, however, he did not know about "the Barrymore frolic," having been out of the country for the duration of it.

Perhaps Evelyn even harbored her own romantic delusions, hoping that Stanny would leave his wife—after all, James Garland had been prepared to do the same. And so, it was rumored, had the producer George Lederer. Or, maybe at age seventeen she simply had no wish for the confines of marriage. As she wrote, "I was quite happy in the enjoyment of the present, quite willing to let the past slip from memory and the future take care of itself." And finally, perhaps she just didn't like his looks.

All she knew was that the closer she could get to Europe, the farther she could be from the disappointments of love and betrayal in New York, where Stanny's divided attentions "inflicted deep little wounds" at regular intervals, and dashing Jack came in a poor second. She also didn't mind abandoning New Jersey, where classes in chemistry and comportment could not compete with haute couture and the Champs-Élysées.

Evelyn at the time of her first European trip, 1903.

CHAPTER ELEVEN

The Worst Mistake
of Her Life

In Domrémy, France, the birthplace of Joan of Arc, Harry wrote in the
guestbook, "she would not have been a virgin if Stanford White had been
around." —*Evelyn Nesbit,* Prodigal Days

Topsy, an elephant that had killed three men, was executed on the boardwalk
at Luna Park by electrocution, "providing entertainment in death as in
life." —New York World, *1903*

According to Evelyn, it must have been "the whim of Fata Morgana"
to snatch her away from stage then school in virtually one capricious life-threatening swoop. An impartial observer might wonder, however, what fickle celestial forces were at work with regard to the girl
destined to "put one man in the grave and another in the bughouse."
Although Evelyn eventually came to learn that Thaw's perceived rivalry
and his resentment of White's potent presence in her life (as well as the
virile life of the city) predated her involvement with either man, she
believed at the time that they were the exclusive and harmless products of
Harry's hyperbolic, hyperactive brain. She never considered until it was
too late that Stanny was the reason Thaw had intentionally fixed his
sights on her; after all, Harry Thaw almost always seemed to be going off
half-cocked on one subject or another. Nor did she consider that Thaw

was driven more by envy and loathing of the great White than by her siren charms, which lured so many men her way and drove so many others to distraction. She was also not conscious that her own conflicted but intense emotions on the subject of Stanford White were mirrored, if grotesquely, by Harry. Like the insanely conflicted Montresor out of Edgar Allan Poe's "The Cask of Amontillado," Harry actually admired and envied the man he claimed to hate, and was plotting revenge for similar albeit darker sins that he himself had committed.

In early 1903, neither Evelyn nor Stanny had any idea of the depth or virulence of Harry's inflamed hatred and swelling obsession, even though he had spoken zealously but in vague generalities on several occasions to his Angel-Child of White's diabolic deeds. Evelyn refused to be provoked or speak badly of Stanny, who she said was not, as Harry's informants claimed, "a sybaritic blight on the girlhood of Gotham." She defended Stanny's unwavering generosity to her and her family, of which there was ample, untainted public evidence. But the evidence Harry wanted so badly was irrefutable proof of White's prodigious appetite for *jeunes filles* and what Thaw imagined were unrelenting wholesale debaucheries in the Madison Square Tower "lust nest" and elsewhere around the city.

Yet in spite of all his money and best efforts, Harry was little more than a whirling dervish, spinning his wheels in fanatical pursuit of his own truth regarding Stanford White and going nowhere. In turn, Evelyn tried to speak well of Harry to Stanny when White cautioned her about the pasty-faced playboy and his offensive proclivities, although, inexplicably, Stanny didn't offer any cogent or specific details that might have convinced her (and perhaps thwarted Fata Morgana). A gullible Evelyn insisted that Harry had been nothing but a gentleman since she met him and was also very generous in offering to pay for her recuperative journey.

Evelyn's appendectomy, performed hurriedly under what today would be considered atrocious and primitive conditions, left her highly susceptible to infection and so enervated that she "couldn't lift a hairbrush." At least, however, unlike the late president's medical team a year and a half earlier, Evelyn's doctor and his assistants wore gloves and masks. Harry rewarded an astonished nurse with a diamond Tiffany brooch. But even though the surgery was declared successful, there was a traumatic and peculiar side effect within days of the operation. Evelyn's crowning glory, her luxurious hair, had begun to fall out in wisps, then patches. The doctor assured Mrs. Nesbit that this was a temporary condition, the result of her daughter's weakened system and inability to tolerate the opiates for pain and morphine-laced sedatives given to her in excessive doses under such irregular conditions. In the meantime, it was decided that she needed to be moved to a sanatorium, where she would be instructed to drink only lithia water, take milk baths—and have her head shaved. This, Mrs. Nesbit was told, would facilitate a quicker, even growth of new hair and "revive her follicles." But once she was told, the very idea of cutting off her profusion of curls sent Evelyn into a convulsive panic as she pushed against the blurry edges of semiconsciousness for several days.

A remarkably understanding Harry assured her that he would provide the best wigs money could buy until her hair grew back. Evelyn, at times almost cataleptic, was too listless to put up a fight. A week after the operation, her mother sat her up in bed and gave her some laudanum (against the doctor's advice, since similar drugs that had been given to her were at the root, so to speak, of her dilemma). Mamma Nesbit also held her still while Harry's valet did the shearing. Unable to watch as her hair fell to the bedclothes and floor, a woozy Evelyn turned her head away from the mirror and then dropped off into a fitful sleep, her hair now in a schoolboy's crew cut. Bedford shook the sheets clean, swept away the locks, which coiled like grosgrain ribbon at his feet, and threw them into the dustbin.

Although annoyed and unhappy that Harry Thaw was the figure behind the European trip, according to Evelyn, Stanny seemed reconciled to her departure if only for the sake of her recovery. He probably was relieved to see Mrs. Nesbit safely out of the country, out of the range of her unrelenting requests for favors (or so he thought), and out of his slightly graying hair. Perhaps wanting to show Evelyn that he could be the bigger man, Stanny gave her a Thomas Cook's letter of credit for $500 just before she and her mother were to leave. Mrs. Nesbit kept the letter with her, and suggested that Evelyn "not mention it to Mr. Thaw." Knowing the bad blood between them, Evelyn also considered it sensible not to mention it. Her mother assured Evelyn that having the letter was a good thing, since they didn't want to have to be beholden to Mr. Thaw while abroad. White's letter of credit gave them, she said, "a sense of independence."

Within a matter of days, a frail and overwrought Evelyn was on her way to Europe, with her mamma in tow as chaperone and Harry Thaw scheduled to follow on another ship two days later. When she boarded the ship, Evelyn wore, of all things, a blond wig that Harry had picked out for her. With the yellow press always near and always angling for a story, this little morsel became tantalizing grist for their rumor mill (most of which never made it into print). Subsequent speculation was that the reason Evelyn was being whisked away to Europe in disguise was due to the fact that she "was due," although her still slight figure, which she did not try to hide, said otherwise. Others speculated in private that she might be recuperating from an "unsanctioned operation" that had been performed in secret and in haste at Pamlico, also hinting that Mrs. deMille had accepted bribe money for keeping it quiet. Some conjectured much later that while at the girls' school, Evelyn had given birth, which accounted for the hair loss she had suffered (since this can be a side effect of pregnancy); speculation was that the infant had been quickly given up for adoption. Still others simply suggested that Evelyn was wearing a wig to conceal the fact that she was going to Europe with Thaw as his lover, although the fact that her mother was chaperoning spoiled that notion and threw the other scenarios into doubt as well. All the legitimate papers said that the budding chorus girl was "minding her mamma" and going off to continue her education in Europe. They were half right. Evelyn would certainly get an education while abroad, but not the kind they assumed or she expected.

In 1915, Evelyn wrote, "Some women have a conscience; some have a sense of self-preservation; they frequently exist together, but most often one does duty for the other." Having been forced at such an early age to choose self-preservation, not to mention the preservation of her precarious family unit, Evelyn the child-woman saw precious few examples of conscience in action from the so-called adults or guardians in her life.

Her mother was perfectly content to let one objectionable but wealthy man pay for their trip while holding a letter of credit from another man in her purse. The latter, her ersatz pater-protector, had taken her both literally and figuratively and showed no remorse, only a fear of being found out. So seventeen-year-old Evelyn did not question the morality of the progress of events, especially since she was still in a haze of post-operative pain and distressed over her lost tresses.

The first night alone in her stateroom, a brooding Evelyn took off her wig, stripped herself bare, and approached the full-length mirror on the back of the door. As she stared at the naked, small-boned, slim-hipped, and startlingly boyish reflection, it struck her that with her hair so severely shorn, she looked uncannily and disturbingly like her fourteen-and-a-half-year-old brother, Howard.

Initially, Harry Thaw reached into himself and pulled out his best behavior as he would another new Brooks Brothers suit from his closet, hoping to make a good impression on Mrs. Nesbit as much as to woo Evelyn successfully. He seemed content to be "the best of friends" with her in London. But, within a few weeks he again began to press his old suit for Evelyn's hand. He was like a man possessed, and "nothing else, nothing less, would satisfy him." It was also in London that Evelyn got her first glimpse into what lurked behind Harry's façade of easy liberality and facile sophistication—a cruelty and malevolence to which she would be subjected all too soon.

Whether for propriety's or publicity's sake, Harry had arranged for Evelyn and her mother to stay at one hotel while he stayed at a different one several blocks away with his manservant, Bedford. But the constant pressure of having to be on his best behavior for such an extended period was too much for the easily ignited Thaw to contain. He craved gratification of his uglier impulses and needed release.

A few weeks into their stay, while Evelyn and her mother were at high tea at Harrods, Harry put a pile of coins upon a side table in his suite and waited behind a Japanese screen as the bellboy was summoned. The boy stepped into the room and looked around, eyeing the money left in plain sight. The temptation was irresistible, and the boy picked up two coins.

As he stared at the heavy gold pieces in his palm, Harry pounced on him from his hiding place. He dragged the boy by the collar of his uniform to the bathroom, put him in the tub, "told him to remove his clothes, and brutally beat him with a riding crop." Since neither Evelyn nor her mother witnessed the attack, it was the tearful boy's word versus that of the richest guest at the hotel.

In a routine Thaw was all too familiar with, a doctor was called in, then a lawyer, and finally he had to pay $5,000 "to square the matter." In hindsight Evelyn wrote: "There can be no doubt that Harry's object in laying a trap for the boy who had shown no disposition to steal was to administer a flogging," a malicious act that "in some way seemed to gratify him." Unfortunately, both distracted and delighted by London, for the time being Evelyn remained blissfully unaware of the details and implications of the bizarre and unprovoked assault, coming to believe, as Harry told her, that the beating was greatly exaggerated, that this was his lot in life as a millionaire. No matter where he was, Harry claimed, people came out of the wallpaper to provoke him in the hopes of claiming bodily injury and therefore remuneration. He would eventually relay the specifics of the London incident "with much too much relish"—on their honeymoon.

Within a week or so of the flogging incident, the Thaw party moved on to Paris in June, where Evelyn had her pick of the best human-hair wigs as promised and Harry arranged for an apartment for Evelyn and her mother on the avenue Matignon. Having convinced himself by some wild pricking of his imagination that Evelyn was in love with him, Harry asked the overwhelmed Angel-Child to marry him, again. She reacted this time with tears, born of frustration and fatigue, which Harry mistook as a reciprocation of his feelings but sensed some obstacle. He believed that he could see in her face how much she was affected by his words and that he was "near victory." But, as before, her answer was "as sable as death," even though, he believed he could read "consent and more" in her doelike eyes.

Undaunted, Harry took Evelyn and her mother to the races at Longchamps. There were festive parties and elegant suppers where the head-turning adolescent model-turned-actress was nicknamed "Le Bébé" by Harry's society friends. No one knew, in fact, that she was wearing a wig and that her own celebrated locks were still in the earliest peach-fuzzy stages of downy growth. Yet as a week or so passed, in spite of the shopping trips on the rue de la Paix, visits to the Louvre, and drives through the Bois de Boulogne, tensions mushroomed between mother and daughter. Finally, Harry had to hire a chaperone from a tourist agency, since Mrs. Nesbit began to refuse to accompany them on any excursions. He had to, for the time being, keep up the image of decorum.

One afternoon Evelyn squirmed when Harry asked about how the day's shopping went with her mother. Sensing her discomfort, he pressed her and she told him that before leaving New York, White had given them a Cook's letter of credit. Although Evelyn assured Harry that she had no need for it and hadn't used it, her mother had finally used it, spending $200 on clothes for herself that morning. A livid and jealous Harry, who felt the superior stretch of White's arm even across an ocean, exploded with anger and promptly confiscated the letter of credit. He knew what effect that would have on Mrs. Nesbit, and although she never said anything about it in Thaw's presence, Evelyn's mother privately railed against the phony aristocrat and his colossal nerve. Mamma Nesbit also complained of the pace of Harry's eccentric itinerary, which was deliberately intended to whittle away at "the Mamma's last nerves" (not taking into consideration, it seems, the potential injurious effect it could have on the post-operative Evelyn).

A decision was made, ostensibly to please Mrs. Nesbit, to return to England, where, she said, "the natives could be understood and the citizens [were] civil." Back in England, according to Evelyn, she and her mother were put up, temporarily, at the Claridge Hotel while Harry stayed at the Carlton and tried to keep the intentionally irksome movable feast moving.

Once back in London, Evelyn and her mother were obliged to call on Harry's younger sister, the twenty-eight-year-old Countess Alice, at Berkeley. To hear Harry tell it, Evelyn and the countess "found no antipathy towards each other," even if they were "not especially friendly." From Evelyn's point of view, the disaffected countess, with her bovine stare, made her feel incredibly uncomfortable, especially since she looked like Harry in drag, but with none of his gift for unpatronizing gab. As far as Evelyn's mother was concerned, the countess of Yarmouth was simply a paler if less pudgy version of the humorless, humiliating Mother Thaw. Luckily for Alice's titled husband (whom the press back home jokingly referred to as "Count de Money"), he and Harry were not there at the same time, so Harry could not follow through with the threat he made on Alice's wedding day to kick him down any one of their aristocratic staircases.

At a time when traveling between countries (even civilized ones) and taking day trips to remote natural wonders, ancient cathedrals, and historic ruins was time-consuming and uncomfortable at best (depending on the weather and the number of steps one had to climb in voluminous skirts and torturous, high-buttoned shoes two sizes too small), the accoutrements of travel required nothing short of sherpas; everywhere the Thaw party went, there were people and problems to contend with—chaperones and interpreters, porters, personal maids, and foreign hotel personnel, packing, repacking, lugging trunks, claiming baggage, and muddling through customs. It was wearing enough on a convalescing Evelyn, but at seventeen, she could rise above the jumbling and crowding, the snarling bureaucracy, and language barriers with the purchase of a new hat. But her aggravated mamma, feeling Harry's unspoken enmity always burning at her back, found the constant upheaval of switching into different hotels, often in the same city, maddening and pointless. As tensions rose, a vexed and cranky Evelyn, pulled between the two, also began to bristle. From the Claridge, Harry moved mother and daughter to yet another hotel, the Grand, with no explanation. If his plan was to bring Mrs. Nesbit one straw away from her breaking point, it was working. What he didn't plan on was that Mamma Nesbit had her own campaign in the works.

As each day passed, the quarreling between mother and daughter escalated, until finally Mrs. Nesbit demanded that Thaw send her back to America. Harry knocked on Evelyn's door. She answered, and when he told her of her mother's demand, she said she couldn't take the strain any longer; she said she would go off either by herself or with Harry if that's what her mother wanted. The desperation in her voice made Harry hopeful that once again he could rescue his damsel, this time from a distress he had carefully orchestrated.

Harry moved Evelyn and her belongings to another hotel near Oxford Circus. When Harry went back to reason with "the unreasonable Mamma," he found her talking to his "acquaintance turned cad," Craig Wadsworth, the man who had invited Harry to White's Tower party several years earlier and who, coincidentally, was an attaché at the American embassy. Wadsworth told Harry that Mrs. Nesbit had been in touch with him and wanted to make a complaint against Thaw at the embassy—and if need be, against Evelyn. Harry feigned surprise and laughed, but secretly wished he could widen the rift between "the stupid mamma" and his "Boofuls," who knew nothing of either's machinations. The wedge, however, had been solidly driven between Evelyn and her mother, and it was sufficient enough for Evelyn to agree to leave her mother stewing in London while she and Harry returned to the City of Light. Harry arranged for the two of them to have separate but adjoining suites in the Ritz Hotel. He said he would hire a new chaperone from an agency as soon as possible, all the while plotting the next phase of his own grand, nasty scheme.

THE CONFESSION

Having achieved what he had set out to do—have his Angel-Child entirely to himself by cutting all but the one cord he was tightening around her (having severed her completely from friends and family who were either a channel or an ocean away)—Harry then seized the opportunity to force the issue of marriage with her. Again.

After only a few days in Paris, Harry entered Evelyn's suite as evening approached, looking haggard and worried.

"I want to speak with you," he said in great earnest, and then without any preliminaries, he blurted out: "I want you to marry me!" With her

Evelyn on arcade postcard frequently
titled The Dawn of Hope.

mother gone, and alone in the room in a foreign city "without a sou," Evelyn realized there was no exit. As she describes it, there was "no fending him off with excuses, with reasons or with explanation as to why marriage was not desirable," especially since he had been so kind, so gentle, and so amazingly patient and understanding. He insisted he had to know why, since he had already shown her he was willing to lay the world at her dainty feet, and she in turn had begun to respond favorably to his tokens of affection.

Like a songbird in a Pennsylvania coal mine, a trapped Evelyn on the verge of physical exhaustion began to get light-headed. She gripped the arms of her chair until her knuckles turned white and she felt as if the floor, along with the Ritz's elegant Persian rug, was about to be pulled out from under her. She had the sensation of being dragged "down and down into a dark rabbit hole."

"I must know the truth," Harry suddenly insisted, thumping his fist on the back of her chair. Her mind sprinted, then raced to weigh the consequences of actually telling him the dreaded truth. Moving to the other side of the room, Thaw began to babble incoherently under his breath and performed a kind of figure eight, almost knocking over an expensive vase. Knowing his preoccupation with virginity, Evelyn figured that Harry would surely and swiftly brand her wanton and unworthy of his attentions if she revealed "the secret." Her mother's shuddering rage after her night out with Jack flashed into her mind. She considered that at best, Harry might leave her stranded in Paris just as he had left her mother in London. Or, even worse, he might become violent, as he had with the bellboy. Like a spoiled mastiff, Thaw was a yelping and tenacious interrogator, and Evelyn could take his "Harrying" no longer. Frightened yet almost oddly relieved that the abominable truth she had carried for so long was about to be unleashed (after all, following White's directions, she had never told a single person), an emotionally, mentally, and physically exhausted Evelyn wavered. She stated one more time, "I cannot marry you."

"Why not?" Harry pleaded. "Do you not love me?"

Evelyn shook her head, indicating that it was something more serious, although she didn't say that she loved him, either.

"Then why?" he repeated.

Evelyn hemmed and hawed and hemmed, then began slowly and deliberately, saying, "Because." But she paused, as if trying to catch her breath. Harry ran his hands violently through his hair in an exaggerated version of one of Stanny's characteristic gestures, and waited as oily perspiration began to form on his upper lip.

After months and months of Harry's hounding and challenging her to explain her stonewalling, Evelyn's resolve crumbled and her common sense collapsed into dust. And then she made the worst mistake of her life. She decided to tell Harry the truth about the "Burglar-Banker-Father" who had stolen her innocence in the guise of guardian and friend.

As she began again, Harry, who was still on the other side of the room pacing with nervous agitation back and forth, walked toward her and laid his large, soft, and clammy hands on her slim shoulders. He looked straight into her frightened eyes with a lemurlike stare and asked (as if he didn't know), "Is it because of Stanford White?"

Evelyn hesitated, then nodded in the affirmative. He prompted her: "It's all right, you can tell me about your relationship with Stanford White. . . . Tell me everything," he said, in a strange, panting voice filled with dread and anticipation.

"All right," Evelyn said, again faltering. "Sit down and I will tell you everything."

The moment Harry had feared, obsessed over, squirmed about, and prayed for was upon him. Finally he would have incontrovertible proof of White's reprehensible behavior with vulnerable, unsuspecting young girls. And he would have the Angel-Child, White's most prized possession, as his trump card. A wave of ecstasy washed over him.

As she described it in 1915, Evelyn told him the tale of her ruination slowly and with great deliberation, unintentionally fanning Harry's already smoldering torment. It was a difficult story to tell, not only because she remained with White as his mistress after his disgraceful seduction of her, but because she feared what Harry's reaction would be once she confirmed his worst fears. The frequent pauses, while not calcu-lated, teased and goaded him. He gaped, openmouthed; would shudder, then go limp; he rose and fell with each tortured sentence and hung, moist-eyed, on every word. But as Evelyn described it, "[I made] no excuse for myself, giving no place to prejudice against White," which was not what Harry wanted to hear. Once she started, she found she could not stop: "I told him all that had happened since the very beginning."

As she proceeded with her narrative, Evelyn sat stiff-backed on the edge of her chair, her hands in her lap nervously working into tight knots an Irish lace handkerchief Harry had given her. Evelyn told Harry how her mother had been convinced to go out of town by White, who assured her he would watch over her (even though family on her father's side had offered to take both Evelyn and Howard in with them). She described the mirrored room and bed, and how White had given her several glasses of champagne. How the next thing she knew, he had "had his way with her" while she remained unconscious. The moment she reached the cli-max of her tale, Evelyn watched in amazement as Harry rose slowly, then pitched himself with his full force into a chair; he buried his face in his hands, and began to paw at his cheeks and sob hysterically.

"Poor child!" he muttered repeatedly. "Poor child!"

Then, instead of spontaneously combusting, Harry's body went momentarily limp. His hands began to shake uncontrollably. His face "was ghastly. . . . He rose and walked up and down the room, gesticulat-ing as he muttered." Affected by the vehemence and apparent sincerity of Harry's distress over her ordeal and her own overwhelming cathartic tur-moil at having finally told someone about that night, Evelyn also burst into hot tears. She held her stomach, fearful of becoming sick or ruptur-ing her stitches. Periodically Harry would get up and prowl across the room, biting his thick bottom lip and emitting loud moans. He walked back toward her, crying, "Oh, God! Oh, God!" and then prompted her with, "Go on, go on, and tell me the whole thing."

The two of them sat up all night, with Evelyn crying off and on for hours, until the hour arrived when her tongue turned to sandpaper. Then she fell silent. At first, Harry whimpered almost imperceptibly. Then he began to make wounded-animal noises eerily reminiscent of the sounds her mother used to make during her "attacks of grief." He began to wring his hands like a ham actor in a cheap melodrama. He gnashed his teeth, pulled at his hair from the roots, and then turned his anger on Mrs. Nesbit.

He accused Evelyn's mother of horrifying negligence and sinful abuse. Evelyn tried to defend her mother, saying that her only fault was naiveté. She told Harry that she had willfully deceived her mother in accordance with White's orders since that awful night (and perhaps began to consider how she had obeyed her mother's orders that night as well). Then she fell silent again. Harry, too, finally became quiet, and Evelyn began to mull over what he had said about her mother's foolish, self-serving neglect. Evelyn knew that she had frequently felt her mother silly, which in turn caused the hardheaded girl to act with deliberate impudence. A nearly spent Harry breathed heavily as if on the verge of a stroke, yet continued to question Evelyn as to her mother's knowledge of the "horrid affair." Did she know anything about her child's maidenly downfall at the hands of a satyr? he asked several times. Evelyn put her head down, but insisted her mother did not know. Harry then assured his Angel-Child that any decent person who heard this story would say that it was not her fault, and that he didn't think any less of her because of it. But he wasn't as sure as he sounded. Nor was he decent.

Evelyn looked at Harry, who made for a pious picture on his knees, his hands folded together like Christ in the Garden of Gethsemane. His red-rimmmed eyes stared heavenward as he began to speak out loud, but in curses rather than prayers. He had known all along that he was right about Stanford White. He had been horribly yet triumphantly vindicated. He rambled incoherently at times, as if speaking in tongues, then knelt at Evelyn's side as he had when they first met and as he had just before she went under the surgeon's knife. He gently took her hand and stroked it in sympathy. Evelyn was overwhelmed and saw Harry in a significantly sympathetic light—"all that was best in Harry Thaw . . . all the womanliness in him, all the Quixote that was in his composition . . . a shining light." But it was a ghost light, and in her own confused and turbulent state, Evelyn did not see how her story also excited Harry in a very different way.

Harry assured her that he would always be her friend. He said that at that moment in the huge drawing room, in her long blond wig tied loosely with a ribbon, Evelyn looked to him like Alice in Wonderland, "so lovely and truly so innocent, it singed one's soul." He told himself that, "all would have been so natural if her father had lived," that her mother was guilty of hideous negligence, and that her mother's behavior in response to White was "unnatural" (a word that would reappear with frequency during the trials). He also said he believed that poor little Evelyn had never acted "[of] her own volition unless she had refused point blank her mother's order to obey a beast."

In his own account of his reaction to Evelyn's "hideously awful tale," Harry claims (disingenuously) that he tried "again and again, moment by moment to find some possible excuse" for White's behavior, but realized once and for all that the admired and fêted architect was a vicious sexual predator.

Throughout the marathon confession, Harry pressed Evelyn to tell him every detail she could ever remember about White. As the night wore on and Evelyn stared out the window, the fabled lights of the city of love seemed to dissolve. Neither she nor Harry heard the rumblings of carriages or the sounds of an occasional motorcar, which gradually faded, then returned with the first light of day.

After the harrowing night of Evelyn's admission to "filthy ruin," the other unpleasant situation, the stewing Mrs. Nesbit in London, had approached its boiling point. Having been "stranded" for almost a week, with the faithful Bedford acting as gentleman-in-waiting for her and Harry paying $1,000 for expenses that had been run up in that week alone, Mrs. Nesbit took matters into her hands the only way she knew how—she cabled Stanford White for money to come home.

Mrs. Nesbit also began official proceedings to charge Thaw with the crime of "corrupting the morals of a minor," whom he had transported from country to country. Insinuating that Thaw had kidnapped her daughter, Mrs. Nesbit found herself in a position of power, if only temporarily. Initially, Harry laughed and tried to pass it all off as a "tempest in a teacup." Then he called his business lawyer, a Mr. Longfellow, who said he would look into it, but that Harry should be very cautious of criminal charges, especially in a foreign country. Since technically Evelyn was "seventeen and three-quarters old," the charge Mrs. Nesbit made against Harry was valid. And if he continued on his present course, there would an armory full of legal ammunition aimed against him. He needed to be scrupulously careful "while traveling with the girl on the Continent." He told Harry in no uncertain terms that he could not cross any more lines. It fell, of course, on wild, deaf ears.

Back in New York, after receiving Mamma Nesbit's angry request for passage home, and after some calculations regarding his own risk (and more than a few curses), White, fearful that his illicit relations with Evelyn would somehow become public if the matter of her irate mother wasn't handled quietly, decided to send Mrs. Nesbit the funds to return to America. The charge she finally lodged against Harry was, in effect, kidnapping a minor. Of course, Craig Wadsworth was unaware that both Harry and Stanny feared the same thing—exposure on an international level with regard to their unwholesome involvement with the still-underage Evelyn. But, once Mamma Nesbit was safely back in New York, Thaw would interpret White's intervention as further proof of the architect's guilt and misdeeds with regard to "the minor child" and her mother's complicity.

So Mamma Nesbit left her teenage daughter. Again. This time in another country and in the hands of a man she knew could easily come unhinged and was prone to violence. With her thankless and wearying mother out of the picture, an exasperated Evelyn decided to make the best of the situation. An alternately euphoric and tortured Harry was now free to continue the European holiday with his Angel-Child unencumbered, all the while letting the image of her sexual ruination fester, then run through the murky channels of his brain.

At first Evelyn's emotions ran the gamut from elation to relief to cautious apprehension to anxiety, waiting instinctively for the sword of

Damocles to come down on her pretty neck in retribution for her own shameful behavior in her affair with Stanny. Although he hadn't expressed it, Evelyn knew that Harry must have harbored some ill feeling toward her, however much an innocent victim he said he believed she was when White plied her with alcohol and stole her virginity. But in place of anger or chastisement or punishment, Harry seemed doggedly determined to fill their days with a frenetic and expensive agenda. Just as before, they snaked their way through countries. They crossed the Channel back to England and visited the cathedrals in Lincoln and York. As they studied one magnificent series of stained-glass windows, Evelyn considered mentioning how she had posed as an angel for Violet Oakley on several occasions. She decided not to mention it.

GRIMMER THAN GRIMM

Almost imperceptibly at first, then far more noticeably, Harry shed layer after layer of his solicitous demeanor. He began to make oblique references to Evelyn's "deflowering." Wherever they went, if the opportunity presented itself, Harry would sidle up behind her and point out the statues or icons of the Virgin Mother, virtuous saints, and young girl martyrs who chose to die rather than give in to sin and temptation. In Domrémy, France, the birthplace of Joan of Arc, Harry wrote in the guestbook, "she would not have been a virgin if Stanford White had been around." There were fleeting moments when his sharp gaze and occasional incoherent murmuring made the hairs on the back of Evelyn's neck tingle, even though "he had done nothing untoward at that time." Wherever they traveled, Harry maintained separate rooms, in accordance with proper custom and a show of respectful decency, unable, he said, to find a suitable chaperone in each city, particularly given their almost frantic pace. They crossed to Holland, went down the Rhine to Munich, moved on to Innsbruck—and then came to a bona fide castle in the Tyrol. It was anything but enchanted.

After following Harry's ridiculously frenetic and tiring itinerary, visiting a new city nearly every two days, Evelyn discovered that Harry, in his usual display of entitled excess, had rented a castle, the Schloss-Katzenstein (and its serving staff of two), for three full weeks. After such a frenzied pace, Evelyn was grateful for the idea of an extended respite and imagined something with storybook charm, something that might look like the "quaint backdrop of a musical comedy. Or a Brueghel." Instead, wholly isolated a third of the way up a steep mountain, the ancient structure was a huge Gothic nightmare of cold stones and dimly lit, drafty passageways, grimmer than anything in the Grimm brothers' tales, and for the last two hundred yards or so reachable only by a narrow footpath.

Acting fully the part of the meister, with straight-backed "Teutonic severity," from the minute they arrived, Harry ordered the servants to carry out his every wish, as if he were right at home. After a day or two of somewhat strenuous sightseeing in the surrounding densely forested countryside, the couple returned to the castle. Harry casually mentioned that he had dismissed the staff for the night. Fatigued and preoccupied that her hair, while growing back beneath her wig, was still extremely short and positively unfeminine, Evelyn did not give any thought to the fact that she and Harry would be utterly alone in their remote part of the castle. She decided to go to bed before the flush of Harry's good mood disappeared and his thoughts turned to Stanford White. Immediately after finishing the dinner that had been prepared and left for them, Evelyn said that she was retiring for the night. Harry raised no objections, kissed her chastely on the forehead as he had throughout their European holiday, and sent her off to bed in her room where, having barely taken off her wig, she fell into a deep sleep almost immediately, her head characteristically beneath her pillow.

Since the fallen Angel-Child had folded herself so quickly into sleep, she did not hear the lock turning only fifteen minutes or so later. Nor did she see the shaft of bluish white light that was thrown across her room. Before she had any idea what was happening, a bug-eyed, seething, and startlingly naked Harry, who loomed directly in the light, threw the pillow and covers aside and woke Evelyn with an angry slashing blow across her legs with a leather riding crop. A startled Evelyn sprang up with a scream, whereupon Harry tore furiously at her nightgown. He broke off the small, pearly buttons and tossed the gown to the floor, next to where her pillow and some of the buttons had landed.

Before she could even react, he pulled at, then ripped apart her delicately made underclothes with one hand while hitting her repeatedly with the other, wielding the small whip with a savage and practiced dexterity. The stripped and cowering Evelyn, looking so much like a prepubescent boy with her slender figure and cropped hair, seemed to both agitate and excite Harry, whose not-so-deeply buried affinity for boys had already emerged in London (it had been discussed in hushed tones among certain of the darkest circles he traveled in since his late teens).

With each bruising lash to her soft skin, Evelyn pleaded with Harry to stop, but the more she protested and tried to fend off his blows, the harder he came at her, railing about sinfulness and shameful indecency. He seemed completely insensible to her panicked distress, and afterward she would swear there were moments when he didn't recognize her at all, his pupils unnaturally marked and dilated. At one point, the sweat-covered Thaw stopped, but only to catch his breath and regain his momentum. And then what was already terrible turned horrible.

Harry, whose chest was nearly hairless and shining with moisture, pinned the stunned and bleeding once-golden girl on her back. Holding her down with the riding crop across her narrow shoulders, he proceeded to rape her. Throughout the incident, as she tightened her eyes and every muscle in her body, she fought against the smothering acrid cigarette smell of his breath and overpowering heaviness as he pushed on her small frame. Evelyn's mind raced as she also struggled against consciousness. She wondered irrationally in blurred flashes if this was punishment she deserved for her wicked and immoral behavior as Stanny's mistress. She wondered if this was her fault for taking advantage of Harry's generosity under false pretenses. She wondered if, in her post-operative condition, her life was going to end in a castle in Bavaria—or if she would be able somehow to obliterate this awful scene from her mind if she did survive.

As the rib-bruising episode jerked forward with its own insane force in ruptures of light and dark, Harry pressed grossly and awkwardly upon her, grunting garbled phrases and screaming about penance and retribution, Stanford White, and blackened innocence.

After his fit of divine wrath passed as quickly as it came, a suddenly and disturbingly calm Harry pushed himself off the shaking girl and proceeded to interrogate her, swollen, then spent with his domination. The entire nightmarish assault had taken all of seven minutes. As more sweat dripped from his chin onto the chaotic heap of bedding and torn clothing, he bent over Evelyn, who was in an embryonic curl. He was vehement, his face corkscrewed in disbelief, asking, "Did you really believe White when he told you everybody did the things you had done? Did you? Is it possible?" When she stammered back "Yes," an outraged Harry reared up to his full height and she put up her hands, thinking he was about to repeat his attack. Instead, he shouted angrily that it was not true, that it was a filthy lie. He screamed again into her face that there were lots of decent women in the world, "like his mother and two lovely, decent sisters."

He towered over the bed where Evelyn lay whimpering, wholly defenseless, grabbing instinctively at the pitiful short ends of her hair, which he seemed to be fixated on. She shook convulsively and stared in disbelief at the streaks of blood on her outer thighs and arms, where she had tried to deflect Harry's blows. After several more minutes of interrogation, which seemed an eternity, Harry left the room as suddenly as he had entered, without saying another word. And locked the door behind him. It was a pointless gesture, since with no Mamma, no Stanny, no chaperone, no money, no friends, no servants, and no way to contact anyone even if she could speak German, Evelyn was already a hostage to Harry as well as to her own fears and near hysterical confusion.

His deliberate barefoot steps made a heavy, hollow thrum as he disappeared into the blackness of the hallway. Evelyn writhed on the bed, exposed to the chilled air and tattooed with scratches, her stomach, hips, and buttocks striped with welts. Seeking some rational explanation, she wondered if there was something she had said at dinner to provoke the

vicious attack, since it had been more than two weeks since Harry had
pried the guilty confession from her. Her brain kept burning with the
same questions: Was she to blame? Had she asked for it? Didn't she
deserve punishment for having kept the truth of her lost maidenhood
from the charitable and dutiful and virgin-obsessed Harry? She then
began to wonder, did Harry mean to disfigure her and ruin her career?
What would she do if he came back? Or if he didn't? Overwhelmed by
the severity of his repulsion and frightened by the speed of his self-
appointed justice, Evelyn shivered all night uncovered, not wanting the
sheets to adhere to her lacerated skin once the blood dried. As she stared
for several hours into the deafening silence that surrounded her, the
sparks of pain gradually subsided and settled into a kind of electric numbness, while the absolute darkness outside gaped at her through the lone
leaded window high in the room. Nothing she had ever read, not even
the most ridiculous dime novel, could have prepared her for such an
unbelievable scenario.

The next day and for the next two weeks, Evelyn simply sat pale and
still in her room, as if turned into a pillar of salt. The telltale scabbed-over
marks of the Angel-Child's all-too-mortal sins lingered. Although not
visible unless she was totally undressed, her usually pliant and unblemished torso and legs formed a sick, stiffened mosaic of faint pinkish welts,
greenish blue bruises, and threadlike reddish-brown scratches (to which
Harry had applied stinging ointment). At the end of the third week, a
desolate Evelyn was informed that they were leaving the castle. She had
already come to the conclusion that Harry had either premeditated this
attack or taken advantage of the situation, knowing in either case that he
would be safe from discovery in the secluded castle for a full fortnight.

Acting as if nothing happened, a chipper and garrulous Harry took
her to Zurich, where she immediately asked to see a doctor. He complied,
sending to her room a physician by the name of Mendes-Ernst, with
whom he was acquainted from previous trips to the area. It was clear to
Evelyn that Harry felt no remorse for his brutish cruelty, nor did she have
an ally in this doctor, who, like so many others, was obviously on Harry's
long payroll.

In the middle of the week, while out for a drive alone, Harry was accused by one of the locals of having run the man's horse-drawn Victoria carriage off the road and into a ditch with his rented automobile. According to Harry, the accident happened before his car ever arrived on the scene. Nonetheless, those at the scene claimed it was Harry's fault. He ended up paying 2,000 francs to settle the matter. Evelyn, meanwhile, confined to her hotel room, was immediately reminded of the flogging incident in London, which Harry also had dismissed as nonsense and motivated by blackmail. She thought about the poor bellboy and his defenseless position in an incident so easily "taken care of." Unable to move about much and trying to figure out how to free herself from Harry's grossly but effectively wrought web, Evelyn remembered feeling like "a firefly caught in a Mason jar by a cruel and wicked schoolboy."

So the trip continued into September, and Evelyn came to see that Harry's route included sites of symbolic significance. One such instance was when he insisted they make a special side-trip miles out of their way to see the Jungfrau. The highest peak of a series of mountains located in the Swiss Alps, the name in German means "virgin." The couple returned to Zurich via Bern, then Lucerne. Evelyn saw the same doctor, who pronounced her healed and well—from her appendix operation. He said nothing about the vestigial signs of her vicious assault, where small patches on her body still looked like too-tender bruised fruit.

A solemn and at times virtually catatonic Evelyn spoke very little during the next week; she was only half-aware of the magnificent scenery that passed before her eyes from a string of carriages, railroad cars, and rented autos. Catching Evelyn crying quietly at times, which increased as the week progressed, an oblivious and deluded Harry offered his own explanation for the distraught and silent seventeen-year-old's black mood. He wrote, "Yet even when we were going along beautiful roads, I remember poor Evelyn crying because we could not settle down and live like other people. I did too; but you know when a girl dies one is saddened to think how pretty and happy she might have been . . . and yet it is a hundred times worse when it is not death but the hellish selfishness of Stanford White that ruins girls' lives."

Clearly, the minute Evelyn told him of her deflowering, confirming Harry's worst fears, the shining angel of his fantasies died. He could never forget. And never really forgive.

What should have been a magnificent introduction for Evelyn to the cultural wonders of the Old World had turned instead into a wretched initiation into Harry's particular brand of sadism (one that she later couldn't help feeling was also inspired by the obvious androgynous picture she presented without wig and clothing). The enormity of another appalling and perverse betrayal by someone she trusted, and her own absurd isolation and powerlessness, broke upon Evelyn one day like a sudden July storm as her tears fell fast and heavy. No matter where they went, Evelyn wondered if or when Harry's outrage would erupt, since he was skilled at veiled threats. With invisible bars surrounding her wherever she went, she was a bird of paradise trapped with a cuckoo. To make matters worse, she was dependent upon Harry for the "smallest female necessity." And, adding injury to injury, her insides burned periodically in spite of the doctor's assurance that she was healed.

Evelyn finally found the opportunity in a less shrouded and mobile moment to ask Harry if Miss Simonton, the woman he had engaged as her chaperone after her mother's initial departure, could meet them back in Paris. He agreed. Evelyn and Harry arrived there on September 3, and met up with Bedford, who had finally left the peeved Mrs. Nesbit after Stanny's funds arrived. Evelyn and Harry then visited Elizabeth Marbury's estate in Versailles, where, mercifully out of Harry's earshot, an acquaintance from New York, Gordon Fellows, asked Evelyn, "How is Stanford?" Another person staying there was Elsie De Wolfe, the celebrated interior decorator whom Evelyn had met back in New York at one of Stanny's parties.

The next day, Marbury and De Wolfe returned with Evelyn to an apartment in Paris, where she broke down and told them her mortifying story of Harry's sadism. It was decided that Evelyn would return with them to New York (while Annie Crane replaced Miss Simonton as chaperone). A sullen Harry provided the money for her ticket and accommodations, only dimly and intermittently aware that he might have done something to injure her.

THE SHORES OF AVALON

Evelyn sought refuge back in New York, which she had hoped might prove to be "the shores of Avalon." But her only luck continued to be bad. She arrived on October 24 on the *New Yorker*. Thaw had asked that his attorney, Mr. Longfellow, meet Evelyn at the dock to help her through customs. But they missed each other, and, according to Harry, Evelyn was "swindled" by the officials out of more than half the money he had given her to settle back in. At first she simply tried to recover from her so-called holiday, which had done nothing to help her improve her nerves or heal her damaged psyche. She realized that she needed to go back to work, but remembered that the doctor who had performed her operation at the deMille School said she should not dance for a year. Stanny was still paying for her mother's and brother's "expenses" (both of whom were now effectively estranged from her), and the teenager now looked at Manhattan forlornly as little more than a house of cards, whose chief architect she assumed would offer solace upon her return, but more than likely accompanied with a regular dose of sin.

Little by little, Evelyn began to learn disturbing things about Harry that she had not known before, although by then she certainly had evidence to support the rumors of his perverted propensities. She wondered why, as with Stanny, Harry's "peculiarities," which had been public property, had been kept from her or were so easily hidden or dismissed. The reason, of course, lay with both White and Thaw themselves, as the bizarre triangle they formed with their American Eve closed in upon her.

Before she left for Europe, Evelyn of course had heard of Harry's reputation as eccentric and knew firsthand of his extravagance, as did a lot of showgirls. But as she had told White before she left, Harry had shown her nothing but kindness and almost womanly consideration for her welfare for nearly a year. Nor did any of her so-called friends warn her about his monstrous side. White, who was aware of Harry's attempts to expose his own alter ego, never really spoke seriously about Thaw to Evelyn, since he considered him such a buffoon (another thing Evelyn grew to resent after having been subjected to Thaw's vicious buffoonery). Stanny had warned her to stay away from Thaw, but Evelyn considered that as coming more from her mother than Stanny at the time. She might have even interpreted Stanny's concern as evidence of a kind of knee-jerk jealousy on his part, harking back to the Barrymore incident, which was still a sore spot for her. Perhaps, since he didn't consider the craven and usually ineffectual Thaw much of a threat to himself, Stanny never considered the real threat he posed to the petite and vulnerable Evelyn. Then again, she had been warned by James Garland about Stanny the voluptuary and ignored the warning with unfortunate results.

As Evelyn found out too late, although Harry was no artist, he had taken great pains to surround her whenever possible with people who painted him only in the best of lights. There was also the Thaw family's art of doing damage control for most of Harry's life, so that any misdeeds were minimized—or erased altogether, like the infant brother who died in his mother's bed. And, like all successful sociopaths, at times Harry was capable of fooling even his closest acquaintances. It had not been that difficult to hide his nasty side from Evelyn initially, especially since, from the time he met her, he lulled her into the warming sense of security she desperately craved. He took extraordinary measures to put his best-polished shoe forward, and as was his habit, reasonably explained away indications to the contrary.

Now no longer within Harry's labyrinth of deception and manipulation, Evelyn heard from "one man and another that he took morphine, [that] he was crazy." Since no one had bothered to tell her these details before she became involved with him, a beleaguered and frazzled Evelyn took in everything, but had no one to ask for help or guidance. As in Europe, she had no family or close friends of any kind she could trust or who could offer her advice, save other chorus girls, whose words, she knew, were "substitutes for real thought." With any sense of well-being torn to shreds once again, it felt to Evelyn as if Stanny and his city were waiting to swallow her whole. And on certain days she welcomed the idea. In yet another awful twist of the screws, upon her return, Mamma Nesbit joined forces with White.

Harry had received a number of anxious telegrams from his lawyer, who had met him when he returned from England several weeks after Evelyn. As soon as he set foot on the dock, Harry had asked about her, but Longfellow could talk only about her mother. According to Harry, "though now she knew, she still pretended to trust White" not to save him but to save herself, "to disguise her own unwisdom, like an ostrich puts its head in the sand." Harry tried to laugh it off as he had in Paris, but Longfellow insisted that White's lawyers, with the help of Mrs. Nesbit, were out to make serious trouble. Harry said he wanted to see Evelyn, but his panicked legal counsel tried to dissuade him. He immediately began to rant and fix as much blame on Evelyn's mother as on White, remembering, selectively, things Evelyn had told him in Paris: "She had broken with her own and her husband's families who wished to keep [Evelyn] and Howard for the ten days she was going to visit back in Pittsburgh. But instead, she told Evelyn to do anything Stanford White said and left."

As the days passed, a besieged Evelyn didn't really consider that she was now back in White's equally calculating sphere of influence and spin control; that she was living in hotels still paid for with money that had been given to her by Thaw or White. On certain dreary days, Evelyn felt as if she were covered with a blanket of heavy stones, hearing now and again the wearing strain of her mother's constant praise of White's character (while continually pressing him for support and getting on average about sixty dollars a week from him, more than twice what he gave Evelyn). And yet, even in her confusion, Evelyn continued to resist running back into Stanny's waiting arms.

But within a week or so of her return, while riding down Fifth Avenue in a hansom cab, the architect passed Evelyn. Soon after that chance passing, he phoned her.

"It's good to hear your voice again," he said.

He went on to say that he had to see her and at first she refused, feeling the pull of the same tangled strings she had felt when she left. But White told her it was very important that she see him, because her family (i.e., mother) had caused him much trouble. Evelyn, having had her relationship with her mother effectively severed, asked if she was ill. White replied that it was a matter of life and death, but that he could not discuss it over the phone. Evelyn agreed to meet him at her hotel, the Savoy. He drummed on her door in his too-familiar way, and as soon as he entered the room, Evelyn asked him if her mother was ill. In reply, Stanny grabbed her face and tried to kiss her. She rebuffed him and he blinked in disbelief, seeming surprised at her brusque coldness to him, and asked her what was the matter. Evelyn told him to sit down, then asked again if her mother was ill. White shrugged his shoulders and said, "Your mother isn't ill. I've come to talk to you about Harry Thaw."

Evelyn threw her hands up, then sighed. Several actress friends of White's had told him some rumors about Evelyn's trip abroad with Thaw.

"Don't you know he takes morphine?" White asked her. "Why would you go around with such a man who is not even a gentleman? You must have nothing more to do with him."

An emotionally battered Evelyn sank back into her chair, wondering why Stanny hadn't been this forthcoming and edifying before. She felt herself beginning to tumble back immediately into old behavior patterns as well—including taking the path of least resistance, which for her also meant shutting down like a Ford engine ready to seize.

Once again, she was being forced to take sides. Stanny said he would set her up for some auditions. Within a week, she was offered a minor but featured part in a new Shubert production, *The Girl from Dixie,* and was about to begin the grind of rehearsals in spite of her physical condition and the doctor's warning. Not knowing whether White's rekindled interest in her affairs, which seemed to have been sparked by the chance encounter on the street, was the result of legitimate feelings for her, an act of simple kindness, a way of placating her mother, or set off by his extreme distaste for Thaw, Evelyn, by then almost eighteen years old, was in an alternately listless and frantic quandary. White proceeded to send people to her hotel who told her more stories about Harry. Stanny himself constantly came to see her, and while Evelyn later offered no evidence that they had renewed their sexual relationship, he must have been hoping for a move in that direction before she turned the corner out of girlhood forever. After all, Evelyn was approaching the age when her girlish—or boyish—charms, might be less appealing to the discriminating voluptuary and therefore less of an irresistible force.

In the meantime, the teenager was so nervous and worried over her new work schedule, her mother's estrangement, and the Thaw stories that she began to suffer from headaches and insomnia and began taking "sleeping powders," eventually even succumbing to having a "nerve burnt" by a doctor to allay the neuralgic pain she had been suffering from for weeks.

During the time they were ostensibly together again, White also told her the saga of her mother's return to America, how her mother had tried to cause trouble for Thaw at the American embassy in London, and how a huge incident had been averted by his bringing her mother home. Back in his saddle as sinful savior, White took every opportunity to support the tales about Thaw that Evelyn heard at every turn, waving them at her like a big stick. According to her, "He was very vehement in his indictment of Harry's iniquities. He was a little frightened, too, I think, and went to great pains to remove any influence which Harry may have had upon me."

White told her in no uncertain terms that she needed to hide from Thaw and cut all ties, and seemed saddened over the apparent loss of that part of her girlish innocence even he hadn't eclipsed.

Since Evelyn could not ignore the evidence piling up around her, making Thaw out to be a monster and a dope fiend with no redeeming qualities, following White's counsel, she avoided Harry, who had been back for about five weeks. In what must have seemed at times an absurd and exhausting exercise, Evelyn hid from Thaw and his detectives, finding ways to elude the men Harry always boasted as having bested Pinkerton's. Her mother, not surprisingly, was nowhere to be found. Having washed her hands of her willful, troublesome daughter, she became more deeply involved with Charles Holman, the old family friend and stockbroker, who made frequent visits to New York on business. Before the end of the next year, Mrs. Winfield Nesbit would become Mrs. Charles Holman,

where, relocated to a comfy Pittsburgh suburb and snug in her new husband's money, she could sit back and watch her daughter's predicament
from afar, like a spectator at a Madison Square Garden boxing match.

THE AFFIDAVIT

In early November, a month before Evelyn's eighteenth birthday, Stanny
telephoned to tell her that he was sending a carriage for her. When it
arrived, she got in and quickly found herself at Broadway and Nineteenth
Street, at the offices of Abe Hummel, a lawyer Thaw described as a "slimy
shyster." As was invariably the case whenever Stanny was orchestrating
things, Evelyn was hurried through a side entrance. Stanny, who met her
at the office a few minutes later, urged a puzzled Evelyn to swear to
Thaw's cruelty in an affidavit. He then left just as abruptly, telling Evelyn
not to be afraid of Hummel (whom even his client White described as
"looking like an abortion"). Although technically he was not a dwarf,
with his large balding hydrocephalic head, wormy mustache, and "a face
like a rotten apple," Hummel's appearance was indeed disconcerting. To
avoid looking at him, Evelyn stared around at the office walls, which
were covered with autographed photos of actresses she recognized, most
of whom were Hummel's clients in divorce or breach-of-promise cases.
Until that moment, his most celebrated case had involved Olga Nethersole's
production of *Sappho*, which had caused a stir a few seasons earlier.

Evelyn told the lawyer everything she could remember, and Hummel
prepared to draw up an affidavit in which he intended to detail Harry's
beating of Evelyn, her virtual imprisonment throughout their trip, and
his general criminal behavior. Hummel produced documents, which pur-
portedly discussed other suits pending against Harry for similar crimes.
He emphasized to Evelyn that she was still a minor and that Thaw should
have been more careful; that he was not only "very wicked" but also a
"nuisance." As if on cue, Stanny returned, stating curtly that he needed
to "keep Thaw out of New York." They asked if Evelyn had gone of her
own accord, to which she replied, "Certainly," knowing that one of her

mother's charges at the embassy was that she had been kidnapped. White of course knew this wasn't true, since he had given Evelyn and her mother the letter of credit for their trip. Hummel then sent for a stenographer. When the stenographer came into the room, Stanny left again. But it was Hummel, not Evelyn, who started dictating.

Within minutes, Evelyn began to tremble and cry, feeling the awful drag of hopeless weight on all sides. But Hummel told her sourly not to interrupt. She became nervous and excited as she listened to Hummel's ludicrous and inventive version of her European experiences. According to Evelyn (in 1915), in spite of the fact that it was already an unbelievable story, he made it sound in effect as if Harry had carried her away "kicking and screaming in a sack." When she tried again to interrupt, he put his gnarled and stunted hand up like an aggravated librarian. The scenario that Hummel dictated was as bad as any hoary nineteenth-century melo-drama; it was filled with such phrases as "I besought him to desist," and "he also entered my bed, and without any consent, repeatedly wronged me." It is doubtful that anyone in 1903—much less a seventeen-year-old—spoke in such archaic and stilted terms. After he finished his version of events, Hummel told Evelyn about a number of breach-of-promise suits he had won for other young actresses, a common practice in those days. He seemed intent upon convincing her to file such a claim against Harry, but when he pressed her, Evelyn gave a little nervous laugh and said if there was any breach of promise, it was on her part, not Harry's. An angry Hummel called her foolish and dismissed her to the waiting cab.

Several days later, Hummel called her up and asked if she had any let-ters from Thaw. She said that she did, but wanted to know what business that was of his. Within minutes, Stanny called her and said that if she was not willing to help him, there was no way he could protect her from Thaw. So Evelyn took a bundle of Harry's love letters down to Hummel, who sealed them in a big envelope in front of her. He said that they just wanted to have something to hold over Thaw's head in case he made any trouble. A mortally confused and depressed Evelyn tried to come to terms with the idea that Harry was, as White and others now painted him, an unrefined blackguard (the same term Harry had used against White, although Harry couldn't spell it). White appeared to be bitterly angry that Thaw had taken her away from her mother, and ironically that Mamma Nesbit, who should have known better, had disregarded his opinion about the crazy Thaw. The perverse rivalry that now seemed somehow mutual began to escalate as each man tried to use Evelyn to intimidate the other.

White's decision to use Hummel, a lawyer with a reputation as checkered as his suit (he would eventually be disbarred), was not made out of ignorance or carelessness. He of course knew many a prominent and respected lawyer. But even as he recognized the illegality of Thaw's actions in terms of his underhanded and criminal behavior with Evelyn, White's position was equally precarious. For he too had taken advantage of her (as well as countless others). This was one can of treacherous worms he wanted sealed, and he needed a lawyer who would do what he paid him to do and ask no questions beyond the matter at hand. White also needed insurance that Thaw would not be a threat to his professional or personal life, armed as Thaw now was with Evelyn's tale of seduction. Getting Evelyn to swear out the affidavit about Thaw's physical abuse and emotional mistreatment of her in Europe could only help his own cause and keep Thaw, ostensibly, at bay.

Evelyn went into seclusion in various places, settling at the Hotel Navarre, but inevitably, with the help of his ubiquitous private detectives, Harry was able to discover her whereabouts and he asked over the phone to meet with her. Although she agreed to see him, reluctantly, after much whining and pleading on Harry's part, Evelyn said she would not meet him alone. So, on the appointed day, Harry brought a friend, Thornton Warren, who also happened to be a member of the New York Bar.

When they arrived, to his dismay, as with White, Harry found a changed Evelyn. Distraught and jittery to the point of nervous exhaustion, she told him the things she had heard about him. A fretful Evelyn sat on her steamer trunk near the door, her feet not touching the floor, her synapses stretched to their final centimeter. In stark contrast, a gentle

and seemingly sanely lucid Harry was the picture of relaxed concern. He
sat down next to her on the trunk, took her hand, and asked quietly,
"What's wrong with you, Evelyn?"

Evelyn pulled her hand away and put her head down at first. Then she
shook it, looking up at him.

"I don't know what to say to you," she said, her voice breaking with
distress. "I have heard such dreadful, dreadful things about you that I feel
that I can never speak to you again."

Harry stared at her, unblinking and frowning. By this time, in spite of
his peculiar and violent behavior in Europe, Evelyn realized that she
had grown "genuinely fond of Harry" and, as she said, the stories she had
been told about him affected her to a surprising and "extraordinary
degree. . . . I hardly suspected how dependent I was upon this new influence which had come into my life." With her mother gone and her health
and thus livelihood at issue, a despondent Evelyn could hardly believe
how indispensable Harry had made himself to her over the course of a
year while reminding her throughout that same time how reprehensible
White had been.

She then told Harry about going to Hummel's office, which gave him
a start. He became fidgety and wanted to hear what had transpired.

"Tell me everything," he said.

In what must have seemed to Evelyn a scene ridiculously reminiscent
of the one in Paris, she proceeded to haltingly tell Harry about White
and Hummel, the letters she had given them, and the statements she had
made about their time in Europe. Each time she hesitated, Harry urged
her on. After repeating Harry's supposed unholy litany of previously
unknown offenses (which included beating young girls, scalding them in
tubs, and taking cocaine and morphine), Evelyn fell silent. Throughout,
Harry said nothing. Then he got up and shook his head.

"Poor little Evelyn," Harry said. Laying his hand upon her shoulder as
he had so many times, he then said to her, "Don't be so asinine."

He proceeded to tell her that everything she heard was a lie. And his
respectable counselor agreed. He said with tremendous contriteness that
he felt terrible about his "irregular" behavior in the castle, but that he had

been overcome with anger and confused feelings about her complicity in her sexual ruination. A silent Evelyn listened. He then said it was well known that any woman who wanted to initiate "a blackmailing suit against some rich man always went to Hummel." His lawyer again agreed, shaking his head in mutual dignified disparagement. Harry asked Evelyn whether she had signed anything or not. In what would become a crucial piece of evidence at the murder trial, Evelyn said that she couldn't remember signing anything in particular. Then she said firmly that she had not.

"That's funny," said Harry with feigned thoughtfulness. "If they want to cause trouble, you must have signed something."

Evelyn wavered again, and said in exasperation that she seemed to think she hadn't, but ultimately could not remember. She said little after that and considered what had been said to her and done to her versus Harry's behavior now. With her vision hopelessly narrowed by the bleak circumstance she was in, she rashly wanted to believe in something. As it had when she confessed to him about her "ruin," Harry's earnest tone and apparent depth of feeling for her present distress moved Evelyn once again—so much so that, as unbelievable as it sounds, like the typical victim of abuse (and as part of the oppressive and perverse social pattern that encouraged female masochism), she began to feel that she had actually "wronged him."

Harry then continued to tear down Hummel, and with the support of his upstanding and "normal-sized" lawyer, Harry started to plead his case with such apparent honesty that Evelyn began to question the validity of things she had heard. After an hour or so, Harry got up to leave. He took Evelyn's hand, kissed it gingerly, and said, "If you want to believe these things you may." Having achieved what he wanted—to counter White's smear campaign by planting his own corruptive seeds of doubt—Harry left.

Evelyn, at the time, was less than thrilled about having to rehearse for her role of Bess Jackson in the new show, feeling depressed, drained of energy, and yet unable to sleep for more than a few hours at a time. Either at a dress rehearsal or opening night (she couldn't remember which), Harry came by and saw that she was looking ill. In fact, she was feeling

awful, and didn't even want to be in the show. Harry persisted in making "all sorts of impossible offers," including one to pay any salary she
was receiving. But Evelyn didn't want to "accept all his generosity
prompted." He pleaded with her to leave the stage, if for nothing else
than the sake of her health. The next night, Harry reappeared at Rector's
(where Evelyn was at dinner with a girlfriend), in his effort to change
Evelyn's mind. With some reluctance, she told him once more about the
stories she had heard, especially his drug use. Harry looked at her with
great seriousness.

"You've known me now for some time," he said, "you have seen me
under all circumstances." He paused, then laughed smugly.

"If I take morphine, and in the amounts you have been told, what
symptoms can you see? That sort of thing is not done with impunity. It
leaves some mark upon a man's face and his manner."

Evelyn had no idea if this was even true, although she suspected that it
must have accounted for his unusually distorted face and huge dilated
pupils that horrific night in the castle. But as Harry pressed on, he convinced her that in their time together, no matter whatever else he may
have done, he had never lied to her. He knew the issue of truthfulness
was Evelyn's Achilles' heel after her experience with White, and Harry
played it to his advantage. He assured her repeatedly that his violent
behavior had been the vile product of temporary insanity and would
never, ever happen again. As he looked into her sad eyes, Harry felt his
quest to win Evelyn back and still expose White as a "blaggard [sic]" was
on the verge of succeeding.

Using "every subterfuge" to get back into Evelyn's good graces, for several weeks after his initial visit, Harry called on Evelyn to check on her
health and was solicitous of her welfare; as Evelyn put it, "He watched
my health as tenderly as a woman" and never mentioned White at all.
His behavior stood in stark contrast to her own mother's behavior. And
she suspected that Stanny's renewed concern was motivated as much by
self-protection as it may have been for her genuine welfare.

During the too-brief time that he and Evelyn were effectively separated, Harry had also embarked with increased zeal on his holier-than-

thou mission. With the fervor of a true believer, he was determined to find fleshly evidence he could show the world to prove White's infidelities (not wanting to use Evelyn for a variety of complicated reasons, not the least of which was his own culpability in having "had illicit relations with a minor").

So Harry "went out into the darkness of various ticklish localit[ies]" in the wee hours of the morning to find a willing witness/victim. He claimed that there were a number of girls, very good-looking and very young, whom he had saved from White. Harry spent days and weeks in search of girls and their mothers (when there were mothers) whom he could warn against White or ask to testify to his immoral and illegal acts. In one of the more bizarre passages in his memoir, Harry wrote, "And I found mothers, many, and I got to each alone and told each how Blank the Pimp crawled up each stairway, some in wretched tenements, some better, like Mrs. Nesbit, he minding no cracked doors nor rotten banisters, silk hat and evening dress and suave, and told her that Mr. White was not like other men, that her daughter should trust him.... They ... each knew later, as each daughter had to go to 22nd or 24th Street or the old den or the new one."

According to the results of Harry's fevered "sifting," at least one hundred girls had made their way into the Twenty-fourth Street snuggery. He had even gone to some of Evelyn's earliest acquaintances in New York, including painter James Carroll Beckwith. The artist said he had noticed a "great change" in Evelyn in the late fall of 1901; when she mentioned she had met Stanford White, then Harry understood. According to Harry, a distressed Beckwith, who had warned Evelyn not to go on the stage, "feared that a terrible fate had overtaken her."

And then, "seventeen-and-three-quarters-year-old" Evelyn made the second biggest mistake of her life. She began a tentative process of reconciliation with Harry, in spite of his atrocious sexual assault of her, his bouts of uncontrollable wrath, his awful battery, and all the reports she had heard about his most vicious proclivities. And yet in spite of her cautious capitulation, agreeing to communicate with Harry or meet him only in a public place, Evelyn still refused to yield to any of his offers to leave the stage. After several weeks, a dejected and thwarted Harry retreated to Pittsburgh. And Mother.

UNHAPPY THANKSGIVING

Harry had been in constant correspondence with his mother while he was in Europe. Although there was no love lost between Mother Thaw and Evelyn, Evelyn's reflections in the years after the murder and trials show that she tried not to judge her former mother-in-law too harshly. She may have even envied the unrelenting, overindulgent display of love and concern Mother Thaw had shown her son. Evelyn admitted that Mother Thaw "was in many ways a remarkable woman," whose advice Harry ignored except when it suited him to please her. Evelyn was unaware that Harry had written to his mother from Paris the day after her confession, giving his mother an edited version of the "pathetic events of poor Evelyn's life which had culminated in her cruel defilement by Stanford White." He did not, at the time, mention her name. Once back home, Harry had the opportunity to see how the story affected his mother in person.

As Evelyn came to see it, it must be said Mother Thaw did everything she could to prevent the marriage. She acted as any mother would have done who thought she saw a "misalliance." But it was not Mother Thaw's intemperate concern for her son that bothered Evelyn. It was her snobbery. As far as Evelyn was concerned, the Thaws acted as if they had made their money within one generation from coke and railroad dealings, and could make no great claims to the kind of social standing that comes from "old money," even though they had "more money than God," as one paper reported. And as Evelyn stated, they were "extremely rich, and I . . . was extremely poor. And Society in Pittsburgh is governed by the initials which indicate the Almighty Dollar."

Even as Mother Thaw continued to serve God through various philanthropic activities affiliated with the Third Presbyterian Church, she maintained a rather un-Christian attitude toward Evelyn. For more than a year she resisted Harry's pleas to marry Evelyn, on the grounds that it would be the ruination of the family name. A surprised Harry, who had been so accustomed to getting his way with his mother, persisted. He told her, in what Evelyn called an exaggeration, that she possessed "a beautiful mind." As Evelyn put it, "healthy" would have been a better word to describe her mind, for she had come to the time when she saw things in "their true proportions." But Harry was prone to exaggerating the virtues of his friends and the failings of those he regarded as his enemies. Harry saw the world in those terms—friend or foe. There was no middle ground between the two in his feverish mind.

Once a distracted and despairing Harry returned to Lyndhurst for Thanksgiving, unable to believe that a sickly and fiscally vulnerable Evelyn could continue to turn him down and remain in the "shadow of the Beast," it looked to his mother as if "he had lost interest in everything." At breakfast he seemed unusually absentminded, as if laboring over a grave problem. Without warning Harry got up from the table, went into the parlor and played the piano violently at first, then more softly; a few minutes later he returned, as if nothing had happened. He repeated this several times, even while there was company at the table. After a few days it was clear that he was no longer sleeping; she could hear smothered sobs coming from his room, sounds that must have wreaked their own kind of havoc on her, if only subconsciously. Once when she went into Harry's room at around four in the morning, she found him sitting on his bed, fully dressed, staring into the darkness. But he refused to tell her what was wrong. Finally, she insisted. In a torrent of words, Harry told her all the details of Evelyn's sad tale of maternal negligence and sexual ruin. Mother Thaw reacted somewhat sympathetically, but warned Harry not to get caught up in such a tragic case, one where the sins had already been committed and he therefore could do nothing to change those facts. It was not a situation "that allowed for salvation."

The next day in the new Third Presbyterian Church at Thanksgiving morning services, an odd little scene took place between Harry and his mother as they sat in the back under the gallery. They were the only two from the family at the service, as his sisters were coming for the holiday from England and New York but hadn't yet arrived. Despairing and desolate that Evelyn was effectively avoiding him, having chosen to go back to the theater and the sphere of White's influence, and unhappy with his mother's lack of sympathy, Harry stood next to Mother Thaw throughout the service. Toward the close, the choir began to sing Kipling's Recessional Hymn. Without warning, Harry began to sob, swallowing intermittently and emitting his wounded-animal noises. Mother Thaw gave him a little shake as his tears fell on the hymnal in his trembling hands.

After church, she tried to discuss the matter with the gloomy Harry. Near tears again, Harry told his mother that he had tried to discourage the girl from life on the stage and offered to send her to school and so forth but that "he had very little help or encouragement from her mother in his efforts to protect or befriend the child," as he constantly referred to her. A week or so later, Dr. Bingman, a family friend who knew Harry's medical and "emotional" history, came to talk to him. He was utterly depressed, even more than when he had tried, halfheartedly, to commit suicide by cutting his own throat in his days at Wooster Academy. Finally, fearing a potentially more effective suicide attempt, Mother Thaw relented. She gave Harry her reluctant approval to pursue his fallen angel.

A thoroughly elated and invigorated Harry returned to New York in December. He kept up a steady campaign of penitent courtship; he sent gifts and the contents of an entire florist's shop with notes indicating that he had changed and that he still wanted to marry her. When Evelyn sent some clothes of his that had been in her trunk, one of the pockets had an ivory nail file of hers in it. Harry took this as a sign "that everything was all right."

What developed in the days leading up to Evelyn's eighteenth birthday was a Mexican standoff in the middle of Manhattan. White's lawyers were armed with the affidavit and other evidence of Thaw's concealed criminal behavior, a large portion of it provided by Mrs. Nesbit (including shirtwaists she said Thaw in fits of anger had ripped from her daughter, which she had kept as evidence). Thaw and his lawyers were armed with Evelyn's story, combined with mounting evidence from other young "victims" of White whom Harry, with the help of his detectives and the prehensile grasp of Comstock's Society for the Suppression of Vice, had ferreted out. Thaw was also paying part of his army of detectives to watch White's every movement, while White paid out close to six thousand dollars in several months to his own detectives to find out who was paying to have him watched. But with White's potentially devastating threat hanging over Harry's head, his lawyers advised him not to do anything rash until Evelyn turned eighteen. So, the overwrought Harry waited like an excitable child for Christmas Eve.

In the meantime, what with costume fittings, pre-show parties, and some modeling assignments, Evelyn tried to throw herself into her new role with enthusiasm. But nothing had changed. Even though Stanny was still willing to make himself and his money available to Kittens, his unwavering interest in other girls was too blatant and insulting. Meanwhile, he had effectively diminished her reputation for any potential legitimate suitors within his considerable sphere of influence. Which left her in limbo.

The morning of December 24, Harry sent all sorts of gifts to Evelyn's hotel—Japanese trees, bonsai miniatures—and, according to his own recollection in his memoir, "she cared little." For his part, Stanny was planning a "bully party" in honor of Evelyn's eighteenth birthday at the Tower.

That evening, Harry—along with two friends, Charlie Sands and Lorimer Warden, and an unnamed girl—drove to the Madison Square Garden Theater, where Evelyn's show had opened. According to Harry, they had expected to find Kennedy, the detective from the Grand Hotel (and one of Harry's informants as to Evelyn's comings and goings) waiting outside. Instead, there was a Detective Heitman, who told Harry that White was not there. Moreover, he told Harry that he had overheard four members of the Monk Eastman gang talking and pointing to Harry as he stepped out of the carriage. An anxious Harry, full of false bravado, went into the theater to watch the play. After the performance, Harry went to Evelyn's dressing room, where "a colored maid was helping her." It would be at least twenty minutes before she was ready, so he again went outside.

There he met with Kennedy and the other detective. When they agreed that there had been Monk Eastman gang members in the vicinity, Harry asked one of the men for his revolver. He took the gun and walked with Lorimer across the street into the saloon, where the four gang members were supposedly in a back room. Harry wondered whether or not the detectives might be lying, and went outside just in time to see a large black electric hansom drive up to the theater. An elegant, darkly dressed man got out and ran across the street in a hurry toward the stage entrance. It was Stanford White.

Within ten minutes or so, an apparently "wild and excited" White came out "looking like everything was wrong."

What had happened was that Evelyn had decided she did not want to go to White's party and continue with tiresome and disheartening patterns that held no promise of anything better in her personal future. White had urged her to come to the Tower, and she hotly refused. He then told her that he would give her time to cool off. Soon after White left, Harry picked up Evelyn, and she, along with his two friends and the girl, went instead to dinner at Rector's, the place she and Harry had first met. Harry was flushed with excitement at frustrating White on the very day his lawyer, Longfellow, said he could start his reconciliation with Evelyn without fear of the law. One has to wonder how soon after her fateful decision Evelyn began to regret it, since Harry's description of the evening of her eighteenth birthday seems anything but happy: "The little party at Rector's was one of repentance, not of the food nor of the wine nor Evelyn, but her rape by White."

Another thing that ate away at Harry was the idea that White continued to provide funds for Evelyn's brother even while he, Harry Thaw, was fully capable and willing to do so. Harry had assumed or had been told (it's not clear which) that Mr. Holman, her new stepfather, had taken over the financial care for Howard. But when Harry discovered that it was not the case, that Howard actually worked for White in some minor capacity, perhaps as an assistant to his secretary, he became more disturbed and angry at Evelyn's mother, who had let both her children be "bamboozled" by White. He also took this as a sign that White still wanted to have some leverage over Evelyn, whom he could twist to his will.

Harry knew that the great architect gave her a weekly allowance when she was not working, and "he paid the same sum for that brother—very generous, you see, when he hoped to 'get her back.'" Harry also began to think, as did others, that perhaps White's well-known princely generosity was a way of offsetting deeds "committed out of unscrupulous passion"— that White was "a bookkeeper with the Fates" who tried out of remorse or guilt to salve his conscience and unpleasant memories by doing good deeds.

According to Evelyn, a few days later, Sam Shubert, the theatrical manager and co-producer of her show (who died tragically in a train wreck in May), had told her with innocent amusement that White was in a great state of excitement that night, both at the theater and at the Tower party, where he kept jumping up from the table and checking for Evelyn, "running out and then coming back in again." Finally, he said, White went back to the theater, where, apparently, he had just missed her. When White questioned the stage doorman, Benjamin Bowman, he was told she had left with Thaw. First, calling Bowman "a goddamned liar," an agitated White ran into the theater, and finding no Evelyn, came back out. He then allegedly pulled out a revolver of his own and waved it in front of Bowman, vowing he would find and "kill the son of bitch before daylight." Four days later, Bowman stopped Harry Thaw on the street and told him of the remarks White had muttered about "that miserable puny Pittsburgher."

As the weeks went by, the antagonism between White and Thaw grew like a nasty swollen carbuncle. It was a situation the best alienist— practitioner of the new science of "psychiatrism"—might have struggled with, especially in trying to answer the eternal question: What does a woman want?

Specifically, what did the still captivating and barely legal Evelyn want, assuming she had any legitimate options? And how was she to think clearly while being pulled across one line and then another in the tenacious tug-of-war between White and Thaw? More than anything, Evelyn wanted peace of mind and some chance at financial security, since it appeared romantic happiness was a delusion. This meant she needed to believe that Harry was sincere in his apologies for his violent and offensive behavior—and that he in turn had forgiven her sinful "transgressions." Knowing she was back in White's city, Harry wanted desperately to win her away, permanently, apparently willing to endure the fact that she was more Magdalene than Madonna. And if he thought Stanny wanted her back, Harry wanted her all the more. If Harry wanted her, Stanny wanted her away from him—and wanted Harry out of his playground. Each man suspected the other of some more aggressive movement toward his discredit. And pinned and wriggling in the middle was Evelyn, the key to both men's potential ruin should she decide to go public with her knowledge of either one's "sexual crimes."

But she didn't.

Instead, Evelyn provided Harry with letters White had sent her, hoping that once each side was equally armed, they would cease fighting, sensing the battle a draw. She couldn't have been more wrong.

Mr. and Mrs. Harry Thaw, the "happy couple," in a composite photo, 1905.

CHAPTER TWELVE

⋞✦⋟

The "Mistress of Millions"

"What Is the Fetish of the Fair Young Woman of the Footlights That Makes
Western Croesus Lay His Heart and Gold at Her Feet?"
—New York Tribune *headline*

My heart is not for sale!   —*Song lyric, 1905*

"Gee! But This Is a Lonesome Town"   —*Song title, 1905*

Throughout the following year, as Harry pursued his fallen Angel-
Child in earnest, miraculously maintaining his temper and tem-
pering his obsession with White (even paying for Evelyn to take another
trip to Europe to study art and music, this one scrupulously supervised by
a hired chaperone for the entire time), the papers were filled with speculative headlines. One read: "$80,000 or Espoused to a Fair Young
Daughter of Thespis." The public wondered how much of a sacrifice the
Pittsburgh playboy was willing to make on behalf of the Broadway beauty.
But Harry had routinely exceeded his $80,000 monthly allowance since
that time when his myopic mother had first threatened him with disin-
heritance should he pursue his broken dream girl all the way to the altar.
There were also rumors at the time that Harry and Evelyn had already
gotten married during their first European "holiday"; another said that
Evelyn had been offered a quarter of a million dollars to leave Harry. But
they were all only rumors.

Mother Thaw, along with the rest of the family, believed that nothing good could come from bringing a common "social-climbing soubrette" who had "nothing but her looks" into their gilded family. After all, in her mind, both of the Thaw daughters had married well. Mrs. George Lauder Carnegie seemed at least content with her lot and snug fortune. But things were very down and nearly out for the countess of Yarmouth, who was adrift in a sea of marital troubles. It didn't help that some reporters had taken to calling her husband "the Countess."

Evelyn knew well enough that Mother Thaw was filled with little sympathy for her and her vulgar bohemian baggage: "It was irritating for these strict souls to have a chorus girl in the family, [whose] beautiful mind [which had been cultivated by Stanny] was little compensation for her association with the stage." And, as Evelyn described it, "I certainly had no great sympathy for her. I never regarded Mrs. Thaw as an archangel because she was so magnanimous as to forgive a chorus girl for taking . . . her favorite son."

But if the matriarch Thaw were to give her curdled consent to the marriage, it would be understood that Evelyn could not under any circumstances continue to pursue her modeling or stage career; she couldn't even, as she was explicitly told, participate in the occasional *tableau vivant*. Although popular with the affluent and aesthetically minded rich from New York to Newport, this harmless parlor entertainment was frowned upon by the pious Pittsburgh clan and their fellow disciples. Evelyn responded only with a sphinxlike smile and said nothing.

Moreover, it was also understood by all at Lyndhurst that Evelyn's past was dead and buried. Here today. Gone tomorrow. Out of sight. Out of mind. Although her knee-jerk reaction was to roil against the first stipulation, a now nineteen-year-old Evelyn halfheartedly accepted the opportunity embedded in the latter to put her short but too painful past behind her, especially certain events needing "less closure than obliteration." Nonetheless, Mother Thaw's abrupt amputation of her whole identity and demand that Evelyn bury even memories of the best part of her still young life seemed terribly familiar to her. She flashed back to her father's death and her mother's eventual dismissal of his existence and mandate of silence. This only helped darken the former chorus girl's "beautiful mind" and color the opinion she was forming of her mother-in-law-to-be, whose face like her general demeanor was a grim, tight fist. There were certain days when she considered that she might be merely trading Medea for Medusa.

The popular-culture myth that Evelyn was a scheming, social-climbing, gold-digging "she-wolf" can be dispelled simply by pointing to the magnates and millionaires who had wanted her and whom she had routinely dismissed or ignored since she was sixteen. One then needs to consider the three-and-a-half-year campaign it took the "millionaire scion of steel and such" to finally win her pretty hand. The question of her judgment (or sanity) in finally agreeing to marry "Mad Harry" is another matter.

Having been forced at such a young age to abandon her fantasies to a harsher reality in order to survive, in early 1905 Evelyn considered her narrowing options. She had been the family provider since the age of fourteen; she had come to the unhappy realization that in spite of his generosity, Stanny the unrepentant rounder would never leave his wife and son. To make matters worse, because of her illicit relationship with him, if it ever got out, no respectable man, young or old, would ever take a serious interest in her. The closest thing to a real proposal Evelyn had gotten was from the smitten Bobby Collier, who had offered to send her to Europe to study sculpture a year or so earlier. And then there was Harry.

Having grown up with the specter of the imposing Thaw family mansion hulking on the outskirts of her drab little neighborhood, Evelyn found herself in the enviable position of marrying into that very same family. Unfortunately, in addition to his millions, she was all too painfully aware that Harry's inheritance included a wealth of neuroses. But in pressing his suit ("He wanted to marry. Nothing, nothing less would satisfy him"), Harry smilingly assured Evelyn that once they were married, he would be a changed man, even declaring that he would "become a Benedictine monk." He promised there would be no more scenes like the one in Schloss-Katzenstein, insisting that he had simply been overcome with anger at her former behavior with White. But eventually, as he said, he realized that it was not her fault. So he forgave her.

Contrary to what has been written, rumored, and ruminated on, and however unfathomable it may seem, Evelyn did also care about and even love Harry, for a time. She would write of Harry in 1915, "He was very earnest, no philanderer, no light lover, even in his infidelities he was absorbed and sincere. Such matters were serious propositions, presenting aspects which would not occur to the normal man." There is convincing evidence of what seems genuine affection in the letters she wrote to him when she was in Mrs. deMille's school (admittedly written with a school-girl's immaturity and before he had revealed his true colors). Yet the same affection seems present in letters they exchanged during the trials. One could also speculate that Harry might have appeared to Evelyn, if not consciously, then on some unconscious level, as simply a much more peculiar and debased version of White. Or even Jack Barrymore.

Like Stanny, but to a lesser degree, Harry did possess a kind of charis-matic intensity that undeniably affected those around him. He was at various times given to histrionically romantic, even sweet gestures à la White and Barrymore (the latter having spent money on Evie, although not his own). Like Jack, Harry had pursued Evelyn, knowing White was in her life, although what was unwitting youthful infatuation on Barrymore's part was full-blown calculated obsession with Harry. Of course with his immense wealth, Harry could give Evelyn the financial security she craved and the ultra-comfortable lifestyle she had grown accustomed to under White's "patronage" and considerable influence. In addition, Harry could give her a veneer of respectability she could get nowhere else. He had grown up with the advantages of money, and his cosmopolitan edu-cation and experience made him a frequently entertaining conversation-alist and a minor connoisseur, albeit not in the same league as Stanny (of which Harry was keenly aware). And, after all, Harry had risked losing not only his well-publicized inheritance but also his beloved mother's favor.

And all for "his Boofuls."

Although virtually all descriptions of Harry the demented wastrel and

Stanny the genius architect make much of their differences, the similarities between the two men are uncanny when dissected in the cold light of a hundred years. Both men had a Jekyll-and-Hyde ability to conceal the darker side of their personalities, even from their closest friends and family—and find excuses when it emerged. Each had paid chorus-girl accomplices to facilitate their introductions to Evelyn, and subsequently paid others to watch her in their absence. Knowing that Evelyn had a traumatic and foreshortened childhood as a result of the loss of her father and subsequent poverty, each at first acted the compassionate benefactor, expressing concern for her youthful innocence and welfare. And of course, fully aware of her impoverished background, each showered her with objects of wealth and luxury enough to turn anyone's head, much less that of a teenage girl who had felt real pangs of hunger and deprivation for most of her formative years. Each took advantage of her lack of moral supervision, as both men paid off her mother or maneuvered her out of the picture so that they could have Evelyn all to themselves—and then each proceeded to act contemptibly, eventually contributing to the utter ruination of her reputation. Ultimately, each man controlled her life so effectively that Evelyn was cut off from any and all friends or outside emotional support. And Stanny and Harry had each knelt before her and trembled at the mere touch of her dress, just as each had surreptitiously lured her into a "soft prison," but a prison, nonetheless. So, it seems, as far as Evelyn was finally concerned, if not Stanny, who had taken her first along with her only marital currency, then Harry, the man obsessed with that terrible truth and the man she had loved. And with currency to burn.

And what, after all, did Evelyn know about moral boundaries? Or the opposite sex? About true love? Or honesty? Or normalcy in any kind of relationship, familial or romantic? She had never dated any boys in Tarentum, Pittsburgh, or Philadelphia. With a truncated childhood and maternal negligence as her only experience, Evelyn was ill equipped to cope with repeated betrayal, disappointment, and loss at the hands of fate and her so-called guardians. Thrust into a world of grown-up men and responsibility while still a child, she was invariably surrounded by adults alone, first in the studios and then on the stage, where the emphasis was on her looks rather than her character. Her harried, self-centered mother offered little if any ethical guidance, and exerted just as little control over her daughter after repeatedly placing her in harm's way, then conveniently disappearing.

For better (or much worse), Evelyn's unfortunate choice to marry Harry probably gave her some little satisfaction by "putting it over" on the mother who had repeatedly put her in so many precarious positions—with strange families, strange boarders, strange "artistic" types, strange married men, and finally the strangest one of all, Harry Kendall Thaw.

From the Frying Pan into a Cauldron

Weakened by Thaw's relentless pursuit of her, compounded by the fact that her options were severely limited, that the theater world under Stanny's considerable shadow had lost its patina, and that Harry professed to be madly in love with her (and only her), even though he knew "the horrible Truth," Evelyn finally relented—and went from the frying pan into a cauldron. In February 1905, she had a sudden attack of searing pain where her appendix used to be and had to go back to Dr. Bull's sanatorium for treatment of internal adhesions and a month's rest. One month later, much to their chagrin, instead of a corporation or another coronet, the Thaws of Pittsburgh's Fifth Avenue and Smoky City society, who "might have added further luster to their brand-new escutcheon," got a common little chorus girl. And, as always, Harry got his way.

On April 5, 1905, twenty-year-old Evelyn Nesbit married Harry K. Thaw in a private ceremony at the house of the Reverend Dr. McEwan. The only people in attendance were Mother Thaw; Josiah Copley Thaw, one of Harry's brothers; and Frederick Perkins, the man who could claim to be perhaps Harry's one and only genuine friend from the days of his youth at Wooster Academy. Attempting to initiate her own familial reconciliation, Evelyn also asked that her mother be invited. So, against Harry's and his mother's wishes, Mr. and Mrs. Charles J. Holman came to the wedding. In a startling flaunting of tradition, the young bride wore black (with touches of deep brown), the bridal outfit having been hand-picked by Harry himself; it consisted of "a three-quarter-length opera coat trimmed in rare lace with Persian floral designs and a velvet hat with a silk entwined brim and a gorgeous feather of three shades of brown." The reason for the choice of costume, Evelyn explained to reporters later on, was that she and Harry had to leave immediately for their honeymoon, so it was more sensible for her to wear the traveling outfit. But perhaps she was already in mourning for the life she had to deny ever existed. Or perhaps Harry had instructed her to wear black as a rueful reminder that he was willing to take her as his bride even though Stanny had taken her first. Whatever the reason, if one were superstitious, it seemed more an unhappy omen than a practicality.

Throughout the brief ceremony, Evelyn never even took off her coat or hat. Harry had thrown his coat over the banister near the front door, only blocks from the door Evelyn's mother had been turned away from in disgrace. And now, in another ironic twist of fate, Evelyn would spend the next year living in that same mansion on fashionable Beechwood Boulevard where, as the newspapers saw it, like a number of *Florodora* girls before her, Evelyn had become "the Mistress of Millions."

From Evelyn's perspective, after having done everything she could to prevent the marriage, "after much discussion, after many heartaches, after great searchings of conscience and of soul"—all on the part of Mother Thaw—she had been allowed to marry Harry "in a Presbyterian church, within a larger Presbyterian circle, and sentenced in the terms of my marriage vow to live forthwith in the charmed circle of a Presbyterian home." Like the mirror image of Dante's Beatrice, in her own circle of Thaw hell instead of the brief paradise she had known with Stanny, Evelyn fully understood the Thaws' dilemma, even if they didn't. As she saw it, they were the ones at a disadvantage with regard to her presence. Among the things Evelyn did not fully recognize, however, was that she had traded one kind of monstrous mother for another. And that Harry's monomania regarding the great White was fired up again and threatening to blow.

THE GILDED CAGE

Evelyn and Harry occupied a wing of the Lyndhurst mansion, maintaining separate bedrooms as was the custom for married couples of the time who could afford such a luxury (and much to Evelyn's relief). Lyndhurst's interior was less like an English manor house than a Teutonic fortress, which on certain nights had a subliminal and awful resonance for Evelyn. The requisite predictable ivy, which overran the façade, only added to the damp gloom inside. It was not a cheerful place by any stretch of even a limited imagination. In addition to the ivy, heavy velvet drapes kept the sunlight out of every room, which to Evelyn was not such a great loss, considering "the distinctive lack of any great or even good art in the place." Harry, she said, was the only family member with any artistic side at all, the only one with any sense of how to decorate. Seeming at times morosely resigned to her fate and her "new family," Evelyn recalled in her memoirs that the "Pittsburgh home was never a home for me." But as she also stated unequivocally, she was a patient and faithful wife and Harry was "as good a husband as one might wish for." Compared, one might ask, with whom?

While the Thaws looked down their pug noses at Evelyn, she saw them as "not particularly well bred," and they were not "intellectually and socially among the gods." In her eyes, they moved "on a lower intellectual plane." But even though she claims she would have at least understood it, they didn't even try to patronize her. Underneath their upper-crusty surface, Evelyn suspected that such insecurity was based on the fact that the noble Thaws "had risen on very unsolid foundations. They had become financial aristocrats in a night." Their world was the "plane of materialism which finds joy in the little things that do not matter—the appearance of a new minister, the comforts of a pew, the profits of a church bazaar." No one and nothing so mundane could occupy Evelyn's thoughts sufficiently, especially since even reading novels was frowned upon as immoral, while the Bible left her "with the taste of salt in her mouth."

Evelyn's daily routine was always the same. Lunch and dinner with the family in the main dining room, often minus Harry, who was inexplicably absent for both meals with increasing frequency as the months dragged on. While she knew that, in general, "relations by marriage are seldom in sympathy" and that her situation was not extraordinary, Evelyn was at least bemused by the fact that her in-laws were in a terrible bind. As she wrote, "Socially, they felt they were at a distinct disadvantage in Harry having taken an actress for his wife (call me a chorus girl if you like; it makes very little difference which label you stick)."

Even so, there was literally and figuratively a brief honeymoon period during which time, when Harry was at home, he attended to various duties for his mother and kept his promise to Evelyn about his behavior. As he and Evelyn seemed to settle down to life in Pittsburgh, throughout much of their first year of marriage, Harry appeared to have had a change of personality, like Saul on the road to Damascus, which pleased Mother Thaw and surprised Evelyn. Perhaps Mother Thaw's prayers had been answered, since Harry seemed to have given up his diabolical hobbies and his pursuit of the white devil. Evelyn remembers that Harry was extremely patient and tactful in those early days, and whenever possible, he even shielded her from oblique attacks on her character from other family members. However, he seemed much less bored with the trivialities of church work than Evelyn, and was "a standing wonder—and a cause for admiration" in his various zealous forays into prayer service or organ funds, etc. Evelyn, however, could not work up any enthusiasm. Nor would she pretend. After all, hadn't she been forbidden to act?

Life at Lyndhurst, to hear Evelyn tell it, was a "benign and stately procession" of ministers whose wives "said things with a monotony and a sameness which lead me to suppose that there existed somewhere in America a school for ministers' wives where they were taught to say the same things in identical terms." One can only imagine that after the highly charged life she had known for five years, first with White, then with Barrymore, and then with Harry, life in the mansion at Pittsburgh held no charms or surprises whatsoever for Evelyn. The novelty wore off quickly as the terrible triteness and atrocious taste of those surrounding her pressed in upon her like a corset lined with jagged stones. Evelyn felt both emotionally and intellectually stifled in the "Presbyterian circle," whose members were "victims of tight, iron-bound ritualism." At least, she remembered slightly with tongue in cheek, that others outside the family treated her "with an attitude of forgiveness and charity. They hoped for the best."

Although it was understood by all who served in the household that Evelyn had no past ("as if she were Athena sprung full-blown from Zeus' head"), even though Mother Thaw "had demanded that it should be forgotten," and no one ever referred to her modeling or stage days, Evelyn said that she "lived in an atmosphere of grim consciousness" that she was a sinner whose name was "tacked onto the end of a list of distant relations at prayer time." She surmised that there must have been "a mighty lot of praying" for her behind her back during those days and months. Her own prayers "took the shape of a request that [she] might have the patience to bear the burden of [her] spiritual friends."

At first, Evelyn's curiosity about a type of person she had never known kept her occupied—these people whose views seemed "cute" to her, even though she could not get past the idea that it was somehow all an act. But when she discovered they were in earnest, that they believed in themselves, and that their terrible triteness was real and intractable, she sank into a kind of melancholy that can be read in her face in the photos taken of her during this period. It isn't hard to imagine how uncomfortable it was for Evelyn, constantly surrounded by strangers who pretended not to know what she had been, and whose obvious attitudes of forgiveness and charity were insincere and unwelcome. Even though it was well known that Harry had been thrown out of Harvard on charges of moral turpitude (he had been given three hours to evacuate the premises), as Evelyn recalled, she was the one chloroformed and squeezed under the microscope of moral scrutiny.

No longer blithely mingling in the heady atmosphere of Stanny's luminous Garden or Manhattan's dazzling and capricious midnight supper society, Evelyn now found herself (as she saw it) at the center of a small-minded church movement, where she was paradoxically an outcast in a clique of people whose lives were solely and in her eyes fanatically bound up in God's work. These were people to whom the words "Grace, salvation, light, [and] redemption come glibly," but who all too frequently "reduced to dry husks words that should have moved men and women to tears." This was Evelyn's first real exposure to serious organized religion, and perhaps most surprising to her was that the people who did a lot of organizing, shouting at, and criticizing of others, who "knew the rules of the game from A to Z... could therefore exploit it without exerting themselves to play it." As she saw it, this sanctimonious Sanhedrin "showed the same interest in religion that the public does in baseball."

Not surprisingly, Mother Thaw was a stickler for propriety, and try as she might (although she frequently didn't try very strenuously), Evelyn found it extremely hard to conform to the silly and restrictive social demands made upon her as the weeks crawled into months. As for so-called society life, the insipid and uninspired parties, receptions, and "at-homes," which generally ended by seven, with only the crumbs of crustless tasteless deviled ham sandwiches as a memory, drove Evelyn beyond the edge of boredom toward the catatonic. After escaping from one particularly dull function, Evelyn made her way to the back of the house, where in her exploration she found some rat holes in an outhouse. The prospect of flushing them out with a hose she borrowed from the gardener was more appealing to her than Mother Thaw's reception. And, she felt, as an exercise it put her in the company of creatures that were more honest, "since at least the rats knew they were rats."

Evelyn's life at Lyndhurst did little to change her attitude toward people in general, or her understanding of certain types of people at extreme ends of the social spectrum when comparing Broadway to Beechwood Boulevard. She tells of how the clergyman who married her, "a very nice, very fair specimen of Christianity," was a frequent visitor to the house: "One morning when we were sitting in front of the house, a dog of mine came along, and in its light-hearted fashion jumped upon the knees of the reverend gentleman. His reward was a kick that sent him flying." To his horror and the consternation of those Thaws who were present,

Evelyn jumped from her seat and swore like a sailor in as violent a language as she could summon at the good reverend. She admits that perhaps it was not the most tactful thing to do, but as "a great lover of animals," she just couldn't control herself.

As each dulling day crusted over, the younger Mrs. Thaw (or Mrs. Harry, as she was referred to when at home) began to harden into deep resentment at all the moldy holier-than-thou types she was forced into contact with nearly every day. Luckily she had learned patience in the studios, and so she made the best of an unpleasant situation as she had many times before, occupying herself with "good works" and planning social gatherings for "brainless socialites," if only to please Harry.

In 1915, Evelyn observed that the sob sisters who wrote tearfully during the trial of her tragic circumstances and life's wasted opportunities didn't understand in the least that she had never wanted to be simply "a shining figure in humdrum society." As she put it, she had no desire to be imprisoned by the "four walls of shapeless domesticity," and had assumed, wrongly, that life with Harry would be a series of trips to the Continent, fancy balls, and shopping sprees abroad with some time left for the occasional domestic bash. Admitting that her marriage to Harry was a mistake, she nonetheless asserted that no matter how much the Thaws chiseled and scraped away at her soul with their blunt little instruments in an attempt to fashion her according to their design, they could never impress upon her "unsympathetic surface the dim image of their God." For all their wealth and attempts to recast her, she considered them "puny" and "inartistic." Unfortunately, Harry was even less suitable to prolonged domesticity than Evelyn. And the honeymoon was about to end.

THE BEAST

Possessed by an earnestness perhaps inspired by the omnipresent cabal of professional reformers who surrounded him when home, near the end of 1905 Harry had resumed writing letters to Anthony Comstock and other vigilance societies trying to expose White and others in his crowd. With "boyish enthusiasm" he began an impressive campaign championing righteousness. And then a zealous Harry converted—back to his old ways. After months of seeming miraculously to forget him, Harry was suddenly more determined than ever to paint White as the blackest of sinners whose evil influence upon the young needed to be exposed. Fanatically preoccupied with White's continuing power and influence, and full of his own overblown self-importance, Harry also sank his teeth into a new bone: paranoia over White's movements in New York.

Evelyn recalled that Harry "imagined his life was in danger because of the work he was doing in connection with the vigilance societies and the exposures he had made to those societies of the happenings in White's flat." He was convinced that White had hired thugs from the notorious Monk Eastman gang to "fix him." "Because of this fancy," Harry began carrying a revolver for his own protection. He was advised to do so, he said, by a former policeman turned detective named O'Mara who had befriended Harry somewhere along his twisted road.

Evelyn (and the rest of the household) became aware of the gun only one cloudless day when, to everyone's alarm, Harry started taking pot-shot target practice out back near the carriage house, aiming at and sporadically hitting rocks, leaves, and anything that did not move. She remained unaware, however, that Harry was paying huge sums to private detectives to have White watched, in a vain effort to catch him with some coltish soubrette and prove him a monstrous ravisher of pure American virgins. But while Evelyn saw that her husband's virgin complex was but one of his mental aberrations, as she would later testify, she never thought Harry would have the courage to use the gun or act physically against Stanny. In fact, Evelyn never feared for Stanny's life. She feared rather for her own, on certain nights, usually in the pitch blackness of her bedroom.

It had been too much to hope for that the rivalry Evelyn believed she had ignited between Stanny and Harry would be extinguished with her marriage. Instead, it was still alive and growing frantically, at least to judge from Harry's distorted sights. From Evelyn's perspective, the worst of this new turn of the worm was that even though Mother Thaw had laid down the law about Evelyn's past being a taboo subject for discussion, Harry lifted the ban—but only for himself. And only when they were alone. Each day, he became more obsessed than ever with thoughts of White, and each night, he would come into her bed where he goaded and wheedled and bullied Evelyn into repeating the details of the day she first met White, of her modeling sessions, of her nakedness and horrible discovery that the Beast had violated her sanctity and girlhood. It was nearly as good as a whipping. And just as nearly titillating, if not more so.

One night he issued the edict that she could never speak White's name again—that she could refer to him only as "the Beast."

As she described the atmosphere in the house (in light of Harry's subsequent mad and lethal act), "Although I had no warning of Harry's intention, I had lived so much in this atmosphere of hate that I had no doubt as to the condition of his mind. I was satisfied, however, that things would never come to a climax. There was no reason why the two men should meet."

But at breakfast or lunch or dinner, if Mother Thaw was not around to hear, Harry interrogated Evelyn about her past. He began waking her up in the middle of the night, sobbing himself into dry heaves and demanding from her details he thought he had forgotten, which she was "loath to give." The subject of Evelyn's undoing was never "absent from his mind," and she "began to fear for his reason." Reevaluating her own reason, she also began to confront the terrible choices she had made, and cried to herself at night when comparing Stanny's extravagantly good-natured treatment of her ("in spite of that one thing") with Harry's infantile, petty, and vindictive paranoia.

One morning when they were alone at breakfast for the first time in a week, Harry abruptly told her that he had made an appointment for her at his dentist. She went, figuring any time away from his "White madness" and Lyndhurst, even a trip to the dentist, was better than her living entombment. What she had not figured on was the psychotic extent of Harry's jealousy. Not knowing on that first visit that Harry had explicitly directed his dentist to undo all the work White's dentist had done four years earlier, an unsuspecting Evelyn was subjected to having her teeth "fixed." Once the work was begun, it had to be finished or she risked infection and possible disfigurement. So, at some expense to Harry and nausea-inducing pain to Evelyn over the course of a month, any suspected trace of the dental work "the Beast" had paid for was drilled, pried, extracted, filed, and spit away. And then all redone exactly the same. (This would eventually weaken Evelyn's teeth and damage some irreparably; little of its effect, however, was initially visible in pictures.)

PHOTO OPPORTUNITIES

On his better days, Harry had one or another photographer come to Lyndhurst to take more formal portraits of his Tweetums than those Evelyn had become accustomed to with Stanny. Harry's first choice was his friend Burr McIntosh, who was a part-time New York actor and who had begun a high-class theatrical picture magazine, although McIntosh's schedule made it difficult to comply with Harry's often impulsive Pittsburgh requests.

Invariably, Harry insisted that Evelyn dress in white, preferably in ermines or starched white shirtwaists and skirts that made her look more like the innocent schoolgirl she had once been rather than a twenty-one-year-old despoiled former mistress turned repentant wife. Then, one day, Harry told Evelyn at breakfast that he had a photographic surprise for her and that it didn't matter what she wore. An apprehensive Evelyn entered the "salon" (living room) an hour later, with a cautious attitude and Harry's soft ham hands covering her eyes.

As he pulled his hands away, Evelyn saw the local "society" photographer whom Harry frequently hired, setting up his equipment. There was a large sheet hung somewhat haphazardly at one end of the room with a

slit cut about a foot and a half wide in its center and about seven feet off
the floor; one of Mother Thaw's ugly carved oak chairs was positioned
behind the sheet. Puzzled, Evelyn turned to Harry.

"It's the thing," he said excitedly, rubbing his hands together and grinning, "the thing. I am Bluebeard!"

Instead of panicking (and thinking perhaps he might rush at her with
a scimitar), Evelyn realized what Harry meant. One of the more ghoulish
fads at the time, popular with college girls, was to pose as one of

EVELYN'S MOODS

Evelyn posing as Bluebeard's wives
at Lyndhurst, 1905.

Bluebeard's wives. Girls would stand on chairs or boxes behind a sheet or quilt and stick their heads through slits made in the material. A girl would then have her crowning glory pulled up into a ponytail and pinned over her head onto the sheet, creating the illusion of a decapitated head. Some, to enhance the effect, added fake blood dripping from where the neck was supposedly severed and dusted flour or chalk on their faces to mimic the pallor of death.

But in deference to his mother, who grudgingly indulged Harry's recurrent desire to have his "little girl-wife" photographed within the confines of the home, there would be no gore on the sheet. Nor would he mar Boofuls's face with makeup of any kind. That morning and into the early afternoon, Evelyn stood on the chair, her head through the slit, her abundant uncombed mane fastened loosely above her head. As directed by a keyed-up and giggling Harry, the former professional poser assumed a different practiced expression each time the photographer took her picture. Several weeks later, he produced for Harry a small portfolio of the shots he had taken and the "special effects" he had achieved in several of them. One of those photos, *Evelyn's Moods,* shows her as the multiple wives of Bluebeard, her "severed" head reproduced five times in the same photo with different facial expressions. It was Harry's favorite, perhaps since he could forget she even had a body. He liked it so much that he included it in his book *The Traitor* twenty years, two asylum stays, and one divorce later.

Meanwhile, much to the socially sensitive Mother Thaw's utter dismay, Evelyn's ugly past kept rearing its pretty and still-attached head. The first time was Evelyn's reappearance on a polar bear rug, in an image known popularly as *Beauty and the Beast,* used for a sausage ad on a calendar sent out by a local butcher, Haudenshields's, that Christmas. The happy butcher thought this would be a superb New Year's present and sent them to all his customers throughout Pittsburgh. The horrified matriarch tried in vain to have them recalled, and shuddered at the thought of so many people being reminded of Evelyn's "polluted upbringing." Evelyn, on the other hand, was tickled pink and red, thinking it might be one of the best Christmas/birthday presents she had ever gotten. Then, in January 1906, the more infamous Eickemeyer photo, *In My Studio* (also known on postcards as *Little Butterfly*), was displayed at the Second American Photo Salon in none other than the Carnegie Art Gallery. The catalogue description reads, "The sultry showgirl, dressed as a Jap, is stretched at full-length on a magnificent polar bear rug."

In March 1906, much to Evelyn's delight, Harry announced that a trip to England was in the offing. He proposed that he, Evelyn, and his mother sail together, and proceeded to make the preparations. The fact that Mother Thaw announced a week later that she would go ahead on a different ship only sweetened the deal for young Mrs. Harry. The date of departure was finally set: June 28. The week of June 19, Tommy McCaleb, a friend of Harry's who had come for a visit to Pittsburgh, accompanied the newlyweds to New York, where they would spend the week before sailing.

Postcard advertisement for Mamzelle Champagne, 1906.
Handwritten on the card,
"Scene of White murder by Harry Thaw."

CHAPTER THIRTEEN

Curtains:
June 25, 1906

"I Could Love a Million Girls"
—*Song title from* Mamzelle Champagne, *1906*

It was so unseasonably hot that day that the hippopotamus in the
Central Park Zoo (who over time had become acclimated to New
York's weather) collapsed and later died from heat prostration. The
abnormal temperatures drove hordes of people out of the oppressive city
to the more inviting shores of Coney Island and the tent city of the
Rockaways. There, at the poor man's Newport, they could forget their
jobs for a few hours and distract themselves in any number of gaudy, conspicuous, cheap ways, enjoying two-cent root beers off Surf Avenue,
holding the towlines at Rockaway Beach, or riding the Tickler at Luna
Park. Meanwhile, down at the pier in Manhattan, John D. Rockefeller's
new imported French wig, ordered for a costume ball, was held up by
customs officials until a $75 duty fee was paid (which was ten times the
average working man's weekly salary). Gradually, the inhospitably muggy
afternoon melted into a sultry June evening. Although not the longest
day of the year, to some that night it would seem interminable.

A little before six o'clock, Evelyn, looking forward to a rare night out,
prepared herself in her hotel suite, the most expensive one at the emi-

nently respectable Lorraine on Forty-fifth Street and Fifth Avenue. Nellie Leahy, Evelyn's Irish maid for the last year, drew a second bath only a few hours after the first in the hopes that it would counteract the effects of the heat. The large windows in the suite were wide open, but all they let in was late-afternoon humidity. The burgundy moiré drapes hung limply. It seemed there wasn't a breath of air left in New York City. Evelyn immersed herself in the cool water and smiled at the bar of Fairy soap that Nellie handed her; she had modeled for one of their ads. It seemed like a lifetime ago. Or two, even though it had only been three, perhaps four years.

Afterward, Nellie helped Evelyn slip on a new white satin summer gown covered from its high neck to the long trailing Directoire skirt with hand-embroidered English eyelets and trimmed with black grosgrain ribbon. The dress was of the type denounced only recently by the *New York Tribune* as "little short of revolutionary in its application of such searching sculptural indiscretion to the female figure." As Nellie finished fastening the last of thirty pearl buttons in back, which ran from the waist to the neck, Evelyn swept her auburn-flecked hair into appropriate Gibson-girl stylishness. The slender Evelyn struck a familiar pose before a full-length mahogany cheval mirror as Nellie added the perfect finishing touches—a fashionably oversized ebony picture hat, a sterling silver hatpin from Tiffany, and sable gloves. The effect, as always, was stunning. As she studied herself in the mirror, she was reminded of Harry's insistence on their honeymoon that they stay at a particular hotel in Chicago simply because it was named the Virginia. At least Evelyn was sure Harry would approve of her costume, as long as he didn't realize that the hatpin was from Tiffany (whose building had been done by McKim, Mead, and "the Beast").

As they had numerous times before, the Thaws were to go to dinner and a show, one of Harry's choosing. Since coming to New York City a few days earlier for a brief stop before their European holiday, Harry had invariably controlled every detail of their daily routine—and with more vigilance than usual. Therefore, it was still a mystery to Evelyn which show they were going to see. She was sure, however, that it would be some musical comedy or comic operetta, since Harry maintained a single-minded soft spot for chorus girls and preferred *Higgledy-Piggledy* to *Hamlet*. Since her banishment from "theater-land" the year before and hibernation in the ivy-covered cave with her socially insecure mother-in-law, Evelyn attended the shows Harry selected with an air of wistfulness mixed with a whiff of regret and more than a little resentment.

Harry had gone early in the morning to the steamship office down on lower Broadway to get their tickets for the trip. He met a friend there, Jimmie Gerard, who was also booking passage for himself and his wife. They briefly chatted about the unusual weather, then Harry went back uptown, had lunch with Evelyn in their hotel suite, and spent the rest of the day at the Whist Club, or so he said. It was one of the few men's clubs in New York City where he was still allowed entrance, in spite of his outlandish antics in the past—and his imagined blackballing by "the Beast." Today, however, he seemed quietly engaged in making last-minute arrangements for their *bon voyage*.

The primary object of Mother Thaw's trip abroad was to attend, as had been announced in the Pittsburgh papers, the "fourteen-hundredth anniversary of the Hertford family, where she would join her daughter, the countess of Yarmouth." Evelyn suspected that the matriarch and moral juggernaut was going to assess the state of the troubled marriage between Harry's unfortunate sister, Alice, and "Count de Money." Happily for Evelyn, Mother Thaw, who had replaced Evelyn's mother as a cheerless hovering entity in her life, was already on her way to Liverpool "by cattle boat, which she preferred," Evelyn recalled, because it was cheaper and thus in keeping with her professed Presbyterian sensibilities (although Evelyn saw a certain aptness to that mode of transportation for other, less Christian reasons). Mother Thaw's pleasure-seeking son, however, would have none of that. He made sure he and his wife would follow in grand style on the German luxury liner the *Kaiserin Augusta*. Harry preferred the Teutonic ships to all others.

As they also had for several nights, the Thaws were to be accompanied that evening by Truxton Beale, a journalist, and Tommy McCaleb, the old family friend who had come to New York with them. Harry had of late developed a particular fascination with Beale, who several years earlier was rumored to have killed a man in California and was apparently acquitted under the "unwritten law" that a husband, following a "higher law," has the right to punish, even kill, another man with impunity who has dishonored a wife or sister. Evidently, as Harry had related with great enthusiasm to Evelyn a number of times, "public opinion had been with [Beale] from the start." Evelyn considered it a rather spurious basis for a friendship, but she had given up trying to figure out Harry's particular whims when it came to his erratic social relationships.

Ordinarily (when she wanted to), Evelyn was easily ready before Harry, having learned to change costumes in a breath as a result of her stage days. Harry, mired as Evelyn described in perpetual "babyhood," generally took longer than most women to prepare himself for an evening out. This time, however, Harry claimed to have grown impatient waiting for Evelyn to finish dressing. He left without her, telling her where she could meet up with him. Sporting a black tuxedo suit with pearl studs and a custom-made white straw boater, Harry also wore a hopelessly impractical long black overcoat. But this eccentric touch did not strike his beleaguered valet, Bedford, as particularly peculiar. Harry had of course done much worse, and Bedford had been witness to an unfair share of it all.

The couple met up at Sherry's, situated at Fifth Avenue and Forty-fourth Street, only a block from their hotel. The ultra-fashionable restaurant, like Tiffany, was another of the jewels in the crown of McKim, Mead, and White, which didn't occur to Evelyn at the time. She found Harry at the bar, where he had already polished off three drinks. In typical fashion, Harry had paid his three-dollar tab with a hundred-dollar bill as he took another cigarette from the gold case in his pocket. Together in their black-and-white costumes, the couple made for a noticeably strange and striking contrast—baby-faced Harry, over six feet tall, was completely muffled in black, save for the white straw boater pulled almost to his eyes, which darted nervously around the room; Evelyn, barely five feet, looked both doll-like and grown up in her ankle-length snowy dress, long black kid gloves, and large hat swathed in ebony black gauze, which surrounded her head like a dark cloud.

It was there they met up with Beale, who apparently was "not dressed," so they decided to go to another, less formal restaurant. The trio made their way to the Café Martin. The Café Martin, located in Delmonico's former building on Twenty-sixth Street between Fifth Avenue and Broadway, was a popular eatery in the theater district with a decidedly French ambience, whose wedding-cake interior consisted of charming layers of white and gold. A man could take his wife (or mistress) to the café without fear of exposing her to the less savory element of the city in the nearby Tenderloin district. Unlike the men's clubs, with their exclusionary policies, Martin's was decidedly democratic in its clientele. Annie Oakley and Buffalo Bill Cody frequented the place when his Wild West Show was in town. But on this particular night, when the Thaw party arrived, there were only the usual customers and a few of the gossipy gaggle of anonymous chorus girls.

Entering from the Twenty-sixth Street side, the trio was seated in the main dining area, where they were joined at around eight o'clock by Tommy McCaleb. Evelyn faced the elegant part of the room, whose huge windows overlooked Fifth Avenue, where the restaurant had a second entrance. Daylight still filtered in from the terrace and cast a lovely glow on Evelyn's face, described by one columnist during her modeling days as needing a blazing light to "bring out the soul of eternal loveliness unrivaled in any other's eyes." Harry sat directly across from her. During the course of their dinner, according to the waiter, who gave the Thaw party his exclusive attention while they were there, Harry "ordered three cocktails and drank them himself in rapid succession, in addition to a glass of wine." He also talked steadily and vociferously about everything from his mother's charity work to mountain climbing. Evelyn barely said a word.

Sometime during the main course, an impressive figure in natty evening dress entered the restaurant from the Fifth Avenue side with two young men in tow. The older man maneuvered his way through the sea of tables, almost as if the room were a bit too small for him, while the younger men followed in his wake. As he headed toward the balcony tables, the man's robust build and brush of reddish hair, "which stood up like velvet pile" flashed suddenly upon Evelyn's consciousness from across the room. She flinched involuntarily.

"He was an unexpected vision," she recalled.

"He" was Stanford White.

Whenever White entered a room, there was usually a flurry of activity and salutations. With him were his nineteen-year-old son, Larry, and a friend of Larry's, Leroy King, both of whom were in town for a visit from Harvard. White's wife, the former Bessie Smith of Smithtown, was at their country home in St. James, well out in Suffolk County, on the picturesque north shore of Long Island. Evelyn stole a look from behind her menu to see if Harry had noticed the small commotion caused by White's entrance. Apparently, he hadn't.

As Evelyn described it, "In spite of the heat, I went cold with fear." She began to shiver unconsciously. "I dared not make one false move, dared not cease my smiling and exchanging repartee" with Harry and the other two men. At first she thought it best not to say anything with regard to White's presence in the restaurant, since she knew Harry's insatiable and obsessive jealousy of the architect would most certainly ruin their dinner. The last thing she wanted was a public scene. Nonetheless, Evelyn could not keep her eyes from inadvertently wavering once or twice in the direction of the terrace.

"I thought my nerves would crack from the tension," she said.

With Harry's "help" and more than three years of hindsight, the former Kittens had come to see that Stanny's carefully designed seduction of her was perfectly suited to an architect of his ingenuity and potency, qualities that had drawn her to him, and that someone as disturbed as Harry would both admire and resent. As she sat, trying to fix her automatic sphinxlike stare at nothing, Evelyn couldn't help but hear Harry's words, uttered compulsively and incessantly for those same three years regarding that "depraved monster and defiler of tender girlhood," forcing certain phrases from her late at night in her bedroom as if part of some mad pagan ceremony. Over time, Evelyn had in fact begun to wonder which number on White's list she had been when he had plucked her ripe from the chorus. As she sat silent and (she thought) imperceptibly shivering, however, she suddenly recalled small flickers of Stanny's tender conversations in the Garden at night and clenched her napkin tightly in her lap.

In the past, Harry had instructed Evelyn to inform him whenever she saw White, and demanded that she refer to White as "the Beast" or "the B" for short. Those few times (before moving to Pittsburgh) when she had passed White on the street or in a car since their final parting on Christmas Eve, 1903, Evelyn made sure to tell Harry. Even though she considered it ridiculous, she suspected, correctly, that she was under surveillance. In her memoirs Evelyn describes the incident, which confirmed her suspicions:

> One day, I awoke with a sore throat and went to a specialist to have my throat swabbed. Coming out of the building, I ran into Stanford White. [They exchanged tentative looks.] That evening, dressing for dinner, I said to Harry:
>
> "According to my promise, I must tell you that I passed Stanford White on the street to-day." His face darkened.
>
> "Did he speak to you?"
>
> "No," I replied, "he just looked at me for a moment, and then I ran into the building. That was all."
>
> "You're sure that was all?" he asked suspiciously.
>
> "Yes."
>
> "Your word of honor?" he asked, remaining oddly unruffled.
>
> "Yes" was my reply.
>
> "That's right," he said approvingly. "All I ask is that you tell me any time you see him. If you don't tell me, I'll find out anyway. There are plenty of people who will tell me."

Harry, in fact, had mobilized his veritable web of professional spies and amateur informants throughout the city in anticipation of their arrival in June 1906. The actual purpose was threefold. The first was to keep a watchful eye over Evelyn's every move when he wasn't with her. (He had little to fear, since the combination of Harry's paranoia, possessiveness, and controlling behavior had managed to cut Evelyn off from virtually all family, friends, and acquaintances.) The second reason was to protect himself from the real or imagined enemies he believed were plotting to do him bodily harm. The third reason was to try and gain proof of White's debaucheries in order to discredit him publicly. Evelyn was unaware that earlier that very day, four of Thaw's detectives had followed White home and had tailed him for several hours.

A small ripple of relief passed over Evelyn once Stanny was clearly out of sight on the terrace. Harry asked her if she was ill, having noticed her involuntary tremors. Not wanting him to do anything rash should he suddenly become aware of White's proximity or think that this convergence was no coincidence, Evelyn asked one of her dinner companions for a piece of paper and pencil. On a small slip she wrote something like "The B was here but has left," hoping that would settle the matter. She passed the note surreptitiously to Harry. He read it and asked her if she was all right, noticing, he would later tell reporters, "that she was shaking like a reed." She replied that she was fine. He then smiled an inscrutable smile, pocketed the note, and ordered another "quart of champagne" even though he would recall in his own memoirs that he was "wild at missing him" and wondered to himself how the "blaggard had entered while he was unaware of his presence?"

"He had got out, how did he get out?"

The meal ended with only a minor incident. According to the cloakroom attendant who had checked Harry's coat and straw hat, "When I handed him the hat he literally jerked it out of my hand and in putting it on he crushed it down over his forehead and his eyes with a crashing sound which indicated that it had been broken by the violence of his treatment." As they emerged from the café, Evelyn eyed Harry with his cracked brim and winter coat and casually asked him if he felt hot.

"No," he replied coolly.

She then asked where they were going. Harry said he had procured tickets for the opening night of a new musical, *Mamzelle Champagne*. The color drained from Evelyn's cheeks. She knew that this particular show was opening at the rooftop theater of Madison Square Garden, just as she knew that, until that night, Harry had petulantly and defiantly refused to set foot in any building connected with White, which was next to impossible in the city Stanny had almost single-handedly redesigned. Evelyn was suddenly more than just dimly aware that the evening's itinerary had an uncanny pattern; first Sherry's, then this near close encounter at Martin's, and now the Garden.

The foursome strolled the single block to the Garden, and Evelyn felt light-headed from the combination of heat, wine, and general nerves. As they took the elevator to the rooftop, Evelyn asked Harry if he wanted to check his overcoat. He said no, and smiled in the same disconcerting way he had the day they first met. Evelyn closed her eyes, and Beale commented that it was already a little past nine o'clock. Harry, apparently oblivious to everything, chatted away about trifles with his two friends, his hands deep within his coat pockets.

Evelyn, who had memorized every click and grind of the elevator gears, knew without seeing that they had arrived at the roof. The party was shown to a table about three-quarters of the way back from the stage. Harry muttered something under his breath about the rotten seats. Evelyn said absolutely nothing. As the show began, while everyone else turned their attention to the noise and lights of the stage, Harry stared up at the illuminated Tower, which dominated the theater and rose in the gathering shadows on Twenty-sixth Street. Like some unconscious symbol of White's potency, it "loomed," and it seemed to Harry that "its bigness increased in the darkness." Harry followed it high up to the "little windows where she suffered," and imagined as he had a thousand times how horrible those memories must be for her, that sacrifice of her whole life which he never let her forget.

Even though she had looked out over the enchanted Garden from White's Tower countless times before, Evelyn was always struck by the magic and splendor of the place, as if seeing it for the first time. In an age when spectacle was the rule of the day, the open-air theater, like everything Stanny ever did, was electrifying, glamorous, and almost overdone. She sighed as she stared at the familiar scene before her, as if temporarily mesmerized by the twinkling lights of various colors; she remembered how they would sway rhythmically at times when a breeze lifted them, the undulating strands resembling fireflies noiselessly hovering in the air. Large and luxurious potted plants were strategically placed throughout the tables that faced the stage to create a feeling of intimacy under the canopy of the vast night sky.

Of course, one special table several rows from the stage was always reserved for the creator of the Garden, but when Evelyn and Harry sat down, to her relief, that table sat empty.

As Viola de Costa, a plumpish and pretty chorus girl whom Evelyn had known, popped out of a giant papier-mâché bottle of Pommery Sec, Harry and his companions ordered champagne. He held his glass up to Evelyn, who turned and feigned interest in the show to hide a swelling sense of uneasiness. As she later put it, "We were there just long enough to be bored." It was apparently clear to even novice theatergoers and first-

The murder scene: the Madison Square Garden rooftop theater.

nighters that *Mamzelle Champagne* would probably be short-lived. Some of the patrons, in fact, took to booing and hooting periodically, while other critics in the audience merely drank and chatted rudely in Irish whispers, oblivious to the performance taking place.

A number of people had begun milling about among the aisles, making it difficult for the waiters in their white aprons to bring patrons their drinks. This added to the audience's general restlessness. Suddenly, without a word, Harry also left the table and was instantly hidden from Evelyn's line of sight by one of the large, leafy plants.

What had drawn him away was a man he had spied sitting alone at a table near the back. Harry recognized James Clinch Smith, Stanford White's brother-in-law, from across the theater and stopped at his table. Smith, who knew Thaw only in passing, said that he was there for lack of anything better to do. Harry engaged him in some mindless small talk, then the conversation ended. Harry came back to his table and took a few sips from his glass of champagne, then left again and disappeared just as quickly as before into the crowd. Beale had also left the table, and as Evelyn sat and listened to McCaleb's critique of the uninspiring performances and music, she watched Harry fade into the glare of the stage lights against the evening sky beyond. The next day, several witnesses said that an agitated Thaw could be seen pacing back and forth at the rear of the roof garden "like a caged tiger."

A little before eleven o'clock, with the show nearly over, a small disruption like the one in the Café Martin drew some people's attention to the elevator. Evelyn glanced in the direction of the noise, where to her dismay, out stepped Stanny, alone this time, who headed for his usual table. She immediately scanned the faces in the audience for Harry, but could not find him. White had originally planned to attend to some business in Philadelphia that evening, but since his son had come to visit, he stayed in town. Several people who recognized him applauded, and White acknowledged their greeting with a wave of his hand. He then took his customary seat five rows from the stage, and began to watch what was left of the performance, resting his chin in his right hand and throwing his other arm casually over the back of the chair.

As the director of the Garden, White had seen the show several times in rehearsals. In fact, he had already been at the Garden that day. About five hours earlier White had made an appearance behind the scenes, where, during a break in their final run-through, he observed the chorus girls huddled around a water cooler, some of whom were wilting from the heat. White directed the stage manager, Lionel Lawrence, to fill the cooler with ice and lemonade for the girls. He also reminded Lawrence that he wanted to be introduced to a particular girl, "a little peach" named Maude Fulton, "Evelyn-like and seventeen," who was new to both New York and the stage. But Lawrence was unable to oblige, because of the bustle over last-minute preparations for opening night. He didn't even notice his employer's departure.

A preoccupied Evelyn jumped when Harry abruptly reappeared at their table. Harry, who again seemed not to have noticed White's entrance, sat down and almost immediately began fidgeting in his chair. Neither Beale, who had also returned, nor McCaleb thought this unusual, since some part of Harry was almost perpetually in motion. Onstage, several of the featured chorus girls, dressed in fencing costumes with cartoonish red-heart appliqués on their white shirtwaists, were singing a song about dueling over a woman's affection, "I Challenge You to Love." It was, Beale commented, "bloody awful." Evelyn shot a furtive glance at Harry, who suddenly stood up again, a somewhat dazed look in his eyes. Less than ten minutes had passed since White had entered.

Evelyn nervously looked up at Harry, who now perched over the table like a huge, distraught crow. She suggested in a somewhat faint and strained voice that they leave. Beale and McCaleb readily agreed. Appearing to comply, Harry, who hadn't taken off his coat all evening, helped Evelyn with her wrap. The four began walking toward the elevator, leaving the general noise of the music, conversation, and clinking glasses behind them. The golden Diana, shimmering with the hemisphere of mirrored lights at her feet and the theater below her, serenely gazed at the city from her privileged spot, her bow arched in ceaseless readiness. At his table below, White spoke briefly to the Garden's caterer, a man named Harry Stevens. He asked Stevens to arrange an introduction after the show to the little peach he had his eye on and who had just finished her debut song, "Could I Fascinate You?" Stevens obligingly headed backstage.

It wasn't until she was nearly inside the elevator that Evelyn, her arm in McCaleb's, noticed that Harry had once again vanished. Drawn away, perhaps even urged on by the lyrics of the song "I Could Love a Million Girls," which the tenor Harry Short was performing onstage, Harry Thaw had doubled back:

> *I've heard them say so often they could love their wives alone,*
> *But I think that's just foolish; men must have hearts made of stone.*
> *Now my heart is made of softer stuff; it melts at each warm glance.*
> *A pretty girl can't look my way, without a new romance ...*

Having just spoken with one Harry while another sang onstage, White was unaware that a third was advancing upon him swiftly and silently from behind. Trying to see over McCaleb's broad shoulder through the archway to the elevator, Evelyn stood on her toes and frantically scanned the audience. A rush of pins and needles ran up the pearl buttons on the back of her dress. Less than thirty feet away from where she stood, the darkly muffled figure moved within a few feet of the unsuspecting architect in his seat.

Seconds later, a startlingly loud gunshot pierced the torpid night air. The musicians faltered. Evelyn recoiled and stared stricken in the direction of the sound. Suddenly everything melted into slow motion and the world stopped on its wobbly axis. She opened her mouth in a silent scream. In the flash of those seconds, which seemed to last an eternity, she saw everything. She raised her trembling hand to her lips. Two more shots followed in searing rapid succession, forcing everything into spinning, pointless motion again and causing her to flinch with each blast. Evelyn looked up at McCaleb.

"He shot him!" she finally cried.

Before anyone else knew what was happening, Stanford White's body was covered with the scarlet spray of his own blood, which began to deepen almost immediately into a sickening dark burgundy. As it edged around his toppled body on the floor, the overturned table lay next to him, having been pulled over with the force of the body; the architect's blood began to seep into the twisted tablecloth. Those closest watched in horror as the jagged crystal shards of his wineglass disappeared in the mushrooming puddle. Part of his face was torn away, and the rest was blackened beyond recognition by powder burns. Harry had stood less than two feet from him when he held the muzzle of the pistol to White's head at eye level and pulled the trigger. One bullet lodged in his brain behind his left eyelid. A second, penetrating his nasal cavity, broke part of his jaw and three teeth, while the third struck him in the right shoulder and then passed through his elbow. Harry stood transfixed, his right hand and starched white cuff and gold cuff link spattered with White's blood. Some witnesses said the victim looked at his attacker in amazement at the last second; others said he never saw it coming. By all accounts, however, they had exchanged no words. The *New York Times* reported the next day that White, whose body had been jolted upright by the force of the bullets before it fell in a heap, was unquestionably beyond any earthly help instantaneously.

Immediately afterward, like some demented avenging angel of death in his black coat and broken white halo of a hat, Harry, his own face deadly white, held the barrel of the gun over his head and let the unused shells fall with a brassy clink to the floor. For a second or two there was a dreadful, penetrating silence. White's blood, mixed indiscriminately with the wine from his shattered glass, began to spread toward Thaw's feet. Harry K. Thaw "of Pittsburgh," with a glazed yet triumphant look in his eyes, shouted to terrified witnesses:

"I did it because he ruined my wife! He had it coming to him. He took advantage of the girl and then deserted her!"

At that very instant, twenty-one-year-old Evelyn's fragile fairy-tale world, which had always edged too close into nightmare, evaporated forever like a childhood dream. And at fifty-two, Stanny was dead.

At first, a majority of the nine hundred people in attendance thought the gunfire was part of the show. But as the grisly reality of White's murder became evident to those seated closest to him, horrified screams now cut through the thick air. The refrain of "I Could Love a Million Girls" froze on the lips of the tenor as the orchestra, some of whom could see White's toppled body, continued to play confusedly in fits and starts. Some people seated near the back of the theater, still unaware of what just happened, shouted, "Go on! What's the matter?" thinking the gunplay was part of the show.

But among those nearest the murdered man, a panic ensued. Within moments, frightened theatergoers from all corners of the Garden scrambled to reach the elevator. As Evelyn described it, time had compressed and now unnaturally expanded; it was like riding the el seated backward and rushing at breakneck speed but going nowhere.

"People were running about, herding into safe corners, calling for help. The ushers and waiters tried to calm them, to get them back to their seats."

From Harry Thaw's perspective, as those nearest him tried to move away, stunned and frightened by this stark black apparition of death, their eyes were riveted to him and the gun he still held over his head in manic triumph. The crowd surged so close to the roof's edge he feared for an instant "that some might be forced over the railing and plunge to the street eighty feet below."

The scene took a decidedly surreal turn as the stage manager, Lionel Lawrence, still not sure himself what had happened, ordered his orchestra to continue playing. Three of the chorus girls, upon seeing White's lifeless body, fell in a dead faint to the stage floor. The other girls, who hurried to the edge of the stage, their painted faces distorted into masks of horror illuminated by the footlights just below, ran hysterically into the wings in a blur of silk and feathers. The music trailed off pitifully. The mother of the lyricist, attending her son's first opening night (and having witnessed throughout the evening the hostile or disgruntled audience's unfavorable reaction to the show), feared he might have been the target of a particularly harsh brand of criticism, and screamed, "Oh, they've shot my son!"

Terrified and confused people were still stumbling and nearly trampling over one another in a frenetic attempt to reach the central elevator while Lawrence jumped up on one of the side tables and announced rather pointlessly that "a most serious accident has occurred." The closest official to Thaw was a uniformed New York City fireman from Engine Company No. 60, Paul Brudi. The fireman gingerly approached a wide-eyed, pasty-faced Thaw and asked him to "relinquish his weapon." Thaw seemed almost relieved, and handed the fireman the sweat-covered gun, as if giving some waiter a particularly generous tip. He was then escorted briskly in the direction of the elevator.

A dumbfounded Evelyn, her face ashen, screamed abruptly in disbelief as Harry walked toward her, "My God!" and "Oh, Harry, what have you done?"

She repeated this, crying, "You're in a terrible fix now." Harry smiled his idiosyncratic smile, took hold of Evelyn, kissed her on the cheek, and said, "It's all right, dear. I have probably saved your life." McCaleb, also pale and shaking, said, "My God! You're crazy!" Beale stood by, mute and amazed. As Evelyn described it years later, "A complete numbness of mind and body took possession of me. . . . I moved like a person in a trance for hours afterwards."

In contrast to the tragedy above, an absurdly comical scene was taking place one floor below. Albert Payson Terhune, a husky young newspaperman for the *New York Evening World* who was covering the opening for the paper's honeymooning drama critic, had witnessed the murder from a mere few yards away. After running at breakneck speed down a flight of plush red-carpeted stairs to the corridor, where the sole telephone booth stood, he found it occupied by a man engaged in "a smirking conversation with one Tessie." After the man refused Terhune's polite request to relinquish the phone, the muscular reporter yanked him away, eager to break the unbelievable news of the murder to his editors. While pleading with an apathetic operator to connect him to the city desk in a hurry, Terhune suddenly found himself under attack by the man whose conversation with Tessie he had abruptly ended, accompanied by a friend armed with a chair. People rushing past in their attempt to escape the theater saw the agile Terhune fending off both men with one leg and his free arm, shouting his unbelievable scoop into the phone.

As some of the less squeamish or more inebriated patrons pushed forward to stare in morbid fascination at White's corpse, someone ran back toward the dressing room to look for something to cover him with. A somewhat bemused and exhilarated Harry Thaw waited for the elevator, his hands twitching nervously. Asked by the fireman Paul Brudi, to whom he had given the gun, "Why did you do it?" Harry calmly stated, "He deserved it. He ruined my wife and left her helpless." At that moment, Officer Anthony L. Debes, whose beat was the theater district, emerged from the elevator and put his hand on Harry's shoulder.

"You're under arrest," he said.

"It's all right," replied Harry strangely.

They stepped into the elevator, and just as it was about to close, Evelyn, ghostly pale and trembling violently, ran into the car and threw her arms around Harry. Beale and McCaleb followed in astonished silence.

"Why did you do it, Harry?" she asked.

"It's all right," he repeated mechanically.

Harry then turned to the policeman and said, "Here's a bill, officer. Get Carnegie on the phone. Mr. Andrew Carnegie. And tell him I'm in trouble."

The policeman ignored him.

When the elevator reached the ground floor, Evelyn, appearing stunned and shrunken, was swallowed up by a large touring car that Beale had hailed at the curb. Meanwhile, as Harry Thaw emerged from the Garden, he calmly lit a cigarette. For some reason, Debes had agreed to Harry's request not to be handcuffed, and the two walked in the direction of Fifth Avenue through the disoriented and distressed crowd, virtually unnoticed. Finally, Harry and his escort arrived without any fanfare at the nearest police station. It was the Tenderloin precinct. The millionaire turned murderer was handed over to another policeman. When asked by the desk sergeant to present himself, Harry, still looking oddly dazed but dapper in his tuxedo and bent skimmer, approached the sergeant nonchalantly.

"Did you know the man you shot?" the sergeant asked.

Harry looked at the floor as if in profound deliberation. After some thirty seconds' reflection, he replied, "Yes."

Back at Madison Square, the lights of the Garden were dimmed as the last of the patrons were escorted to the crowded street, many of whom, insensible to their surroundings, stood in shock and disbelief in the path of oncoming traffic. A discordant noise from the motorists and carriages could be heard up on the roof, where White's body lay in thick and awful silence. Due to the gunpowder burns and gruesome nature of the architect's wounds, when James Clinch Smith had walked past the body, he was unaware that the murder victim was his own brother-in-law. Six years later, Smith would be one of the doomed passengers on the *Titanic.*

Summoned by the police from his father's Gramercy Park house at 121 East Twenty-first Street, a stunned Lawrence White, who had just returned from another theater, arrived at the Garden. When asked, he said he had never seen Harry Thaw in his life, nor had he ever heard his father speak of him. After that, the traumatized nineteen-year-old simply stood throughout the mercilessly humid night as silent sentinel over his father's unbearably still body, now covered with a dressing gown soaked and stiffening with clotted gore. With the street below evacuated and the sky above the deserted rooftop a stagnant vacuum, it was as if the world had stopped again. Even Diana seemed paralyzed.

"If only he had gone!" White's son later cried, feeling pangs of guilt for inadvertently postponing his father's business in Philadelphia by his arrival in New York. Once the news of White's brutal murder hit the newsstands the next morning, some reporters already were beginning to speculate that the architect had "reaped the whirlwind." But it was the former model and chorus girl who would stand at the eye of a gathering storm unlike anything anyone had ever experienced.

Mamzelle Champagne, which by most accounts would have closed that opening night or soon after, had an astounding surge of ticket buyers throughout the rest of the year, with eager patrons requesting to sit at Stanford White's table to see for themselves "the scene of the blood-spattered tragedy." No one, however, could have predicted the "journalistic circus," the "orgy of misplaced sentimentality," and unparalleled theatrics that were to follow in the wake of White's murder.

Seven months later, when questioned on the witness stand, both the Madison Square Garden doorman and a Tenderloin cabdriver said essentially the same thing. They weren't surprised White had been shot. They were just surprised that it had been a husband.

"Everyone always figured it would be a father."

THE NATIONAL POLICE GAZETTE

THE LEADING ILLUSTRATED SPORTING JOURNAL IN THE WORLD.

RICHARD K. FOX, Proprietor.

NEW YORK: SATURDAY: JULY 14. 1906.

VOLUME LXXXIX. No. 1500. Price, 10 Cents.

EVELYN NESBIT THAW.

Mrs. Harry Thaw on the cover of the Police Gazette
two weeks after the murder.

CHAPTER FOURTEEN

⟲✤⟳

Aftershock

A rich man has been killed, a rich man did the killing, and so a world sits up
to hear the tale in every red and dripping particular.
—*Alfred Henry Lewis, Newspaper clipping*

According to the righteous Reverend Charles A. Eaton, John D. Rockefeller's
pastor, "It would be a good thing if there was a little more shooting in cases
like this." —*Newspaper clipping, 1906*

Less than an hour after the crime, rogue reporters alerted to the
murder and hungry for immediate gratification grew to a fearsome
pack. They began prowling throughout the city, "scavenging for the puniest morsel of information," "purveyors of salacious and demoralizing
minutiae of vice." A large number waited outside the Hotel Lorraine
along with an almost equal number of photographers, hoping to get an
exclusive shot of the "lethal beauty." Others waited impatiently outside
the Tombs for some word about the "playboy killer" who had yet to
appear. Frantic efforts were under way to find every photo ever printed of
the lovely younger Mrs. Thaw, while editors were equally anxious to
secure the best sketch artists available to capture the effect of such "harrowing circumstances on her fragile beauty"—once she could be found.
Because the child bride had vanished, as if into thin air.

Some editors were in a quandary, not knowing whether to refer to her
as Evelyn Nesbit or Evelyn Thaw. Several journalists questioned indi-

viduals loitering in the vicinity of the Garden, where people who had not
seen a thing cheerfully offered their version of the events. Some of the
more resourceful reporters began to ferret out the haunts of anyone who
might have had contact with the three principals in what was already
being referred to as "The Madison Square" or "Garden Tragedy." Maneuvering their way up and down Broadway, through the Tenderloin district
and the surrounding areas, newspapermen invaded saloons, restaurants,
and hotel lobbies in search of anyone who had a story to tell, some for the
price of a cigar or a Rheingold.

Back at the Tenderloin station house on West Thirtieth Street, the
police who had confiscated Harry's valuables looked them over: a fine-
grain leather wallet containing $166 in bills, $2.49 in change; a gold
watch; a solid-gold cigarette case; several blank checks; and an empty
leather holster hanging like a lifeless black tongue. They also found in his
coat pocket several letters and calling cards, all of which identified him as
"Harry Kendall Thaw, Pittsburgh." To everyone's surprise and amusement, when asked to identify himself for the desk sergeant, thirty-five-
year-old Harry, perhaps hoping to take advantage of the public opinion
that he had the babyish unwrinkled look of the perpetual sophomore,
replied "My name is John Smith. I'm an eighteen-year-old student from
Philadelphia." (Harry claimed in his memoirs that a reporter from the
Herald who spoke with him briefly on the way into the police station had
advised him not to use his real name.)

He was then taken to a back room in the station house while the desk
sergeant wrote his age down as twenty-eight. Harry was told by those in
possession of his calling cards, checks, and letters, "Look, it's useless to
try and hide your identity. Is there anything you'd like to say about the
shooting?"

Thaw gazed at the floor again, as if trying to make something out of
the pattern in the well-worn planks, and then said he would wait for his
lawyers. The police shrugged their shoulders and took him back to his
seat. Since he was obviously a gentleman, they still didn't feel the need to
handcuff him.

Harry sat in a stifling back room on a long bench between two hefty policemen who regarded him with only passing interest, neither caring about the tuxedoed, blood-spattered celebrity they had in their midst (he had lost his topcoat at some point). After a few minutes, Thaw pushed his partially cracked hat back on his head at a comically rakish angle, stretched out his long legs, and coolly lit another cigarette. He never asked about the fate of the "fat scoundrel," having seen for himself the gruesome results of his arm's-length shots. At the trial one of the policemen would recall that he had "a far-away look" in his "bulging eyes," and looked "kinda spooky," a black shapeless mass shrouded in the haze of his own smoke.

True to form, Harry had sent the policeman at the front door to buy some cigars for him with ten dollars and instructions to find a bar that sold his special brand. He asked almost as an afterthought for either Mr. Longfellow or Mr. Choate, his lawyers of choice at that moment. He was wise enough to continue to refuse to make any statements without the presence of his lawyers (a fact that would be offered at the trial as evidence of his sanity). At one-thirty a.m. the coroner, a Mr. Dooley, reached the police station and asked to see the prisoner. After some witnesses were brought in to make statements at three a.m. and identify Harry as the shooter, Thaw was officially charged with murder and escorted across the Bridge of Sighs two stories up from the street into the Tombs, where he was locked up. The reporters who had waited on the street below had been effectively and deliberately ducked and thus deprived of an exclusive first shot at him, much to their disappointment.

As he sat in a cell choked with humidity and "beleaguered by the shouting of drunken prisoners," Harry believed that night he heard the voices of young women, sounding uncannily like his little wife, from adjoining prison cells. "A girl cried and her voice seemed young and another shouted to someone 'She's enercent!'" (It is unlikely that he heard anything sounding remotely female, unless it was echoes from the other side of the Bridge of Sighs, since there were few women prisoners and they were in a separate section of the prison.)

Harry interpreted these voices as a heavenly sign that his deadly act had divine approval, and folded his tuxedo jacket neatly under his head for a pillow. In spite of his situation, a confident Harry believed that a carefree, immaculate life like a clean slate was now going to open before him and his Angel-Child. He considered that Evelyn was safe at last from the "tentacles of the Beast." In his euphoria he even thought that they might consider having children. At the same time, detectives had finally been dispatched to the Hotel Lorraine with instructions to "pick up the accused's wife." But as the mob of reporters already there infesting the lobby and the sidewalk informed them, "the lady had vanished."

By two a.m., reporters in Pennsylvania had wasted no time in seeking out Evelyn's mother, Mrs. Charles Holman. A handful were so bold as to knock at her "pretty cottage door." Described the next day in the papers as "prostrated," Evelyn's mother at first refused to believe the story that reporters were telling her, then she broke down and wept bitterly. After she had been quieted with some mild sedatives, the paper reported, "She said she did not know White, had never seen him, and that so far as she knew, her daughter did not know him." Soon after, it was reported that she left for New York and most people assumed it was to join her devastated daughter. In fact, Mrs. Holman went to meet her husband, Evelyn's stepfather, who happened to be in New York on business. He had been there for several days, unaware that Evelyn was also in town. Contrary to everyone's expectations, however, there would be no family reunion.

HEADLINES

In spite of the fact that the murder had occurred so late the evening before, an astonishing assortment of facts and half-truths were already printed in the morning newspapers and delivered along with the milk to an unsuspecting public. Some reporters described in thrilling detail the panic that had ensued on the rooftop, while one of the most sober of the more than twenty-eight daily papers, the *New York Times,* reported that there had been no panic whatsoever among the theatergoers. The *Times* was wrong. Its headline read simply:

A crowd gathered beneath the Bridge of Sighs,
connecting the Tombs prison to the courthouse,
the day after the murder, 1906.

THAW MURDERS STANFORD WHITE
Shoots Him on the Madison Square Garden Roof
ABOUT EVELYN NESBIT

Unsubstantiated rumors began to leak out in the press about the "Garden Tragedy," some wildly speculative—that Harry Thaw had been obscenely intoxicated or doped up on opium, that his wife had refused to break off her friendship with the dead architect, that White had spoken disparagingly about Mrs. Thaw at the Café Martin and had boasted about their past relationship in front of her outraged husband—even that Evelyn had shot White! Almost anything was considered newsworthy. It was reported in another paper that more than a dozen women had fainted in Madison Square Garden (not counting the chorus girls), but that happily, no one had been run over by any electric motorcars or beer wagons. One paper, in an unintentional play on words, reported that one of hard-drinking Harry's sisters, Alice, was the "Countess of Vermouth."

Just as quickly as information spilled onto the streets, the district attorney's office was flooded with misinformation. Some of the more inventive witnesses insisted that a beautiful, young, and slim dark-haired woman in a large white hat and a filmy white veil, which "fell about her shoulders like wings," sat with White at his table just before the shooting. Others insisted, accurately, that he was alone from the moment he sat down until Thaw shot him, which was all of fifteen minutes. It was seriously suggested that perhaps the mistaken witnesses had seen the ghost of other young girls White had destroyed. Or that it might have been the angel of death in disguise.

The *World* quoted a Mr. Nott from the D.A.'s office: "I get a new tale every minute . . . and so far neither the police nor the force of this office has been able to substantiate one of them. . . . I never knew of a case in which there were so many rumors which were without a grain of truth."

The glint of Thaw's gun in the air under the hot lights of the theater caused some witnesses to swear that the millionaire murderer had used a golden gun. Upon closer inspection of Harry's .38-caliber revolver, however, they noticed that it appeared slightly rusted, as if it had been carried in his pocket for some time without a case. When questioned about it, Harry offered that indeed he had carried it with him for more than a year. The police, who seemed always half a step behind even the greenest reporter, puzzled over a reasonable motive for the murder.

Anthony Comstock, who saw a golden opportunity to promote his own causes, issued a statement two days after the murder about how Thaw had "cherished enmity against White" for some time prior to his marriage to Evelyn. Apparently, Harry had phoned Comstock after the inquest (against the advice of his counsel). It was subsequently revealed how Harry had for the last year and a half (and previously) supplied Comstock with funds and information regarding White's suspected practices.

"He seemed very anxious to punish White," Comstock was quoted as saying. He then added darkly, "In more than one instance, when it seemed a clear case had been made against White, the victims of the man were spirited out of town."

Comstock did not stop to think that his statements could be used in court to prove premeditation on Harry's part. Neither did Harry.

Far from the almost hilarious pockets of noisy, disorganized activity ripping open around the city, a much more somber and virtually silent scene was being played out as young Lawrence White made his way by train to his parents' home in St. James. It took him about three hours to reach the house, and after that, he sat for several more hours outside his mother's bedroom door, waiting to break the terrible news to her. The papers the next day reported that Mrs. Bessie Smith White had taken the news calmly. But it was a different story for Stanny's aged mother, Mrs. Richard Grant White, who like Mrs. Holman, was "prostrated" by the news of her son's death. The family thought it best not to tell her the circumstances of his death, eventually settling on the suggestion that it had been done by an anarchist. The next day, the Gramercy Park house was besieged by sympathetic callers. Messenger boys ran themselves into a full sweat as they delivered cablegrams by the score from as far away as Japan and Russia.

The *World*'s headline told the story:

Stanford White Stretched at the Feet of Venus
Architect's Body Lies in His Beautiful Drawing Room in City Home,
Near the Ancient Statue of the Venus Genetrix,
Taken from the River Tiber

Ultimately, White's family decided to cancel a memorial service scheduled for St. Bartholomew's Church, one of the architect's most splendid designs, out of fear of an expected crush of the "morbidly curious." The papers continued to hint at the now crumbling façade of the dead man's life. The *World* on Thursday, June 28, 1906, read:

Men in White's Set Shiver and Keep Silent
Twenty of Them, Some with Brains and Others with Money,
Are Keeping Close Watch for the Dreaded Subpoena-Server
Not a Word in Eulogy of Dead Intimate
From Millionaire's Parties to the Morgue

Mother Thaw, meanwhile, arrived in Liverpool. The minute she stepped off the boat she was informed of her son's deadly performance at the Garden's rooftop theater. Far from being prostrated, she promptly and stoically got on the next available ship, the *Baltic*, and sailed back to New York. Her daughter Alice would follow a short time later.

The Victorian picture of mournful maternal concern, Mary Copley Thaw would be the only one consistently depicted with unqualified sentiment and sympathy throughout the trials. Few but Evelyn, however, knew that she was also a vain and obstinate woman, and that Harry's inheritance from his mother also included a tendency to erupt into violence. As described by one writer years later, not only was she "ungovernable in her abuse" of servants, of the law and its representatives, and of Evelyn, but her "inordinate social ambition" often provoked an unholy wrath. Mother Thaw had been known on several occasions to heave the bulky Pittsburgh city directory at the head of her secretary when displeased with her tardiness in tending to church business. Evelyn had also seen evidence of Countess Alice's familial if latent aggressive tendencies: Once, when poking into unused rooms at Lyndhurst out of boredom and curiosity, Evelyn discovered Alice Thaw's girlhood mahogany boudoir table. It had a deep rut worn into it and several other spots that had been made by Alice with her ivory-boned hairbrush after consistent and repeated beating.

THE "CAUSE OF IT ALL"

A horrendous and surreal night dissolved into squinting, painful early morning for Evelyn, who had not slept for even five minutes. Having had a good deal of practice avoiding Harry and his detectives over the last few years, Evelyn managed to escape detection by police and the press as she left the scene of the crime, earning her the nickname of "the girl Houdini" by one reporter. She wondered for a moment if perhaps she hadn't just had a horrible dream. But she knew she had been awake all night, and that instead of packing her things and relaxing in a plush stateroom on a luxury liner, she was in the tiny cramped apartment of her only real friend, former Weber and Fields chorus girl May McKenzie. After having seen Stanny's bloodied face blackened into a horrific and unrecognizable death mask before her eyes, she had gone instinctively to the only other home she had—to the heart of the theater district Stanny had once shared with her. She realized May's apartment, run by a no-nonsense woman named Mrs. Molloy, could provide only a brief refuge. For two days, the sound of the gunshots echoed through her brain as the throbbing in her head became unbearable. Increasingly prone to migraine headaches (which doctors called neuralgia), Evelyn would not sleep for two more nights. The usual sleeping powders were useless.

With a heart like a leaden plumb line, Evelyn knew she could not stay in hiding any longer, even though she wanted to "bury herself forever beneath six feet of concrete." The first time she appeared in public, pale and wan and dressed in a somber brown outfit, "with a thin soft veil hanging from her hat to her delicately formed chin," she had to run the gauntlet of cameramen who had camped outside the prison steps. All the papers speculated as to whether Evelyn would be forced to offer testimony at the inquest to be taken later that morning in front of the Grand Jury. Grim and tight-lipped, she was told, much to her relief, that she was not required to answer any questions after refusing to say anything that might incriminate her husband.

After that ordeal, she ran the same gauntlet of flash powder and shouts from the army of newsmen that would surround her for the next two years. She had hardly reached her rooms at the Lorraine when she fainted. The hotel doctor had to be called to revive her with camphorous smelling salts. As the small veiled figure passed them in the lobby some of the hotel guests indulged in speculation as to the fate of the Thaws' social standing back in their Smoky City. But if the Thaws were about to be "mash[ed] in muck," "poor little Evelyn, faithful and alone," was about to be "trapped in quicksand." And even though she was in New York, her mother had not materialized to offer comfort or support. Nor would she.

Harry's valet brought him a sober gray business suit for the morning's events and informed his employer that he was on some list of the district attorney's. Harry asked about the lawyers, Delafield and Longfellow, who had shown up, as opposed to those he had wanted. He questioned why he couldn't have two of the most famous lawyers in the country, Joseph H. Choate and William B. Hornblower. He protested "politely" to a detective when handcuffed for the first time as he was taken to police headquarters (a novelty for Harry, who was the one usually locking the cuffs). He was told by a thin-lipped, pruny inspector, "We always handcuff murderers," and was whisked off to have his photo taken for the rogues' gallery before being placed with other prisoners awaiting inspection or interrogation by detectives.

After a brief stop in the Jefferson Market Police Court, where he was formally charged with homicide in the first degree—willful murder—and committed to prison without bail, Harry was then taken back to the Tombs to sit on "Murderers' Row." Later that same day, as a team of alienists was being put together, called in from all parts of the country to test Harry's sanity at the request of both the defense and the prosecution, the police extended their net for actual witnesses to the murder, still hoping to find a clear motive while wandering in a fog of ineptness and confusion. At almost the exact same time, the funeral train bearing White's body and a full carload of roses, gardenias, chrysanthemums, and hyacinths left at nine o'clock from the Long Island Rail Road station, bound for eastern Suffolk County. Within the hour, Harry Thaw's inquest would take place.

Evelyn had spent just a few nights in May McKenzie's tiny apartment before reluctantly going back to the Lorraine to be with the rest of the Thaws, by which point Harry had been placed in an eight-by-nine-by-twelve-foot cell that would be his home for the next seven months. Incarcerated in 220 on the second tier on the Centre Street side of the Tombs (as duly reported in the papers), Harry found himself, much to his dismay and displeasure, with a murderer on one side of him and a man arrested for criminal assault on the other. He did not like being in such proximity to common criminals, especially since he still believed that White had paid off vicious gang members to do him harm if they ever got near enough—and both of these men were far too close for comfort.

The police were informed by the Pittsburgh authorities that Harry had been unusually agitated for at least a fortnight before the murder. It came to light that he had "run afoul" of two different people in Pittsburgh, a tobacconist and a streetcar conductor, both of whom got into fistfights with Harry. Not surprisingly, in each instance Harry got the worst of it, even though he had provoked the attacks. He was not good with his fists.

Harry had gone to the district attorney's office two days after the murder, surrounded by alienists hired by his attorneys and the prosecution. The names, when run together, sounded like yet another law firm— McDonald, Mabon, Flint, and Hamilton, the first three being the D.A.'s team of "bug doctors." The novelty of alienists struck many as a "sham" pseudo-science, "voodoo hoodoo." It was the same day the newlyweds had planned to set sail for Europe, but instead Harry sat in his cell and steadfastly refused to submit to an examination by any "bug doctors." As he nervously awaited his mother's arrival in New York, he sent out a barrage of hastily scribbled notes to friends and associates, against the advice of his counsel. And even though it had been only two days since the murder, Harry had already received mail, "consisting of seventeen letters, most of them addressed in the handwriting of women." These were well-wishers who applauded Harry's heroism, based on what they had read in the papers. Guards reported that Harry smiled quite happily as he read the letters and lay back on his cot, although he was still upset that the prison had not allowed Bedford to bring him another change of clothes. Burr McIntosh, his friend who had featured Evelyn's photo a number of times in his magazine, asked the police if he could bring Harry some food, which Harry had requested in one of the notes. McIntosh's request was refused.

It was not long after, however, that Harry's photo appeared on the front pages of every newspaper, sitting in his cell, fork in hand, dining happily on squab and steak brought in from Delmonico's. He had apparently also convinced the prison physician that he required a bottle of wine or champagne a day "for medicinal purposes." The public's response was mixed. Some were outraged by the obvious privileged treatment, others were amused, and his lawyers were beside themselves, trying to keep their bubbly, babbling client and publicity-mad crusader from ruining his case before it ever went to trial. Nor would the transformation of Harry from demented playboy to shining hero happen without a price. As one writer described it, "The gilding of the figure was not effected without gold."

As for the more detached audience across the Atlantic, they were nonetheless drawn into the Garden tragedy at Madison Square, in part because of the connection the Thaws had to British royalty, however slight. And geographical distance seemed to provide some critical distance as well. The London *Telegraph* said that the murder merely created a "mawkish desire to make a virtuous hero out of a degenerate criminal." The London *Times* extended its criticism to an entire class (while commenting on the lack thereof): the murder in Madison Square Garden offered a "glimpse, and not a pleasant one, of wealth without elegance or refinement; luxury without culture ... much costly eating and drinking and fine clothes with coarse manners." Nonetheless, in spite of feigned indifference and a superior attitude, during the first week and a half of the trial, the London papers published more than seventy-two portraits of the captivating Evelyn Thaw. And the stage was now set on both sides of the Atlantic.

Back in Manhattan, Thomas Edison's studio rushed to put a film version of the *Rooftop Murder* into nickelodeons only a week after the actual crime (with wild rumors that Evelyn played herself in the film). With curious audiences eager for an up-close view of the reenactment of the Garden tragedy, the film pushed *The Story of Jesus* out of its spot as the top box-office attraction. Meanwhile, confronted with what was already being called the "crime of the century," no one paid attention to the mention in the papers near the back pages that the hippo who had died a day earlier in the zoo was buried quickly in a quiet nonsectarian ceremony in Brooklyn.

Ad for a film based on the murder, funded by the Thaws, 1907.

CHAPTER FIFTEEN

Dementia Americana

Everyone's record is a secret more or less,
A trifle chequered, although people never guess.
Cut up your capers—
But don't get them in the papers—
For you're done for if you once get in the press.

—*Newspaper clipping, 1906*

And whoso counts me but a fool for leaving a tender maid untouched when
I have her in my house, to him I say he measures purity by the vicious standards of his own base soul.

—*Euripides,* Electra, *translation included in Harry Thaw's* The Traitor

In one of those cosmic quirks of timing, Mother Thaw arrived in New York on Bastille Day, Saturday, July 14, determined to liberate her son from the dungeonlike Tombs. But even the indomitable Mother Thaw could not fight the entire Empire State so easily or quickly. She was met at the dock by Harry's brother Josiah, whom Harry believed had been fooled by his incompetent lawyer, Lewis Delafield. Josiah told his mother that he would not give Harry any more money to pursue a course of action with new attorneys, which Harry had demanded. He also informed her that Gleason, Delafield's partner, had declined to see the "ill-starred Evelyn," who Harry believed could simply declare what White had done to her, whereupon he would be released, with apologies and applause all around.

Harry was immediately disenchanted with his first attorney, Delafield, the man after whom he named his memoir, *The Traitor,* and whom he described as "a creature far meaner and uglier than Stanford White, aside from White's one vice": "White was a type by himself. He was a character that does not appear once in a hundred years. . . . There was a bold audacity about White's vices; there was a slinking putridness about the contemptible tactics of the Traitor."

At the time of his arrest, Harry was worried about Delafield's effectiveness, since none of his own family or friends had ever used him in any of their legal dealings. But Delafield had been put in place by default, since the family's other attorneys, Longfellow and Hartridge, were experts in business and financial law (and at that time the "mourning matriarch" was still somewhere in the mid-Atlantic). In fact, none of the Thaw lawyers was well versed in criminal procedures, which only helped complicate the case right from the start.

At Delafield's request, Harry gave him an initial fee of $10,000 by check and sent for $15,000 more from Pittsburgh. Then it was suggested by someone that he hire a different lawyer, a Mr. Black, who was a family friend. In Harry's eyes, the case should be fought on its own merits. The stunned and shaken Evelyn stuck by her husband, merits aside. But with Harry in prison, Evelyn was at the mercy of the Thaws.

Surprisingly, Harry hadn't wanted his mother to come back from England; he had cabled her not to come, but by that time she was already on the ship headed for New York. Whether or not he wanted to spare his mother the heartbreak of seeing her son in such a dire place or he considered her a liability at this point (since he believed her emotions might cloud her judgment), Harry thought he had everything under control. He didn't. He knew his mother would find a way of spending vast amounts of money wrongheadedly. She did. He also dreaded the inevitable confrontation between his mother and Evelyn, who was being touted in virtually all the newspapers as "the cause of it all."

But after three or four days had passed, it seemed to Harry that his nominal counsel was only pretending to represent him and was in reality working for "the head of that nest of degenerates in 22nd and 24th Streets." Harry believed that Delafield's intention was to "railroad [him] to Matteawan as the half-crazy tool of a dissolute woman." When Lewis Delafield suggested halfheartedly that Harry hire Delancy Nicholl, a man more familiar with criminal law, to replace him, Evelyn reminded Harry that Nicholl was one of White's many lawyers. Reports began to surface in the papers that perhaps Thaw would not fight the charges against him and would plead insanity. Harry was convinced that the source of this speculation was his own counselor, and decided that Delafield was in cahoots with the dead man's guilty partners in perversion.

After three weeks Harry dismissed Delafield, which meant that at the inquest, Harry was represented by an interim counselor, who "the baby-faced millionaire murderer" said "looked more like a janitor." Refusing to talk until he could have a lawyer he would be satisfied with, Harry unwittingly stopped himself from offering testimony that could have been used to prevent the case from going to trial. With stenographer at the ready, the district attorney had planned to save the state an enormous amount of time and money by declaring Harry insane. After all, there was no doubt that Harry was mentally unbalanced. He had killed White in front of nearly a thousand witnesses and was now happily taking credit for it.

In fact, Delafield had been perfectly willing to allow the insanity defense. And as Harry suspected, he had indeed been working with the district attorney's office for a swift end to the whole ugly mess, not only to save Harry's life but also to protect others whose reputations might be tarnished or even ruined should the case go to trial. Perhaps Delafield also suspected that there was no other way for Harry to avoid the electric chair, especially given Evelyn's past as a model and a chorus girl, which would make any defense based solely on Harry's claim that he was protecting her innocence difficult at best. Even Harry's own alienist, Dr. Allen McLane Hamilton, hired under Harry's protest by his defense team (and who would prove embarrassingly ineffectual on the witness stand), wrote to Josiah Thaw in early August: "I am quite at sea as to what to do as in your brother's case. By the papers I see that your mother has unreservedly committed herself to his [unsound] . . . and futile defense, which will eventually land him in the electric chair. I am in a position to know that the district attorney is in possession of facts that will flatly contradict Evelyn Thaw."

But no one could appease Harry, who was hopelessly obstinate throughout the months leading up to his trial. By the time Hamilton wrote his letter to Josiah, the firm of Black and Olcott had already been "turned out" by Harry and replaced by Hartridge and Gleason. Nor would these new attorneys represent Harry at trial.

In the meantime, friends and enemies alike, as well as Comstock's revitalized and omnipresent Greek chorus of conscientious righteousness, seemed to scurry or bluster their way out of the wainscoting to offer either assistance or character assassination of the trio involved in the Garden tragedy. Stories quickly began to make bolder accusations about Stanford White's character. One headline read, "White Reaped the Whirlwind and Paid the Ultimate Price."

Lurid tales of White's incredible proficiency at womanizing also began to surface. One reporter asked facetiously if there were some phrase he could use other than "womanizer," since the issue wasn't women but girls: "He attended musical plays where there was likely to be the grandest display of irresponsible beauty," one paper reported. Another anonymous source, referring to Evelyn, stated that White had "made every attempt to thrust himself upon the child's notice."

"White was a rounder," or so said producer George Lederer (in whose second divorce Evelyn was named a co-respondent—along with ten other chorus girls). Lederer also offered opinions on the Thaws. He described his former "Wild Rose" as having a "frivolous disposition," while he characterized Harry as "a cigarette fiend [who] always seemed half-crazed."

Unflattering or increasingly hostile descriptions of White accumulated at an astonishing rate; he was labeled "a sybarite of debauchery, a man who abandoned lofty enterprises for vicious revels." He was "an engine of creation and destruction," "a charming companion, a man of kindliness possessed of many talents . . . but not bound by scruples." Hearst's paper reported that he was "the most oriental and luxurious rake in his subtle and splendid equipment for the ruin of women." According to the Thaw family's hired publicist and apologist, Benjamin Atwell, White was "as respectful to women of the stage who demanded respect as he was to his wife's friends. But when they were young and powerless and posed no threat . . . he was capable of revolting mistreatment." During his life, White had dreaded public exposure of his infidelities and had worked furiously to prevent them from leaking to the press, but now as the proceedings moved forward with a frightening momentum, an avalanche of negative publicity threatened to crush his formerly sterling reputation into gravel.

The prosecution quickly found in preparing its case that it could not maintain control over the situation. Rampant dark rumors and dim innuendo purported to be facts about White were happily offered by unsavory inhabitants of the Tenderloin, some of whom wanted to shine however briefly in the glare of publicity, while others were paid by the Thaws for their "cooperation." Sadly, few friends came to White's defense publicly. His closest friend, Gus Saint-Gaudens, was incapacitated, dying from cancer up in New Hampshire, and only one other man was brave enough to defend White's memory publicly. It was Richard Harding Davis, the model for the Gibson man, a popular war correspondent, and the author of a number of adventure novels. After a devastating *Vanity Fair* editorial, which painted White as nothing short of diabolic, Davis wrote a response in *Collier's*, August 8, 1906. He angrily accused the tactics of the yellow press of being "hideous" and "misshapen" in their attempt to denounce White and forever stain his memory:

> Since his death White has been described as a satyr. To answer this by saying that he was a great architect is not to answer at all. . . . What is more important is that he was a most kindhearted, most considerate, gentle, and manly man, who could no more have done the things attributed to him than he could have roasted a baby on a spit. Big in mind and in body, he was incapable of little meanness. He admired a beautiful woman as he admired every other beautiful thing God has given us; and his delight over one was as keen, as boyish, as grateful over any others.

As far as the press was concerned, all they knew for sure was that their circulation figures were "leaping by the hundreds of thousands" with each new twist to the story. The D.A.'s office also tried to defend White's character, stating to the press, "It is ridiculously easy to besmirch the character of a dead man who cannot reply or institute a suit for libel." But these pronouncements were lost amid the hectic tumbling circus of noise and misinformation, the "orgy of misplaced sentiment" and "homicidal hysteria of yellow journalism" that the Thaws and their millions were financing.

Even White's professional reputation began to suffer. The *Evening Post* stated that he was "more of an artist than an architect," and that at least in some of the buildings he left as his legacy, there was evidence of the moral decay and "social dissipation" that undermined his life. The *Nation* expressed a similar opinion regarding White's plummet from grace: "The follies of his time and his own frailties did everything possible to undo the great artist in Stanford White. . . . Severe moralists will find the cause in his devotion to pleasure. . . . He adorned many an American mansion with irrelevant plunder."

White's sins also offered a convenient platform for more radical social critics who could use the dead architect as their scapegoat and as a symbol of the not-so-starving but rather self-satisfied if thwarted artist, co-opted by decadent consumerism at its most debased by those who neither knew nor respected the splendid things their money procured. As the days pressed full speed ahead before the trial even began, critics seemed unified in their judgment: by "shutting himself up in the musky atmosphere of adoring cliques, building residences, clubs, and mausoleums for the rich," Stanford White had frittered away his genius. And sold his soul.

DISAPPEARING ACTS

On the other side of the gilded gates, Mother Thaw, who had worked as strenuously as White to keep her own secrets locked away (including a family history of insanity as well as her son's immoral escapades), was alternately apoplectic and dyspeptic as she watched the Thaw name thrust daily into a glaring and notorious public spotlight that she was, ironically, financing. Within a week of the murder, surprising or disturbing Thaw-related developments and rumors began to fly just as fast and furiously, as if on the express track out of Pennsylvania Station.

The first occurred when Harry's faithful valet of eighteen years, William Bedford, died suddenly and mysteriously. Everyone suspected that the loyal Bedford had witnessed more than his share of Harry's aberrant behavior, and wondered if his abrupt and final departure wasn't part of some twisted Machiavellian plot by the Thaws to protect Harry's tinseled image as defender of the blameless and the innocent. Apparently, no one was aware of any preexisting malady—except Harry, who blamed the district attorney's office and its tactics for hastening Bedford's death. Although the exact nature of the valet's illness was never disclosed (peritonitis was suspected), Harry wrote, "Knowing that my poor valet was very ill and should be in bed and receiving proper care if his life was not to be endangered, the district attorney's staff made him sit and sit in their offices for days and days. Mortally brutal, they made him sit when deadly ill until he had to be taken to the hospital at once. He was operated on the next day. The following day he died."

This happened only one week after Harry's arrest, and to an already traumatized Evelyn, Harry seemed disturbingly and incomprehensibly unemotional about the death of Bedford, the man who had been closer to him than anyone (save his mother) for half his life. The only emotion he showed was to rant at the D.A. "and his minions."

Coming hard on the polished heels of Bedford's suspicious demise was the abrupt resignation of Evelyn's maid, Nellie Leahy, who had been with her for more than a year. Nellie was "wrought up" over the "unintentional murder" of White. Bedford's sudden death, coupled with feeling a chill on a warm day, stoked Nellie's Irish superstitions. Convinced it was time to leave, she came up to Evelyn in the drawing room of the hotel, blurted out, "Someone has walked over my grave!" and promptly quit. Harry maintained that the district attorney's office had arrested one of her relatives as a way of suppressing any favorable testimony she might offer, "in that way getting rid of her as they did of Bedford, even if it was not so drastic."

"I Told You So"

In spite of such disturbing events, for his part, Harry seemed annoyingly cheerful and buoyant to Evelyn when she came to visit him in his cell: "He had no doubt as to the righteousness of his act or . . . its wisdom. He never then or at any subsequent time expressed the slightest regret for his act." (One of the few times in his life that Harry ever even alluded to the incident, or so it has been told in a now famous anecdote, occurred in Florida, near the end of his life. Supposedly, when confronted with a monstrosity of a building newly erected on the fringes of Miami Beach, Thaw remarked to a companion, "I shot the wrong architect.")

But if Harry was suffering at all in prison, and on most days it didn't seem so to Evelyn, she was suffering a far more miserable and paradoxically public confinement, having merely been maneuvered from one gilded cage to another. Even when surrounded by the mounting number of hangers-on who battened themselves to the Thaws and their millions, Evelyn was utterly alone.

The attitude of the Thaw family following the murder was, not surprisingly, one of unwavering united support for Harry as they offered an ivy-covered uniform brick façade to the press and the public—Mother Thaw; the countess of Yarmouth; Mr. and Mrs. George Lauder Carnegie; Josiah Copley Thaw, Harry's financier brother; and Edward, the youngest sibling. But their attitude regarding Evelyn was a relentlessly stinging and reproachful "I told you so." Evelyn, subject to what she described as only a handful of "isolated instances of kindness," soon saw that any small act of nicety on the part of the Thaws was the result of their realization, after consultation with lawyers, of how much depended upon her and her testimony.

Initially, Evelyn and Mother Thaw went together to the Tombs to visit Harry in a show of solidarity for the battalion of reporters who watched their every move. One of the days when Evelyn was still riding with Mother Thaw to the Tombs, their car was stopped in heavy traffic. A policeman strolled up to the car at the crossing, Evelyn having become a familiar figure to the police. Evelyn and the traffic cop chitchatted for a little while, although she noticed out of the corner of her eye that Mother Thaw sat with rigid face and stiff back in the corner of the automobile. When they had moved on, Mrs. Thaw turned to Evelyn with a shocked expression.

"Evelyn," she said reproachfully, "how can you speak with these people? Don't you realize the social position you hold?"

Having no illusions anymore about the social status of the Thaws, an angry Evelyn retorted, "Mother Thaw, you have got to realize that the social position your son now holds is associated with the Tombs Prison." She continued, telling the glaring woman that "with reporters watching our every movement and on the hunt for 'copy,' what kind of a story do you imagine it would make if I turned up my nose at men whose social position is, at the moment, infinitely superior to Harry's?"

Mother Thaw remained unmoved, and sat like an Easter Island statue carved out of ebony instead of stone and covered in imported black lace.

Because Mother Thaw was spending the majority of her time in New York, she was unable to control the Pittsburgh press. It soon began to surface in the hometown papers that Harry K. Thaw had been for years considered more than just "a mild sort of degenerate." The headlines read, "Pittsburgh Rent by Thaw's Act." To add injury to insult, the Thaws' mansion had been burglarized the day after the murder and $60,000 worth of Mother Thaw's jewels were stolen, the thieves having read about the family's absence in the papers.

As for Evelyn, described in the Pittsburgh papers as the "Woman Whose Beauty Spelled Death and Ruin," to the unsympathetic she was now Delilah, Jezebel, and Salome all rolled into one. Nor was she prepared for another blow—her family's abandonment of her, the family she alone had supported throughout her entire adolescence.

At first, between visits to the Tombs to see Harry and meetings with other Thaw family members, between the preliminary consultation with a multitude of lawyers and questioning by the police, a preoccupied Evelyn didn't notice her mother's glaring absence from her side. Neither was she fully aware of her brother's growing bitterness toward her. But Howard had grown extremely fond of White, whom he saw not just symbolically as a kind and indulgent father figure, but as the only father he had known since the age of seven. Howard, who had also become inseparable in the last few years from White's secretary, Charles Hartnett, wanted to repay White somehow and felt it his duty to defend the name of the man who had played such a large role in his otherwise limited, fractured, and insignificant life. For nineteen-year-old Howard (the same age as White's son Lawrence), this meant shunning his sister, the person he too came to view as responsible for White's tragic end. It was Harry, in a rare moment of clarity, who suggested in a letter to one of his lawyers that his lawyer "quietly call" on Evelyn's new stepfather, Charles Holman, to intervene and take care of Evelyn. But if the lawyer ever made the overture to Holman, there was no response, either from the Mr. or the Mrs.

On any given day, Harry was champing at the bit to go to trial; in fact he looked forward to finally having a public forum to expose the "set of perverts" who preyed on upright and chaste young girls, as Evelyn once was. He was sure that the man in the street supported him and Evelyn, as did "every policeman and detective in New York City." "And," he was sure, "the great tide of sentiment could not be turned back." So the idea that there might be no trial, that he would somehow be forced into an asylum not as the conquering hero but as a lunatic murderer, sent him into paroxysms of rage and tears. He went into a purple frenzy at the thought that the public might think he was sitting in a straitjacket and drooling into a spittoon.

The media seemed as schizophrenic as Harry in trying to describe the role of the principals in the case. While many tried to run with the Edwardian notion that Harry was Sir Galahad, others began to report how he had been involved all his life in "costly and humiliating escapades" from which his poor mother had to rescue him, with Mother Thaw often covering exorbitant checks (and hiding his peculiar moral bankruptcy), which Harry tried to cash with insufficient funds on both counts. One story asserted that when in school, he had "taken courses in dissipation," even though Harry believed that he had thousands of years of history on his side, going all the way back to Cicero: "When life or liberty to self, or in those we must protect, is in danger by robbers and enemies, any means is allowable to defeat their nefarious ends."

There was of course other front-page news. A Pennsylvania Railroad express train had rolled into the Philadelphia station with a dead engineer standing at the lever. The man had apparently had a heart attack somewhere between Philadelphia and Trenton. The heroic fireman who had noticed the unusual speed of the train as it approached the station jumped into the cab and stopped the train as it barreled into the train yard, barely avoiding disaster. But there would be no one to stop the Thaw engine as it gathered steam and threatened to crush any who might interfere with the wheels of their particular well-greased defense of heroic Harry Thaw, protector of wife and home. When two weeks became two months, the "Garden tragedy" was still dominating the headlines; little did anyone realize that it would continue this way, with only brief and intermittent periods of relative quiet, for two years.

The murder, coming as it did in the midst of insurance scandals, Roosevelt's trust-busting, and the like, prompted the working class to suddenly look more critically at the "filthy rich." As the young century progressed, one by one the wealthy and powerful were being knocked off their high horses, and increasingly it seemed the greater the fall, the more pleasure it afforded the common man. Uncommon wealth may still have been synonymous with superior social position, but it no longer meant moral superiority. In fact, the rich were experiencing a backlash. Whereas the nineteenth century had upheld the belief that God rewarded the deserving, the young twentieth century, disillusioned by the extraordinary and blatant immorality of the typical millionaire, destroyed that notion forever. New York City in particular, in the words of Irvin S. Cobb, was depicted as "a bedaubed, bespangled Bacchanalia." It was, some glibly proclaimed, doomed to collapse like the Roman Empire.

And with the help of the "new Pandora," in spite of what appeared in black and white in the press, there were far more shades of red than anyone could have predicted.

MRS EVELYN
NESBIT THAW
BY
H Loomis
N.Y. HERALD—

H. K. T. was informed
comber 24th, 1903, S
theatre from which
went to the restaur
a revolver with h
that E. N.
that would
before that
25th day of 1906,
of New York where S
ried a revolver but did
he was not in the City
resided; that in 1904 H
Europe together and re
living together as husb
Autumn of 1904 return
on the return from Eu
H. K. T. they continue
and wife; that from J
first of April, 1905, H
to time his offers to m
ways declined upon the
subjected to such usage
S. W. that it would not
the wife of H. K. T. b
H. K. T. to derision or
friends of S. W. and ot
by E. N. knew of the tr
ceived from S. W.; that
the mother of H. K. T.
of E. N. and H. K. T.
first day of April, 1905,
H. K. T., and that ther
of April, 1905, E. N. a
in the City of Pittsburg
their respective parent
between E. N. and H.
wedding journey and t

Newspaper illustration of Evelyn on the witness stand, 1907.

CHAPTER SIXTEEN

A Woman's Sacrifice

I must tell all that is to be told, because around this night . . . circled the tragedy which destroyed the life of one man, helped to undermine the reason of another, and dragged me into the fierce light of publicity and of criticism. —*Evelyn Nesbit,* Prodigal Days

It is a frightening experience to hear a thought to which you have never given words babbled aloud in the street. . . . It sets you frantically anxious to amend, to contradict, to correct. Your little secret is everybody's secret now. It has gained in importance, has been twisted in detail until it is like nothing you ever knew. —*Evelyn Nesbit,* Prodigal Days

Absolutely no one was prepared for the incendiary media firestorm ignited by Stanford White's murder, not even Evelyn, who had grown used to intrusive publicity and frequently boorish or questionable methods of investigation and speculation on the part of reporters. As she wrote, they could "cover a horse show and an electrocution in one day . . . and give no indication they are impressed by either." But the "Garden tragedy" exploded with an unprecedented molten force upon an unwary public, whose growing taste for tabloidism became clear as they "gorged themselves on every morbid morsel."

Much to her chagrin, it was Evelyn's predicament that took center stage in what would become, among other things, a battle of the journalistic sexes—giving rise to a whole new form of reporting in America and a new labor force, "those women with three names"—the sob sisters.

THE SOB SISTERS

Nicknamed "The Pity Patrol," the sob sisters shared a spiritual kinship with Nathaniel Hawthorne's "damned mob of scribbling women" fifty years earlier. As aspiring writers, their only hope to break through the male bastion of the fourth estate was to replace tough, cynical, hard-nosed coverage with a softer alternative, which in this case meant offering a "womanly perspective," filtered through the sympathetic gauze of an overly sentimental style of writing befitting their "feminine skills" and "intuition." Hired to cover the Thaw case by three of New York's biggest newspapers, the sob sisters sprang up virtually overnight to provide day-to-day tear-jerking, heart-tugging reportage. Aided and abetted by the social and political climate of the day, the sob sisters entered the journalistic arena by fixing their sights on Evelyn (who would have preferred to remain in the shadows). And they did so with a florid, maudlin vengeance:

> Her baby beauty proved her undoing. She toddled as innocently into the arms of Satan as an infant into the outstretched arms of parental love. And she is not to be blamed for it. As well may the frail girl martyr be blamed for not having successfully defended herself against the ferocious attacks of the hungry wild beasts when placed in the arena to be their prey for the pleasure of the populace.

The sob sisters sought different angles from their male competitors with which to approach the crime of the century. For many, the cast for a bodice-ripping melodrama turned morality tale was perfect. White was the typically reviled, mustachioed, lecherous older married man who had seduced, deflowered, and abandoned the unworldly young country maiden. There was the maiden's husband, Harry of Sooty City, the knight in tarnished armor who had killed for the sake of American womanhood and the love of his angel wife. And there was the child bride, the girl who had been victimized by a cruel fate and a crueler voluptuary. Not surprisingly, a number eventually turned the spotlight on the mothers in the case, both of whom proved to be deliciously sensational fodder. But while the elderly and histrionically widowed Mother Thaw got the mawkishly compassionate best of it, Mrs. Charles Holman eventually got the worst. As the drabs and dribs of Evelyn's sorry childhood spilled into public knowledge, Evelyn's mother was branded an "inhuman monster and a wretch," "an unnatural unwise horror of maternal concern," as the pity patrol's general take was that "the poor child was bartered to satisfy a mother's cupidity and a man's baseness." One enterprising newswoman spoke to Evelyn's relatives on her father's side, who were happy to offer their own slant on the former Mrs. Winfield Nesbit:

> She knew better. She also knew she was sacrificing her child's soul for money by which to live without effort. She could have taken in washing or done a thousand other things that would not have placed her child in harm's way. . . . Even a dumb brute would protect its young. . . . She was the degenerate.

With the exception of Harry and Anthony Comstock, nearly everyone else connected to the case dreaded the daily throng of reporters groping and hunting for an exclusive or new angle. Evelyn spent her exhausting days and sleepless nights dodging the press wherever she went, calling the sob sisters "special kind of lunatics," while from his cell, Harry deliberately inflamed their interest in her with his praise of Evelyn's bravery, hinting almost gleefully at what had befallen her and "how all would be revealed!"

To make matters worse, the Thaws had been approached early on by a publicity firm in Pittsburgh, McChesny and Carson. When they refused the offer, the firm turned to Thaw's opponents, the D.A.'s office, who gladly accepted and began a campaign to smear both Harry and Evelyn in the press. The Pittsburgh firm was in an ideal position to repeat stories that had only made the local or regional papers, such as the rumor that Harry had killed a horse in anger (he claimed the horse had run wild and broken its leg and had to be put down). Or that a physician passenger on a Pullman car traveling between Albany and Buffalo remembered seeing Harry "intoxicated and probably doped." Women came out of the wallpaper, eager to talk about their past relationships with Bathtub Harry; it was the same for Evelyn, only in her case men who had only fantasized about her spoke as if they had known her, and women who resented her beauty or "good fortune" saw a chance to get their names in the papers. And they did by the streetcar load.

During the earliest days of preparations for the trial Evelyn's sole friend and confidante was May McKenzie. Appearing in the courtroom each day in long-trailing, form-fitting lavender outfits, topped with ostentatious ostrich-plumed hats that enhanced her chipper, birdlike demeanor, May was a constant presence next to Evelyn and made for great copy. But, viewed against the sea of sedate black suits and mahogany browns of the courtroom, May's colorful presence seemed wildly inappropriate. The press couldn't resist comparing her to either the stylishly subdued but still bewitching Evelyn, dressed always in dark navy blue, or Harry's unfortunate sisters, who invariably came off as dowdy at best and as looking like Harry in a fright wig at worst. Described by the sob sisters as "rosy, round-faced, bright-eyed, well-groomed, cheerful, chattering and full of a birdlike but good-humored curiosity," May was "a friendly jimson-weed, fine to shade the fading tuberose [Evelyn] from the too searching glare of the sun . . . while on the other side of the child bride sat Mrs. George Lauder Carnegie and the countess of Yarmouth, commonplace, round-featured, steady-eyed, plainly dressed," each of whom who "could pass in any crowd without being observed in any way," "pie-faced and plain," and only able to "smile with difficulty." Since the Thaws were nearly manic to avoid at all costs any unnecessary reminders of Evelyn's "prodigal days," within a matter of weeks, like a girl in a vaudeville magician's trunk, the purple-plumed and flamboyant May McKenzie disappeared from the young Mrs. Thaw's side, banished from the courtroom by the Thaws and their lawyers as if she had never existed. The sob sisters took dainty purple-prosed note.

While Evelyn may have seemed to a deluded Harry in the early days after the murder like "one of the Princesses in Fairyland," between the lawyers on both sides trying to build their case and the various "moles and weasels" in the newspapers raising questions about her past, Evelyn found herself in a nightmare landscape where even Harry came to see that "her own plight was cruel beyond degree." Surrounded, according to Harry, by "hosts of evil" rising up around her, Evelyn was once again distressingly and entirely without guidance and support. Harry dimly considered there might have been women friends he could have called to come to her aid. But he didn't.

On certain days Evelyn shuddered to think what would happen if Harry got the electric chair, since she was unprepared to deal with the Thaws all by herself over the long term. They were a gloomy and repressed tribe under the best of circumstances, and as Harry described it, at first they were "woozy" with the bad publicity, which they blamed solely on Evelyn. Harry saw from his cell that his family was shunning Evelyn: "My family, who you think would have outdone themselves in extending their friendliness to her left her almost alone; she had to dine by herself for all most of them cared."

According to Evelyn, only Harry's sister Margaret and her husband, George Carnegie (who agreed privately that Harry was crazy), had any common sense. They treated Evelyn civilly, in part because they recognized how necessary she was to Harry's defense, although there might have been an inkling of genuine compassion as well. But in spite of the surging force of people around her night and day—all on the Thaw payroll and all engaged in preparing and dissecting the case that was about to come to trial—as it seemed so many times during her short life, Evelyn had to fight her battle virtually alone.

Contrary to popular myth, Evelyn had little access to any money. Josiah prevented his brother Harry from obtaining any additional funds while he was incarcerated; as such, Evelyn had to save "every [shekel]" that came to her by way of Mother Thaw (even while Harry foolishly insisted that she retain their rooms at the Lorraine and the electric car). Mother Thaw, in an effort to keep tabs on her daughter-in-law and to keep her from running up a tab at Delmonico's or Lord & Taylor, decided to hire an unfashionably dour lump of a woman to "keep Evelyn company." Her name was Mrs. McMillan, and she charged up hefty bills under the heading of "expenses," which irritated Evelyn, who had no such account, and who knew that Harry was paying for McMillan's rooms and Josiah Thaw for her meals. But Mrs. McMillan was dismissed after a month once the Thaw tribe decided to close ranks as tightly as possible. The fewer eyes there were to witness what was going on backstage, the better.

JURY SELECTION

Unlike any previous criminal trial in America, the Thaw trial—even the process of jury selection—made headlines virtually every day, especially when it was announced that, because of the sensational nature of the case, the jury for the first time in American history would be "incarcerated" (sequestered) for the duration of the proceedings. The sole person who seemed practiced in this process was a lawyer named Dan O'Reilly, the only down-to-earth member of the Thaw legal team and the only one who befriended Evelyn. As Mr. Penny, the court clerk, shouted prospective jurors' names over the unruly noise of a hundred reporters crowded into the room along with the rest of the two hundred or so spectators, one by one the talesmen (prospective jurors) entered. And one by one they had to be dismissed, either for having connections to White or Thaw. When it was suggested that the trial be moved to a more neutral location, one observer quipped, "How about the moon?"

It took a week and three hundred prospective jurors before even a solid number four could be agreed upon. Then number two complained he could not wait for weeks and was dismissed. One man, who had initially been selected as an alternate juror, began making disparaging comments about Evelyn and was promptly "mashed" under the jury table by number nine. Neither, however, was dismissed, although the question of potential perjury regarding the man who made the remarks about Evelyn hit the newspapers the next day. It was discovered that his brother-in-law was employed at Madison Square Garden. As described by Harry, he and others like him still deferred to the deceased White's "evil presence in his eagle's nest in the Tower." All told, a whopping six hundred prospective jurors went through the process before an unwavering twelve men could be selected. (Women, of course, were not allowed to serve on juries.)

During other preliminary proceedings (discussing the admission of handwriting experts and additional alienists, ballistic experts, and issues of spousal privilege, etc.) it became clear to everyone, even Harry, that his newest main counsel, Gleason, was absolutely and hopelessly inadequate, "expressing good thoughts . . . but unaccustomed to Criminal Courts," while his partner, Hartridge, seemed more concerned with finding the nearest watering hole. There was a tremendous amount of hearsay as to how both the defense and the prosecution would proceed. What would be their line of defense? What would Thaw be tried for? According to Evelyn, those who knew the D.A. stated that he would "confine the issue to one point: Did or did not Harry Thaw kill Stanford White on the evening of June 25th?"

"If this is the only question to be decided," she wrote, "the case will not last very long."

The pivotal issue for everyone was the question of sanity. Was Harry Thaw insane, either temporarily or genetically?

The question of bug-eyed, baby-talking Harry's sanity for anyone who knew him, even casually, was easily answered without the calling of a lunacy commission. Yet Mother Thaw, in spite of all mad evidence to the contrary, wished fervently "to avoid a scandal" with regards to the issue of insanity, a fact that Evelyn found ridiculous, "given the tremendous and electrically charged consequences" hanging over Harry's head. In her 1915 memoir, Evelyn derisively described the Thaw family's thought process regarding a plea of insanity before the trial: "If it comes to that, the Thaws will put the biggest lunacy experts that money can buy on the stand." They will "prove that Harry was a madman, but they will prove it nicely. There will be no suggestion that he can be unpleasantly mad, or that his madness can take beastly shapes."

As the weeks ran on, Mother Thaw spent an insane amount of money hiring an inordinate number of experts in insanity, who were there only to confirm that Harry's illness was a "temporary brainstorm." By the end of the trial, the twelve alienists, whose fees totaled close to $1,000 a day, cost Mother Thaw half a million dollars alone to aid the cause of saving her son's life.

And what of the lingering notion that Evelyn was paid a handsome price for her testimony? There has been much speculation about the amount of money Evelyn must have been paid in order to testify as she did. The amounts mentioned have ranged from $25,000 to $1 million. At the time, almost no one questioned the likelihood that there must have been some pot of gold waiting for Evelyn when all was testified to and done. Certainly as Mrs. Harry Thaw, Evelyn was necessary and thus supported throughout the course of both trials by the Thaws, if for no other reason than to keep up appearances, a game the Thaws played exceptionally well. But Evelyn had no money she could call her own—no savings, and no control over the amounts they might give her to keep her in good spirits and finer clothes. Time and again she had to go to Harry in his cell and ask him to intervene on her behalf for basic spending money. More than likely they promised her a comfortable lifestyle, the kind she had become accustomed to—should things turn out well for Harry, but only under those conditions. Otherwise, they would have little use for her and feel no obligation to be charitable, professed Presbyterianism aside. Especially if Harry was fried.

COURTROOM TIGER

In a notions store in the vicinity of the Tombs, a man who worked in the courthouse who knew the district attorney and his ability to make short shrift of everyone from well-respected doctors to lawyers to established lunacy experts recognized Evelyn (she had ducked into the store in search of some headache powders). He pointed to a rack of picture postcards.

"Do you know that man, Mrs. Thaw?" he asked, gesturing to a photo of the D.A. "That is Jerome."

By 1906, William Travers Jerome had carved out an impressive reputation for himself in wiping out corruption and vice in New York City. He was known as a tiger in the courtroom, relentless in his questioning of witnesses, and as a man who cut his teeth on experts of any kind. However, Jerome had been on vacation when he was called back to New York to take charge of the case for the state. As a result, having only read a handful of newspaper accounts of the murder, and having had only a few hurried phone conversations with his office before returning to Manhattan, at the outset Jerome seriously underestimated the implications of the case, the power of the Thaws' money, and the media feeding frenzy that had already started. There was also a personal "situation" that might have an effect on his thinking and behavior, one that some might consider a conflict of interest and threat to his objectivity in the case. For Jerome had known White—they had belonged to several of the same clubs in the city and thus shared the same social circle and friends. More significant, however, and one of many great ironies of the case, was that Jerome himself was leading a double life of sorts. He was involved in an extramarital

D.A. William Travers Jerome,
circa 1900.

affair with a woman twenty years younger than himself. If he feared at all the revelation of this fact (which would certainly hurt his chances of winning the case, since any number of political enemies, as well as the press, would have loved to expose him as a hypocrite and an immoral fraud), he didn't show it.

As Evelyn looked at the picture postcard, the store owner cautioned her: "Jerome loves lunacy experts. . . . I should not back the lunacy bugs if I were you."

He then suggested that she hightail it out of town until the whole thing blew over. Evelyn thanked him, fearing that soon enough she might have to occupy the witness box "and face this remorseless man," this "square-jawed lawyer, all brain and ice-cold logic."

A pensive Evelyn bought the penny card and took it home with her, not aware that her own lovely face occupied every slot on the other side of the revolving rack. She studied the picture for hours, trying to shore herself up for what the newspapers were already predicting would have to be "the performance of Herself's life to save Himself." Several days later, Evelyn read what Jerome told reporters in anticipation of his cross-examination of the fair young Mrs. Thaw: "Those who find pleasure in the mental anguish of their fellows [should] prepare for a treat." The cocky D.A. also bragged that if she took the stand, he intended to tear Evelyn Thaw "limb from limb and exhibit the interesting remains triumphantly." Asked by reporters in Atlanta, where he had been vacationing, if he thought this would be a difficult case to prosecute, Jerome answered that it was simply a case of one man killing another out of jealousy: "Why, it's just an everyday police court story." But as Jerome would quickly learn, nothing about this case was ordinary.

Day after day, as the papers kept the story on the front pages, pounding away at the popular theme of "moral lepers in high places." The "thundering from pulpits across the land grew positively deafening," while the outpouring of denunciation and insinuation was astonishing. Anonymous girls who had never moved from the back of the chorus suddenly emerged to tell tales about the hive of depravity inhabited by White and friends in his corrupted Garden. There is little doubt that at least some of them were paid by the Thaws. Irvin S. Cobb guessed correctly when he wrote in the *World* that money was "poured out by the Thaw family, and sucked up, like water in a bed of sand."

As the trial date neared, the district attorney Jerome described the conditions under which his office was operating in terms of eager witnesses willing to tell all:

> As you know, the witnesses so far—most of them—have not been gifted with reticence. These women love to talk. Miss Doris So-and-so, or Miss Irene Such-and-such, will come down to the office and tell Mr. Garvan or another of my assistants what she purports to know. But the matter doesn't end there. Just outside the office there will be a newspaperman lying in wait. He takes Miss Doris or Miss Irene . . . and carries her off to some cafe. Then comes a bottle of wine. Over the wine they talk. Naturally what the young lady has to say becomes somewhat embellished. . . . It's a great game.

A Narrow Escape

In the last week of January 1907, a stunned Jack Barrymore received a summons from the Manhattan district attorney. Barrymore, who had surrendered to the genetic pull of acting, had been preparing for a role in his sister Ethel's revival of *Captain Jinks* in Boston. But the Manhattan D.A.'s office had a juicier off-Broadway role chosen for him. Jerome and the prosecution expected him to appear as one of the "dozens of men" Evelyn had known before she married Thaw. Barrymore obeyed the summons and came to New York.

In his brief preliminary discussion with Assistant D.A. Garvan, Jack offered little in the way of essential information. He said he had not known Thaw at all, nor had he ever heard Evelyn mention the name; as far as he knew, her relationship with White was "like a daughter." The image of their fateful all-night "frolic" and White's stern, unwavering gaze the next morning leaped to his mind immediately. To his relief, he was told he was not yet needed as a witness, and he went back to Boston. But it soon dawned on Jack (or his family's lawyers) that he might cast himself in a bad light if he returned to testify at the trial, since he would have to admit to their *affaire de coeur* and perhaps say under oath things he would rather leave unsaid in open court, if not for his own sake then for Evelyn's. Jack knew well enough when to make his exit. Within a matter of days, the press reported that young Jack Barrymore had been "threatened with pneumonia" and had gone to a sanatorium. And even though the headlines identified him as the latest figure in the "Thaw, White, and Nesbit Case," he would make no grand reappearance at the Thaw trial. Jerome was livid; as he grabbed at the slick roots of his hair, he more than suggested that Barrymore was pulling a fast one. "Who goes to Maine in February to combat pneumonia?" he yelled.

But in spite of Jerome's frustration, a relieved Jack sequestered himself as far away from the trial as he could for the duration. After a brief stop in Rockland, Maine, on February 8, Barrymore arrived at his destination, the Mansion House Hotel, situated in the little-known town of Poland Spring.

OPENING REMARKS,
MONDAY, FEBRUARY 4, 1907

The naive and seemingly desperate need by a significant percentage of the citizens to hang on to outdated stereotypes made it easy for them to accept the image of the gallant husband and innocent wife versus the suave and insistent seducer who threatened hearth and home. But more cynical spectators dissected the latest rumors that filled the daily columns regarding the so-called hero and his Angel-Child. Hadn't a girl named Ethel Thomas brought suit against Thaw in 1902? (At that time, Thomas had recounted the day when she and Harry were walking down the street to his apartments at the Bedford Hotel. He stopped in a store and came out with a dog whip. When Ethel asked him what it was for, he replied

laughingly, "That's for you, dear." She thought he was joking, but once
they got to his room, with a wild look in his eyes, he beat her until her
clothes were in tatters.) Wasn't this the same Harry Thaw who was a
suspected dope fiend? Hadn't Evelyn, the studio model and chorus girl,
been named in not one but two divorce suits before the age of eighteen?
And hadn't Evelyn been involved with the rakish and increasingly and
publicly dissolute Jack Barrymore? With most indications to the contrary
brushed aside, such as those published in the generally impartial *New
York Times*, the reactionaries and radicals on all sides seemed intent upon
viewing the story as the last grand performance of Victorian theater. And
everyone wanted a front-row seat.

The most remarkable thing about the opening remarks in the trial was
their brevity, on the part of both Garvan, Jerome's assistant, and the
defense. They seemed downright anticlimactic in light of all the hoopla
leading up to that day. The reason, many figured, for the relative briefness
of the respective openings, which finished before the noon recess, was
that neither side wanted to show its hand. It took Garvan all of ten minutes to offer that the state intended to prove that the defendant "shot and
killed with premeditation and intent to kill one Stanford White" and that
"the purpose of punishment of crime is to set an example" for the community. Throughout this, Harry sat flushed and fairly immobile, his head
downcast, as if studying something on the blank pad just beneath his
nose. He began to drum nervously on the table with his fingers, a habit
White had also possessed.

The first witness was called, a grim-faced Lawrence White. Harry did
not look up once at the nineteen-year-old as he sat in the witness box.
The next witness was Myer Cohen, musical publisher of the *Mamzelle
Champagne* score, who had witnessed the murder and imitated Thaw's
stealthy approach to White's table seconds before the shooting. Several
witnesses later it was Paul Brudi's turn. Dressed in his fireman's uniform,
Brudi related the brief conversation he had had with Thaw in the
moments after the shooting. Soon after, it was Officer Anthony Debes's
turn, who repeated what Brudi had reported. He stated that Thaw had

proclaimed with great gusto, "I killed him because he ruined my wife!" He then paused briefly, and said perhaps Thaw had said, "He ruined my life." He was dismissed.

The procession of witnesses continued with the coroner's physician who performed White's autopsy describing the gruesome nature of his wounds and his death by cerebral hemorrhage. The bullets he had taken out of White were entered into evidence, and when they were passed to the defense table for inspection, everyone but Harry looked. His eyes wandered back and forth, but as one reporter close to his table wrote, "not even a fleeting glance was thrown in the direction" of the deadly bullets.

And then a shocked courtroom heard from the coroner that, based on his postmortem findings, Stanford White hadn't had long to live. Had White not been murdered, the doctor stated, he would have succumbed very soon to Bright's disease, incipient tuberculosis, or a "serious degeneration of the liver." After a few more witnesses, the prosecution rested. His head down, Harry stared, as if boring a hole into the table.

When Thaw's hopelessly outmoded lawyer, Gleason, took the floor, his old-fashioned thunderous orator's voice, compared to the easy conversational tone of Garvan, provoked snickers and nudging smiles from a number of the reporters. The crowd was once again astounded when Gleason stated that Harry Thaw believed he had acted upon the command of divine Providence. As a hush fell over the three hundred spectators, Gleason said that Thaw was insane at the time of the killing, because of both stress and heredity. As reporters wrote furiously, Gleason further stated that Thaw had acted in self-defense and without malice, believing that White had made threats against his life. He finished by claiming that Thaw did not know the wrongful nature or quality of his act at the time he committed the offense. Harry Thaw cringed in his seat at the confusing and contradictory remarks, delivered like a dotty old maid schoolmarm's recitation. This was not what the Pittsburgh tribe had agreed upon in weeks of pretrial powwows. The defense was supposed to be a temporary brainstorm, but Gleason offered at least four defenses—and all of them horribly wrong, as far as Harry was concerned.

Then the elderly Dr. C. C. Wiley, the Thaws' family physician since

Harry was a child, was called to the stand by Gleason to firm up the case for Harry's insanity. Dr. Wiley would prove to be anything but what his name suggested under the pitiless cross-examination of Jerome. He was but one of several physicians and alienists who would be called to describe Harry's various ailments as a child. Harry, pale and nervous, twitched at the slightest unusual noise in the courtroom, and the frequent scrape of a chair was like fingernails on a blackboard to him. It didn't take long before Wiley was stuttering and faltering under Jerome's hail of questions, aimed at discrediting him as an expert in matters of insanity since he was a general physician and not an authority on the brain. By the end of the day, the only thing clear to those in the courtroom was that an exhausted and shriveled Dr. Wiley needed a vacation. Harry's sanity remained open to question.

The next day, Gleason wandered off the topic so much that even Jerome quietly but firmly tried to get him back on track. The need for a specialist in criminal law was obvious. But a perverse Harry, feeling bad for Gleason, and having already fired the "Traitor" as well as Black and Olcott, wouldn't dismiss the rattled man unless he asked to be fired. After the fiasco with the physician-not-alienist Dr. Wiley, Harry, Evelyn, Mother Thaw, and half a dozen other members of the legal team gathered in the anteroom next to the court, where Gleason, in tears, asked officially to be discharged as chief counsel.

NAPOLEON COMES EAST

Sitting in his cell as precious moments ticked by, Harry Thaw foamed over his own lawyers' attempts to paint him as a madman. His whole self-image was tied up in the belief that he had killed White to protect the young girls of New York. To claim he didn't know what he was doing when he shot White threw him once again into almost spastic convulsions, much to the amusement of those inmates of the state in the adjoining cells who didn't have their food sent in from Delmonico's.

Tearing at his soiled shirt collar and denouncing his legal team for

attempting to proceed with the insanity defense against his specific direc-
tives, Harry saw to it that within a matter of hours after Gleason's resignation, through his mother, a new head counsel was hired, one whose
old-fashioned but far more cunning sensibilities fit snugly with the
Thaws' paradoxically outmoded yet nouveau riche ideas as to what was
acceptable and what was not—and how to bend the media to their advantage. He was Mr. Delphin Delmas from San Francisco. Once he was at
the helm, he assured Mother Thaw over the phone, there would be no
more talk of madness.

Although there were times when Evelyn was barred from hearing certain pretrial testimony in the courtroom, what she couldn't hear in the
actual courtroom, she was nonetheless able to read, verbatim, in transcripts of the daily proceedings in the papers. So could the rest of the

Thaw's head counsel, Delphin Delmas.

country, much to the vexation of President Roosevelt, who tried to sup-
press (unsuccessfully) the printing of the transcripts on both moral and
practical grounds; he feared that reading accounts of the sordid and
depraved subject matter of the case would cause further moral ruination
of the citizenry, and that Americans were so preoccupied with the Thaw
trial they were ignoring their own work. So it was from the newspapers
(and not her in-laws) that Evelyn first learned just who Harry's new head
counsel would be—a short-statured, eloquent, and shrewd barrister who
the papers said deliberately accentuated his resemblance to Napoleon,
with both his hairstyle and his characteristic pose of putting one hand
inside his vest. More important, in his illustrious West Coast career,
Delphin Delmas had never lost a case, including one in the not-so-
distant past in which he had earned an acquittal for a murdering client on
the basis of the unwritten law—the quaint Victorian notion that a man
can snuff out another man's life to avenge a wife or sister with impunity.
Even so, thought Evelyn, he could very well be meeting his Waterloo
with Harry K. Thaw.

After so much legal wrangling over courtroom strategy and mumbo-
jumbo habeas corpusing and maneuvering, the day finally came when
Evelyn was delivered by car to Mother Thaw's hotel early in the morning. She was greeted at the door by Delphin Delmas. With only a minimum of polite preliminaries, he sat her down in the parlor of her
mother-in-law's suite. Evelyn could read nothing in his inscrutably impe-
rial look but sensed that something was terribly wrong as he began to
speak in a somber silken voice. She fixed her gaze on the distinctive oiled
forelock on Delmas's large head as he leaned toward her, meeting her
eye-to-eye. And then he told her of "their" plan.

When she understood what he was asking her to do, Evelyn was
dumbfounded. It was quite simple, really, Delmas told her. All she had
to do was tell the story of her relationship with Stanford White—the
whole story, in living, lurid detail. A wave of nausea passed through her
and her hands began to tremble. Mother Thaw, completely motionless,
sat wedged like an overfed crow on a tufted divan against the far wall.
She said nothing.

"But," Evelyn almost whispered, "it is an unthinkable thing that I must stand up in open court and tell . . ." She trailed off.

There was no other way, Delmas told her.

"Nothing less will serve. Your husband's life is in the balance." Then he added, "After all, what does it matter?" Evelyn shivered as a second wave of nausea gripped her near the throat.

"What does it matter? What does it matter?" The phrase reverberated in her brain. To get up in front of a judge, lawyers, a jury, the press, the world—and tell the story of her debasement? Tell all those secrets that she had kept for so long and had been exhorted by Stanny to keep hidden forever?

With the very unfortunate exception of Harry, Evelyn had kept her promise to White for six years and never told anyone. In fact, until he declared to nearly a thousand witnesses that White had ruined his wife, with the exception of his mother, Harry had kept the secret as well. What would everyone think of her? A thousand things tracked sharply through her brain, not the least of which was what Stanny had said over and over about girls who tell such things: "They come to a bad end." Then there was her mother's reaction to consider. And her brother's. Feeling as if she had suddenly seen the Medusa, a blurry-eyed Evelyn barely glanced over to the black silent form on the sofa. Once the tremors subsided, Evelyn also sat completely still and stared out the window. Delmas waited for a response, his hand in his vest pocket.

"What does it matter?"

She looked over Delmas's shoulder without seeing anything distinctly, unconsciously shut-off, just as she had the morning after her undoing by Stanny. The phrase haunted. As she wrote in 1915 of her train of thought on the days following this meeting, "I tell myself this a hundred times a day. Other women have gone into Court and told stories, without so much as turning a hair, which were infinitely more discreditable to themselves." But she knew that wasn't true.

Seeing no other viable defense, a resigned and frightened Evelyn was under no delusion about the nature of what she was expected to do. Or what she would have to endure as a result. Moreover, she realized fully for the first time that for better or infinitely worse, her entire life and identity were inextricably and everlastingly bound up in Harry's psychotic act.

SACRIFICIAL LAMB CHOP

In the handful of days before her testimony was scheduled to take place, Evelyn became obsessed with the awesome, faceless power of the public's "insatiable curiosity." During certain of the darkest moments before her testimony, Evelyn considered that: "Any well-kept secret takes on a new horror" and leaves one feeling "stripped and naked and defenseless—and open for an awful beating." As for the Thaws, Evelyn knew that none of them ever doubted that she would hesitate to bare her shredded soul for Harry: "They took it for granted that I should be pleased to have the opportunity to save him from the electric chair. After all, in their private opinion, I was already a fallen woman who could fall no further . . . they expressed their hope that Harry would be shown through [my] testimony in the light of a saint, and that is enough."

During one early meeting with Harry's defense team, Evelyn weakly hinted that the evidence might reveal Harry to be something other than what they were making him over to be, but she was "sshhed out of the room" by the Thaws, who had spent such a long time covering up for Harry that it was an automatic response.

Evelyn soon came to comprehend fully not only the terrible fix she was in but that the fix was in. In weighing all the facts and her options, Evelyn saw that there was little room for choice in the matter. In spite of what he had done, she didn't want to see Harry electrocuted. She flashed on the hideous, shuddering image of the pitiful elephant Topsy, whose electrocution on the Coney Island boardwalk had been captured by Edison for the nickelodeons a few years earlier. And she needed no further evidence that Harry was indeed crazy, but an insanity plea seemed out of the question as far as he and his clan were concerned. She also knew enough about the law and a wife's lack of rights in marriage and property matters (in those days before pre-nuptial agreements) to see that as Harry's widow she would get as little as possible from the miserly Thaws. Perhaps even nothing. Their formidable battery of high-priced lawyers would see to that, and she had no money of her own to mount any kind of defense. And if Harry was found insane and sentenced to an asylum, at best she might have to live indefinitely with the Thaws in dismal repentant dependence on them until such time as Harry was released. Knowing Harry as she did, she knew that day might never come. Her best and only hope was that he be acquitted.

Although she wrote years later with nostalgic bravado that she was "determined to tell all that [would] help him," at the time Evelyn also considered "a very patent alternative." She questioned whether any human being, no matter how momentous the issue, should be made to undergo the humiliation she would surely suffer on the witness stand. Considering all Harry had said and done in the name of her so-called honor and American girlhood prior to the murder, Evelyn wondered why the issue of preserving her honor no longer applied. Of course, she knew the answer, but still she contemplated the heroic actions she had read in books of "prisoners who have risked death rather than the honor of their wives should be questioned." But Harry's heroism was "not of that variety," nor was he the kind to be satisfied with "posthumous honors." If his lawyers wanted to preserve the image that he was sane, Harry would have to be kept as far away as possible from the witness stand, while Evelyn would have to be, as one Broadway denizen wrote, "grilled like a sacrificial lamb chop."

As the day of her testifying neared, Evelyn appeared to those around her like someone in a trance, acting just as she had the night of the murder. Some started to speculate that the ethereal Evelyn Thaw was on the verge of a nervous breakdown. It would also become clear enough to even casual observers that Evelyn's only other acquaintances, theater people and Bohemian types, were powerless, not very reliable, and not likely to come to her defense—described in the *World* as "nauseous representatives of the common types of the Tenderloin—waiters, chorus girls, bell boys, cab drivers, private detectives, chauffeurs, doorkeepers, theatre hands, models, valets and other habitués of that part of the city." In this Evelyn shared the fate of White, whose highbrow friends at the other end of the social scale suddenly became merely clients who found it convenient to remove themselves from the city for the duration of the Thaw debacle, "high-tailing their high-toned arses to Europe or South America while the Thaw circus was in town."

The fact that Harry Thaw continued to speak confidently about Evelyn, considering all he had done to her (and countless others), reveals Harry's mad capacity for self-delusion. Of course, the same could be said about his family and attorneys as well, even if they believed Evelyn would be able to come through successfully in the face of William Travers Jerome's ferocious tenacity, withering prosecutorial style, and years of experience. He had reduced older, much more experienced men to real tears, so what chance did little Evelyn stand? Surely no amount of coaching or prompting or prior performing as a utility girl in the chorus could prepare her for Jerome's inevitable onslaught. And it was all to be conducted in front of the watchful eyes of hundreds in the courtroom—and by extension the rest of the nation and the world beyond.

Throughout all the preliminary discussions about her testimony during visits to Harry in the Tombs, Harry seemed to Evelyn increasingly, ridiculously pleased with himself. In her account in 1915, Evelyn spoke of Harry's enthusiasm, of how he looked forward to her appearance in the witness box, "where she was to introduce him as if he were one of the knights of the Round Table." Although he remained obstinately silent in the face of alienists and medical doctors who he said, "haunted him while in the Tombs," Harry was absolutely and girlishly chatty when reporters visited. Speaking to a *Times* reporter one day while Evelyn was there, Harry said proudly, "Wait till my little wife gets on the stand and you'll hear a story such as you have never heard before."

Evelyn's reaction was slightly understated: "I [did] not share Harry's enthusiasm."

Thursday, February 7,
"Human Sacrifice on the Altar of Love"

Prior to her appearance on the stand, the general professional opinion around town was that Evelyn's talents as an actress were unremarkable. As a result, at first there was a great deal of speculation that she would be coached and that her answers would have to be "rehearsed" by Harry's defense team. But not even this could make her ready for every possible issue or question that would be raised (as Delmas told her without much emotion). Evelyn fretted in her chair at the hotel, her head pounding and her eyes burning with the force. She asked Delmas one more time what she could expect.

He looked at her solemnly: "My dear child," he said, "I cannot tell you, no one can tell you what questions Mr. Jerome will ask you. He himself does not know as yet. You must do the best you can, and I will protect you to the best of my ability. That is all."

On Thursday, February 7, the moment Evelyn dreaded and an entire nation had been waiting for arrived. As she described her feelings, "I went into Court that morning with all the sensations of one already condemned. . . ." Outside the building and in the corridors, a crush of people tried every possible means to force their way into the courtroom, past both the animate and inanimate barricades. In the days before Evelyn's testimony, the security had been somewhat lax, but on the day she was to be the star witness, bars had to be installed to keep the curious crowd of thousands from streaming inside. Mounted police strained to push back near hysterical women who kept surging forward to get a glimpse of the "lethal beauty." "Half a score" of the most aggressive females actually succeeded in getting seats in the back of the noisy courtroom, as befuddled policemen were unprepared to physically restrain ladies, many dressed in their "gayest Sunday best."

And then over the commotion a court official shouted: "Evelyn Nesbit Thaw!"

As if everyone in the packed courtroom had been struck dumb simultaneously, a miraculous palpable silence fell. The only exception was the sinister "rustling of paper from the Press tables." Evelyn emerged from the judge's chambers, walked slowly and gracefully toward the witness stand, and took her seat. A court attendant handed her a Bible, which she held while being sworn ("which is a rather impressive business").

"You do solemnly swear to tell the truth," he said earnestly.

She bowed her head mechanically and sat down as the scrape of the chair leg echoed through the large room. Even Harry sat quartzlike and uncharacteristically immobile.

Dressed as she would be throughout the trial in a plain dark navy blue ankle-length suit with a white linen Peter Pan collar and a stylish broad, soft-brimmed black velvet hat trimmed with artificial violets, Evelyn appeared to some like "Beauty in Distress," and to others a "small, frightened mouse" as she sat on the edge of her seat. She removed the dark veil she had worn until then, and a murmur ran through the room as some got their first look at the still-astonishing girlish beauty. Her mass of dark hair tied in a loose knot at the back of her neck was in stark contrast to the pallor in her "daintily molded features."

It didn't take long for several reporters to speculate on the theatrical effect her decidedly subdued "costume" might have on observers, particularly the twelve male jurors. The outfit certainly made the slight and fragile-looking Evelyn seem little more than a schoolgirl of thirteen, even though she had turned twenty-two a month and a half earlier. Her appearance made a powerful impression on all spectators in the courtroom and "intensified a hundredfold the dramatic climax of the trial." She sat perfectly still, her complexion as white as "finely sifted sugar."

As she surveyed the scene, it took all of Evelyn's strength to hide the fear that had welled up inside her; panic bobbed and hovered near her throat and threatened to escape any minute in a primal scream. Her heart was beating at an abnormal pace as her hands shook. She could hear the scuffling and wrestling of those barred from entering the room just beyond the imposing doors that led to the corridor. The enormity of her task hummed through the room. There was nothing to obscure her view of Harry, who sat about forty feet away, behind a railing in the center of the court. His eyes met hers as she shifted nervously in her seat on the stand. He smiled encouragingly, but Harry's smile frequently had an unsettling effect on her, and this was certainly one of those times. Harry was surrounded on either side by "a great deal too much counsel," six in all. There was also a handwriting expert as well as numerous medical "experts" and "specialists . . . all charging small fortunes merely to lend their presence to the scene."

Immediately in front of Evelyn sat the district attorney, Jerome; his assistant, Garvan; three more alienists; and some friends of Jerome. To her left sat the sober-looking jury; to the right, the equally sedate and heavyset Justice Fitzgerald. Then there were the long tables of reporters, a number of whom she knew; others were merely part of the sea of anonymous faces that stared up at her as if she were "in the monkey house at the zoo." In the extreme right corner of the room sat "the sob squad" and as the hundred newspapermen and -women leaned forward eagerly in their section, all held their collective breath so that "not even the random jingling of a coin or the buzzing of a fly could be heard." Even though she thought she had become used to people gawking at her (and had posed for Stanny numerous times "in absolute shameless nakedness"), nothing could have prepared Evelyn for this "spectacle of over-exposure" as the tyrannical gaze of the press and the public watched like vultures as her brief and too colorful life unraveled in front of them.

True to form, the Napoleonic Delmas, hand in vest, wasted no time. He stood up, approached Evelyn, and said: "Please state exactly what you confessed to Harry Thaw that night in Paris with regard to your prior relationship with Stanford White."

Evelyn took a deep breath as Harry let out an involuntary smothered yelp. She would later write that in many ways she found the first day the worst of all, worse than the cross-examination that followed. Her ordeal would last two uninterrupted hours that first day during direct examination alone. No one thought to offer her a glass of water during those times when her mouth was "turned to sawdust," and as she put it, "I was too afraid to stop, sure that I would never be able to start again."

She thought, having sat through a number of days in court as a specta-

tor, that she had adjusted to the whole scene—the predatory crowd, the
staid judge on the bench, the keen and impatient reporters packed into
every corner of the large room, the flash-happy photographers, even the
various Thaws sitting rigid in their row of reserved seats behind Harry
like a cold convergence of deceptively treacherous icebergs, their threatening heft hidden well beneath the surface. But, she recalls, "as I sat on
the bench in the witness chair it was all the difference between watching
the sea from the beach and viewing the beach from the sea."

Half-Truths and Justice
the American Way

With a new cotton handkerchief in hand, her head sometimes downcast,
and her trembling voice at times barely audible, Evelyn began to tell her
terrible tale. Delmas slowly unfolded the story from her lips, moving
backward from the events on the night of the murder to her meeting with
White "and all that followed." With only one exception, she spoke in a
clear, soft voice, occasionally brushing wisps of her hair from her eyes.
While relating the story of her first meeting with White, in the course of
her narrative Evelyn mentioned the name of Edna Goodrich, the other
chorus girl who had facilitated and attended the lunch. Suddenly there
was a burst of shouting and a furious conference on both sides. A brief
discussion at the bench ended with a directive to Evelyn: "From this point
on, you are instructed not to speak out loud the names of any people not
directly involved in the murder. Any names you include in your narrative
will be whispered to the attorneys. . . . This is to spare them from public
embarrassment."

It must be a dreadful thing to be associated with this case, Evelyn
thought to herself ironically.

Delmas asked her to relate the events that preceded their marriage,
culminating in the night she confessed to Harry about her seduction by
and subsequent affair with White. Almost as soon as Evelyn began to
describe the mirrored room, the champagne, and so on, Jerome leaped to

his feet and objected violently. But Delmas only smiled and waited for the judge to put the district attorney in his place, secure in the knowledge that his defense strategy was brilliant. Yet amazingly simple. By asking Evelyn to state what she had told Harry during that long night, Delmas could introduce into evidence a great deal of information that would not have otherwise been allowed. And, while circumventing any possible objections Jerome might make as to inflammatory or prejudicial remarks introduced about the murdered victim, Delmas's strategy also stymied the irate D.A., who could not object on the grounds that something Evelyn said was inaccurate and untrue. What mattered was that she had said it to Harry. And that Harry had believed it.

To Evelyn, having to tell the humiliating story of her deflowering and subsequent corruption on the witness stand was "rather worse" than either the night she confessed it in lurid detail to Harry or having lived the event itself. And, to many spectators in the court, including Evelyn, it seemed that the repetition of the sordid facts was worse the second (or hundredth) time around for Harry. He strained forward in his chair and periodically gripped the table convulsively, his large knuckles alternately beet red then blanched. Halfway through her story, tears began to well up in Evelyn's eyes, something she had promised herself she wouldn't allow. She knew enough about the press to know that some would construe her crying as theatrical. But as she repeated the story of "the modern Nero" (so said the papers) and how "he had ravished her sixteen-year-old flesh" while she was unconscious, Harry's terrible anguish exploded with choking unexpected force. Unable to stop herself, Evelyn also broke down crying, and restoratives had to be administered before she could go on. Tense, nervous, overwrought, and "thrilled with emotions of pity," the spectators also made incomprehensible exclamations as they hung on every word that Evelyn uttered. With each revelation or disclosure, a gasp could be heard from the jurors. Some of them had tears in their eyes. And the sob sisters sobbed. Vociferously.

Finally, as Evelyn finished recounting her "wrenching tale of betrayal and debauched innocence," Harry broke down again and bawled, making the same wounded-animal noises he had made that night in Paris. Adjournment for lunch was called, and as a shaken and exhausted Evelyn got up from the witness stand and walked along the narrow passageway a court official had made for her behind the jury box, her face turned from crimson to ghostly white. She felt for the walls with her gloved fingertips as if she were about to fall into an anemic swoon. Luckily she didn't, since all the physicians at the defense table were tending to Harry as he heaved to and fro in his seat, blubbering. Evelyn, however, hadn't noticed the reactions of anyone else in the room. She was too consumed with her own terrible emotions, which the papers the next day gleefully printed in explicit black and white.

FRIDAY, FEBRUARY 8

On the second day of Evelyn's testimony, the crowds outside the court-house swelled by several thousand more than the previous day. The corridors of the building itself were completely congested with bodies hoping to catch a glimpse of the "Child-Bride." In the cobbled street under the Bridge of Sighs that connected the Tombs to the courthouse building, an equally large crowd had gathered, hoping to see "the defender of American womanhood."

Inside the courtroom, only Edward Thaw, Harry's brother, was present to represent the family that morning. A more pallid, haggard-looking Harry was brought in. Instead of walking briskly to his place as he had the previous day, "he seemed to move in a hesitating way, looking about to right and left in the crowded courtroom." He smiled as he recognized his brother, but as Evelyn later learned, Harry had slept little that night, agonizing once again over the story she had told the day before, a story he had made her repeat to him countless times. But on this day, Harry was "heavily medicated and not by his own hand."

Evelyn was also feeling much worse than the day before, trying to combat a tight, drawn feeling that seemed to want to "wring her insides out." As she gripped the sides of her chair in the witness room, waiting for her name to be called, razorlike pains shot through her slim wrists.

Her nervousness increased, and she felt a weakness along her spinal column that threatened collapse. She was grateful to be sitting, feeling for the first time that she might faint if she had to stand at that moment. If anyone spoke to her suddenly, her heart "began palpitating in a frightful manner." And then, the court clerk's voice rang out, "Evelyn Nesbit Thaw."

Delmas approached her again with a benevolent smile on his face, one hand in his vest pocket. Letters that Harry had written to Evelyn during the period she had avoided him were read out loud. One was signed, "From one about to die," which was so like Harry in a certain mood that Evelyn almost smiled. Other letters were read, revealing not only how troubled Harry was about White, but how his troubled mind had worked in trying to make Evelyn accept his honorable advances more than five years earlier.

At times during her testimony, Evelyn would glance over at Harry, who suddenly looked "wonderfully cheerful" during those moments when both lawyers were enmeshed in wrangles over the inadmissibility of evidence or when Delmas succeeded in making a point about White's "diabolical ingenuity." Occasionally, Harry would give her a nodding smile, which was subdued for Harry—as Evelyn described him, it was "his way to go to the limit either in joy or sorrow." But as the day wore on, Harry too seemed, if nothing else, increasingly annoyed by the circuitous arguments taking place.

Delmas began to jump back and forth "with startling abruptness" and at a "breathless speed" from America to London and Paris and back. At times Evelyn's lips trembled involuntarily. The day dragged on, with constant interruptions, protests on both sides over the introduction of evidence, and explanations. Through it all, when she was permitted to speak, "the tiny, shrinking figure" spoke of the "horrid details of the repeated criminal outrage" committed against her. And since she did this with virtually no hesitation, if there were any who questioned the truthfulness of Evelyn's testimony, they were in great part silenced by her precise recounting of certain events that clearly had been "seared and branded" into her memory. She never wavered.

Finally, the session ended. But when the court rose, the door through which Evelyn was supposed to exit was entirely blocked with bodies. She had to wait while a path through the crowd was cleared for her, as those who had no official reason for being in the courthouse were roughly escorted out. But when she reached the street, before she could get in a hansom, a frightening scene occurred. Impelled by curiosity, hundreds of people, the majority of whom were women, pulled and pushed and fought to get close to Evelyn, breaking through even the mounted police cordon. Some shouted that they just wanted to touch her dress. Others seemed caught up in mob hysteria, as if they wanted to tear her dress from her. Policemen armed with their nightsticks had to beat back the surging crowd as people screamed at Evelyn to look their way. Eventually the bloodied fanatics gave way and watched as she was driven off in a cab.

FEBRUARY 20

Evelyn was due back on the stand, but this time it would not be the supposedly friendly lawyer asking the questions. It was painfully clear to Evelyn from the start that Jerome did not intend to spare her feelings. He began by asking her insinuating questions about her days as a model in Philadelphia and New York, pressing them upon her quickly and sharply in rapid succession, barely giving her time to respond. He squeezed her as to details of the dresses she wore or didn't wear when posing for artists in the studios when she was fourteen and fifteen. He persisted in certain queries, insisting on definite answers despite the protests of Delmas and Evelyn's inability to remember specific details of what had been a monotonous and seemingly endless parade of similar days of posing. As Evelyn put it, "He credits me with a memory I do not possess. . . . I am a terrible girl by inference. My no's sound very feeble in comparison with the detailed and impressive questions Jerome puts."

In question after question, Jerome asked her about the company she kept, the dubious stage society she was surrounded by, raising more insinuating questions about when she "first became ambitious to become a great actress." He asked Evelyn what her mother thought about her young daughter going on the stage.

Evelyn responded, "Mother said I ought not to go out without her. She said the 'show' was all right, but she ought to go along with me."

Jerome tried to emphasize a moral slackness on Evelyn's part and yet not her mother's. The reason, which Evelyn would soon discover, was that Mrs. Holman was at first secretly then openly providing the prosecution with ammunition and evidence to help their case against Thaw. Jerome therefore didn't want to alienate Evelyn's mother as long as she was telling him private details and helping his cause. Although she was eventually silenced, it was not because of a guilty conscience. The Thaws and their money saw to it that Mrs. Holman retreated. And, even though Evelyn must have resented the position that her mother's "moral slackness" or ignorance had helped put her in (in addition to her taking the D.A.'s side), she could not bring herself to condemn her mother on the stand. So in trying to defend her mother's indefensible actions while justifying her own, Evelyn only made herself seem worse.

Jerome produced the famous Eickemeyer photos of Evelyn in the kimono on the bearskin rug.

"Are these fair types of all the pictures taken that day?" he asked her, hoping they would be risqué enough to raise eyebrows, but sensing that these and others he had might strike people as "disappointingly proper."

Before Evelyn could answer, he followed with, "Are there none suggestive of any more impropriety than these?" Jerome seemed "aggrieved" that he could find no truly scandalous photos. Evelyn replied that there were "some taken with a low neck."

He persisted, encouraged by her answer. "Was there any further exposure?" he asked, waving the photos in her face.

"They were very low in neck," she said quietly, which only fueled his exasperation.

It was clear to Evelyn that Jerome had hoped the issue of her modeling in compromising positions and costumes would throw her into a panic and upset her amazingly calm demeanor. But Evelyn had been

hounded and beleaguered and raged against by the best of them in Harry
Thaw for so long that any badgering Jerome could muster, however fierce,
paled in comparison. Aside from Harry, to the rapt courtroom spectators
it seemed that the district attorney was the only one in a visibly agitated
state.

In fact, while Evelyn's testimony was at times selective or twisted by
Harry's defense (such as the fact that Stanny must have drugged her
champagne), she told enough of the truth to confound Jerome, who
couldn't find a way to entrap her. Try as he might, with countless questions asked and repeated angrily in an attempt to confuse Evelyn "into
the controversion of facts," Jerome, a man who had aspirations toward
the governorship of New York and even the presidency of the United
States, could not break the "little model-wife" into pieces. Even Harry
declared admiringly, "None can forget what a witness she made! The
simple directness of her narrative as it was drawn from her, and remain-
ing not only unshaken, but emphasizing and renewing the facts, startled
and astounded us at the time."

Jerome moved on to a different topic, which he believed was unsavory-
sounding enough to provoke a reaction from Evelyn and would simultaneously tarnish the girlish image she was presenting on the stand.

"Hadn't Stanford White paid you on a regular basis whenever you
were not engaged in a production?"

Evelyn replied that White's generosity was well known and not confined only to herself, her mother, and her brother. In fact, it was in the
capacity of benefactor and supporter of her career that she knew White
"first and best."

He tried to pressure her for details about the letter of credit White had
given her before her European trip.

"When did he give it?" "What was the amount of the letter of credit?"
"Was it a large or small sum?" To all these rapid-fire questions Evelyn
replied, "I don't remember." She added that she was unconcerned
with the financial details of the trip, that her life was in the hands of
others—namely, her mother, who in turn had put everything in Thaw's
control in arranging the trip. As she repeated for emphasis, she was a

seventeen-year-old schoolgirl recuperating from an operation, barely able to tie her shoes.

An exasperated Jerome asked her if the letter of credit made any impression on her mind. "No" was her reply. Jerome then asked her when she began to doubt the wisdom of accepting such a letter since Mr. Thaw was paying for her trip abroad. She gave him a general answer: "1903."

Jerome sneered. "When Thaw proposed to you, and you rejected him, did you believe yourself to be better than others because of what happened to you?"

Evelyn recalls her reaction, "I could afford to smile. That was not the way to rattle me."

After days on the stand, Evelyn had impressed both seasoned reporters and court officials with her touching and simple recounting of her story, so artless and so seemingly genuine and vivid. Her testimony, offered with restraint and characterized by unexpected moments of understated drama or a simple pathos, not only confounded Jerome but continued to move others in the room to tears. No one could refute the facts of her awful childhood after her father died. And as Harry put it, "For sheer realism there is little that can surpass her description of that night in Paris."

As the days wore on, Evelyn was caught up in a terrible paradox, even though she was not only holding her own with the "courtroom Tiger" but seemed to be beating him at his own game. She was an unsuccessful actress when Jerome wanted to underscore her financial dependence on White, and when he insinuated that the tearful story of her seduction and ruination was made out of theatrical cheesecloth, she was suddenly a phenomenal actress. The fact that Harry's life was at stake seemed to be forgotten in the "duel between herself and the Public Prosecutor." The only question in some people's minds was who would win—the lady or the tiger?

Evelyn quickly learned the kinds of tricks Jerome had at his disposal, one of which was to combine two questions as one, the one demanding a "yes" answer, the other a "no." After several instances of putting such a question to Evelyn, with Jerome shouting, "Yes or no?!" Evelyn began to demand that the questions be separated and asked one at a time. Ordered by the court to do so, with Evelyn being instructed not to answer anything she didn't understand, Jerome would himself become rattled "and pretty sore, which was perfectly sweet of him," Evelyn wrote.

After her initial cross-examination, once they heard from the lawyers that she had done well, the different members of the Thaw family who met her in the witness room were all smiles and congratulations. As she described it, "At the hotel I was 'brave little Evelyn' and 'dear little Evelyn' and 'most courageous girl.'" Mother Thaw blessed her and told her she was wonderful. But, as Evelyn also writes, "had the lawyers told them I made a bad witness they would all have shown unmistakable signs of desiring to shake me." Needless to say, she was not fooled by their praise, although one comment in the press assessing her performance did please Evelyn: "From one point of view, the cross-examination's effect tended rather to strengthen the defense's argument as to the cumulative effect upon Thaw's mind. There was never any faltering, and as her courage rose, more than one answer having every semblance of candor and innocence parried Mr. Jerome's questions by producing an impasse."

LE RAT MORT

During the next session Jerome began with a line of questioning that took Evelyn back to Paris, 1903. He asked her, "Did you continue to believe that all women were unchaste, as White told you, until you talked with Thaw in Paris in 1903?"

"Yes," Evelyn replied meekly.

He then asked her about a café in Paris with the unappealing name of Le Rat Mort.

"Is it a reputable café?" Jerome demanded to know.

Evelyn was surprised by this question, saying that she didn't know. "I don't know, people were sitting about eating," replied Evelyn, "it seemed a respectable thing to do." Some in the packed room snickered.

"Was there somebody dancing?"

"I think so."

"Was it two o'clock in the morning?"

"Possibly," she answered.

"Did you see the cakewalk being danced?" he asked ominously.

"No, I think it was a Russian dance," she answered.

Evelyn knew that it had in fact been the cakewalk, which was considered an outrageously improper ragtime dance by most, performed usually by "colored dancers." She thought it probably best that she remember it as a Russian dance. Unfortunately for Evelyn, she had forgotten "in her exuberance" that she had written to a friend about going to the Dead Rat and watching the cakewalk. Harry had also written a letter stating that a Miss Winchester was persuaded to get up and "do the cakewalk at 2 a.m."

"How many times were you at the Dead Rat?" he asked, emphasizing the name with relish, realizing it made more of an unsavory impact in English.

"Only once," Evelyn replied, which irked Jerome.

However, there came the moment when Jerome finally managed to break through Evelyn's reserves. For the first time he brought Evelyn to tears.

"Had you felt the heinousness of the wrong that had been done to you?" he asked

"I didn't know anything about it at the time," Evelyn said.

But Jerome persisted, asking her a series of rapid-fire questions: "Didn't it outrage every instinct in you?" "Weren't you very bitter against White when you told Thaw?" "When you felt you were giving up Thaw's love, did you not feel enmity against White?"

Again and again the name of White and what he had done was thrown in her face.

"White—White—always White!" she wrote later. "It made me go hard and bitter to hear the name of this man whose dead hand was laid upon me."

"How do you regard Stanford White?" he asked, his piercing eyes fixed on hers.

The courtroom was quiet as a mausoleum. Evelyn then said something without hesitating that shocked everyone, especially the Thaws.

"White had a strong personality. Outside that one awful thing, he had been a very grand man. He was very good to me, and very kind. When I told Mr. Thaw this he said it only made White all the more dangerous." She then began to cry for the second time, but talked through her tears.

"Before the Twenty-fourth Street incident he had never made love to me. He always treated me with the greatest respect and kindness, yet he was also a man of sufficient authority and domination to pack me off to school at his pleasure." Everyone sat in stunned silence.

As each day passed, Jerome's "shameless" "foul and venomous innuendos," his "brutal hounding" of Evelyn began to garner him unfavorable press as well. As one paper described it, "Around the slender form of the unhappy girl-witness the battle rages. Her quivering features attest the agony she suffers." One editorial letter said that his "fiendish persecution of Mrs. Thaw on the stand, taking what appears to be the most cowardly advantage of his position [and] her unfortunate situation . . . is sufficient to elicit the contempt of even the lowest criminal on earth. The man seems to have lost his senses in the insane desire to crush the woman into the gutter. We do not look for such conduct from a gentleman or a man with human instincts." He came off not as "an advocate anxious only to arrive at the truth" but as a "frenzied partisan." Another reporter wrote, "Even we, at this distance, can realize something of the depth of misery into which such a cross-examination would plunge any woman. What must it be to her?"

MONDAY, FEBRUARY 26

After three days of rest and relative quiet, Evelyn was recalled. She had been to the Tombs to see Harry, who was more than cheerful; he was in full-blown heroic mode, which she found "more than mildly irritating." Even more annoying to Evelyn was the fact that Harry seemed to be enjoying his celebrity status. She wrote that "the dreadful seriousness of the position in which he stands does not seem to impress him so much as the sudden fame which had come to him." Harry was just crazy enough to believe the fantasy his own public relations people created and ignore the reality of his actions. More and more it seemed to Evelyn that he considered himself the hero the papers made him out to be. Basking in the false light of positive publicity, his view of himself finally coincided with that of the rest of the world.

That afternoon, Jerome began where he left off, trying to prove that Evelyn was, in her words, "something worse than the dust." He dragged up every incident he knew about and baited her to see if there was any he did not know about, magnifying certain details to discredit her or cast doubt on her credibility. Once more she was asked about White giving her money, under what circumstances, and how frequently. Had he given her presents for her vacations? How did he help her when work was slack? How many suppers had she been to, and with whom? Here again the names of those involved had to be whispered "with a great show of secrecy," which only served to arouse the curiosity of the spectators to a "fever pitch." Were there chaperones? When did these supper parties end? After the theater? By this time, Evelyn's exasperation and mental exhaustion turned into a kind of giddiness; she was possessed by the "absurd desire to make extravagant and inconsequent replies, to say that supper coming after the theater was not remarkable. Had it come before the theater it would have been something freakish." Jerome continued along these lines until he turned his attention to Evelyn's relationship with Harry.

After asking similar questions—about presents Thaw offered her early in their acquaintance, about the fifty dollars he sent her with flowers ("You were accustomed to receiving money from men?")—he then switched gears completely. Jerome stood in front of Evelyn, deliberately blocking her view of Harry, and asked, "Up to February 1902, had you noticed anything irrational about Thaw, either in appearance, in his actions, or in his manner?" Evelyn's reply was that she had not, that Harry's attentions to her at that time were no more marked than those of other men interested in her. Jerome pounced on the phrase "other men" and proceeded to "blacken her by inference." He ran through a list of men, some of whom Evelyn knew by name or met briefly at one of Stanford White's parties, others whom she met through her roles in various companies, and still others who must have wanted desperately to believe they had somehow been an object of her affection. He then jumped back to Harry.

"Did you understand that Thaw was paying honorable courtship to you?" he asked. In reply Evelyn asked, "What do you mean by courtship?" To her surprise and everyone's amusement, Jerome floundered. It was one of the few smiles that she showed during the proceedings.

He then asked her whether she traveled under an assumed name in Europe. Evelyn said, "No." She began to see that Jerome was making his case as he went along, "searching haphazard and for information he did not possess." A series of questions followed about the hotels they went to, about who paid the bills, about her feelings for Harry, about whether or not she knew at the time that her mother had begun a suit against Thaw for kidnapping her. As Evelyn recalled, "The questions were beginning to tire the Court; there was a stirring and a shuffling of feet." Then Jerome came back at her with "a more brutally direct question."

"Did you ever receive money from White after you reconciled with Thaw?"

"Never in any way, shape or manner," was her reply.

It wasn't true.

A RECORD "KEPT CLEAN FOR EVIL MEN" BUT NOT FOR HER

Harry's one quarrel with Delmas throughout Evelyn's days of testimony was that during his examination of her, Delmas was unable to get the names of the others involved in White's atrocious crimes mentioned for the record and for all to hear. He wanted no more of this whispering into

Jerome's ear or expurgating testimony to protect men who were "ages away from being innocent." But Jerome had seen to it that all those not directly involved in the murder were protected, so reporters were forced to print blanks in their stories where names ordinarily would be. As Evelyn saw it, "The record was kept clean for evil men but not for me."

By March 1907, postcards of Evelyn were selling rapidly; the demand reached half a million in a single month. According to one printer, his presses were going "night and day. And night." Evelyn's testimony finally ended, but the Thaw case steamrolled on.

The trial that had begun on January 23, 1907, found itself thrust into April. On April 11, the jury began its deliberations. Thousands milled around outside the courtroom and the prison awaiting the verdict. The sequestered jurors were locked in debate. They were out forty-seven hours and eight minutes. During that time, the crowd waited and speculated and shivered in the cold rain. Some created a makeshift tent city on the streets outside the Tombs and the courthouse. The police did everything they could to clear them out, but the effort was futile. It was like herding cats.

Finally it was announced that a verdict had been reached.

The serious-looking group of twelve, dressed in their sober suits, reentered the courtroom. All eyes were riveted to the foreman as he stood to read the verdict.

Seven votes for guilty and five for not guilty by reason of insanity.

It was a hung jury.

The packed courtroom erupted in cries and shouts. Reporters rushed out the door in one tumultuous wave. At first, Harry buried his head in his hands. He then began to rant and swear. He pounded his fists on the table as several lawyers tried to restrain him and then those left in the room watched as he broke into hot tears, realizing that he would be back in a cell and would not be going home the avenging angel. As a palsied Harry was taken out of the courtroom, back to his cell, past the clutching black-gloved hands of his distraught mother and sisters, a wordless, emotionless Evelyn sat perfectly still in her seat. Only the trembling of her bottom lip indicated that she had heard the verdict. The sphinx once again. The late-edition papers announced to an astounded public that there would have to be another trial. And "the desperate game of life and death would have to be replayed."

© 1913, P. N. CO.

"All I ask is fair play, and a legal solution of my troubles."

Harry K. Thaw

A dejected Harry seeking public support for release from Matteawan asylum on a postcard, circa 1913.

CHAPTER SEVENTEEN

❦

America's Pet Murderer

One night, primed with high-ball virtue, he murders a man of genius. Then for years the courts are full of his fame, and the lawyers of his money. . . . At length the long ignominious drama is ended. The paranoiac walks forth free . . . the idol of "the populace." Cheering crowds crush around him. Women weep over him. —*Newspaper clipping, 1915*

In all this nauseous business, we don't know which makes the gorge rise more, the pervert buying his way out, or the perverted idiots that hail him with wild huzzas. —The Sun, *July 1915*

[Her] future will be a study for psychologists, for despite her achievements of luxury and marriage, she has the appetites of the Tenderloin.
—New York Evening World, *April 14, 1907*

Before the second trial, scheduled for the following January, a battle-fatigued Evelyn, teetering at times on the razor's edge of nervous exhaustion, gathered together the records of every great criminal trial for the last fifty years. "There was invariably a woman in the case, that goes without saying. It was the woman who interested me," she writes, "the woman guilty or innocent; temptress or victim. She and her future were immensely interesting to me . . . and my discoveries were of a depressing nature . . . for every woman had gone down, down, down. Drink, drugs, the hundred and one wild diversions which eclipse sorrow and soothe heartache had been pressed to service, and the poor light had flickered out dully and miserably. And this without exception . . . Said I to myself, Evelyn Thaw, you shall do better than that." It was wishful thinking on her part.

With an awful sense of déjà vu hanging over everyone's heads, the new trial of Harry Thaw began in January 1908. Once again, more than six hundred prospective jurors were summoned in order to find twelve men who could serve. Delmas was gone, having returned to the West Coast half a million dollars richer, with his record intact, since technically he did not lose the case. Another lawyer, Martin Littleton, was engaged as Harry's head counsel. But the second trial would be significantly shorter than the first. This time, as one newspaper stated, "in a turnabout so fast that it almost snapped your neck," the Thaw family helped Jerome's case. Realizing the futility of the outdated "unwritten law" and the weakness of any defense that did not admit to Harry's tainted mental history, in spite of Harry's continued protest, his mother and his legal team supported the idea that Harry was insane—temporarily. Once again Evelyn had to recount the sordid details of her ruination and how it "inflamed the burning embers of her unstable husband's insane hatred for Stanford White." The trial was once more on the front pages of every newspaper every day for a month. On February 1, it ended. The jury deliberated for twenty-four hours.

But in a year's time things had changed. After an unprecedented avalanche of publicity that left "not even a pebble unturned," virtually everyone's name, whether good or bad, found itself "ground into the dirt." It was no longer possible to consider anyone involved in the case as innocent, including the lethal beauty who would for the rest of her life be known as "the girl in the red velvet swing."

This time, thanks to Evelyn's willingness to "bare her soul and share her awful sins with the world again," Harry was spared Topsy the elephant's fate. Instead of going to the electric chair, Harry was acquitted by reason of insanity and sent to the Matteawan Asylum for the Criminally Insane in Fishkill, New York. Evelyn's reward for saving Harry's life was to be virtually cut off from the Thaw money. As soon as Harry was judged incompetent, Mother Thaw took over the finances.

Harry meanwhile began a desperate campaign to have himself declared sane.

A week did not go by without Harry having some communication with lawyers who fought to schedule a hearing regarding Harry's sanity as soon as possible. In the meantime, at Matteawan, Harry was treated with every consideration his wealth could buy. He had a room of his own, all the books and comforts he required, and was given every facility for seeing Evelyn alone, both inside the grim and repressive-looking asylum, and outside, where he was frequently seen tooling around in a touring car with his warders. As she described her feelings for Harry at the start of his incarceration, "I was sorry for him, and pity retains love even as it creates it." There were moments during her visits when old feelings of happier times were rekindled, but as she saw it, "The puny logic of humanity can run with Nature's scheme just so far." She felt the uncomfortable pull of obligation and believed that "to have cut him off just because he was a life prisoner of the State . . . would have been wicked . . . cruel." But she was wrong again.

As months passed with no sign of release in sight, Harry became increasingly moody (even for him) and, as Evelyn described it, hateful to her. He was insistent that she demonstrate her appreciation for all he had done for her. He accused her of not being sufficiently grateful to Harry Kendall Thaw of Pittsburgh for the tremendous sacrifice he had made. With each visit and the swelling sense of the impossibility of leaving the asylum, Harry grew more bitter in Evelyn's presence. There were times when she wanted to scream at him out of sheer nerves, at the "futility of his talk and the extraordinary absence of any sense of proportion." As she put it, "The everlasting strain was sapping me, destroying me."

Harry continued to be his own paranoiac manic-depressive self, "at times in the most exalted mood, full of cheer, jovial, almost optimistic," then suddenly down "in the depths of despair, ready for death, bitter, reproachful and self-pitying." There were days when he was buoyed by the letters received from well-wishers and fans, most of them women, although there was a percentage of people looking for handouts and a share in the Thaw fortune as well. One fan, a man, even offered to take his place for him in the asylum.

Evelyn herself received bagfuls of letters and cablegrams daily, because, as she put it, "my affairs were everybody's affairs." The temptation to offer advice was irresistible to many who wrote to her, as was their desire to pray for her, a subject that had a "certain disflavor" for her as a result of her yearlong training as a "prayer subject" at Lyndhurst. Others wanted her autograph and most her photograph, while some simply wanted to praise her for her courage and devotion. Then there were the insulting letters, the "outpourings of vicious" people who thought she had escaped punishment for her deeds. But as Evelyn put it, "I had been insulted by experts, and the amateur efforts of lesser people left me unmoved."

As for Evelyn, she felt she was the one who had made the great sacrifice, but that no one had appreciated it, least of all the Thaws, who gradually cut off all her funds and made her life a misery. Her own position was becoming increasingly desperate and called up the worst memories she had of her childhood. Financially she was on shaky ground, as the money that came to her grudgingly, in small sums, from Harry's lawyers did so at irregular and seemingly capricious intervals. Her allowance "from Harry and his people" was nothing like the princely sum most imagined she had earned with her "soul searing testimony." The only relief she had was to sculpt, or as she put it, "model in clay," something for which she had a real talent, perhaps a greater one than either her acting or singing abilities.

Inevitably, Harry's resentment turned to absolute hatred, which Evelyn gradually reciprocated to a less obvious degree—at first. As she described it, in the first two years of his incarceration at the asylum, her feelings for Harry were moving more in the direction of "loathing," as he had become "America's pet murderer." In the meantime, Harry pursued his release from the asylum with an angry relentlessness, believing that the formation of a lunacy hearing would find him sane and set him free. Although Evelyn claims that it was not her idea to participate in the weary progression of lunacy hearings that Harry demanded and eventually won over the course of seven years (with the aid of the Thaw money once again), she could exact some revenge herself by simply stating the truth about Harry in hearing after commissioned and costly hearing. He belonged, she asserted with clear-eyed simplicity, in the bug house.

But by the fall of 1909, Evelyn was nearing a nervous breakdown; she was overwhelmed mentally and physically. She saw "history horribly repeating itself" as she imagined a "whole lifetime spent in the choking environment of the courts," where her mother first met with disaster after her father's death. Grudgingly attending one after another in a seemingly pointless succession of lunacy hearings at the Supreme Court in White Plains, New York, as Evelyn described it, "To save his life they proved him mad, and now in telling the stories of his madness to keep him locked up, he is lashed into a fury." But no other evidence, even medical, would be so convincing or damning as Evelyn's testimony at each hearing in keeping Harry incarcerated. If Evelyn had wanted money from the Thaws, this was not the way to get it. But as she initially tried to tell Mother Thaw and the others, no one could convince twelve people that "a man could be sane all his life and a lunatic for the space of three minutes." Even though the discussions of Harry's delusions were terribly humiliating, "only at intervals did he recognize the humiliation." He still held to his fantasy of chivalry in spite of so much evidence to the contrary.

As Evelyn describes it, she and Harry inevitably broke apart—aided by the stress of his being in the asylum and her trying to get money from the Thaws for her daily expenses. And then, as if things weren't bad enough, Evelyn was faced with a terrible crisis that would seal her fate (as far as the Thaws were concerned).

If Evelyn and Harry's relations were inevitably and understandably strained during the first dismal fifteen months of his incarceration, they reached a critical point when Evelyn announced in early 1910 that she was pregnant. She said her condition was the result of a conjugal visit with Harry several months earlier on a day when both were "feeling sad and lonely." She also said that this encounter was perfectly possible because of Harry's money. He vehemently disputed the claim. Already hard-pressed for money, Evelyn now had to endure "the vilest of suggestions"—that she had this child solely to extract money from the Thaws—or that it wasn't even Harry's. As each day passed, Harry refused to admit that he was or even could be the father. The situation with the Thaws became unendurable.

"The awfulness of the innuendos" in regard to her unborn child drove her "almost to a frenzy."

To avoid the anticipated glare of publicity and the Thaw family's cruelty, Evelyn considered going abroad. Hoping to hide herself and at times wanting simply to forget the name of Thaw altogether, she decided to leave all the scenes of her humiliation and "bury herself somewhere" where she would not be known. Eventually Evelyn landed in Germany, traveling on the ship the *Lusitania.* In October 1910, Russell Thaw was born. As Evelyn wrote in 1915, at the time there were easy ways for her to "find oblivion," but that she had determined to work out her salvation in such a manner to "avoid the fate which has awaited other women" in similar circumstances and led them to an "ignominious end." Initially, painfully, and almost tragically, she failed.

While Harry was preoccupied with finding a way to free himself from the asylum, Evelyn came back to New York, seeking a way out of her mounting financial troubles. Amazingly, she reconciled with her mother, who agreed to take care of her infant grandson while Evelyn sought employment. While trying to figure out a way to escape her troubles, Evelyn met a man "who was wholly good, who was neither depraved, prudish nor lax, a broad-minded friend" who recognized how terrible her position was and who helped by setting up some auditions for her in England. In 1911, she left Russell with her mother back in Pittsburgh and sailed for England on the *Olympia.*

Once again, fate grabbed at Evelyn. A man named Albert de Courville, a passenger on the ship, recognized Evelyn. He was the manager of the London Hippodrome and very keen to have Evelyn appear there. At first, Evelyn instinctively shrank at the thought of publicity, of "making capital" out of her troubles. But she considered that things were potentially better for her in England than in America, since she assumed people in

London had already forgotten about the Madison Square tragedy. Trouble, however, was never far behind her.

En route to England, Evelyn was shocked to receive a wireless message, a Marconigram, that indicated that Harry Thaw had publicly repudiated his son's paternity in the newspapers. De Courville was sympathetic. In fact, after having come to a tentative agreement about her salary with his agent, a Mr. Marinelli, Evelyn found that Mr. De Courville generously increased her salary for the sake of her infant son. But once Harry's public dismissal of Evelyn's claim hit the newspapers in England, her relative obscurity was once more rudely shaken. Two days later she received a phone call from her agent back home, who told her there were problems brewing. The *Daily Sketch* had carried an article that did more than hint that the management of the Hippodrome was taking advantage of her notoriety rather than offering jobs to legitimate artists. There was also a suggestion that she was drawing a fabulous income from the Thaws. The papers made it seem as if she had stepped out of the jury box and onto the variety stage with no intervening time or events.

Disheartened by the thought that she might never be able to get a part, Evelyn considered her limited options and also the far-reaching influence of the press: "I have a respect that amounts to awe for the extraordinary nature of the power of the Press." Rather than stay in London during what would no doubt prove to be a new wave of journalistic agitation, Evelyn moved on to Paris. As for the issue of Russell's father, Evelyn wrote, "In reply to those who had the slightest doubt" as to her son's paternity, "no man who has seen Harry Thaw and Russell can have the slightest doubt as to the child's parentage."

Eventually, after a meeting with a reporter from the *Daily Sketch* who found Evelyn's frankness disarming and who then wrote favorably of her desire and the necessity to go back to work, Evelyn was ready to begin again. To that end, De Courville set her up with a dance partner named Jack Clifford, whose experience "ranged from San Francisco to Paris." Clifford was a handsome, experienced, and muscular dancer who was prepared to literally carry Evelyn through the routines they were

Evelyn with dance partner and
future husband, Jack Clifford, circa 1912.

rehearsing. A dancing master was brought in from Italy to work with the couple on their act as dresses were ordered that would enable Evelyn to do the more acrobatic types of moves that were becoming popular in prewar Europe. The show was *Hullo! Ragtime,* and every day that passed before the opening made Evelyn more and more nervous. Rumors that there would be demonstrators ready to disrupt the opening performance caused the management to come up with what they considered an ingenious plan. They actually cabled America and asked them to send twenty girls of Evelyn's height and coloring so that when the chorus appeared, the audience would have to guess at which was Evelyn Thaw. But that turned out to be unnecessary as the opposition to her appearing died down before opening night. Now the only problem was whether Evelyn could perform or not.

They had decided to put her into the show unannounced on the Saturday before her scheduled Monday debut. As she watched the revue begin to unfold from the wings, Evelyn's throat tightened. She sat down behind the scenery near the back of the stage feeling faint. Then, suddenly, the little ritual she used to perform as a *Florodora* girl before going onstage came back to her. It was as natural as breathing.

Evelyn and her son, Russell, in a poster
for Redemption, 1917.

The Fallen Idol

A former head of Scotland Yard . . . said that he wished girls, at the age of fourteen, could quietly be put to sleep by the State and allowed to remain unconscious until they were eighteen and ready to become harmless and normal women. —*Frederick L. Collins*, Glamorous Sinners

A woman like a country is happiest when she has no history. —*Oscar Wilde*

The tragedy wasn't that Stanford White died, but that I lived.
—*Evelyn Nesbit, 1934*

As the child-woman whose age seemed intriguingly indeterminate to some and of great consequence to others, Evelyn Nesbit came to New York on the quivering cusp of possibility. Within a year, her captivating face and figure set a new, modern standard of beauty by which all others would then be measured. Acting as a mirror to the era's deceptively intoxicating and provocative charms, she offered an image of idealized youth and beauty imprinted on the collective consciousness of an America in perpetual and lustful pursuit of "the last horizon of an endlessly retreating vision of innocence." One need only look at the remarkable Rudolf Eickemeyer Jr. photo taken of a sixteen-year-old Evelyn in 1901 (see page 6) to see the timeless and irresistible quality of a beauty that remains astonishingly contemporary, long after many so-called beauties of the past have faded from fashion. And memory.

It was an image too quickly and easily shattered.

Part Little Eva and part nymphet, proto-feminist and femme fatale, Evelyn Nesbit exposed an entire nation's sins from the witness box while her own more startling and intimate transgressions were taken up with purple vengeance by the newspapers and promoted from the pulpits as a sizzling cautionary tale. Eventually spread out like a crazy quilt over six decades of the twentieth century, the details of the rest of her life illuminate not only her own personal strengths and weaknesses, but also the brightest and darkest aspects of the collective American Dream she embodied.

But if Evelyn Nesbit's early life resonated with the intensity and naiveté of Edison's melodrama that rushed to depict *Rooftop Murder* within a week of the rooftop murder, her life after that ghastly night and the trials that followed continued to move along in fits and starts, capturing in brief but vivid flashes an America always deliriously teetering on the brink of self-awareness. Or self-annihilation.

RÉSUMÉ

After she "rocked civilization" (her own words) for a second time, Evelyn's consistently mercurial life lurched forward with the same uneasy, haphazard, and artless misdirection it had since she was ten. Although she tried to pick up the shards of her ruined reputation by embarking on a vaudeville career, Evelyn (divorced from Harry in 1915, and no longer Thaw) Nesbit found to her dismay that she could not escape the tentacles of the press or her own "swinging" notoriety. In August of 1913, Harry escaped from the asylum to Canada, and until he was caught and brought back, Evelyn had to fear for her life since the papers were full of Thaw's "vengeful threats." In 1916, Evelyn married her dance partner, Jack Clifford (aka Virgil Montani), who was by all accounts an attentive surrogate father to young Russell, but who eventually split with Evelyn, when being known as "Mr. Evelyn Nesbit" became unbearable. She would never marry again. She tested the shadowy waters of silent film, the first of which was produced by the Lubin Company in exotic Fort Lee, New Jersey. Titled *Threads of Destiny*, it was, like the dozen or so films that followed between the years 1914 and 1922, a thinly veiled and self-consciously exploitative depiction of episodes from her own life best forgotten. Only stills of those films remain.

Never far from the front pages or controversy, Evelyn suffered again and again in the court of public opinion. She found herself at the center of a censorship battle over her films when some righteous-minded citizens condemned her for allowing her young son, Russell, to appear in several of them, while at the same time tales of public brawls and ether parties with prizefighters at a retreat in the Adirondacks circulated in the newspapers.

Through the teens and the flaming lawless decade of the twenties, although always threatening to burn out, Evelyn continued to be a commodity, even if she was perceived by most as "damaged goods." She met with initial if limited success, enough that she could tour the country in her own railroad car for a time. But to the dwindling audiences who watched her rapid decline, she ultimately became merely a curiosity. Unable to live up to her early phenomenal success (and left penniless by the thankless Thaws), Evelyn paid a hard price for her so-called fame. She descended into drug abuse (morphine) and alcoholism, in part to numb the pain she felt from frequent excruciating migraine headaches. She tried several times to take her own life (once by ingesting Lysol), and twice a then teenage Russell was forced to come to her rescue, one time while visiting her in Chicago on Christmas break from boarding school. Her name appeared with colorful regularity in the papers and in gossip columns due to drunken brawls (her nose was broken more than once), nonpayment of bills and evictions, auctions of her clothes and what remained of any furs and jewelry, car accidents, suspected abortions, speakeasy arrests, and associations with mobsters, etc. Her pet boa constrictor, Baby, escaped to the streets of lower Manhattan while she was living and performing in cabarets in Greenwich Village ("He keeps away the bill collectors," she remarked to bemused reporters).

There was even the occasional rumor that she was getting back together with Harry Thaw, who came to see her several times in nightclubs in Atlantic City, Manhattan, and Chicago (this after he was released from the Kirkbride Asylum in Philadelphia, after nearly eight years of institutionalization for the "Frederick Gump debacle"). But money that Harry promised to give her "for her son" never materialized (although he did buy Russell a bicycle one Christmas). As time passed, by his twenties, Russell, having inherited his mother's devil-may-care attitude in his approach to life, became a well-known and daring test pilot whose acquaintances included Charles Lindbergh and Amelia Earhart. Sadly, it was around this same time that Evelyn's unfortunate brother, Howard, from whom she had remained estranged and who always seemed to exist on the periphery of life, succeeded where Evelyn had failed. He hanged himself.

A devastated Evelyn struggled as a single mother in the Depression and the war years, during which time her mamma died. She made varied and valiant attempts to regain control of her life between the late twenties and 1945. She "sobered up" on a milk farm, ran her own Club Evelyn Nesbit in Atlantic City, opened a tearoom on Fifty-seventh Street in Manhattan, and started a line of cosmetics—all of which eventually failed. Gradually, the nightclubs and cabarets she performed in, doing songs like "I'm a Broad-minded Broad from Broadway" and "I'm No Man's Woman Now," were seedier and farther away (as far as Panama City) from the fickle and unforgiving limelight. A serialized account of her life in the New York *Daily News* was part of the inspiration for Orson Welles's depiction of the pitiable has-been alcoholic singer in *Citizen Kane*, which many believe is based on Marion Davies. When Harry Thaw died of a heart attack in 1947, he left Evelyn $10,000, the same amount he left a waitress he barely knew who worked in a coffee shop in Virginia. Then, just as she had immediately after the murder that fateful night in Madison Square Garden, Evelyn Nesbit seemed to vanish from the scene. Far from the prying eyes of a capriciously curious and unsympathetic public, Evelyn moved to southern California to live with her son, Russell, and his wife and family, which eventually included three grandchildren.

A little more than two decades after the Madison Square Tragedy,

F. Scott Fitzgerald had proclaimed, "There are no second acts in America." But he was wrong.

In 1954, in true Hollywood fashion, Evelyn Nesbit emerged from the shrouded depths of insignificance and infamy when she sold her story to Twentieth Century–Fox. Hired as a consultant for the film, *The Girl in the Red Velvet Swing*, with a twenty-one-year-old Joan Collins in the title role, Evelyn basked once again, however briefly, in the twilight of kinder and nostalgia-inspired publicity. After a decade-long career as a sculptor and ceramics teacher, Evelyn ended her days confined to a wheelchair and then a bed in a series of convalescent homes. Nevertheless, her mind remained sharp and vibrant as she kept contact with the outside world through hundreds of letters written to several friends. She died in 1967 "of natural causes."

FINALE

In those hypocritical years when the scandal she ignited simultaneously shocked and titillated the public, Evelyn attempted to wear her notoriety with tenuous, shrinking dignity, though she barely succeeded in keeping her head above water. And although in some ways she remained hopelessly naive and childlike until her last days, she was, however, shrewd enough not to reveal "the whole truth" about her story while she lived. Perhaps this enabled her to negate her past and any guilt she may have felt about the murder of Stanford White, the only man she said she ever truly loved. Perhaps she came to realize that the only control she would ever have over her life was how much or how little of it to disclose, telling the truth, but (as Emily Dickinson might say) telling it slant ("success in circuit lies").

She resented being considered merely a cultural oddity "like something in Barnum's museum," but the questionable publicity she was routinely engaged in did ultimately provide a living for herself and her son, whose paternity Harry Thaw denied to his dying day. She had, according to all those who knew her personally in her later years, "great presence and an assured manner and she could never, never become an obscure house-wife." Into her eighties Evelyn was, as described by her daughter-in-law, "a free spirit," even though she was forever bound up in the mythology surrounding the "girl in the red velvet swing." Her name now resides in that realm where fact has fused with fiction.

Florence Evelyn Nesbit lived more than most in the first twenty-one years of her early turbulent life and then spent the next sixty contending with the myth she had become and helped invent. And reinvent when the occasion presented itself. Yet even at eighty-two, one could see the spirit of the young model come to life when someone produced a camera; she instinctively struck the characteristic pose that made her famous—her head tilted slightly back and to the side, her eyes seductively half-closed, an enigmatic smile on her face.

American Eve.

ACKNOWLEDGMENTS

There are so many people over the course of a decade who helped me with this book that I am sure to forget to thank someone; I apologize in advance.

I want to thank Greenpoint, Brooklyn, for my parents, Martin and Estelle. I'm indebted to my mom and thank my sister, Pam, for her unwavering faith in me, and although I miss my dad, who offered his keen endorsement at the start of my book, I am very happy to have Michael Martin, my nephew, born halfway through this process, who seems at uncanny moments to channel my father's spirit. I want to thank the Winks of Seaford Manor for their continued encouragement, and the Pittsburgh branch, who offered a base of operations for my research in what seems a lifetime ago. Then there are my own "kids," who not only understand my madness but share it—Tammy Baiko, Eric Chiarulli, Nick Mougis, Allyson Smith, and Brian Smyth. And of course, none of this would have mattered as much were it not for Lisa Cardyn and Lorri Ford, whose friendship and perseverance in the face of seemingly insurmountable odds are a constant source of inspiration.

This book would not have been as meaningful and vivid were it not for Russell Thaw, Evelyn Nesbit's wonderfully supportive grandson, and his mother, Barbara Thaw; their generosity and assistance with this project from its inception made me fearless in the face of a hundred years of mythology. I also would not have been able to complete this book were it not for continued institutional support from Hofstra University, its Faculty Research and Development Grants, and leave time. As for creative minds and kind hearts, I am particularly grateful to Paul Baker,

Kevin Brownlow, Carl Charlson, Stuart Desmond, Ed and Helen Doctorow, Adolph Grude, George Hatie, Suzannah Lessard, Joe McMaster, Jay Maeder, Jim Petersen, and Ira Resnick. Their assorted acts of benevolence, encouragement, and advice have helped me greatly.

I am of course extremely grateful to my agent, Katharine Cluverius, at ICM, my editor, Sarah McGrath, whose instincts are right on, and her assistant, Sarah Stein, at Riverhead Books; each has helped me immeasurably to make this dream a reality, and I wish Katharine and Sarah M. the best world possible for their own new additions.

There is no way I can qualify the unconditional emotional support and intelligent contributions (editorial and otherwise) made by my friends and colleagues throughout this process (listed here in alphabetical order), so I will simply say thanks to Iska Alter, Dana Brand, Joe Fichtelberg, Bernie Firestone, Brad Hodges, Gloria Hoovert, John Klause, Susan Lorsch, Meghan Molloy, Jean Ng, Karen Schnitzspahn, and Chris Svatba. There have been many times when, immersed in my research or my writing, I have felt like Dorothy stuck in Oz, maddeningly unaware how close I was to home all the time, and I could never have made this strange journey without the brains, courage, and heart of Chris Rubeo, Allan David Dart, and Russell Svatba.

Last, *American Eve* is dedicated to my captain, the person who taught me the exaltation of an inland soul, Brian Molloy. His resolute spirit, fierce intellect, and joyous sense of humor made this all possible, and I miss him most of all.

NOTES

I began working on *American Eve* more than ten years ago as an accidental tourist in somewhat unfamiliar territory. While doing research for a course I teach called "Daughter of Decadence," I looked for iconic images of women that would reflect the period in which the images were produced. In an unGoogled, pre-eBay world, I extended my search beyond the usual libraries and archives into the realm of antiquarian books and postcards, private collectors, and "ephemera" shows. At my very first postcard show I was intrigued by a category labeled Pretty Ladies (sandwiched, symbolically, between Perambulators and Prisons). While thumbing through hundreds of postcards I was suddenly struck by one in particular. The sultry gaze of a young girl poised dreamily in turn-of-the-century fashion seemed almost hypnotic. At the bottom it read "The Debutante—posed by Evelyn Nesbit." Her name was not unfamiliar to me. I had read E. L. Doctorow's wonderfully evocative novel *Ragtime* and seen the 1981 film adaptation based on the book; in both she is a featured character. As weeks, then months passed, the face or name of Evelyn Nesbit emerged with astonishing regularity.

I soon became obsessed with uncovering the facts buried beneath the fictions that had been written about this astonishing-looking young woman and the events surrounding the night that sealed her fate as "the girl in the red velvet swing."

When I began this book, no one had written anything that attempted to distinguish objective fact from subjective fancy or that tried to put Evelyn Nesbit's fascinating and fractured life into the broader cultural context of her "gilded cage" (and certainly not from a woman's perspective). I saw this, then, as my task, and soon discovered that Evelyn Nesbit told and retold several versions of the crucial events that shaped her life, first on the witness stand in 1907, again in *The Story of My Life* (written as Evelyn Thaw in 1914), and then in a second memoir, *Prodigal Days* (written as Evelyn Nesbit in 1934, and published in the UK as *The Untold Story*). In spite of sometimes frustratingly variant autobiographical versions of her story, I now had significant pieces of information as well as self-generated mythology that I could begin to sift through and a historical timeline I could piece together to form a cohesive narrative. As I discovered, Harry Thaw also wrote a bizarre version of the events leading up to his murder of Stanford White in his own book, *The Traitor* (published, appropriately, by a vanity press in 1925), which in its own strange way also helped me stitch together a fuller story.

The New-York Historical Society, the New York Public Library, the Museum of the City of New York, the Madison Square Park Conservancy, the Lincoln Center Theater Collection, the Smithsonian Institution, the Archives of American Art, and the Library of Congress have all been extremely valuable in providing materials that have helped me tie together the "threads of destiny" that hold this book together. It was also my good fortune to have had the support of Evelyn's family (particularly her grandson, Russell Thaw), who gave me full and unprecedented access to personal family archives, including letters and photos. In addition, I am beholden to the private collections of Ira Resnick, George Hatie, Adolph Grude, Lisa Cardyn, and Lorri Ford, as well as Kevin Brownlow and Photoplay Productions, Inc. The list of works that have been invaluable as source materials are listed under "Further Reading."

Just as I have tried to keep my citations as concise as possible, citing directly quoted material and omitting only those citations related to facts that are widely known and accepted (as well as quotations taken from periodicals and newspapers of the period for which I had clippings or parts of clippings but no other identifying source), I have also tried to let Evelyn speak for herself as much as possible, since her voice is the one that has been the most muffled and misinterpreted over the last hundred years in spite of her best (or worst) efforts. I therefore apologize if at times my relating of her recollections leads to some factual errors or seeming inconsistencies, particularly regarding her early life. Unless noted, her quotations are taken from *The Story of My Life, Prodigal Days, The Untold Story,* and unpublished letters in private collections and interviews with family members. Unless otherwise noted, Harry Thaw's quotations are taken from his book, *The Traitor.*

INTRODUCTION: THE GARDEN OF THE NEW WORLD

3. *men like E. H. Harriman* Multimillionaire politician, financier, and railroad magnate Russell Sage was the target in 1891 of a dynamite-toting anarchist. Although miraculously Sage was unharmed, his secretary was killed, along with the would-be assassin. Another member of this exclusive club was Henry Clay Frick, who was the target of an anarchist one year after Sage. A disgruntled worker raided Frick's office armed with a revolver and a steel knife. In spite of several serious wounds inflicted upon him before his attacker was shot, Frick was back at his desk only a week later.

3. *"dishearting middle-brow indifference"* Collins, 86.

3. *potter's field* The Washington Square area was farmland until the Common Council of New York purchased the land for a new potter's field, or public burial ground, in 1797. The potter's field was used mainly for burying unknown or indigent people. But when New York went through terrible yellow fever epidemics in the early 1800s, most of those who died from yellow fever were also buried here, safely away from town, as a hygienic measure.

5. *"Envious, suspicious"* Collins, 110.

CHAPTER ONE. SIREN SONG

8. *"unruly" and "self sufficient"* Whitman, "Mannahatta," from *Leaves of Grass*.

8. *apocalyptic feelings that seem* From Elaine Showalter's insightful study of the sexual anxieties at the turn of the last century, *Sexual Anarchy*.

9. *"loads of babies"* From Stephen Crane's *Maggie: A Girl of the Streets*.

9. *street Arabs* The term, coined by social reformer and photographer Jacob Riis, describes the virtually homeless children (predominantly male) abandoned by their families, and given over to the dirty, dangerous streets of the Bowery and Five Points areas to fend for themselves.

10. *the machine had entered the garden* From Leo Marx's critical study of American culture and literature, *The Machine in the Garden*, which examines the impact of industrialization and technology on a predominantly pastoral America, which saw itself as the virgin wilderness and "New Eden" prior to the Civil War.

11. *image of an age* In homage to Nabokov's Lolita, a girl who also generated a great deal of controversy in her day and whose circumstances,

although fictional, are an uncanny parallel to Evelyn's (including a dead father, feckless mother, precocious intellect, theatrical aspirations, and identity as the sex object of two adult men, one of whom is a dark doppelgänger of the other).

13. *"love, hate, villainy"* Atwell, 12.

13. *"contemporary social types"* Banta, 7.

14. *"a vision who assailed one's senses"* Collins, 62.

15. *"grown wholesomely in"* Collins, 63.

CHAPTER TWO. BEAUTIFUL CITY OF SMOKE

22. *fire consumed all records* In all versions of her childhood, in spite of the fact that Tarentum was known for its glass and bottling industry (in addition to salt and oil drilling and the manufacturing of bricks, lumber, and other such products), Evelyn characterizes her earliest experience as rural, most likely because she spent so much time with relatives on outlying farmland. As for her correct age, the IRS had to rely on the sworn testimony she gave during the murder trial that she was born in 1884 to decide the issue of her receiving Social Security. But Evelyn was never quite sure if that was the correct year and always believed, as she wrote in a number of letters, that she was born in 1885 (which I also believe, given the furor over her turning eighteen in December 1903, referred to in various accounts of events).

25. *Florence Evelyn was around eleven* Evelyn's own memory of her actual age when her father died varies from eight to eleven in different accounts of the story. If, as she testified, she was born in 1884, then she was almost eleven when her father died.

CHAPTER THREE. POSES

37. *hustling bustled and burgeoning* Once the shirtwaist came into being and swept the country as a revolutionary fashion accesory (in imitation of the man's detachable celluloid collar and cuffs), women had greater freedom of choice and slightly more freedom of movement. The colorful shirtwaist was cheaply made and gave the appearance that one had a larger wardrobe than in actuality.

37. *"escagators"* Nickname given to the newly invented escalators that posed a real threat to the long skirts of women shoppers.

39. *ripped down the hems* At sixteen, a girl was no longer considered a child, which meant from that point on, her legs were hidden beneath skirts lengthened to their "proper" height just at the ankle. In a popular poem titled "Goodbye Legs," widely reprinted in various newspapers, a young woman sighs, "I shall be legless until my death," lamenting the end of childhood freedom and the restrictive clothing adult women wore.

40. *Charlie Somerville* Working for the *New York Evening Journal,* he would become one of the most prominent reporters to cover the Thaw murder trial.

41. *"create possibilities for their future"* Habegger, xxxvii. In *Gender, Fantasy, and Realism in American Literature,* author Albert Habegger argues that adolescent girls benefited from their reading of the popular romances that invaded the best-seller lists at the end of the nineteenth century, providing them with both models of behavior and the promise of greater opportunities.

47. *"a dreary adult"* As her grandson Russell Thaw related in one of our conversations, even in her sixties and seventies, Evelyn never really thought much or cared for money in the sense of one who is covetous. When she had little or no money, she made the best of the situation, and when she had it, she was both a soft touch and a spendthrift, which meant she didn't have it for very long.

CHAPTER FOUR. THE LITTLE SPHINX IN MANHATTAN

58. *Miss Florence Evelyn* In her earliest incarnation, Evelyn was identified variously as Florence Nesbit and Florence Evelyn; frequently her last name was misspelled as Nesbitt, which meant she was also sometimes confused with a more mature actress named Miriam Nesbitt.

59. *titled* Miss N. Not to be confused with the famous photograph of Evelyn of the same title, taken by Gertrude Käsebier and discussed at length in chapter 6.

61. *"flash into public view as a famous beauty"* Atwell, 12.

64. *Sandow the strongman* Popular vaudeville performer whose nude muscular posing in photographs (from behind) came under Comstock's fire.

65. *other plays suffered similar fates* When Ibsen's *A Doll's House* premiered in New York City, the first American audiences remained seated after Nora's heroic exit; in spite of the furious blinking of house lights, they awaited Nora's repentant return to provide the expected conventional happy ending. Comstock's unrelenting condemnation of the play led to its closing.

66. *"The Statue That Offended New York"* Title of an article on Saint-Gaudens's Diana and its colorful history from *American History Magazine.*

67. *showgirls bursting out of pies* Stanford White's first close brush with notoriety, which signaled to some that he had experienced "more than a whiff of the Tenderloin," was the "Pie Girl Incident." Along with his business partners and most intimate friends, White gave a party at 5 West Sixteenth Street, the home of society photographer James Breese, founder of the Carbon Studio. The word *studio* itself conjured images of depravity and licentiousness among the general public, and this party would only reinforce that notion once the details of it were made public during the Thaw case. (It also gave rise to the expression "Would you like to come up and see my etchings?")

At the outset, two young models in haremlike costumes, one blond, the other auburn-haired, poured wine, whose color matched their hair and complexion. The centerpiece of the bash was a huge pie wheeled into the center of the room. On cue, out popped four and twenty real blackbirds and a scantily clad fourteen- or fifteen-year-old girl named Susie Johnson. Wrapped seductively in the sheerest of black gauze, the nubile teen also wore a stuffed blackbird on her head and danced seductively on the table, her bare feet adorned with exotic feathered toe rings.

When gossip quickly began to spread about the debauchery of the "Pie Girl Incident" (within two days the Gerry Society began a search for the girl), although White managed through begging and pleading to keep the story out of the papers, rumors of the degenerate party made their way into Hearst's pseudo-moralistic *American.* It was reported that Susie Johnson's mother had found gold coins in her purse and shoes when the girl returned home in the early-morning hours. It would ultimately come out at the first murder trial that "the poor Johnson girl" later married, only to be "thrown off" by her husband when he heard about her role as the infamous Pie Girl. She killed herself and was buried in a potter's field.

70. *a population obsessed with iconographic images* Banta, 7.

70. *Charles Dana Gibson's "Eternal Question"* Probably the most ubiquitous and best-known image of Evelyn as the quintessential Gibson Girl, it made its first appearance as the centerfold of *Collier's* magazine in 1903. It was also the advertisement for a collection of Gibson's prints and drawings called *The Weaker Sex,* and nearly eighty years later was used in the ads for the 1981 film *Ragtime.* Even before Evelyn, Gibson's popular illustrations, gracing the weekly centerfold in *Life* magazine, reigned supreme. Embracing, however naively, Gibson's often satirical vision of themselves, Americans basked in the "stylized and sardonic" national identity depicted in Gibson's drawings. According to the *New York World,* before Gibson synthesized his ideal woman into the Eternal Question, "the American girl was vague, nondescript, inchoate. . . . As soon as the world saw Gibson's ideal it bowed down in admiration saying, Lo, at last, the typical American girl."

70. *much like the Garden's Diana* Thanks to E. L. Doctorow's *Ragtime,* one of the myths that has entered the cultural consciousness is that Evelyn modeled for Saint-Gaudens's *Diana.* She was nine when he created the statue.

70. *Harrison Fisher, Howard Chandler Christy, Henry Hutt, and Archie Gunn* Four of the most prominent, talented, and successful illustrators of the period; each in his own way developed a signature vision of the American girl that complemented Gibson's vision.

73. *the all-consuming desire of manufacturers* Banta, 8.

73. *Restricted circulation of a wholly different kind* The Victorian view of feminine modesty required five layers of clothing for women—beneath the skirt a woman was supposed to wear a slip or petticoat, then a cotton chemise, and then rough underwear. Clothes at best provided for decorous immobility and at worst painfully restricted the ability to breathe, let alone move. The rib-crushing whalebone corset of the nineteenth century was replaced with the technologically advanced metal model.

73. *hair rats* Made of wire mesh, these rat-shaped fixtures were set in place with hairpins on top of a woman's head to lift her hair for the requisite Gibson-girl coiffure.

73. *picture hats* Abnormally huge and unwieldy hats thought fashionable and named for their ability to totally block an unfortunate patron's line of vision seated behind a woman wearing one at the "picture show" or nickelodeon.

This prompted theater owners to insert the card "Ladies must remove their hats" into the opening title sequence of the movies they showed.

CHAPTER SIX. BENEVOLENT VAMPIRE

99. *"Night turned into Day"* To many it appeared that as soon as Roosevelt assumed office, changes took place that reflected the character of the newly appointed young, flamboyant, and fervent president. Roosevelt's leadership signaled the start of a period marked by acceleration in industrial development, land acquisition, foreign trade, immigration, international finance, and unprecedented economic growth in building construction. Ironically, McKinley's untimely death provided Roosevelt with a number of timely opportunities, one of which was to move the United States into the arena of world politics, which included helping Cuba establish itself as a nation, and annexing the Philippines, Guam, and Puerto Rico.

119. *Gertrude Käsebier* Respected and talented portrait photographer and part of the Photo-Secession movement who exhibited at the prestigious 291 along with Stieglitz and Steichen.

123. *"sugar-daddyish mix of altruism"* Michaels, 114.

123. *"selling her to the highest bidder"* Michaels, 115.

124. *"none more fully"* Michaels, 115.

129. *"little butterfly"* This is probably the most famous photographic image of Evelyn. It won Eickemeyer a prize and was the image used at the murder trial as proof of her unsavory character. It was also the best-selling of all the postcard images of Evelyn.

CHAPTER EIGHT. AT THE FEET OF DIANA

146. *"a connoisseur"* . . . *"an apostle of beauty"* O'Connor, 131.

148. *"architect of desire"* Title of Susannah Lessard's engrossing and elegantly written autobiographical book detailing her family history and the legacy of her great-grandfather Stanford White.

149. *"just a fairy out of wonderland"* Atwell, 12.

159. *Svengali and Trilby* The manipulative hypnotist/impresario and his lovely model/victim in George Du Maurier's best-selling 1894 novel *Trilby*.

CHAPTER NINE. THE BARRYMORE CURSE

166. *"In the considered opinion of"* O'Connor, 188.

169. *"By God we'll go to a restaurant"* O'Connor, 190.

170. *"a slick, penniless, hard-drinking ne'er do well"* O'Connor, 189.

CHAPTER TEN. ENTER MAD HARRY

194. *Posing under another assumed* From the second trial transcript.

CHAPTER ELEVEN. THE WORST MISTAKE OF HER LIFE

213. *"I want to speak with you"* This episode, with a few additional details from *My Story* and Thaw's *The Traitor,* is Evelyn's recounting as described in *Prodigal Days.*

216. *"Burglar-Banker-Father"* From an Emily Dickinson poem describing God.

219. *a very different way* Both White and Thaw were also, coincidentally, enraptured by a specific quality of Evelyn's distinctive beauty—her exquisitely delicate and "boyish figure"—which may have had more unconventional implications than Evelyn realized at the time. Each man at different times had expressed to Evelyn his severe distaste for "fat" women of the more voluptuous type that was popular in the 1890s, and there are indications that their love of beauty cut both ways in terms of gender.

228. *"the shores of Avalon"* As a child, Evelyn had read Arthurian romance with her father, who praised the chivalry of knights and the virtue of the ladies whose honor they defended.

233. *Olga Nethersole's production* A shocking drama for its day, *Sappho* tells the story of the "regrettably named Fanny Le Grand." Several scenes after prostrating herself willingly at the feet of her would-be lover (a position normally reserved for maidens begging to protect their purity on stage), Fanny is carried up the stairs in the arms of her lover. When it became clear to the audience that the man had spent the night with Fanny, they let out a collective gasp. Some rose and angrily stormed out of the theater. The next morning, the unfortunate Nethersole was roused out of bed and taken down to the police station. Hummel took up her case and made her the

advocate of artistic freedom during a very brief trial that ended with her acquittal (much to Anthony Comstock's bilious resentment).

239. *Blank the Pimp* Harry's name for White's secretary, Charles Hartnett.

CHAPTER TWELVE. THE "MISTRESS OF MILLIONS"

260. *sob sisters* Before the 1880s, there were few newspaperwomen, and those female journalists who did exist were not permitted to write on important topics. Front-page assignments, politics, finance, and sports were not usually assigned to women. Over the next decade, as historian Frank Mott writes, "women flocked into newspaper work." The Thaw case, with Evelyn as its central figure, was the impetus for an entire generation of newswomen to take their place at the table with the men in covering the "crime of the century." The term "sob sister" was nonetheless a disparaging one.

CHAPTER THIRTEEN. CURTAINS: JUNE 25, 1906

276. *"When I handed him"* From the first trial transcript.

284. *"a smirking conversation"* O'Connor, 191.

287. *"Everyone always figured it would be a father"* From the first trial transcript.

CHAPTER FOURTEEN. AFTERSHOCK

289. *"scavenging for the puniest"* Most of the quotations in this chapter are taken from newspaper accounts that appeared immediately after the murder. There were twenty-eight newspapers in New York alone in 1906.

300. *"The gilding of the figure"* Collins, 99.

CHAPTER FIFTEEN. DEMENTIA AMERICANA

304. *"a creature far meaner and uglier"* The majority of quotations in this chapter are taken from Thaw's account in *The Traitor* of his ordeal after the murder.

307. *Benjamin Atwell* The Thaws' publicist also helped the family mount a play more than just loosely based on the murder case. It opened in Brooklyn while the first trial was taking place. Its central characters are Stanford

Black, a "rounder and roué" who seduces then abandons a young girl, and Emeline Hudspeth Daw, the beautiful wife of the young chivalrous hero, Harold Daw. Several scenes after a particularly lurid one in which Black seduces and abandons a young girl, who is then spurned by her family and dies of a broken heart, Daw shoots Black during a musical performance on a roof garden and awaits trial in the Tombs. In the play, Daw proclaims his own innocence, based on the idea of the "unwritten law": "No jury on earth will send me to the chair, no matter what I have done or what I have been, for killing the man who defamed my wife. That is the unwritten law and upon its virtue I will stake my life."

CHAPTER SIXTEEN. A WOMAN'S SACRIFICE

326. *"thundering from pulpits"* O'Connor, 199.

327. *"poured out by the Thaw family"* O'Connor, 201. The Thaws' well-paid publicist, Benjamin Atwell, who helped mastermind the campaign of slander and vilification against White, also wrote *The Great Harry Thaw Case, or, A Woman's Sacrifice,* published initially in hardcover, then quickly made available to the eager public as a pulp edition during the first trial.

328. *"Who goes to Maine in February"* O'Connor, 200.

329. *"shot and killed with premeditation"* Most of the quotations in this and the following chapter regarding testimony are taken from the original first trial transcript.

349. *Le Rat Mort* This episode is taken from the first trial transcript, with some details added from Evelyn's account in *Prodigal Days.*

EPILOGUE: THE FALLEN IDOL

368. *silent film* The titles of most of Evelyn's films indicate the common theme of her notoriety: *Threads of Destiny, The Hidden Woman, A Fallen Idol, Thou Shalt Not, Woman, Woman!, I Want to Forget, The Woman Who Gave, Her Mistake,* and *Redemption.*

370. *"Frederick Gump debacle"* Harry was arrested for whipping a young man, eighteen-year-old Frederick Gump, in a hotel bathtub. Thaw avoided jail by going to the Kirkbride Insane Asylum in Philadelphia for eight years, longer than the time spent in Mattewan for killing White.

370. *He hanged himself* Although it remained "the love that dare not speak its name" where Howard was concerned, all the signs pointed to Evelyn's brother's being gay. He had clearly developed a relationship with White's secretary, Charles Hartnett, ten years his senior, which lasted through the second trial. But a closeted Howard inevitably married and lived a number of years in an apparently affectionate but sham marriage until he killed himself in despair.

371. *Joan Collins in the title role* In one of the letters she wrote in her later years, Evelyn lamented the casting of Joan Collins to portray her in *The Girl in the Red Velvet Swing*. She felt Collins was "too bosomy" and "too British" to play her. She wrote (perhaps tongue in cheek) that she would have preferred Marilyn Monroe.